T0418467

LITTLE ITALY IN
THE GREAT WAR

An Italian soldier bids farewell to his wife and child at the Vittorio Emanuele
barracks in Rome as he prepares to depart for the front.
(*Evening Ledger* [June 26, 1915].)

LITTLE ITALY IN
THE GREAT WAR

Philadelphia's Italians on
the Battlefield and Home Front

RICHARD N. JULIANI

TEMPLE UNIVERSITY PRESS
Philadelphia • *Rome* • *Tokyo*

TEMPLE UNIVERSITY PRESS
Philadelphia, Pennsylvania 19122
tupress.temple.edu

Cover illustration: Company A of the Third Regiment of the Pennsylvania National Guard,
whose many Italians made it the "Italian Brigade," marches to a local armory in June 1916.
Under Sergeant Frank Attanasio as their commanding officer, James Baldino, Charles
Cianfrani, Victor Cippolone, Victor Bonovolto, "Kid" Missolina, Angelo Maturo, Joseph
Leopoldo, and J. Parri also served as members of the unit. (*Evening Ledger* [June 23, 1916].)

Library of Congress Cataloging-in-Publication Data

Names: Juliani, Richard N., author.
Title: Little Italy in the Great War : Philadelphia's Italians on the
    Battlefield and Home Front / Richard N. Juliani.
Description: Philadelphia, Pennsylvania : TEMPLE UNIVERSITY PRESS, 2019. |
    Includes index. |
Identifiers: LCCN 2019003670 (print) | LCCN 2019004569 (ebook) | ISBN
    9781439918791 (E-book) | ISBN 9781439918777 (cloth : alk. paper) | ISBN
    9781439918784 (pbk. : alk. paper)
Subjects: LCSH: Little Italy (Philadelphia, Pa.)—History—20th century. |
    Italian Americans—Pennsylvania—Philadelphia—History—20th century. |
    World War, 1914-1918—Italian Americans. | World War, 1914-1918—Social
    aspects—Pennsylvania—Philadephia. | Philadelphia (Pa.)—History—20th
    century.
Classification: LCC F158.68.L58 (ebook) | LCC F158.68.L58 J845 2019 (print) |
    DDC 974.8/1104—dc23
LC record available at https://lccn.loc.gov/2019003670

Printed in the United States of America

9 8 7 6 5 4 3 2 1

Contents

Preface

The subject matter of this book has been part of my life for as long as I can remember. When I was growing up in the 1940s and heard my father and his friends talk about "the war," it was not World War II to which they were referring. Leonardo Antonio Iuliani, a corporal in the 70th Infantry Regiment of the Ancona Brigade, 7th Infantry Division of the Italian Army, was a veteran of the Great War of an earlier era. While being moved up with replacement troops, he found himself in Mestre, the jumping-off point for the front line, when the war ended on November 4, 1918. Two years later, having served his country "with loyalty and honor," he was discharged. Like other men finding themselves in senseless wars from which many of them never return, this fortunate soldier never forgot his experiences during his time spent in a military uniform. In 1922, having left one army, he joined another one of "cultural irredentists," sailing on the *Taormina* in search of opportunity in some "Little Italy" of urban America. After meeting a beautiful young lady, Emelia Adriana Torquati, a native of Rome, whom he would marry, he found a new life as a tailor in Camden, New Jersey. I never tired of hearing him talk about his earlier days, and his words had a profound influence on all my work. Even though he is no longer around to hear me say it, I remain grateful to him for introducing me to this subject matter.

Several other persons have influenced my work, perhaps much more than they realize. From the beginning, I exchanged ideas and much information with the late Umberto (Bert) Vorchheimer. During this manuscript's entire course of development, Mario Colombo, my sage and generous friend, has always given me much more than I sought. Raffaello and Gabriella Juvara and their son, Pietro, have similarly provided indispensable published materials, advice, and encouragement in support of my work. Piero Consolati and Antonio Zandonati, unforgettable guides to the trenches in the Trentino and to Forte Belvedere-Werk Gschwent in Lavarone, were great informants on the war. Teresa Cerasuola shared with me the invaluable memoir written by her father, Michele Buccino, a native of Rionero in Vulture in the province of Potenza and a veteran of the war who later became the best cabinetmaker in New York City during his life in America. Spencer Di Scala provided indispensable criticism and advice that could come only from a great scholar of Italian history. Adele Maiello of the University of Genoa has been unflagging with her kind and intelligent support. Leonard Guercio, who embodies the best of South Philadelphia, has always been ready to offer his help in every possible way. Aaron M. Javsicas, editor in chief of Temple University Press, guided my work with great encouragement from its first submission through later review and editing. I must similarly cite Ashley Petrucci whose diligent attention and efforts as an editorial assistant enabled us to reach a final version. I also express my appreciation to two anonymous outside readers whose helpful recommendations I have sought to satisfy. I owe them all far more than I can adequately express. I must similarly acknowledge Rick and Alex, my patient and understanding children, who have had to grow up while their father was writing.

Finally, Sandra Carlotta Juliani, confidant, critic, wife, and best friend, has been with me through every step of this undertaking, as well as our journey through life together. I cannot imagine what it would have been like without her. Nor would I have wanted it any other way.

LITTLE ITALY IN THE GREAT WAR

Introduction

The basic issue of this study, as it should be for all historical research and analysis, is how do we confront the past? And since war especially invites the construction of a mythic past, the writing of history becomes an attempt to correct our collective memory. In the case of the Great War of 1914–1918, remembrance has often taken the form of heritage and celebration rather than more profound learning and understanding. But we do not want to rehash the platitudes of "conventional wisdom." Among the many aspects of a conflict that engulfed much of the world, for the United States, it involved coming to terms with the great diversity within the population as its military forces went off to fight on foreign battlefields. It sent men into combat against the military forces of the lands their families had only recently left but that had become enemy nations. It asked other men to become allies of friendlier states from which they had departed, sometimes with uncertain plans about whether they ever intended to return. How this affected the mobilization of troops for the combat that lay ahead remains to be fully told. But it left a legacy that persisted in national policy and popular culture, even after the war had ended.

In the years after the Great War, performers on the theatrical stages of America would celebrate the victory of the United States and the Allies over the Central Powers. Drawing on a vast repertoire of musical selections that reflected various aspects of the ended but still intrusive war, audiences could hear a catchy song called "When Tony Goes over the Top," whose words intoned:

Hey! You know Tony the Barber
Who shaves and cuts-a the hair
He said skabooch, to his Mariooch
He's gonna fight "Over There"
Hey! You know how Tony could shave you
He'd cut you from ear to ear . . .
When Tony goes over the top
He no think of the barber shop,
He grab-a-da gun and chase-a da hun
And make 'em all run like a son-of-a-gun
You can bet your life he'll never stop
When Tony goes over the top
Keep your eyes on that fighting wop
With a rope of spagett
And-a big-a-stilette
He'll make-a the Germans sweat
When Tony goes over the top.[1]

Recorded in separate versions in the autumn of 1918, by Billy Murray, a son of Irish immigrants, and Gus Van and Joe Schenck, performers of racial and ethnic dialect songs, the lyrics celebrated the exploits of Tony, an intrepid Italian immigrant soldier in the U.S. Army on the Western Front.

On the surface, such entertainment offered a modicum of accurate information. Tony, the Italian, and many other foreign-born men did go over the top as American soldiers. Beneath that basic fact, however, the message held more complicated nuances. Two years before the United States entered the war, other "Tonys" had answered the call by the Italian government to return to Italy as reservists to serve in the war against Austro-Hungarian forces on another front. But an even greater number of them would cast their lot with whatever the future held in America. Many Italians who had defied the order, as well as the American-born sons of immigrants, would eventually find themselves called to military duty after Congress, having declared war, enacted the Selective Service Act in the spring of 1917. And thus Tony, in various representations during the Great War, could be found clad in the gray-green uniform of the army of King Victor Emmanuel III; or as a *renitente*, using his ambiguous suspension between two countries to avoid military service; or as a khaki-clad "Sammy," serving with General John J. Pershing's American Expeditionary Force on the Western Front. But Tony, consciously or unconsciously, was also seeking and sorting out his identity as an Italian and an American. While the journey toward becoming an American remains an unresolved issue in the study of assimilation, it also reflects an aspect of war in modern times that has yet to be fully explored. World War I was a war in which the immigrant presence became an important issue, played a vital role, and underwent a great transformation by an accelerated assimilation process.

In *The Age of Empire*, Eric Hobsbawm raises the often ignored question of the public reaction to modern warfare: "What would the attitude of these masses be when called to the colors, and what would the impact of war be on civilians especially if, as some military men shrewdly suspected—though taking little account of it in their planning—the war would not be over quickly?" Except for events that transformed Russia during the war, Hobsbawm would give little further attention to the question. Similarly, American historian, David M. Kennedy, while exploring the "home front," noted that American society had no longer remained homogeneous, with its cities' "polyglot cauldrons roiling with astonishing various ethnic ingredients" as industrialization "opened the ugly fissures of class." Addressing what Hobsbawm had found to be so important, Kennedy, despite his emphatic recognition of diversity, depicted an American society all but totally devoid of ethnic groups within its population. Although recognizing military service as the instrument to "yank the hyphen" out of Italian American, Polish American, and other immigrant recruits, Kennedy omitted any further consideration of its impact on identities and communities. While diversity as a dimension of modern war needs to be more fully explored, it remains especially germane as an aspect of America's participation in the Great War.[2]

Within a vast repertoire of studies begun even before the war had ended, research that focused on immigrants in training and combat as well as their communities at home has uncovered promising initiatives, without exhausting the subject. Whether from voluntary enlistment or conscription, organizing the new National Army was made more difficult by recruitment from a far more diverse population than ever before in American history. Exploring this problem, Nancy Gentile Ford argues in *Americans All!* that the methods of scientific management and beliefs of the Progressivist movement guided military efforts in promoting Americanism while allowing immigrants to retain cultural traditions during their indoctrination into military life. Relying largely on official reports focused on stateside experience rather than combat overseas, her study abruptly concludes that the integration of immigrant recruits and native-born Americans was successfully achieved. But Gentile Ford isolates the challenge that the nation faced in transforming ethnic diversity into unified military preparedness.[3]

Official policy, however, did not reveal much of the intensely personal experiences that ensued on the battlefield or in the postwar reception of returning soldiers. David Laskin, in *The Long Way Home*, describing the poignant encounters of 12 immigrants who served as doughboys in France, vividly depicts the "reality of the soldier's life in war." In contrast to a more saccharine view of a nation grateful to its foreign-born soldiers, he also recognizes that with restrictive immigration legislation after the war, "the parades had barely ended when the doors began slamming shut." Throughout his narrative, Laskin shows that the ordeal of warfare was widely shared by a sometimes united and at other times divided population.[4]

Applying a more sociological perspective, Christopher M. Sterba, in *Good Americans*, compares the experiences of the Italian colony of New Haven, Connecticut, with the enclaves of Eastern European Jews of New York City. He seeks to answer three main questions: How did the war affect their communities? How did their communities respond to the war? and What was the long-term significance of the war for the "new immigration" to America? While focusing on the indoctrination to military life of Italians and Jews as individuals but also examining the adjustments forced upon their communities at home, Sterba's approach expands the context for understanding the war. Whether concerned with soldiers or civilians, he shows that "foreignness" continued to resonate in the resolution. By his critical debunking of more "heroic" interpretations, Sterba provides a useful perspective on immigrant soldiers and their communities during the war.[5]

In considering the American role in the Great War, Jennifer D. Keene's analysis of issues that challenged military and political leaders exposes major matters of military operation. After decades of disparaging any role for citizen soldiers in modern warfare, regular army officers, suddenly needing to do exactly what they long resisted, had to mobilize and train wholly inexperienced recruits into a force capable of defeating a formidable enemy. Army officials had to establish an institutional setting that weaned civilians from private life and infuse a shared sense of purpose that could support military interests after the war. Repeatedly returning to the theme of how citizen soldiers, many of them reluctant to be in the army at all, forced military authorities to dilute unquestioning obedience by granting concessions to their demands, Keene reveals the reciprocity of power within the ranks. But while recognizing the tragic plight of black soldiers, the large population of immigrants whose presence within the National Army also threatened the goal of integration receives little attention.[6]

This brief review is not meant to serve as a critical appraisal as much as to discern a context for the present work. While some scholars find favorable consequences in the experience of immigrant groups during the war, particularly in regard to assimilation—reflecting what might be called a "unity narrative"—they have left space, although sometimes partly addressed by them, for a more skeptical conclusion. Without being exhaustive, these works provide valuable vectors that allow for the introduction of further research. In the present case, another study, based on the history of Philadelphia's Italians as an immigrant population, is introduced.

While challenging all who were touched by it, the war forced Italian immigrants to confront some difficult choices. Within that community, intellectuals found the need to transcend their usual reflections on personal identity. With the exigencies of political allegiance encouraging more profound considerations than peace had required, they explored the meaning and relevance of Americanization. In December 1915, journalist Agostino De Biasi, an editor of *L'Opinione*, an Italian newspaper in Philadelphia, before becoming an important voice of Fascism, identified the relationship between their country of origin and country of relocation as the key question facing Italians. But, for other Americans, the war brought a reciprocal question in the problem posed by the presence of foreigners who threatened to disrupt the political and cultural unity of America. Unlike intellectuals such as De Biasi, who proposed a pluralistic, simultaneously dual allegiance, advocates of Americanization expected a more acquiescent response from the foreign born. And while the nation would eagerly embrace them as industrial laborers, military recruits, and even citizens, especially if they were willing to adopt "American" ways of thinking and acting, it would remain hesitant if they retained "foreign" identities, languages, and behaviors. In short, native-born Americans believed that newcomers had to be more unequivocally assimilated as Americans if the war was to be won.[7]

Within this framework, the present study seeks to examine the impact of the war on men who served in the ranks of the military and civilians who defended the nation in industrial and civic roles on the home front. In particular, it asks how an immigrant population reacted to the war, especially as foreigners on a path to becoming Americans. The case of Philadelphia's Italians presents a large population of foreign origin still uncertain about its own intentions toward life both in America and in a city that was ambivalent about them. The war forced Italians along with other Philadelphians to seek answers to these questions. Hopefully, the present study provides a better understanding of the relationship of war to such matters as diversity and assimilation, along with a greater appreciation of a previously missing dimension of the history of the Great War and Philadelphia as an American city.

I

Philadelphia's Italians

From Earliest Arrivals to the Great War

The seeds of the experience of Italian immigrants with the Great War are found in their long history as settlers placed within the social fabric of Philadelphia. Beginning in the colonial era, Italians, in search of opportunity and adventure, had brought their knowledge and skills as physicians, musicians, artists, merchants, tavern keepers, impresarios, theater operators, pleasure garden proprietors, scientists, and scholars, as well as a colorful presence that enhanced life and helped to transform Philadelphia from a "gray Quaker lady" to the most important city of North America. By the early nineteenth century, Italian life began to take on more collective and institutional aspects. The arrival in September 1800 of six Ligurians, who had traveled together from Amsterdam on the brig *Tryphena*, and their shared origins in towns of the Val Fontanabuona above the coastal city of Chiavari revealed the first "migration chain" linking Italy and Philadelphia. Such newcomers would form a gradually emerging colony near 8th and Christian Streets in Moyamensing District, just below the southern boundary of the preconsolidation city. In 1853, Bishop John Neumann, a native of Bohemia, founded the Italian Mission of Saint Mary Magdalen de Pazzi on Marriot Street, the first church exclusively for Italians and a prototype of later nationality parishes, as well as an important part of the institutional spine of a nascent immigrant community in Philadelphia.[1]

The Industrial Revolution planted the stimulus for the migration that erupted with the expansion of industrial capitalism, bringing a far greater volume of Italians in the late nineteenth century. With Italy evolving from a collection of self-sufficient local economies to a participant in an international market of goods and labor, the great need of workers in the mills, mines, and factories of more rapidly developing nations, labeled by Karl Marx as the "light cavalry of capitalism," provided a compelling incentive for emigrants to seek overseas opportunities. As the era created a "gigantic machine for uprooting countrymen," Italian emigration took its place, as Robert F. Foerster noted in introducing his classic study, *The Italian Emigration of Our Times*, "among the extraordinary movements of mankind." But among other factors, government policy also facilitated its growth. With manpower co-opted by the Civil War, the main provision of the Contract Labor Law, enacted by the U.S. Congress in July 1864, empowered agents of American industries to recruit foreign labor. While indentured service had been almost extinct since the 1830s, the newly devised padrone system now threatened to restore it. The Foran Act of 1885, supported by organized labor against the threat of competition from foreign workers rather than any humanitarian concern over abuses suffered by them, prohibiting recruitment by promised employment, would not eliminate contract labor but only drive it undercover.[2]

In Southern Italy and Sicily, an increasing population, largely due to rapidly declining death rates, under a natural environment exhausted by hailstorms, crop failures, and inefficient agricultural practices, could not be easily accommodated by local resources and institutions. The unsympathetic government of the Kingdom of Italy, established in 1861, fearful of the threat of popular uprisings after early efforts by landowners to prevent the flight of workers, eventually welcomed mass immigration as a "safety valve" to resolve the "Southern Question." And with such dramatic improvements in navigational technology as the shift from sail to steam power, the determination of nautical position with better instruments, and the introduction of the twin screw propeller, shipping companies entered into a fierce competition for the human cargo that filled vessels with the highly profitable steerage trade. While newspapers, books, and pamphlets disseminating commercial propaganda were used to persuade prospective emigrants in other countries, the low literacy rates of Italy required other devices. And with a large demand on one side, a population ignorant of conditions in the receiving country, and a long distance to be traveled, the recruiter flourished. Upwards of 400 unofficial subagents (or brokers) serving steamship lines, mining companies, and manufacturers roamed the countryside with the complicity of government officials, promising work and wealth across the sea. And thousands of Italians, not searching for an "American dream" but eager to solve the needs of their families, left ancestral villages. Enticed not as docile hostages of the padrone system, these "birds of passage," or migratory seasonal laborers, joined the trek to *l'America* seeking to rescue their families from *la miseria* of a beloved but impoverished homeland. While relief sometimes came from mailed remittances or money carried by returning kin, many immigrants also began to revise their goals from ameliorating the distress of those left behind to building a new life for themselves in America.

Philadelphia in the Era of Mass Migration

Italian emigration, as Philip Taylor has written about migration in general, arose in response to European discontents and American opportunities. While the initiative, skill, and energy of immigrants influenced their adjustment, economic conditions determined their "choice" of new destinations. But American cities were not the same in what they offered immigrants. In Philadelphia, unlike cities dependent on heavy industry, the diversity of manufacturing, along with the promise of homeownership, attracted Italians. Many years after his arrival, Lorenzo Nardi, a figure maker and vendor from Diecimo near Lucca, and eventually a leader of the immigrant colony, claimed that he had searched for several days before finding another Italian when he first reached Philadelphia in 1852. In the U.S. Census of 1850, only 117 residents within the original city and adjacent districts of Southwark and Moyamensing were natives of Italy. By 1860, their number had risen to 485, with 622 found in the entire state of Pennsylvania, second only to New York City with about three times as many Italian residents. With the lure of prospecting for gold, the state of California, with slightly more than 2,800 Italian residents, offered an even more popular destination. But in Philadelphia, the number of Italians, often organ grinders and fruit vendors, living mainly within the Second, Third, and Fourth Wards of the consolidated city, rose to 516 by the 1870 census. Having reached the eve of mass migration, the number of Italians in Philadelphia would rapidly accelerate in further growth.[3]

With the outbreak of the Civil War greatly reducing the flow of immigration, the scant cohort of Philadelphia Italians, along with other foreign-born residents, joined the ranks of the Union army. After military service, more of them were seeking naturalization as American citizens by the late 1860s. Their value as citizens became enhanced by solicitation as voters on the eve of elections. But local Italians were not only being organized by others; they were also beginning to take organization into their own hands. In September 1867, emulating other immigrant groups, Italians founded *La Società di*

Unione e Fratellanza Italiana, the first of several hundred fraternal and beneficial associations that would follow in subsequent years. Along with Saint Mary Magdalen de Pazzi, the *Società* provided a bulwark for community development. By seeking to preserve traditional culture and language, such communal institutions eased adjustment, a task that would become even more daunting as a huge volume of immigrants began to reach America.

While a respected demographer had described Italy in 1861 as a place where "history has not in fact recorded . . . any important outward movement of population," natives of Southern Italy and Sicily, under a government indifferent to their needs and suffering, would soon begin to pour out of their homeland. With departure facilitated by the same mechanism that would mediate their adaptation in a new destination, prospective emigrants increasingly relied on relatives and friends who had already been or were currently there. And with the birth of what might be called the "*paesani* system," interpersonal relations, serving as informal "chains of migration," decisively influenced their coming to Philadelphia. When asked why they chose the city as their destination and how they got there, they would often reply that "my people were all there." Relatives and friends, who had returned to native villages or had sent letters from America, now provided incentive, information, and passage money that induced others to emigrate. With origins that made them not only newcomers to America but also to city life, the same *paesani* enabled them to find employment, housing, friendship, religion, recreation, and even a familiar language in Philadelphia. The reliance of *paesani* upon each other, sharing personal identity and culture, offered protection from an often hostile environment. And by clustering, not in a monolithic pattern of settlement but as distinct subcommunities, particular localities of Italy were reconstituted as neighborhoods of South Philadelphia, offering "urban villages," both real and imagined, that resembled the *paesi* of the native land. In short, "Little Italy" was actually a composite of "Little Italies."

By 1880, the rapidly growing population of Italians in the United States had increased from 17,157 to 44,230, with slightly more than 60 percent of them, a larger proportion than any other immigrant group, living in the 50 largest cities of the nation. While Irish and French immigration had fallen off greatly and Germans slightly within the urban population, Italians were among several groups that had notably increased. And Philadelphia, as Taylor notes, with only one-half of its streets paved, less than one-sixth of its houses with indoor plumbing, and sewers nearly a half-century old, despite being far from the city of later years, was increasing as a destination. But while the 1,656 Italian-born residents had more than tripled, they still ranked far behind the Irish, Germans, English, Scotch, and French.[4]

As Italian immigration grew in volume, other related conditions also changed. Early Ligurians had usually departed from Genoa, but with the shift of emigrant origins to Abruzzo-Molise, Apulia, Basilicata, Campania, Calabria, and Sicily, the port of Naples became the point of embarkation. While immigrants of Northern European or British origins often landed at Philadelphia, they usually paused for only a day before the Pennsylvania Railroad carried them to their final destinations in the Midwest and West. For steamship service from Mediterranean ports, Philadelphia, about 140 nautical miles and a day longer, and with inadequate navigational and docking facilities, was a less desirable port of entry. Except for a brief span from 1908 to 1914, when the Italia Line offered service to Philadelphia, Italians were far more likely to arrive at New York, before trains brought them to the Broad Street Station of the Pennsylvania Railroad or the Market Street depot of the Reading Railroad. And after being greeted by relatives and friends, they began the final stage of their journey on foot over city streets, toting baggage in colorful processions that brought them to the figurative gates of "Little Italy."

In 1890, the number of Italians, along with Russians, Poles, and Hungarians, almost nonexistent in immigration statistics 20 years earlier, had increased with "extraordinary rapidity." But less than 200,000 in total number, Italians remained well behind nearly 28,000,000 Germans and more than 18,000,000 Irish, with almost 65 percent of them in northeastern states. Of slightly less than 25,000 Italians in Pennsylvania, some 6,799 of them lived in Philadelphia, comprising 2.52 percent of its population. But the Census Bureau, after introducing ancestry, also reported 10,208 offspring of full or part Italian parentage, with some 7,620 foreign born and 2,588 American born in the city. In 1900, some 17,830 Italian born, or 60 percent of the total foreign-born population, were residents of the city. (Contrary to U.S. Census findings, the Italian press claimed their population as being 80,000 in the city and another 20,000 in the suburbs in 1907, figures also deemed as more accurate by the Italian consulate of Philadelphia.) By 1910, it had burgeoned to 45,308 immigrants and 28,942 more being children of Italian-born parents. While Italian natives remained larger in number, the census, by including American-born offspring in the tabulation, officially recognized the presence of an Italian American generation. But Italians remained much lower on the economic scale, unlikely to hold occupations requiring fluency in English or education that enabled them to deal with other Americans, as Taylor states, "across counter or desk." Beyond working in factories and railroad maintenance, however, their skills as barbers, tailors, cobblers, and bootblacks gave them high visibility in personal services. Although resting on its lower rungs, Italians had gained a foothold on a ladder that held the promise of upward mobility for future generations.[5]

Despite being concentrated at the lower end of the urban economy, Philadelphia's Italians, on the eve of the Great War, already showed some internal differentiation. Some of them, whose roots stretched back to the Ligurian pioneers of the previous century, having reached white-collar, entrepreneurial, or professional careers, occupied the upper echelons of the stratification system of Little Italy. But they also varied in their responses to life in America. For some of them, Italy had already become a faded memory; for others, it remained a place from which they were only temporarily separated as they toiled in hopes of rescuing their families from the miseries of an impoverished but enduring "homeland." Unlike Jews and Armenians, who fled oppression, violence, and the threat of extermination, Italians, who often returned to their place of birth, shared with Greeks and Hungarians the highest rates of repatriation. In Philadelphia, the low wages they earned as unskilled laborers or seasonal employment in clothing factories enabled them, or perhaps forced them, to be "birds of passage." The *paese* remained for them a village or town or, at best, a province or region that gave them their identity as individuals and cohesion with other immigrants. For many of them, their localistic orientation also obscured their sense of loyalty to any national government, whether its center was in Rome or Washington, DC, especially when nation-states decided to go to war. But even for sojourners who hoped to retire in Italy at the end of their working days, the first of several important pivots—a shift toward more permanent life in America—had begun to alter their intentions. Other events would accelerate that adjustment even more.[6]

By 1914, with immigration halted by the outbreak of the Great War, Philadelphia's Italians were largely concentrated in the southeastern quarter of the city but also dwelled in several outlying "satellite" communities. Three years later, the *Evening Ledger*, in describing the scene, could memorably declare, "Philadelphia, a city which has in its borders an Italian city of 150,000." That estimate of the Italian population, higher than more official sources but widely repeated, would take on a life of its own. The war would also force Italian residents to ask whether they preferred to face the future as Italians or Americans. When Italy joined the Allies in the next year, several thousand Italians responded to the order to report as reservists at their consulate in Philadelphia. Despite the desperate need of forces to confront the Austro-Hungarian enemy on the Italian front, the slow conversion of passenger vessels to troop ships, and the inability of their government to provide funds for passage, impeded their return to Italy. With the belated entry of America into the war in the spring of 1917, Italians, unable or unwilling to answer the call of their own nation, including men who had emigrated specifically to escape military duty, were now being summoned by the Selective Service and enlisting or being inducted into the army of the United States. From their experiences in basic training to commendable service in combat, Italian "doughboys" would find themselves in a cauldron that eventually brought them home, much like their comrades in arms, as "American" veterans of the Great War. The broader determinants of this process would begin not on the streets of Philadelphia but with a violent act in a far-off Balkan city that ignited the maelstrom that eventually changed the entire world.[7]

2

From Sarajevo to Little Italy

In the summer of 1914, diplomacy in Europe failed. In June, when the young Serbian nationalist Gavrilo Princip assassinated Archduke Franz Ferdinand, heir to the throne of the Austro-Hungarian Empire, and his wife Sophie in Sarajevo, the incident provoked a trajectory of unanticipated disaster. Criminal proceedings, conducted with a spirit of compromise among concerned parties, might have resolved matters. Although states had found peaceful solutions to previous disputes, this event, tragic in itself but not a sufficient cause of further damage, would provoke far greater consequences. In Vienna, Berlin, Belgrade, Saint Petersburg, Paris, and London, emperors and kings, prime ministers, cabinets, and parliaments sought to mediate disagreement and reduce tensions. But with the mobilization of armies by supreme commanders, unrestrained by constitutional limits or higher governmental authority, inducing similar reactions by other nations, the momentum toward war as the solution was irretrievably released. While diplomats pursued their futile efforts, the generals had won the opening skirmish of a conflict that had yet to be declared. The Great War had begun.[1]

By August, only a few weeks after the assassination at Sarajevo, the leading powers of Europe, having devised plans to attack other nations or to defend their own borders, were poised to enter the battlefield. By September, after German troops overwhelmed Belgian defenses, entered France, and approached Paris, the war was widely expected to be a brief adventure that would not last more than a few months. But with French resistance against the Germans in the First Battle of the Marne, it became a protracted struggle with huge losses of men and marginal yields of territory often regained by the other side in counterattacks over another four years and three months. During that course of time, its boundaries widened until it involved most of Europe as well as Japan and the Ottoman Empire. It required the largest armies ever placed on battlefields. The duration of battles, with renewed assaults, counterattacks, and defensive maneuvers, stretched into weeks, months, and years. It saw a widened use of new instruments of warfare—steel helmets, machine guns, long-range artillery, tanks, airplanes, submarines, and nerve gas. It destroyed masterpieces of art and architecture, ancient universities, and entire cities. It displaced vast populations from their homes and towns. It took millions of lives in military and civilian casualties while leaving countless others forever mutilated. Its impact on life and environment shattered the human spirit.

Early Responses to War in Europe

The United States, away from the tinderbox of old animosities, unsettled feuds, and new provocations, could refrain from choosing sides and momentarily escape the conflict. But it was not as remote from the woes of Mother Europe as was first believed. In its own development as a nation, America had witnessed much of the turmoil that would explode when Kaiser Wilhelm's army crossed the Rhine into Belgium. From New York to California, from the Canadian border to the Gulf of Mexico, the kaleidoscope of population, fueled for more than a century by mass immigration, reflected the peoples who would engage in conflict on the Western Front, the steppes of Russia, and the Italian-Austrian border. As the Great War began, ethnic diversity within the population posed a challenge, as immigrant communities sorted out their allegiances to disparate homelands as well as to their adopted country. Germans, who had long been the largest component of the American population, could not be enthusiastic about going to war against their homeland. With the Irish second in volume, the possibility of supporting Great Britain would not easily inspire the consent of a people seeking Home Rule. With a sizable number of immigrants from the various peoples of the Austro-Hungarian Empire, any decision to oppose the Central Powers would risk further alienating workers who had already been much abused by heavy-handed factory owners and mine operators. Seeking to remain apart from the war, America initially hoped to follow a course of action guided by the widely held conviction that "the quarrels of Europe are not our quarrels." In the autumn of 1916, the reelection campaign of President

Woodrow Wilson used a similar argument, "He kept us out of war." Yet, while attempting to avoid the dispute among European nations, even Wilson recognized the growing likelihood of an eventual shift in policy.[2]

In Philadelphia, a huge population of Italian origins, many of whom had arrived in recent years, along with the material challenges of their relocation, struggled to discern personal identity and political allegiance. In Italy, government officials, attempting to raise an army capable of defeating an old enemy and gain long-disputed territories that would consolidate its own sense of national geography, had to determine the military obligations of thousands of young men who had departed for remote destinations where they had found work, wages, and new lives. And Philadelphians of older tenure as Americans, with their first major encounter in international war, faced the need to finally decide how far they would allow Italians with their duskier complexions, quaint customs, and lusty demeanor to enter civic life. The Italian community in South Philadelphia and its satellite clusters would become laboratories for social and cultural initiatives in which such issues would be tested.

In September 1914, the local press, along with coverage of the recently started war, reported the departure of Italian reservists who, despite the fact that Italy would not enter the conflict for another seven months, were among the 400 passengers on the steamer *Ancona* as it headed for Genoa. By the time the vessel reached New York City, their number had grown to 1,900, precursors of other recruits on a similar path before the year had ended, with Naples as the destination. In early December, when another 1,500 men boarded the *Ancona* at the Municipal Pier at the foot of Vine Street, newspaper accounts placed the scene within an unfortunately familiar context used for events in the Italian colony. A police detail, assigned to maintain order over an estimated 5,000 persons who had come to bid farewell, despite a driving rain, harbored another task. While ostensibly "going home for Christmas," as many immigrants routinely did at this season, informants had convinced police that the "reservists" were heavily armed with concealed weapons. As onlookers cheered passengers who claimed to be going to join the colors, a search on deck reportedly recovered "a good-sized arsenal" of revolvers, stilettos, and ordinary knives, enabling authorities to conclude that nearly every man had some kind of weapon. With the reprise of the image of potentially violent criminals, readers could only be relieved that so many Italians were leaving Philadelphia.[3]

For departing Italians, it meant leaving an America that had not welcomed them with open arms but had been ambivalent if not hostile to their presence. And with the entry of the United States into the war looming in the near future, the aversion to immigrant groups that did not "fit" expectations of what being "fully American" meant was gaining salience across the nation. In April 1915, *The Inquirer*, fanning the flames of xenophobia, expressed that point of view in its opposition to a bill in the Pennsylvania legislature that would require the publication of official notices in German, Italian, and Yiddish in any county where more than 40,000 immigrants spoke one of those languages. While objecting to the proposed act because "the language of the United States is English," *The Inquirer* more broadly argued that immigrants were welcome, but, when they settled down and took the oath of allegiance to become citizens, they should learn to speak its tongue. And while allowed fond recollections of their parent country, "they are no longer—or should not be—German-Americans, Italian-Americans, Irish-Americans, English or French-Americans or anything else but just plain Americans. The hyphen has no business being placed before the word American. This is not a hyphenated country."[4]

Even while the conflict remained a European war, some observers recognized what the future held for America's diverse peoples. In Philadelphia, amid clamorous voices expressing a wide range of judgments, the erudite Judge Joseph Buffington, of the Third Circuit Court of Appeals, argued that the greatest consequence of the war would not be found in military preparedness or in the extension of international trade but in the absorption of the large foreign population that had migrated to America. He noted that some 22 percent of all immigrants had made Pennsylvania their destination. Despite their overwhelmingly rural origins, new arrivals settled not only with others who shared their language and provided companionship but where they were likely to find employment in urban industries. As the foreign born learned to appreciate favorable conditions found in America, Buffington expected that after the war they would seek to bring families and friends to their new country. And Americans, despite their opposition to immigration, could not fail to be impressed by the ambition and industriousness of the newcomers. Buffington's analysis, however, was not new or especially prophetic but part of an older dialogue expanding with urgency under the impact of the war.[5]

Italian immigrants presented a distinctive challenge for America, partly because Italy would join the Allies nearly two years before the United States did. As they embraced that cause while America hesitated, Italians momentarily separated themselves from other Americans. And undeterred by American neutrality, they would, when beckoned by Italy, parade in the streets before marching to the docks where erstwhile tourist steamers, serving as impromptu military transports, waited to carry them back to their homeland.

In March 1915, Little Italy, undisturbed by news and opinion swirling about the city in recent weeks, remained "quiet and peaceful" despite the clouds that loomed over the mother country. Rumors that the Italian government had begun calling up reserves from within the immigrant population in the United States had so far proved to be unfounded. The *Evening Ledger* blithely observed that "everybody in the little colony is happy and doing business with the usual diligence," with many people expressing the opinion that Italy would come through the current diplomatic crisis with Austria without a declaration of war. But it was a tranquility that would not last. Before the month ended, another article reported a noticeable shift: "The war fever gripped hundreds of Italians this morning, and they gathered on the Municipal Pier at Vine Street to witness the sailing of the Italian liner Ancona." With departure scheduled at noon, reservists had begun arriving at 6:00 A.M. to board the vessel taken over by the Italian government to carry food supplies and some 600 men from Philadelphia and New York to Italy. Port officials were said to be amazed by men and women conspicuously displaying national colors who had come "to say farewell to a father, son, husband or sweetheart." The reservists, somehow already trained, reportedly would be immediately given guns and uniforms upon arriving at Naples, while the *Ancona*, after being refitted at a New York shipyard, was expected to be converted to a troop transport or auxiliary cruiser.[6]

The reaction to the inevitability of war partly reflected whether one lived inside that immigrant community or only vicariously experienced it from the outside. Although the call for mobilization had not yet been officially issued, when volunteers boarded the *Ancona*, another newspaper account noted that as "padre" went off to war, "madre" began to weep. It described Elena Gasparo of South Percy Street whose "five bambinos play apathetically and wonder what the matter is with 'madre'" as her husband Guglielmo went to the "bigga war." But beneath attempts at condescending humor, as men gathered on corners and sidewalks, neglecting their work to discuss the war with excited gestures and raised eyebrows, and stoic women faced its meaning for them, tensions emerged in Little Italy. The newspaper writer added: "It might be safe to say that if patriotism depended solely on women, it would soon become an obsolete virtue. Somehow they seem to love their husbands and children a little better than a faraway country." But as long as the United States remained a nonbelligerent nation, instead of empathy, jocular accounts of dining in an Italian restaurant were more typical of what was being reported. And a new shape of spaghetti that challenged the dining skills of cosmopolitan Philadelphians who ventured into Giuseppe's Restaurant at "South Eighth-and-a half and Somewhereselse [*sic*] streets" would find space in an evening edition. While "opera buffa" journalism had long amused Philadelphia, it now also trivialized the anguish of Little Italy.[7]

An Appeal for Peace—and a Disaster at Sea

The approach of war, however, did not convince everyone of its inevitability or desirability—and Philadelphia's Italians would share in the dissent. Appropriately, on Easter Monday, 1915, "An Appeal to the American People," appearing in *The Inquirer*, *Public Ledger*, and newspapers throughout the nation, and signed by 390 editors and publishers representing the foreign language press, religious bodies, organized labor, and Socialist factions, called upon American industries and workers to not manufacture, sell, or ship powder, shrapnel, or shot of any kind to any nation already at war. The signers implored: "Let us alleviate human suffering and preserve life—not help to destroy it." Recognizing the arms industry as essential in making war possible, they were protesting its impact on their own people in lands from which some of them had only recently left. Sponsored by the American Association of Foreign Newspapers, its endorsers claimed to express the views of immigrants and their families who had written thousands of letters "demanding that the United States observe the spirit as well as the letter of neutrality." Although calling for neutrality, it was actually a plea for peace—advocating action by which waging war would become impossible.[8]

While his "Appeal to the American People" stirred controversy throughout the nation, much of the dispute focused on Louis N. Hammerling, an Austrian-born immigrant who had worked as a mule driver in the coal mines of Northeastern Pennsylvania before becoming a millionaire, and the question of who had actually paid for the advertisement. In Wilkes-Barre, where he had once lived, a local newspaper, disputing his claim that he had paid $100,000 for the cost of publication, charged that the money had actually come from the German government. But within a few days, his supporters had increased to the editors and publishers of 481 foreign language newspapers, with 113 Italians being more than twice as many as the next group, Poles with 47 names, and others mostly represented by only a handful of signers. Despite the absence of German signers, some critics believed that the appeal was propaganda financed by a German fund in New York City. Vehemently denying such charges, Hammerling insisted that no foreign government had anything to do with the appeal. With his town of birth having been destroyed and no relatives involved in the war, he claimed to care only about America and that the foreign language press association was neutral in every way.[9]

Controversy had also been fueled by disagreement over trade policy. Despite many Americans being profoundly uneasy and some industrialists even rejecting the pursuit of profits from such trade, Congress refused to ban the manufacture and sale of arms to belligerent nations on the grounds that altering national policy would mean taking sides. But while the Central Powers were blocked from obtaining arms by British and French sea power, American manufacturers continued to sell arms and ammunition to the Western Allies. This inconsistency, along with Wilson's wavering commitment to neutrality, showed that the United States was destined to join the Triple Entente.

The dispute over Hammerling's appeal to the American people, meanwhile, reached well into the Italian community. With 105 Italian signers, the manifesto transcended differences that normally separated them into antagonistic blocs—for it embraced labor, Socialists, Catholics, monarchists, and republicans. In Philadelphia, Father Tommaso Terlizzi, the pastor of Our Lady of Good Counsel Church, signed the appeal as editor of a parish bulletin that served the community as a newspaper. What made Terlizzi's advocacy, whether of neutrality or peace, even more notable was that only three years later he would be one of the organizers of "Italian Flag Day," an enthusiastic celebration of the Italian cause in May 1918. Other supporters of the appeal for an end to war would undergo a similar transition to this more bellicose position.[10]

But the signers of the proposal did not include every influential voice within the immigrant population. Agostino De Biasi, now editor of *Il Carroccio*, a New York review, charged that Hammerling had greatly misrepresented his support among Italian journalists. Contending that many Italian editors had opposed the appeal, De Biasi declared, "He surely is not the leader of the Italian press, which would revolt at such a thought." Moreover, the American Association of Foreign Language Newspapers existed in name only, without Italian editors and newspapers as supporters to promote the interests of Hammerling's advertising agency. De Biasi regarded the appeal as being a pro–German and Austrian propaganda effort, paid for by unknown sources, intended to cripple and damage American industry. In the end, even though unsuccessful in reaching its objective, the appeal afforded some glimpse of the opposition toward the war within the Italian community.[11]

Whether being what it was purported to be or serving a less honorable agenda, the peace initiative would be undermined by another event with far greater consequences than any rhetorical opposition could have achieved. Only one month after the appeal for peace appeared in newspapers, a German U-boat attacked the Cunard liner Lusitania off the southern coast of Ireland, sinking the ship less than 20 minutes after the first torpedo struck, with the loss of 1,198 of the 1,959 passengers and crew, including 128 Americans aboard. Although the vessel carried a large cargo of war supplies intended for

England, which had been openly declared on the ship manifest, and despite German warnings of the dangers of Atlantic crossings to prospective passengers, the enormity of the tragedy discredited any argument in favor of neutrality. But its impact went even further. While Wilson and other politicians displayed restraint in their reactions, the sinking of the Lusitania galvanized American sympathy for Great Britain and animosity toward Germany. And for Italians in Philadelphia and elsewhere, Italy's intervention against the Central Powers loomed with even greater certainty.

3

Little Italy Goes to War

By May 1915, anticipation and apprehension had visibly increased within the Italian colony of Philadelphia. As the Chamber of Deputies in Rome deliberated the decision that would bring their nation to war, Philadelphia's Italians gathered to discuss what the outcome would mean not only for Italy but for themselves as well. Widely recognizing that war was now inevitable, they awaited the return of Consul General Gaetano Poccardi from meetings at the Italian Embassy in Washington, where he was expected to receive instructions to release an order for the mobilization of reservists. By Saturday May 22, with rain driving them from streets and sidewalks to more sheltered places where claims and counterclaims could be exchanged, Italians, along with sharing the rumor that reservists intended to charter a ship to take them back to Italy, waited for Poccardi to announce the names of the first men being summoned from Pennsylvania, Delaware, Maryland, and New Jersey.[1]

The events of far-off Italian cities would be echoed by similar demonstrations on the streets of immigrant colonies. With the "days of May," as George M. Trevelyan later wrote, being nothing less than "an ever-memorable event in Italian history," Italy, while not a great parliamentary nation but nonetheless a democratic nation, would see its people, "endowed with remarkable sense and vigour" in moments of crisis, attempt to take matters into their own hands. Whether supporting Camillo di Cavour and Giuseppe Garibaldi in 1860, or Antonio Salandra or and Sidney Sonnino in 1915, the "popolo" once again clamored in support of war. With characteristic eloquence, Trevelyan recalled,

"The politics of Italy since the time of Romulus have been the politics of her cities," and then with glum prescience of what was to come, "The cities of Italy made the war; but the peasant has had to fight it." The "politics of the *piazza*" were also to find expression on street corners and in cafés of Philadelphia.[2]

. . . Until the Last Austrian Is Killed or Surrenders

Within the next few days, the "war wave" suddenly swept across Little Italy. While discussing the likelihood of Italy entering the war, Italians had initially remained unwilling to believe that their homeland would take up arms. The origins of many immigrants in provinces of the Abruzzi where Socialist sentiments prevailed had also discouraged belief in war. But with news that Parliament had voted to authorize the king to declare war being posted at newspaper offices, banks, and travel agencies, along with reports that even Socialist deputies had already offered to enlist into military service, dispositions quickly changed. And like the crowds clamoring for war in cities across Italy, Philadelphia's Italians openly voiced their concerns as they joined in the call for military action against an old adversary. They gathered at Palumbo's Restaurant on Catharine Street, at the nearby Mascagni Hotel and Restaurant, and on the sidewalks between South 7th and South 9th Streets to talk excitedly about recent events. A small boy, dressed in a Bersaglieri uniform, wearing a hat with green feathers and wielding a wooden sword, elicited repeated outbursts of cheers. Men and women, old and young, could be heard singing the "Royal March," along with the hymns of Goffredo Mameli and Giuseppe Garibaldi, as people poured onto the streets. And as the crowds shouted salutes for King Victor Emmanuel III and Queen Elena, photographic images of their royal majesties became visible in the windows of shops and homes. At least, that was what one reporter claimed to have seen and heard.[3]

If more residents of Little Italy had been able to read the newspapers, their early enthusiasm might have been tempered by accounts of what their native country faced. As Philadelphia's Italians eagerly plunged toward imagined encounters, a more sober assessment of Italy's military capability on actual battlefields reached less optimistic conclusions. While the call up of various classes of reserves could mobilize nearly 2,000,000 men, the need for arms and ammunition, growing more acute over time, would require aid from other nations. A detailed appraisal of Italy's strength produced a grim prognosis: "Many an Italian regards the struggle to come with a lamentable lightness. He fails to realize that tens of thousands of his countrymen will leave their bleached bones in the mountain fastnesses of the Austrian Alps before the Italians can hope to see Vienna in subjection, even before they cut off the 'water-rats' at Pola." Anticipating that any attack by Italy had to come through Alpine passes, Austria had already deployed troops and fortified the mountainous salient of the "unredeemed" Trentino. The "bleached bones," as fully literal as it was metaphorical, that captured the core of the argument were as much a warning to the enthusiastic crowds on the streets of Philadelphia as on any piazza in Italy. But fervently convinced that destiny made victory inevitable, its costs, particularly in young lives, could be ignored—at least for the moment—and no crowd of "patriots" could be dissuaded from marching on the safe streets of an American city.[4]

As Little Italy shifted to more careful reflection, "the first flush of excitement [had] given way to sober thought and definite planning to aid their government." New concerns went further into the minds of people whose origins had shifted from the Abruzzi alone to Calabria and Sicily as well. And news that the Italian government had decreed pardons for all "military offenders," presumably evaders of their obligations to serve, if they would answer the call within three months beginning May 7, invited a mildly facetious observation: "This makes it possible for many an outlaw to rehabilitate himself." With an estimated 175,000 Italian residents, including as many as 25,000 of them ready to volunteer for duty with Italy's army, Carlo D. Nardi, an editor at *L'Opinione*, declared that Philadelphia would become the center for a great mobilization with any declaration of war. But with men seeking to know when and where to report, the answer also depended on finding a way to implement this task without incurring opposition from American officials.[5]

In late May, some 8,000 participants, hoping for good weather, prepared to celebrate the annual feast day of the patron saint at Saint Mary Magdalen de Pazzi, the mother church of Philadelphia's Little Italy. With events to begin at 2:00 P.M. what would transpire could not be entirely foreseen, beyond the expectation: "If the sun shines, there will be a bewildering display of uniforms and banners to augment the martial spirit that has swept over the district in the last three days." Father Antonio Isoleri, its longtime pastor, would lead a special service with the statue of the saint being carried in a procession, followed by 100 religious and military societies. From the sidewalks, the large crowd, anticipating the entry of their native country into a great military struggle, enthusiastically cheered as men in Italian uniforms marched by. But what gave the occasion even more significance was the first public announcement that Italy had declared war against Austria. And in an instant, Little Italy itself proclaimed war against the enemies of the *madrepatria*. As news flashed across newspaper bulletin boards, it was greeted by cheering onlookers. Carrying American and Italian flags, marchers, along with hundreds of children, displayed allegiance to homeland and faith. Inside the church, Isoleri, who as a seminarian had written patriotic poems in support of Savoy in earlier wars with the Austrians, now offered prayers for the Kingdom of Italy against the same enemy.[6]

The selection of flag bearers who would carry Italian and American flags side by side projected the spirit of the day. While the customary auctioning of the privilege usually reached about $25, the Italian flag on this day was awarded to a bootblack who operated a stand near city hall for his bid of $100. When bidding for the American flag peaked at only $5, angry spectators shouted "Shame!" until someone proclaimed: "The United States is Italy's friend, and the one who carries the Red, White, and Blue shall pay the same sum as the bearer of the colors of Italy." With an offer of $100, the anonymous winner declared: "It is an honor to carry the Stars and Stripes and I will not disgrace the flag by advertising myself as its humble bearer." His gesture, as well as the entire event, suggested that the imminent war was reshaping not only religious observance but personal identity as well. With sentiments of the crowd shifting from religion in America to the war in Italy, a newspaper noted that "most of the prayers were made for the safety of relatives abroad, who soon will be in battle."[7]

Isoleri, no less patriotic than his parishioners, responded with similar fervor, as younger priests were returning to Italy to serve as chaplains. He was, at 70 years of age, too old for military service, but with the declaration of war, Isoleri took up his pen on the following day to write "Il 24 Maggio 1915—Viva L'Italia!" a poem in which he exhorted the sons of Italy to answer the call. Mindful of the lingering tension between church and state, as well as the territorial claims of Italy, he united pope and king in the same cause and called for the inclusion of Trieste and Trento within the boundaries of an expanded nation. He began his final stanza with the words "O Guerra Santa, Guerra Benedetta" (O holy war; blessed war), before ending his poem by linking the crosses of Savoy and Calvary. And if poetry was not enough, Isoleri claimed to have also seen "the extraordinary spectacle" of the Italian tricolor radiating around the sun in his own version of what had happened on this day in South Philadelphia.[8]

As Italy's declaration of war was being embraced in South Philadelphia, it inspired Italian residents of other sections of the city. In the Italian quarter of Germantown, sometimes referred to as Little Italy North, some 100 or so "patriots" gathered at a street corner then marched to Germantown Avenue as Italian women and children on sidewalks cheered. They boarded trolley cars

FIGURE 3.1 Ottavio D'Angelantonio (*top*), having shed the first blood for Italy in a street fight in Philadelphia, was expected to leave to enlist in the Italian army. His brother, Tommaso (*bottom*), was already serving as a sergeant, stationed at Bari. (*Evening Ledger* [May 29, 1915].)

that carried them to the Italian consulate and offered their services as aspiring soldiers to their native country.[9]

While unsubstantiated rumors that Austrian and German "spies" were gathering information on Italians elicited apprehension but little harm, more direct encounters became violent. In the evening of the day that brought news of war, an incident would galvanize Philadelphia's Italians with patriotic zeal for their native land. It began when a group of young men scanning bulletin boards in search of war-related news encountered an Austrian at 7th and Chestnut Streets who disputed Italy's chances of success against his own nation. As their argument escalated, the Austrian allegedly stabbed Ottavio D'Angelantonio, reputed to be one of the eager stalwarts who had already volunteered for military service in Italy. Released from the hospital where he had been taken for medical treatment, the first casualty of the war joined incensed friends who clamored to launch another counterattack on any one who looked German or Austrian. In recognition of "the first blood spilt for Italy in Philadelphia since the war began," friends toasted D'Angelantonio at Palumbo's Restaurant, while their hero, medicated by Chianti, proudly displayed the wound on his arm to admirers. But D'Angelantonio had a more personal reason for his actions—his brother, Tommaso, was already in military service, holding the rank of sergeant and stationed at the city of Bari with the Italian army. And with news quickly spreading among Italians, a cry rose from Little Italy: "More than 25,000 soldiers for the Italian army from Philadelphia."[10] (See Figure 3.1.)

With Italians ready to back words with action, D'Angelantonio, on the day after being stabbed, had reportedly sought information at the Italian consulate on how he might expedite his intention to join the army. But by then fervor had reached a broader audience. It was being rumored that all men between 18 and 45 years of age would be obliged to report for duty, while men who refused would be prohibited from returning to Italy. It was also said to be unnecessary to speak of this openly in the Italian colony in order to spur young men into action. A group of them had called upon editor Nardi, at the office of *L'Opinione*, with plans to organize a Philadelphia Regiment that would enable them to face the enemy as a group representative of their adopted city. When another committee of young men called upon Poccardi at his office, seeking information on the presumed declaration of war, he had reportedly answered, "Not a word! Not a word." With his staff clearly occupied with preparations related to military mobilization, Poccardi had been instructed by his embassy in Washington to remain silent on what the immediate future held for Italy and its reservists in immigrant colonies.[11]

As immigrant reservists, uncertain but impatient, waited for clarification, their situation became even more confused. Some men had already been summoned to military service. In a letter from Rome where he had gone to visit relatives, Giuseppe Donato, another editor of *L'Opinione*, wrote that he had been detained by an order to join his regiment as a lieutenant. Meanwhile, before a general summons of reservists, a call had been made for physicians overseas. The first Philadelphia Italian to be officially beckoned was identified as Dr. Joseph Pasceri. Although in the United States for only seven years, he had married an American woman from Richmond, Virginia. From his residence on North 63rd Street, Pasceri had served the Italian community in West Philadelphia. As a captain in the Italian Royal Medical Corps, he had received an order to report to the Fifth Army being mobilized in Verona. Along with Pasceri, at least nine other Italians, practicing in the community or studying at local medical schools, now ready to offer their skills on battlefields, indicated their willingness to answer the summons. But a more general order for mobilization remained to be issued.[12]

With the Italian Parliament voting on a declaration of war in May 1915, the mobilizing of military forces became urgent. While most recruits would come from its own inhabitants, Italy, with a population greatly depleted by immigration, faced the need to persuade its young men to return home. While meager opportunities in an underdeveloped Italian economy, particularly in the South and Sicily, had encouraged many men to abandon their native land, emigration had also enabled them to escape their military obliga-

FIGURE 3.2 Little Italy discusses developments in the war news. (*Evening Ledger* [May 26, 1915].)

tion to a government widely viewed in unfavorable terms. But despite having once sought to avoid military duty, immigrants would answer the summons to arms. While some reservists responded out of loyalty, others feared arrest or forfeiture of their right to return to Italy after the war if they ignored the call. And of those who sought to remain as civilians within the apparent safety of an immigrant colony for the duration of the war, the government of the United States would eventually induct many of them as the largest foreign component of its armed forces during World War I.

With residents gathering in cafés and on street corners to discuss the fate of their native country, patriotic enthusiasm remained high in Philadelphia's Italian colony. As a newspaper reported, "Every hour brings forth a new hero in Little Italy in these days of wartime excitement." On May 26, when Mario Cotellessa of Salter Street in South Philadelphia led another group of 60 young Italians to the consulate seeking assistance for their plans for military service, a more familiar name, Ottavio D'Angelantonio, who had become a "popular idol" in the Italian quarter, appeared among them.[13] (See Figure 3.2.)

Italian reservists, however, quickly learned that no arrangements had been made for any special provisions to convey them back to Italy. The Italian government could provide only what was available during times of peace, a half fare of $23, for reservists who wished to complete their military service. Since no official call for volunteers had yet been issued, the consulate had no authority to provide any cheaper passage. But on the same day that the reservists received their disappointing news, other Italians rallied to Italy's cause. Professor Saladino Vincenzo Di Santo, an instructor of Romance languages at the University of Pennsylvania, announced that he was ready to go on a moment's notice to serve his country. Having already volunteered two weeks earlier, Di Santo had prepared a list of others willing to answer any call up. And with news that Italian forces had captured five towns on the path to Trieste, veterans of earlier wars, "Garibaldi men," who had fought in the cause of "liberation from the Austrian yoke" but now being beyond the age of military service, donned old uniforms and marched before cheering crowds. And as another parade of Italian and American flags passed over downtown streets, reservists invaded shipping offices, seeking passage on the *Taormina*, scheduled to sail for Naples on May 31.[14]

While transporting men to war remained urgent, the community found itself threatened by chaos. With the Italian government expecting volunteers not only to enlist promptly but to pay their own way, or at least one-half of the fare, stalwarts eager to serve their native country confidently insisted that transportation would be provided without cost when the time came. But as long as consular officials had not yet issued any call, the matter remained a premature question. In late May, with religious celebration again becoming support for war, patriotism grew in momentum. As the igniting of firecrackers in front of Our Lady of Good Counsel filled the air with dense smoke, the martial airs of La Banda Rossa di Grassano, in bright red coats and under the spirited baton of Luigi Lucantonio, stirred crowds as another feast day of a patron saint "cannonaded" into a more bellicose occasion. Meanwhile, Sons of Italy leaders sought to defuse fears that an unlawful demonstration or even a riot was being planned, as had recently disrupted their convention in Pittsburgh. In the midst of turmoil, a committee of prominent citizens, led by Charles C. A. Baldi, announced plans for Italian American physicians and American women, organized as a Red Cross unit to be sent to Italy, along with a campaign to collect food, clothing, and other necessities for families of soldiers left behind.[15]

By early June, as news of the first call up of reservists reached Philadelphia's Italian colony, Pasceri and other men with officer's rank received orders to report for military service. An otherwise unidentified Dr. Kramer, Italian despite his German-sounding name, was a druggist who operated a pharmacy at 11th and Tasker Streets. Lieutenant Costantine was a journalist who worked as an editor for *L'Opinione*. Dr. Vincent De Virgilis was a dentist who only 10 days before had been depicted in a photograph as one of "Five Leaders of Thought and Action in the Transplanted Italy of Philadelphia," which appeared in the *Evening Ledger*. Each man's professional skills gave him a dubious priority as Italy sought to mobilize a military force that could be quickly dispatched to the front. But the call, coming several weeks earlier than expected, along with the fact that some recipients were already in their 30s, an age not usually liable for duty, indicated that Italy intended to place an army of fullest strength without delay in the field against the Austrians.[16]

When the Italian Embassy finally issued the first general call for mobilization by a telegram to consular offices in American cities, it carried instructions to be published in Italian language newspapers. In a detailed statement to the press of the immigrant colony on June 3, Consul Poccardi directed men between 20 and 39 years of age to report for further instructions. In response, Italian reservists, although still uncertain about what was asked of them, began registering at the consulate. The announcement was aimed at all men who had not yet been naturalized as American citizens, who were regarded as reservists and obligated to answer the call to military duty in Italy. Recent figures reported precisely 712,813 male Italians at the age of 21 or older in the United States, with 126,523 of them already naturalized as American citizens and not subject to the call even if they visited Italy, and nearly 600,000 others who were eligible. In Pennsylvania, some 111,536 Italian men had been counted in the 1910 census, with the number estimated to be about the same five years later, and slightly over 78,000 of them were still aliens in 1915. Of the more than 57,000 Italian men in New Jersey, about 35,000 remained aliens. In June, when the *Duca degli Abruzzi* left New York, it carried a vanguard of 3,000 men called up by the Italian government. A few days later, upwards of 500 more reservists boarded the *Ancona* in Philadelphia before it picked up another contingent in New York. About the same time, a large number of reservists in New England also answered the call to arms. Altogether some 2,300 reservists were expected to sail on the vessel. Along with the Philadelphians who had boarded the *Ancona*, most men had been called from the central and western sections of the state, with others from the Midwest and as far away as Colorado. On the overcrowded ship, accommodating far more passengers than in normal crossings, men were "doubling up" in berths and sleeping on floors of saloons and other areas of the ship, which carried no travelers other than reservists. But the task of getting men back to Italy remained clouded by confusion over related matters. While men were reported as believing that only half of their expenses would be paid by the government, the offices of the shipping line received inquiries about whether families would be taken along with them or left in this country.[17]

The use of the *Ancona* as a troop carrier prompted other concerns at its point of departure as well as along its anticipated route. In Philadelphia, Italians eagerly hoped to honor recruits by a festive ceremony at their embarkation. But the plan was abandoned, reportedly at the order of Consul Poccardi on the grounds that it might provoke American authorities. Amid rumors circulating that British warships, waiting at the three-mile limit, would protect the *Ancona* from enemy attack over its course until Italian vessels could escort it safely through Mediterranean waters, the vessel departed without any formal send-off. But the *Ancona* was on a special kind of voyage—with its complement of "tourists" answering the call of their native country, bound for a very different trip to Italy than the carefree travelers who ordinarily took passage on it.[18]

Reporting the departure of the vessel, a newspaper portrayed the scene:

All that is inspiring in patriotic fervor, the strains of martial music, the brilliance of waving flags—all the beauty of conflict without its sordidness and pain—reached its height today when 4000 sons of Italy gathered at the Vine Street wharf to bid god-speed to 1000 of their compatriots who sailed on the Ancona shortly after noon to join the armies of Victor Emanuel in their campaign against their arch-enemy—Austria.

There were no weeping women, no sorrowful faces. The sunny browed young men laughed because they were on their way to service for their Italia. Those who said farewell, perhaps forever, rejoiced because their friends were glad to risk their lives and their fortunes in their country's cause.

One of the first reservists on the liner was the Rev. Antonio Garritano, rector of St. Anthony of Padua Catholic Church, of Chester, Pa.

Before 1 o'clock this morning the first eager Italians were clamoring for admission to the pier of the Italia Line, where the Ancona lay, getting up steam for her 11 day journey to Naples. An hour later the little stream had become a river of humanity, pouring in from every street to the common centre.

Afoot they came and by trolley. Vegetable carts and automobile trucks bore loads of agile young men, the occupants wearing red, white and green rosettes and ribbons in their lapels. The vehicles themselves were decorated with Italian flags and the Stars and Stripes side by side.[19]

If there was any doubt about the mission being undertaken by the reservists boarding the *Ancona*, Joseph Marcella, who lived at 7th and Wharton Streets, put them to rest as he waved an Italian flag from the rail of the vessel and loudly declared: "Viva Trento! Viva Trieste! We will fight until the last Austrian is killed or surrenders!"[20]

On its return to Philadelphia in late July, the *Ancona* reflected the realities facing Italy and its people. With war sharply reducing emigration, its 79 passengers represented the smallest number the ship had ever carried into the port. But the *Ancona* had come not as much for the purpose of bringing civilians to the United States as it did to carry reservists as quickly as possible back to a nation at war. And two days later, another contingent, reportedly from 700 to 1,000 more men, mostly between 20 and 23 years of age, prepared to depart. Along with them, the *Ancona* loaded 30–40 cars of canned meats in Philadelphia, with more meat, 500 horses, and 700–800 reservists to be put on board in New York. Far from the loading site, Italian forces were striking across the Isonzo in a 60-mile front from Tolmino to Salgrada, dislodging the enemy by bayonet attacks on Monte San Michele and capturing Gorizia in "sanguinoso combattimento," leading to the illusion that Supreme Commander Luigi Cadorna and his troops had already achieved the decisive victories that would end the war. In Philadelphia, as reservists began the journey that would transform them into replacements for exhausted troops at the front, elation over the war was being tempered by the disconsolation that separation brings. The scene at the Vine Street wharf, bathed in brilliant sunlight, was animated by human emotion as men embraced their families, some for the last time, turned away, and filed onto the ship. A young wife held up a baby for a parting father to see; a gray-haired mother wiped away a tear; a sweetheart sank under her heavy heart; each and all shouted "arrivederci." On the deck of the ship, a soldier who could laugh, free from care, because he had no one on the pier crying for him, struck up a spirited air on a wheezy accordion, which the crowd enthusiastically picked up. Alongside him, another man wiped away fast-falling tears as he waved farewell to his wife and children. As noon whistles blew, the vessel slipped away and disappeared downstream on the river. A journalist's words found the deeper meaning of the moment: "There were tears, many of them. The men were going to war. But there was enthusiasm, such as only Italy knows, for the men were going to fight for their sunny Italy. Many of those who were going away and those who came to bid them god speed were transported in their mind's eye to their native country, for the flashing eyes and teeth, sparkling white against swarthy skins, and the blue skies mirrored in the water spoke eloquently of Italy."[21]

For the men who left Philadelphia on that July day, the first risk was not waiting on the battlefield but as soon as their ship had left port. Although the *Ancona* had been disguised by her buff funnel painted black, her name obliterated, and her characteristic markings altered, the threat of enemy vessels on the Atlantic was immediate. The sinking of the *Ancona* four months later would confirm these fears. And even a laughing accordionist could not entirely erase that peril.

The call for mobilization had brought a "fever of excitement" among Italians. About 30,000 men in Eastern Pennsylvania, Southern New Jersey, and Delaware were said to be eligible for military service. One report placed the 30,000 into the estimated 80,000 population of the "local colony," presumably referring to Philadelphia alone. When the Italian consulate issued what was intended to be its final call in July 1915, some 3,000 reservists from the Philadelphia Consular District had already returned to Italy. The second manifesto was addressed to all males, whether Italian-born aliens, naturalized citizens of the United States, or even American born, with August 19 as the deadline for leaving Philadelphia and August 31 as the final date on which they could present themselves in Italy, before they would be redefined as deserters and much worse as "traitors" to the cause of Italy. As advertisements of "Neapolitans," seeking to sell their belongings before departing, filled pages of Italian language newspapers, the largest exodus of reservists was expected to begin.[22]

As the second call was issued, businessmen pledged support for a program intended to generate funds to aid the growing number of families left behind who were at risk of becoming destitute because of the military mobilization. When they convened at the Society for Italian Immigration at 10th and Bainbridge Streets, proprietors, shopkeepers, and merchants attempted to assess the needs of the families of an estimated 10,000 reservists who lived in Philadelphia and other parts of Pennsylvania. It was an obligation for the community that was almost as important as the need to don the uniform.[23]

With patriotic fervor growing, Philadelphia's Italians again converted religious observance into a political event on the feast of Saint Rocco on August 16. After special Masses at Saint Mary Magdalen de Pazzi, Our Lady of Good Counsel, and Saint Rita's, about 800 members of the parishes joined together in a parade through the streets of the Italian colony. Money ordinarily used for social activities was being redirected to the War Relief Committee. One observer noted: "For many of the Italians of this State, New Jersey, and Delaware, this will be the last celebration of any kind they will take part in before their departure for Italy, on Thursday next, when the reservists will sail from this city to join the army. . . . Prominent members of the colony here say practically all those subject to this call have responded and there will be few laggards."[24]

For men seeking to serve their country, their voyage to Italy still had complications. On the day after the Saint Rocco festival, upwards of 600 reservists who gathered at the Italian consulate on Spruce Street, carrying soiled envelopes with passports and other identification papers, overflowed from its steps onto the sidewalk and into the street. Inside of the building, the shorthanded staff, augmented by temporary workers, frantically processed applicants. This army of recruits, not yet in uniform, then moved on to the Frank Di Berardino Company on Christian Street and to the Agenzia Generale di Navigazione on South 9th Street to settle matters of money exchange, transportation, and dates of sailing. On the next day, the *San Guglielmo*, with 2,000 reservists aboard, then in another two days, the *Stampalia* of the Veloce Line, and in early September, the *Sant'Anna* of the Fabre Line would leave New York for Naples. Men with families, who began selling their household belongings, were learning that they could only depart for Italy from New York with their wives and children, as ships were no longer leaving from Philadelphia.[25]

The summons to reservists to report for military duty required more than finding passage and disposing of personal possessions. On one hand, Italian authorities had to find inducements for the significant number of men who were reluctant to answer the call. In its decree of early July, the Italian government suspended the issuance of the *precura*, the document prepared by consuls that allowed relatives to leave Italy in cases where applicants had not reported for military duty. By blocking the departure from Italy of a parent, prospective spouse, or actual spouse, or other relative seeking to join someone already abroad, it prevented the reuniting of the family of any reservist who refused to meet his military obligation. The suspension of passports would end the practice of prearranged weddings, long a feature of immigrant life, of newly arriving women to men already here. It was believed that hundreds of Italian men were betrothed to women who expected to join them for such expeditious rites of marriage. While requiring anyone who wished to see his family again to return to Italy as a reservist, the plan would only partly succeed in preventing men from refusing to answer the call to arms.[26]

If the Italian government had placed immigrants and their families in a difficult situation, it would be further complicated by American authorities when the U.S. Department of Labor announced in late July that any alien who joined the military ranks of a belligerent nation would be denied American citizenship. Since any American who swore allegiance to a foreign state

ITALIAN RESERVISTS ANSWER LAST CALL BY CONSULATE HERE

FIGURE 3.3 Men reporting to the Italian Consulate at 717 Spruce Street in response to the summons issued to reservists (August 1915). (*Evening Ledger* [August 18, 1915].)

was regarded as having abrogated his original citizenship, the same principle was now applied to the foreign-born petitioner. But if the federal government had restrained the options of reservists, City Solicitor Michael J. Ryan's reply in early August to an inquiry from Dr. S. Lewis Ziegler, the director of the Department of Health and Charities, that, without assurances that families left behind would not become public charges and be arrested for abandoning legallybinding obligations, further aggravated their predicament.[27]

At the core of the matter, the reservists faced a lingering dilemma. Would they prefer to be deserters from military service and banned from ever returning to Italy by the ruling of the Italian government or repudiators of their family obligations and subject to arrest by Philadelphia authorities? Their difficulties had become even more complicated by reports that the Italian consulate had run out of funds to provide for the transportation of reservists back to Italy. When asked by the press about two men said to have applied for but been denied such assistance, consular officials refused to discuss the specific cases or the more general matter. With reservists leaving for New York City in order to embark for Italy, confusion grew with the apparent impasse. In mid-August, as hundreds of men flocked to the consulate seeking to register as reservists, believing that it was the last day before they would be classified as deserters, officials became vague on the actual deadline, as claims circulated that a weekly high of 20,000 new registrations had been reached. For uncounted others who chose not to report, it meant giving up the hope of ever being allowed to return to Italy. But another threat to mobilization had emerged with growing signs of even broader efforts to oppose the war.[28] (See Figure 3.3.)

The Antiwar Movement in Little Italy

Despite widespread support for intervention in the war, it was not shared throughout the Italian community, where an undercurrent of radical political opposition also existed. As in Italy itself, another faction opposed to the war sought to dissuade eligible reservists from reporting for duty. In late July, when Carlo Tresca, the fiery orator of the Industrial Workers of the World, attempted to address an audience at Fulton Hall at 8th and Fulton Streets in South Philadelphia, a mob of angry Italians, estimated to be as many as 10,000 strong, which had gathered nearby, burst into the building, smashing chairs, breaking windows, and attacking attendees. It might have become one of the most disastrous riots in recent years in the city, which had long avoided collective violence, without the quick action of a force of upwards of 150 policemen, who prevented Tresca from speaking. As sporadic disturbances broke out in other locations, with an even greater riot looming at South 8th Street and Passyunk Avenue, the police again intervened. Although blame was placed on "New York agitators," the actual organizers were anarchists and Socialists who had come from local neighborhoods. And although it was reported that the program had been arranged by a Socialist club, erroneously identified as the Circolo Ferrari, located at South 11th Street near Carpenter Street, the incident revealed that antiwar sentiment had gained a place in the immigrant community.[29]

The narrowly avoided riot also provided an opportunity for more conservative "patriots," whose Italian and American flags that hung from the windows of their homes asserted a presence that newspapers eagerly reported. Emmanuel V. Nardi, identified as a court interpreter and erroneously as editor of *L'Opinione*, arriving on the scene shortly after the first outbreak of disorder, declared that Socialist efforts had agitated many Italians who remained loyal to the cause of their country. Claiming that Tresca, known to be in the city, had organized the event, Nardi commended the police for preventing a more serious outcome. While Tresca had attempted to convince reservists to defy the mobilization order, other Italians sought any means to prevent his message from reaching them. And by arresting a Tresca ally and three other men who had come to his aid but failing to protect the rights of radical speakers, accused of being German and Austrian agents, along with suppressing their meeting, the actions of the police had mainly served to implement the objectives of the mob.[30]

Two weeks later, Italian radicals again asserted their opposition to the war by distributing an "ad hoc" newspaper, *La Comune*, published by what was now accurately identified as the Circolo Francisco Ferrer, with headquarters at 1212 Passyunk Avenue, the local branch of a worldwide movement named for the Spanish anarchist executed in Barcelona in 1909. Convinced that they could not receive fair treatment from the American or Italian American press, its editors intended to continue efforts against the recruitment of Italian reservists and war in general, as well as to warn partisans to be prepared to defend themselves. In an impassioned plea, as "champions of the proletariat," it would be a matter of treason and base dishonor to remain neutral against those who preyed on labor, sought to carry out an ignoble swindle, and took a tribute of blood. Calling on all laborers and honest men to help with whatever means was at their disposal, *La Comune* proclaimed: "The time has now come to defend the dignity, the supreme interests and the life of the laboring classes from the jaws of militarism. . . . Let the agitation against the war, stopped for a moment by reactionaries, be resumed with new vigor, and let us prepare ourselves above all to defend our personal safety."[31]

In language strikingly reminiscent of Marx and Engel's *Communist Manifesto*, but in this case coming from an anarchist rather than a Communist pen, *La Comune* conveyed the need for exploited people to consolidate themselves and resist repression. And while other newspapers used the opportunity to draw attention to the Circolo Ferrer, they also confirmed not merely the presence but the possible menace of anarchism in the Italian colony. Yet, it remained less clear whether such reporting had not actually inflated the occasion by a depiction that converted a less serious danger into a more exaggerated threat. Although agitation against the war would not evolve into the kind of massive resistance based on ideological principles that its leaders had hoped for, opposition resting on more personal concerns would have a far greater impact on the recruitment of immigrant Italians into military service. And while efforts to mobilize immigrant reservists would produce far less than what the Italian government had sought, it would only temporarily deter matters before the United States entered the war—with many of the same men who had successfully evaded military service in Italian uniforms in 1915 finding themselves as American soldiers only two or three years later.

Stringiamci a coòrte, siam pronti alla morte, l'Italia chiamò, si!

For reservists who answered the call and boarded ships that brought them back to Italy, the war enabled them to reconnect with their origins as Italians, while expressing some sense of their experiences in America. In his diaries, Gino Speranza, the Italian American activist, recounted what he witnessed on the *Taormina* when he accompanied some of those men on their trip back to Italy in the summer of 1915: "Each group of men I speak to has a surprise for me, some unexpected bit of the American life of these 'aliens,' an assurance from unexpected quarters that, no matter how divided the views and interests of the nations are, even in these tragic days, Italy and America have been welded together in an apolitical, natural and deeply human sense by the life, work and hopes of humble immigrants like these."[32]

Speranza described one man whom he believed to be the leader of a group of about 40 Italians from Hartford, Connecticut, as "a capable, business-like chap," who had been forced to choose between going to summer camp with the state militia or to the real fighting already going on in his native land. The young New Englander had decided to follow his brother, who had sailed for Italy a week earlier after telling his father that he was only going to New York for a good time but took a ship for Naples instead. Speranza colorfully portrayed another reservist, "a tall fellow wearing—would you believe it?—a baseball suit showing considerable wear. He looked like a Westerner and was an Italian from Kansas; he was sure that he would be back in time for the next baseball season."[33]

Speranza also found a Minnesotan who intended to become an aviator so that he might drop bombs on the enemies of Italy. He carried with him a poem entitled "The Farewell of an Italo-American Aviator," composed by an earlier returnee who paid tribute to his American hometown:

> *Hibbing, beloved Hibbing,*
> *Town of my thought, Adieu!*
> *Farewell to joy and pleasure,*
> *And friends most kind and true;*
> *Remember, in some measure,*
> *One ever true to you!*[34]

With only a slight substitution of another locale, the refrain could have been sung by Italian reservists departing from New York, Philadelphia, Boston, and countless other places where they had found the kind of opportunities sought by migrating but had not yet cut their ties to Italy. Speranza described Alexander Tirelli of South Washington Square in Manhattan and his companions, speaking with unmistakable New York City accents, as they disembarked from the *Taormina*. They were also singing the words of Goffredo Mameli, the soldier poet of the Risorgimento, written for "Il Canto degli Italiani," the hymn that would become the national anthem of Italy: "Let us join together! We are ready to die, Italy has called."[35]

Other observers reaffirmed Speranza's description of Italians returning to their native land with a sanguine spirit, almost in denial of the ordeal to be encountered on the battlefield. A newspaper account of the 2,000 men, as they boarded the SS *Dante Alighieri* on its voyage from New York to Naples in July 1915, stated: "These men didn't look as if they were going to war as they walked the steerage gangplank." They were mostly very young men with bulging bags, knobby luggage, and leather trunks, traveling with their families, including a young chap with his wife, mother, and two babies. Among dozens of men with green-covered guitars and mandolins, one reservist "sat idly on the deck, outside the gates, and played languorously upon his guitar while he waited his place in the line which seemed to wind in and out through the bales and barrels." As Speranza and others depicted it, when Italians came together, even for the grim calling that awaited them, they could manage to convert the occasion into a festa.[36]

Moved by his own observations, the prescient Speranza insightfully examined the more serious meaning of these events. He asked if these men, "bound for an embattled continent, and leaving behind a land of peace and plenty," were not "the product of unprecedented conditions of civilized life." Replying to his own question, he declared: "Are they not the resultants of that very modern mobility and flux of labor which have created, faster than the jurisprudence which should discipline and protect them, a peculiar internationalism, not supplanting but substantially modifying the old legalistic nationalisms?" He found the answer in the reasons given by the men themselves: "Italy calls us today," they seemed to say, as men who had weighed and considered essential facts of life, "Italy calls us today, but tomorrow we shall come back to serve America again." Although they were going to where they were urgently needed at the moment, it did not constitute their entire world or even their entire *patria*. While legally recruits for the armies of Victor Emmanuel, spiritually they were "doers of hard, practical and good deeds." With concise determination, Speranza noted that "they were not absolutely Italian as the stamp of American life was ineffaceably upon most of them; they were not, in the deepest sense, American because the tremendous forces of Italian history and tradition were powerfully though unconsciously working upon their spirits." He succinctly concluded: "They were, in fact, and in deed, a little army of reliable men who today happened to be sent to Europe to help fight the battles of freedom while yesterday they were helping work out the problems of industrial life in America."[37]

As the figure of speech "all in the same boat" would have it, Speranza recognized that these reservists, although very American, were returning to Italy as Italians. And sensing that they had become bicultural in not only their political loyalties but also their personal identities, he anticipated a new type of character emerging from their experiences, an early version of what would later come to be called "transnationalism."

Little Italy as a Home Front

Winning Hearts and Minds

With the departure of men for duty on the Italian front, the war was not removed from the lives of those whom they left behind but recast with Little Italy as a distinctive "home front." While the study of the Great War has brought the home front into focus, it remains to be fully explored, especially in specific local settings, and even more so as an aspect of immigrant community life. Similarly, the tendency to see the war almost exclusively on the Western Front has not only neglected the conflict being waged on other fronts, such as Russia, Turkey, the Middle East, and, of course, most relevant to our interests—Italy—but has almost erased its implications for immigrant groups of these "neglected" origins who found themselves in America. It is made even more anomalous by the salience of the Americanization movement during these years. America's diverse population meant that there were many home fronts, made distinctive by numerous national origins and ethnic consciousnesses, that felt the impact of the war in different geographic and social locations. Philadelphia's Little Italy was one of them.[1]

Even before, in fact long before, America entered the war, the question of what to do about the millions of foreign born within its population had been recognized as an important issue. As the war approached, it only became more urgent as the issue of their loyalty emerged. By 1916, even President Wilson had joined into a dialogue of increasingly high intensity that made Americanism a central theme of his campaign for reelection. And after the United States entered the war, faced with the exigency of mobilizing its armed forces, advocates of assimilation saw conscription and military train-ing as opportunities to solve the problem of the alien presence. As David M. Kennedy has noted, the military camp could be seen as the way to "yank the hyphen" out of Italian Americans and other unassimilated peoples. Theodore Roosevelt, a zealous advocate for Americanization, could predict that the mil-itary tent, where men of different origins slept side by side, would someday rank with the public school as a great agent of assimilation. A member of the U.S. House of Representatives could describe compulsory military training as a "melting pot" that would break down distinctions of race and class, mold a new nation, and bring forth new Americans. It was an ambitious agenda that held promise for success among Italians. But while the entry of Italy into the war had encouraged Italians to look favorably upon the prospect of America joining with the Allies, whether it also meant a willingness to commit them-selves to the same cause was less certain. After all, some of them had migrated to avoid military service. But once the war came to America, Italians would give an unequivocal answer that bought them to the tents where assimilation awaited them.[2]

Philadelphia's Italians dwelled in a multilevel home front in what was for most of them a new nation, city, and neighborhood. They responded first to the entry of their ancestral homeland into a war taking place in that country, before answering the call of an adopted nation as it entered the same conflict on another front. But in several respects, their situation had a different char-acter than any home front in Europe. For one thing, unlike such countries as France and Belgium, as well as Italy and Austria, where battlefront and home front were in close proximity, it was for Italians in America, like other Americans, far removed from the scene of the war. It was even different from England where artillery barrages at the onset of a great battle, despite being separated by the English Channel, ominously resounded. Moreover, within the diversity of urban America, populations of foreign roots, many even with origins in enemy nations, could be found. This aspect, in particular, based on a presumed if not real threat posed by some of those peoples, made loyalty a conspicuous issue for the duration of the war. It is impossible, for instance, to fully relate the narrative of the domestic situation without some attention to the unfortunate German American experience. But America also was a home front that was not invaded or ever threatened on its borders by the encroaching army of any enemy. And without a provocative incursion, it remained similar to the Central European nations that could have gone, at least during an early moment, into either side of the war. In short, at some point, America had to make a choice. And that decision was, in no small part, affected by the struggle among its diverse peoples, positioned on opposing sides, seeking to convince America of the merit of their own cause. And while the United States would not enter the war until April 1917, Italy had gone to war almost two years earlier in May 1915. In sum, America already had a complicated home front, with a confusing array of foreign components, long before the United States declared war. And the streets of Little Italy reflected the imprint of that reality.

But neither Philadelphia as a whole nor Little Italy as a community was left on its own in the matter of mobilizing support for the war. From its beginning, the Great War had brought war itself as another commodity to the home front in cities across the nation as no other conflict had ever done before. It would be advertised, marketed, and sold to potential consumers who sought information but also had to be persuaded and properly prepared for the possibility that they themselves might be asked at some time to become more active participants. When the United States entered the war, the audiences of motion picture theaters and lecture halls had already learned much about the alleged barbarity of the Hun against helpless victims in Belgium and France. And while press coverage reported political and military events, it also provided an agenda that solicited the support of readers. In addition to recruiting men to wage war on the battlefield, the effort had to be materially and emotionally aided through bond drives, parades, and rallies. While it was relatively easy when the fighting was taking place on the borders of their homeland, the same efforts had to convince Philadelphia's Italians that the war, when it shifted to American involvement on the Western Front, remained their war, too. And in order to sustain that premise, it had to infuse the foreign born and their families with the belief that they were Americans, too. But that shift of consciousness had other consequences. Whether they were young men donning the uniforms of the armed forces or civilians who remained on the home front, the war, by strengthening their identities as Americans, would facilitate their acculturation. It was not a new process but one that had long been going on, although in a more gradual and undirected manner. With the crisis invoked by the war, it became expedient to hasten that transformation. By being asked to demonstrate their support of the war, Italians were also given the opportunity to manifest their allegiance as Americans in a manner that they previously had not been asked to do. As Italians themselves became more enthusiastic participants in the campaign to promote and support the war, they also became more active participants in their own assimilation as Americans. And as their identities as individuals were being altered, the collective entity that had poured onto the streets as an immigrant colony in enthusiastic support of Italy's war against Austria had entered a path that led to becoming an Italian American community that would occupy public space with similar rage against Germany.

Community Responses

By autumn of 1915, Philadelphia's Italians were continuing to adjust to the alternating rhythms of familiar routines and the newer priorities that Italy's entry into the war had brought. On September 20, Little Italy renewed its observance of the capture of Rome, some 45 years earlier, in the final battle of the Risorgimento with parades and festivities in what remained an important day for Italians throughout the city. And on October 12, they celebrated the day set aside to honor Christopher Columbus, regarded by many of them as the first immigrant, in a holiday that by being increasingly shared with other citizens offered a broader consciousness of themselves.[3]

Earlier in October, the Italian consulate issued a third call for reservists previously excused by a government now even more pressed by the need for manpower. These untrained men of the "third category" were to be assigned to guard railroad lines where military operations were being conducted, but not to be placed into active service in the near future. The new summons created a stir of some magnitude in Little Italy, because it mainly affected men who had been deferred from duty by reason of being the sole support of their families. Italian language newspapers disseminated the unanticipated call, instructing them to report to the nearest consulate as soon as possible. With the war having already taken a heavy toll of able-bodied men in Italy, while the new recruits were expected to replace them in home guard duty, it was also aimed at immigrants who had escaped military service by departing for overseas destinations. With a reported 30,000 eligible men in the Philadelphia Consular District at the time of the first order, the 3,000 or so who had answered that call represented a small proportion of the population. And while the Italian government would fail to find a full solution, the call to arms by the United States would partly deflect the issue in another two years.[4]

With patriotic fervor dampened by news from the Italian front, more somber observances further tempered the exuberance that had marked earlier public demonstrations. In November, Philadelphia's Italians gathered to honor the memory of Alfonso Apice, sergeant major of Italy's 30th Infantry Regiment, a son of Mrs. Maria Apice, of South Carlisle Street in South Philadelphia, as the first soldier of Little Italy to be killed in the war. Having returned to Italy, he had fallen in battle on the Carso as a member of one of the first regiments to move into Austrian territory. The program at New Lyric Hall on South 6th Street now solicited funds for his widow and son who had gone back to Italy with him, with the aim of enabling them to return to Philadelphia. While an enthusiastic crowd applauded songs and speeches, the main event was a four act drama, *The Italian Austrian War*, written by Frank Bova, a well-known playwright of the colony. His play, set in Trieste and the Trentino, depicted swaggering Austrian military officers and civil officials uttering threats against Italy before being foiled by an Italian hero, much to the delight of the audience. In act 3, King Victor Emmanuel III joined other Italian leaders in condemning Austrian perfidy, before the final act in which Bersaglieri completed the performance by routing the enemy in battle and undoubtedly pleasing the audience even more. In another feature of the evening, Michele Strizzi, an editor of *L'Opinione*, delivered a lecture, "A Soldier of the New Italy," in which he not only praised the fallen Apice but Italian war policy as well. The crowd was also entertained by Antonio Scarduzio, a popular baritone, and Felice Romano and Lucrezia Pace, drawn from the nearly inexhaustible font of Italian musicians of the city. With some irony, Eugene Apice, the brother of the dead soldier and organizer of the program for the evening, would be employed as a machinist at the Remington arms factory in Chester when he registered for the draft in another three years. From one brother who died on the Carso in an Italian uniform to another who worked in the arms industry in America, it reflected the arc by which the war grasped Italian American families.[5]

With the new year of 1916, Philadelphia newspapers continued to project images of life, at least in the minds of their editors, in the Italian colony. In his columns, Tom Daly, a popular poet and humorist, promised: "If you would know your city and its sunny human side—Rittenhouse Square and the Walnut Street Clubs as well as 'Little Italy' and the streets of crowded humanity, know it through the Philadelphian who speaks to them as one who knows." And so, readers were promised the antics of "Antonio Sarto," presumably of South Philadelphia. Local news included the annual gala masquerade ball of the Stella d'Italia Society, representing the Italian Barbers' Beneficial Society, at which several hundred "beaux and belles" enjoyed themselves at Horticultural Hall in Fairmount Park. And the press could not ignore such colorful romantic escapades as the impending marriage of a 13-year-old girl, which undoubtedly simultaneously shocked and titillated genteel sensitivities of more proper Philadelphians. It also covered even more sensational moments such as a reported "bomb" explosion that tossed inhabitants from their beds and damaged a home on South Warnack Street but left the police without any clues. Or when it reported the shots of "cammoristi," who turned out to be only excited neighbors, after the oven of a pastry shop on Christian Street exploded—what good journalist could resist declaring: "Bomb explosions in 'Little Italy' have become quite frequent in recent years and the police have determined to stamp them out."[6]

For the Italian colony, with many men having departed, the war had become a matter of gravest concern, but with even greater urgency after the major assault launched by the Austrians in the Trentino in May 1916. With florid rhetoric, the *Evening Ledger* reported that Philadelphia's Italians were not so much worried as they were astonished by the sacrilege of an Austrian offensive in "the land of Julius Caesar and the immortal Garibaldi." And anyone who even suggested that the enemy might reach Rome risked being "biffed" by an irate son of Italy. But a generation gap separated the opinions of older men who still gathered to discuss the strategy of generals from younger men who preferred to talk of baseball and boxing. For the latter, it was not Italy versus Austria on the Isonzo but Connie Mack's Philadelphia Athletics versus the Cleveland Indians in the ballpark or the next prize fight of boxing champion Jess Willard that had become more important. And the *Evening Ledger* could use sports metaphors to make light of the situation: "They are in the melting pot. And the great emotionalism of the Latin ought to make him a far better baseball 'fan' than the calmness of the Teuton or the matter-of-fact spirit of the Anglo-Saxon. It's a case of the older generations 'rootin' hard for Italy, with the younger men strong supporters of the Mackites."[7]

This almost incongruous, if not incoherent, interpretation of generational differences suggested that the spirit of the older Italian toward his native land was the same as that of the baseball fan with the comment: "The team's just got to win that pennant." And although the "team" had fallen into a slump, which placed it in the lower division of the league, the *Evening Ledger* declared: "The season isn't over yet by a long shot and soon you will see Italy slamming out hits in great style, not singles, but triples and home runs galore." Despite its banal analogy, the *Evening Ledger* recognized that assimilation was luring younger members of the community away from the concerns of an ancestral land and replacing them with the distractions of a newer culture. But Italians, whether young or old, were not likely to find any kind of amusement in the Austrian offensive.[8]

The Austrian military offensive of the spring of 1916 tested efforts of the "mainstream" press when the outlook of Little Italy became less receptive to inquiry and Italians chose to give belligerent responses or refused to talk about the war at all. But if reluctant to share his own views, an Italian could designate others in the community as voices "who do all his talking for him." Directed by such an observation, the *Evening Ledger* asked the opinion of Pietro Jacovini, an editor of *L'Opinione*, who believed that Austrian advances were merely part of an Italian strategy akin to "that famous invitation from the spider to the fly," before dismissing the matter with a shrug of his shoulders. While skeptical that the Austrians actually occupied Italian territory since news reports were coming mainly from sources in Berlin and Vienna, Jacovini admitted that the enemy had found, along the 600-mile frontier of the Alto Adige and Trentino, the easiest avenues to invade Italy. But he remained convinced that Italian generals, knowing the route of invasion, would draw the Austrians further into Italy until, with deployment of every available man and support of four impregnable forts, "we'll batter the devil out of 'em."[9]

C.C.A. Baldi, the titular leader of local Italians, was similarly hesitant to discuss the war with an *Evening Ledger* reporter, almost as if he would be revealing privileged information about military strategies. But after first refusing to discuss Austrian progress, Baldi opined that the enemy offensive was nothing at all. With the help of a roughly penciled map, he showed how the Austrians would soon find themselves overextended from supply lines and forced to withdraw from Italian territory. He offered his view: "In a few days you will see the Italians chasing the Austrians over the border in true pell-mell style." Baldi proposed an elegant comparison that might enable an American reporter to better appreciate what was happening: "Why, this is simply like your own battle of Bunker Hill. . . . The Italians are waiting to see the whites of the eyes of the enemy before they open fire. . . . Yet the Italians in Italy and in America have every confidence in victory for Italy. Their thought toward the Austrian invasion is very similar to 'I should worry?'"[10]

Americanization . . . and *Italianità*

When the Austrian offensive stalled, the war resumed its more stalemated character. But with the approaching involvement of the United States, Philadelphia's Italians found matters of concern closer to home. As America turned its attention to issues involving immigrants from countries that might soon be among its enemies, a consciously deliberate program of Americanization sought to replace the slower course of undirected acculturation and assimilation. In January 1916, the National Americanization Committee opened a two-day conference in Philadelphia with its principal aim being: "the patriotic business of driving the hyphen out of life in America, now and in years to come." While the 6,000 delegates in attendance differed on means and goals, a consensus shared a clearly defined agenda: "A definite campaign for

Americanization is to be launched along lines laid down by men and women whose business it is to see that the United States assimilates the human ingredients of all nations in the melting pot."[11]

As the program culminated with a banquet that featured several speakers, a liberal priest, Father Joseph M. Corrigan, of the Saint Vincent de Paul Society, brought the views of Cardinal James Gibbons, the leading American prelate, to the delegates. From his days as a seminarian in Rome to a more recent time as director of the Catholic Missionary Society of Philadelphia, Corrigan had come to know Italians well. In his speech, he declared that "God made this a shelter house for all nations." Corrigan eloquently noted: "He comes, indeed, in poverty; but we would have departed from our ideals if poverty was a bar to him." Before an audience eagerly seeking to make Americans out of the foreign born, if not to exclude them entirely, Corrigan had asked for kindness, patience, and consideration for the immigrant.[12]

The next speaker, former president Theodore Roosevelt, after offering enthusiastic applause for Corrigan, was actually determined to refute the priest. In far-ranging remarks, Roosevelt condemned the "promise everything and do nothing policies of the Democratic Administration," before he maligned pacifists as "persons of indeterminate sex." Reaching his real target, Roosevelt declaimed that hyphenates made America "a polyglot boarding house." Repeatedly turning to face Corrigan, Roosevelt declared: "The hyphenate is incompatible with patriotism." The former president's antipathy toward the foreign born, shared by many in his audience, foreshadowed the increasing difficulties of anyone with origins in nations that would be opposing, but even for those who would be aligned with, America in the near future.[13]

The Americanization conference did not project a welcome message for Philadelphia's Italians for whom its main objectives meant even less than Roosevelt realized. When their own leaders spoke to them, it was to Italians in America not to Italian Americans. And when they paraded in the streets of Little Italy in support of troops at the front, despite the flags that might be carried, they did not march as Italian Americans but as Italians. While other Americans might claim to know what a hyphenated American was, most Italians did not. In an ethnic enclave where language, family and friendship ties, religious worship, and street life were still defined by and confined within Italian parameters, they could not anticipate the assimilation of later generations. Despite what others might seek, whether at Americanization conferences or elsewhere, the residents of Little Italy, citizens of a unique community, probably believed, if they thought about it at all, that they would always be as Italian as they were at that moment.

Philadelphia's Italians asserted their distinctive identity and cohesion on public occasions as war in Europe drew even closer to America. When they gathered at Saint Mary Magdalen de Pazzi on a Sunday in late May 1916, their esteemed pastor, Monsignor Isoleri, after greeting them in Latin with, "Da, Domine, propitius pacem in diebus nostris" (Grant us graciously, O Lord peace in our days), spoke to them as he usually did in Italian, but his message followed a circuitous path. After disclosing a plan for moving the body of Father Gaetano Mariani, its first pastor, from Saint Mary's Cemetery for reburial alongside the church and then for replacing the cross on the old outer wall that protruded through its roof, which he wished could have carried in the day's procession, abruptly he changed his topic and the meaning of the program, stating he would have preferred that it be a day of thanksgiving for final victory and peace, as much as one of prayer and penitence. He praised "i nostri soldati" (our soldiers), who had fought so heroically on the Isonzo, the Carso, Monte San Michele, and other places, and astonished the entire world, before reaching the boundaries assigned by God to "Il bel paese, che Appennin parte, il mar circonda e l'Alpe" (Beautiful country parted by the Apennines and surrounded by sea and Alps) (again with an allusion to Dante). He described the Carso as bathed by so much Italian blood and now the tomb of so many sons of Italy that it had become a sacred place where others would come in search of inspiration. Isoleri beseeched the God of armies to bless these soldiers, to free Italy from foreign enemies, to make her prosperous and happy again, and to bring her soldiers safely back to their homes and families.[14]

Shifting to a more local focus, Isoleri implored the patron saint of his parish to protect those in America, and especially in Philadelphia, who had answered the call to duty, offering their blood and lives by a patriotism that would be recorded in gold in the annals of the Italian colonies. While professing his love for America as the land that had welcomed Italians, with his inevitable gloss that it had been discovered by one of them, he emphatically reasserted, "We will always love our dear Italy." After other intercessions, calling for both flags to be brought to him to be intertwined and kissed, Isoleri declared: "For all of you, as well as for me, still Italian, after 46 years in America . . . we all know that if we love Italy, we also love Columbia, and we wish that the peace and friendship between them never be disturbed, but may endure as long as the world."[15]

After Isoleri's impassioned oration, the large but orderly crowd marched under nearly perfect skies of late afternoon through the streets of the neighborhood, affirming their faith, patriotism, and ethnic identity. But rather than yield to the supplications of Philadelphia's Italians, the war could come only more fully into their lives. While many reservists had returned to Italy, other Italians would soon find themselves in American uniforms after the United States entered the war. Whether in military service or on the home front, the future could only bring further challenges for Italians who had chosen to test the tension of their character and customs within an American setting. The most important issues remain related to the role that military experience and the war-related activities of a home front enflamed by war, which tested the identity of Italians as individuals and their cohesion as an ethnic group. But for men who had already joined the Italian army in its struggle against the Austrians, it would not serve to make them more American but only to restore and strengthen their *Italianità*.

5

News from the Italian Front

During the course of the war, several major sources brought news from the Italian front to immigrant colonies. Beyond the carefully monitored letters of men in uniform, the dispatches of the press, despite also being censored by military authorities, provided regular and extensive information. And along with the limited circulation of the Italian language press, the principal newspapers of Philadelphia, even before the United States entered the war, presented political and military events to a broader reading public. In the days leading up to the war, readers found themselves saturated by extensive coverage of events in news articles, background features, and editorial commentary that supported the Italian cause. In May 1915, as Italy prepared to announce its decision to join the Allies, an *Evening Ledger* editorial, melodramatically titled "Italy Crosses the Rubicon," expressed a point of view that could have easily appeared in any other major newspaper in the city. After noting the risks that would have been incurred by remaining in the Triple Entente, it declared that Italy had made the right decision. Assessing the relative strength of Germany, as well as the vulnerability of Austria, it recognized a pragmatic basis for the direction that Italy had chosen. But its more philosophical endorsement of Italy's course of action anticipated a future alliance with the United States: "It is our Italy, the land of poetry, the oppressor of the world for centuries, the oppressed of Europe for generations . . . in whose glory all nations share and all humanity exults, mother of arts and civilization, in whose bosom genius has been nurtured, the holy of holies of history, whose soil has reddened with endless romance and whose fingers have touched the strings and brought there from invisible beauties of sound! Who can be without a thrill as she arms herself and marches in solid phalanxes again to write history in humanity's great book of records."[1]

The *Evening Ledger* editorial reflected an appreciation, shared by Philadelphians since colonial times, of Italy as a civilization of ancient roots and culture and a place for personal fulfillment and cultivation—especially for the scions of upper-class families who made the "grand tour." But aware that the United States and Italy would soon find themselves at war against common enemies, it now sought a bridge by which to reach the Italian community of the city. While morning and Sunday editions of the *Public Ledger* and the weekday *Evening Ledger* kept readers well informed with news of the war, they remained less accessible to Italians until the introduction of an unprecedented innovation. On May 20, 1915, the *Evening Ledger*, in its lead article, announced that the Italian Parliament had overwhelmingly voted to authorize King Victor Emmanuel III to declare war against Austria. Alongside that news, another article, accompanied by a photograph, described the citing of strange rings around the sun, the same phenomenon that Isoleri had regarded as a sign of divine approval of the recent demonstration in support of his homeland. Under the headline, "Tutto In Italia È Pronto Per La Guerra Contro L'Austria," another article, written entirely in Italian, provided details of deliberations that had brought Italy to the edge of war. It was not the first time that a major newspaper had published articles in Italian, with the *Public Ledger* having presented at least two news items on the devastating earthquake, centered on Avezzano, which had taken more than 30,000 lives in Southern Italy in January 1915. But in its groundbreaking edition of May 20, another *Evening Ledger* article in Italian described diplomatic negotiations with representatives of likely allies as well as of imminent enemy nations, along with military mobilization in Italy. It also revealed that the Italian government had published a summary of the so-called Green Book, the diplomatic dossier that explained Italy's withdrawal from the Triple Entente. And auspiciously for future relations, it reported that Ambassador Thomas Nelson Page had been among the diplomats who had called upon Baron Sidney Sonnino, the Italian minister of foreign affairs. One day later, the *Evening Ledger*, again in Italian, reported shops and stores in Rome with window signs proclaiming, "chiuso per gioia nazionale" (closed for celebration of national joy), along with less pleasant news that Austrian troops had fired on Italians in Dalmatia.[2]

The use of Italian was not a temporary experiment that would be quickly discarded; it became an enduring practice. Such articles, first appearing before Italy entered the war, held even greater significance with over 250 to be published by the *Evening Ledger* in Italian, often alongside English-language versions. In attempting to reach Philadelphia's Italians, both newspapers provided news of the war by articles written in Italian usually with a dateline from Rome several times each week over the next six years until March 1921. Briefer items were often accompanied by the postscript, "Leggere in 2a pagina le ultime e piu dettagliate notizie sulle guerra dell'Italia, stampate in lingua italiana" (Read on page 2 the latest and most detailed news on Italy's war, printed in the Italian language). In its Saturday edition, the *Evening Ledger* often reminded Italian readers to turn to its sister paper, the *Public Ledger*, on Sunday for a more extensive account of news from Italy. Philadelphia's Italians were now able to find the almost immediate coverage of events that Italian language newspapers were unable to provide. And despite being based on releases packaged by the Italian government, it provided readers eager for information with news from Italy.[3]

Although the *Evening Ledger*, waiting for fuller disclosure of failed negotiations, had moderated its earlier enthusiasm for Italy's "verdict for war," it remained strong in its support for the Italian cause. On the day following the decision by the Italian Parliament, the lead article, under the headline, "Italians Shot by Austrian Troops in Dalmatia Capital," described the violence inflicted against Italian civilians as they demonstrated on the streets of Zara. In the center of the same page, a photograph, spread across the space of four columns, showed what was identified as "Italian Infantry in the Trenches on the Firing Line." Under the photo, its caption informed the reader: "The picture reveals the young and well-equipped troops who within a few hours at most will direct a sheet of flame against the Austrians drawn up on the frontier. Italy has something over 2,000,000 men, including reserves, ready to hurl into the conflict." But it was hyperbole as well as factual information. The relaxed postures of men sitting on exposed slopes, in a war that had not actually begun for them, revealed an obviously staged scene, far away from actual combat, as well as propaganda from the Italian government. In text and images, the *Evening Ledger* left little doubt of sympathies and support, which would be further confirmed by editorials that augmented the recently introduced policy of publishing news articles written in Italian.[4]

The Immigrant Journalist

If reporting news in Italian represented an unusual undertaking for an American newspaper, the *Evening Ledger* took an even more extraordinary step with an editorial in that language on the day after the Italian Parliament had voted in favor of war. Longer than any other editorial in that edition, it explained why Italy had chosen to enter the war. Beginning with the disagreement between the interventionist government of Prime Minister Antonio Salandra and the neutralist opposition led by former premier Giovanni Giolitti, it argued that war was the device by which Italy would oppose the Austro-Hungarian Empire, the traditional obstacle to the unity and independence of the Italian people. The crucial factor was the violation of neutrality by Germany's invasion of Belgium and Luxembourg, along with the sinking of the Lusitania and the consequent loss of women and children among its passengers. It asked if anyone could believe any longer that Germany and Austria would not be likely to attack Italy at a later point, especially if it were isolated by the absence of any alliance or friendship with England, France, and Russia.[5]

Although the editorial on Italy's decision to enter the war was unsigned, its author almost certainly was Pasquale Adalberto Caporale, an occasional contributor to the *Evening Ledger*. In addition to his own articles, he also probably edited the news sent from Rome by an Italian press agency. During slightly more than two years, under the name "Adalberto Caporale," he wrote at least 12 items, sometimes news stories but more often feature articles resembling the op-ed items of today. From his first article on May 18, 1915, in which he described how Giolitti's opposition to war had brought about Salandra's resignation as prime minister, Caporale clarified the intricacies of Italian politics over the next two years. In a later article, Caporale described the appreciation of Francesco Nitti, a member of the special Italian War Mission of June 1917, for the warm reception found in every city, especially in Philadelphia, along with a detailed analysis of Italy's current condition. Given the significance of the mission and the stature of Nitti, who would become prime minister after the war, Caporale strengthened his own role as a journalist, which allowed him to be a spokesperson for Italy and the Italians of Philadelphia.[6]

In what may have been his most important contribution as a journalist, Caporale examined the impact of immigration on the war effort. In "Immigrants Fighting Italy's War," he described how Italians in America, sending money in postal deposits to banks in their native land, were subsidizing the Italian government in its efforts to finance the war. With the great amount of money from workers overseas reducing the annual deficit by one-half, emigration represented an enormous asset for Italy. In 1906, the record year for emigration, of 788,000 who left, about 500,000 had gone to the United States, Canada, or South America. Claiming 3,000,000 persons in the United States of Italian birth or parentage, well above the officially reported

2,000,000, who were found in every state but heavily concentrated in New York and Pennsylvania, and with modest numbers in the Midwest and California, he cited Luigi Rossi, the former royal commissioner general of emigration, who said they had sent annually no less than $100,000,000 back to Italy. Whether used to pay debts, to be deposited in banks, or to buy small houses and farms, it greatly increased the money available for loans, reduced interest rates, and returned an enormous amount of bonds formerly held by foreign investors. Statistics for September 1913 showed a total of $1,186,000 in postal savings banks, private savings banks, and other financial institutions in Italy. While it was not possible to determine how much of that could be attributed to emigrants in the United States, the only available figures, published by the state-controlled Banca di Napoli, showed that they had remitted nearly $2,400,000 in 1912. Since it was only a small part of the total sum coming from America, with much more being sent directly to wives, Caporale asserted that about one-fourth of the money was swelling the funds of savings banks in Italy. Whether directly converted by depositors or savings banks, he attributed the more than $200,000,000 loan recently launched by the Italian government to fund military preparations as being largely due to emigrant deposits. In sum, Caporale argued that the emigrant was an important contributor to Italy in times of peace when savings fostered economic development and war when savings were used "for the realization of national aspiration and probably to save the country." (Note that remittances actually greatly fell once the war began.) This also helped to explain why Italy would not summon emigrants working abroad, especially in the United States, until absolutely necessary; their savings supported the war effort. Noting that he had not included money being collected to relieve the suffering of destitute families of soldiers, Caporale pointed out that the Italian colony of Philadelphia was expected to contribute no less than $100,000. He asked what New York's Italians, four times greater in population, as well as the millions of Italians scattered throughout the nation, would do in response to the same need. In his deft analysis, Caporale had partly reversed the usual stream of information by focusing on what Italians in Philadelphia and elsewhere were doing for their homeland rather than only presenting more news from Italy to readers abroad. Instead of blaming them for being in America when their own nation needed them, he had grasped the opportunity to extol their contributions to Italy. And the *Evening Ledger* had found an authoritative voice and capable advocate for the immigrant community.[7]

Pasquale Adalberto Caporale, born in Altomonte in the Cosenza Province of the Calabria region in 1879, had migrated on the *Sicilian Prince* from

Naples at the age of 25, with his younger brother Cesare. With his occupation appearing to be as a tailor on a blurred line, he gave the address of an uncle in New York City as his final destination on the ship's passenger list in November 1904. When he submitted his declaration of intention for citizenship in October 1913, Caporale had become a journalist, living on South 12th Street in Philadelphia. In June 1917, his petition for naturalization listed his wife Adelina, whom he had married in Naples in 1897, and their two children, Francesco and Amalia Maria, both born in Philadelphia, in residence in Pennsylvania since 1905. His witnesses were two other journalists, neither of whom had an Italian name, who also lived in Philadelphia. When he registered for the draft in September 1918, Caporale's occupation was listed as a restaurant manager, with his place of employment at the 12th Street address and his employer as Filomena Basta.[8]

In November 1918, Caporale, along with other prominent Italians, placed his name as proprietor of the Leoncavallo Restaurant on a full-page tribute, appearing in the *Evening Public Ledger*, to "Triumphant Italy," saluting the role that his native country had played in the war. While expressing the pride shared by all of its signers, and strongly, it again probably reflected the writing and public relations skills of Caporale, the erstwhile journalist turned restaurant proprietor, more than of anyone else.[9]

Caporale's visibility to the Italian community and the wider public rested upon a reciprocity that linked him to both the *Evening Ledger* and the *Public Ledger*. As much as he contributed by his writing, these two pillars of local journalism gave him prominence. In late October 1916, the Society Section of the *Evening Ledger* noted the birth of Amelia Marie [*sic*] as a hefty 10-pound addition to the household of Mr. and Mrs. Adalberto Caporale. Although such an announcement usually was submitted by a family, it was a rare notice for a child born to Italian parents. But attention to the Caporale family would become even more generous. A later photograph, incongruously placed between articles on labor problems in navy yards, ship plants, and coal mines and the explosion of an Austrian mine on Monte Nero, showed his four-year-old son Francis, in a summer suit and wide-brim sombrero, on his return from spending the summer months with his grandparents Mr. and Mrs. Frank Basta in late September 1917. And lest the ongoing war be forgotten, another image of young Francis, dressed in a military uniform, holding a dress sword, and identified as "the youngest officer in the Italian army," appeared on a page of photographs with more bellicose themes in May 1918. Such notice of Caporale and his family far exceeded the attention given to other families of the Italian colony.[10]

In June 1917, Tom Daly, the Italophile Irish American, whose humor appeared almost daily in the *Evening Ledger*, extended a backhanded compliment as he celebrated Caporale's naturalization as an American citizen. With the recent abdication of King Constantine I of Greece, Daly's poem, in which an Italian speaks in broken English, proposed a successor: "Don't you know da 'Cap'? Why he's da brighta chap dat write about da battle een da valley an up da heell agen. . . . Oh, he's da guy to sand; I nominate my frand, Pasquale Adalberto Caporale." With a pencil sketch of Caporale and the signature of "Guinea," Daly appeared to have concluded his poem, before further down in his column picking his verse up again: "Signor Caporale only recently became the equal of keengs. The official at city hall spoke somewhat as follows: 'Puty'rhanontheBible—brum-mum-mum-mum-mum-$4.' 'm I a cit'zen.' 'Yeh! Yer a citizen. Nex!'"[11]

Although Daly more explicitly ridiculed the official administering the oath and the process itself, it expressed an ambiguous regard for his Italian friend. Yet, while it would not have been surprising if Italians, perhaps many of them, saw it as annoying or, at least, holding latent hostility, it also reflected the respect that Caporale had earned from his colleagues as a journalist.

In a letter to the *Evening Public Ledger*, Caporale resumed his role as an advocate in defense of Italians in May 1918. As the third anniversary of Italy's entry into the war approached, he asked why the flag of Italy, despite a recent recommendation of Pennsylvania's governor, was not being displayed with the banners of the other Allies. Caporale noted that Italian troops, deployed in France, occupied the same sector as American forces on the Western Front. And while the colors of England and France were easily seen, with the absence of Italy's tricolor, "One might even think, if he has not read carefully his newspaper, that the Italians had not been in the war but in that unfortunate period in which they were thrown back of the Piave River, or that they have quit the game altogether." Eager to wear a patriotic lapel button with the colors of Italy, he had been unsuccessful in finding one but told in the leading jewelry stores of Philadelphia that its absence was due to the fact that Italy had not yet joined the war at the time they were being made for the other nations. How, he asked, could people left in a state of ignorance, whether purposely or carelessly, appreciate the help that Italy had given to the Allies or that America was giving to Italy? Caporale ended by posing an even greater question: "Don't you think that the American people should be reminded of the fact that Italy is still in the war, is still giving away, without a wailing, the lives of thousands of her sons for the very same ideal for which America is now in the war?"[12]

In reaction to Caporale's letter, an editorial in the *Evening Public Ledger* on the same day heartily agreed with his argument. Citing the letter, it declared that the observance of Italy's entry into the war, which would occur on the next day, required a generous display of the Italian colors. Admitting to being remiss in the failure to include the Italian banner in public displays, the editorial noted that "none of the Allies has shown more magnificent spirit and energy in her campaigns than Italy." Recognizing neglected bonds, it concluded: "The ties of blood and spirit that link us with our Italian kinsmen are many and indissoluble; let us give public testimony thereof by the proper display of their gallant colors."[13]

On the next day, the anniversary of his homeland's entry into the war, Caporale, in another lengthy article in the *Evening Public Ledger*, "What Italy Has Done," expanded his argument. At a time when Italian military forces sought to regroup, and Italy as a nation to recover, after the defeat at Caporetto, he offered a highly optimistic view of the future. Reviewing the past three years, Caporale declared that Italy remained in battle with youthful ardor, unshaken determination, and an undying faith in the ultimate ideals of national unity and democratic government. Despite the recent setback, its soldiers, whether boys of 18 or men of 40, retained their enthusiasm. And Italy, still a powerful partner in the alliance for liberty and democracy, would remain in the fight because its people had answered the need to destroy a caste system that had been a pillar of autocracy. Although deep penetration by enemy forces left the appearance that little had been achieved so far, Italy had stymied the kaiser's plan to end the war before America could enter the field. Despite their nation's earlier hesitation, the Italian people, never holding any sympathy for the German and Austrian plan of conquest, had always been "heart and soul" with the Allies. Moreover, Italy's moment of neutrality, Caporale asserted, may have been decisive to the Anglo-French defense of the Marne.[14]

In seeking to clarify the war's meaning, Caporale argued that Italy had begun to reach national unity and to put millions of men on the battlefield, despite lacking the equipment and resources to face the military power of Austria. After 10 months of intense preparations, it launched an offensive, scaled mountain heights, crossed the Isonzo, and approached Trieste, only to be repelled by an enemy, strengthened by German reinforcements after the collapse of Russia. Yet, even the defeat at Caporetto, he insisted, could have been avoided if it had not been for subversive propaganda and Socialist influences. (It was the same rationale that Chief of Staff Luigi Cadorna would offer in his own defense.) But with the economy at its worst, bread and fuel almost entirely exhausted, and withdrawal from the war a tempting solution, the Italian people found moral unity. Recognizing that surrender would allow Germany to overwhelm France and England, gain a victory before help arrived, and put the world at the feet of the kaiser, Italy again decided to save the Allies. Limited by the failure of the Allies to provide coal and steel for her factories and food for her people, resulting in ammunition and arms shortages on the battlefield and starvation at home, the situation remained difficult—but Caporale found cause for hope: "The Italian army is still struggling with the problem of doing much with as little as possible. . . . The only weapons the Italian soldier has in plentifulness are his morale and his unshaken determination and faith. . . . And it is this faith in the final victory and in the justice of his cause that keeps him in the shell torn trenches and makes him go to his death with the words 'Italy and Freedom' on his lips."[15]

While accurately assessing some aspects of Italy's recent history, Caporale undoubtedly exaggerated the resilience of the men who, with their morale all but shattered, were abandoning the trenches in increasing numbers, leaving the future quite uncertain in the spring of 1918. But from his distant vantage point, he was writing more to bring comfort to Little Italy and the rest of Philadelphia than to capture the mood of a dispirited army. In his assessment of the situation, he was projecting his own hopes that it would greatly improve. But it was not the "fog of war" as much as the incense of patriotism that had reached the banks of the Delaware. Being naive rather than dishonest, his words were likely to only enhance his reputation among Italians and other Philadelphians.

Caporale's exegesis on Italy's wartime role contained his final byline but probably not his final editorial work. While the absence of corporate archives leaves the full extent of his services uncertain, he had established himself as a capable journalist. He had also connected his skills as a writer to his proprietorship of a successful restaurant and to his influence in the Italian community. Having well served two major newspapers, they had reciprocated by magnifying his visibility and authority. The frequent advertising that kept the Leoncavallo Restaurant before the eyes of the public did its part as well. As an entrepreneur, Caporale helped to bring one of Little Italy's most important institutional contributions—the Italian restaurant—to the American public. As a journalist, he made himself the wartime voice of Little Italy.

Other Voices from Little Italy

With articles in Italian often paralleled by what was being published for the larger audience of Philadelphians, such coverage appeared to successfully reach readers in Little Italy. The new initiative was favorably acknowledged, almost immediately after its introduction, by Consul Poccardi, who noted that local Italians, including many who could not read English, were now able to keep up with news of the war as a result of the articles being published in the *Evening Ledger*. In the same edition, two Italian readers offered similar comments in letters to the editor. Alba D'Amore simply wrote: "Bravo for your news printed in Italian in your newspaper. All sons of civilized Italy are grateful to you." Salvatore Angelo, after reading the articles of the past two days, expressed: "Heartfelt thanks for your kind thought toward us," before adding: "You have given the Italians of this city, who cannot read English, the opportunity of reading the Italian news of the day in their own language, and we Italians must feel very grateful to you for this."[16]

From such responses, the editors of the *Evening Ledger* could easily conclude that providing the news in Italian had produced desired results. Two days later, using almost the same words as the grateful readers, the *Evening Ledger* announced, under the headline of "War News from Italy," that it would continue to publish letters from Italians who appreciated the opportunity to read the news in their own language. If that gesture was not sufficiently ingratiating, the *Evening Ledger* went even further by extolling not only Italy's cause in the war but the immigrants that it had sent to America: "Italy is destined to play a great part in the great tragedy now being enacted in Europe and interest in her destiny is all the greater in America on account of the number of her native sons who have made this country their home and have contributed so largely to its development." While such praise was obviously intended to gain new readers, it also quietly endorsed the presence of Italians in the city and nation.[17]

The messages, appearing in English, despite often coming from writers claiming to be unable to use that language, and evidently translated by someone with fluency in Italian, continued to applaud the *Evening Ledger*. Lorenzo Fuoco enthusiastically expressed his appreciation: "Sir—I take pleasure in writing this letter in order to express to you the satisfaction and gratitude of many Italians who have been able to read in their own language the news of the Italian war, and to say that *Evening Ledger* essays great popularity among my countrymen" [*sic*]. Another reader, Luigi Zucchi, whose letter began: "I am an Italian and not able to read English," wrote that he had not been able to find firsthand news of the war in Italian papers, and thanked the *Evening Ledger*, convinced that he was expressing the "general feeling among Italians here." Guido Aceto indicated his gratitude "for the news that your newspaper is giving the non-English-speaking Italians of this city," with his hope that the policy would be continued. Luigi Corona, claiming to reflect widely shared sentiments of "the entire Italian colony," praised the newspaper for its support of the nations that were fighting for civilization but especially for publishing articles in "our own language," which enabled readers like himself "not familiar with the English language" to read about the war. Commending the people of Italy for having entered the war, not only for their national aspirations but for feeling obliged to support "the cause of civilization against modern barbarism, and to end once and for all the German militarism and imperialism renovating the 'glories' of Attila," Corona ended by congratulating the "richest in news" among Philadelphia newspapers for having "quickly conquered the heart of the Italians."[18]

Corona had also correctly surmised that, although Italy had declared war only against Austria, it would inevitably involve Germany as well. While a misspelled reference to Leonida Bissolati, the Reformist Socialist, suggested that, while being a part of the immigrant masses, he was perhaps a Socialist himself, the substance of his letter refuted any impression that its writer was drawn from an illiterate population. In another message, Nicholas Cannoe, after the seemingly obligatory genuflection to the *Evening Ledger*, declared: "I can assure you that it has been highly appreciated by the professional and business men of this vicinity." He too revealed more about himself: "Although I am an American citizen, which I consider above all, I still have a patriotic feeling for the land of my birth." Such self-portrayals served as a social survey of a small sample of articulate Italians, who were making themselves more visible as Philadelphians.[19]

As accolades mounted, Charles M. Bandiere, president of the Atabol Country Club, an organization of young Italian Americans, claimed that a "tremendous wave of enthusiasm" was sweeping over the Italian colony as a result of the articles. He declared that "the most prominent men, as well as the most humble in the Latin Quarter, have almost come to look upon your paper as their official organ and are delighted with the well-written, authoritative articles, both in English and Italian, which are daily a part of your issues." But by the slightly patronizing tone of their messages to a highly respected newspaper, Bandiere and his colleagues had also turned the tables on establishment Philadelphia.[20]

Joseph A. Lombardi, the corresponding secretary of the Madonna Catholic Club, reported that a recently passed resolution of its members expressed the hope that the *Evening Ledger* would continue publishing news in Italian for the benefit of the non-English-speaking Italians of the city. Such letters recognized the new policy as being welcomed not only by the writers personally but by Italians throughout the city. And within such messages, younger leaders of the community, introducing the term "Italian Americans" to describe themselves, were proffering a new identity that reflected what the future held for later generations.[21]

Praise grew even more profuse as another reader proclaimed: "It is the first time . . . that I have seen Italian news in the Italian language printed . . . in an American newspaper. Good. I and many other Italians highly praise the *Evening Ledger* for that, and I hope that it will continue to do so. I believe that there should not be one Italian in this city, who, being able to read, does not get the *Evening Ledger*." While the increasingly redundant letters looked like the marketing ploy of an eager effort to find a place among readers of a previously untapped audience, their publication also offered recognition that Philadelphia's Italians, growing in size and power, could not be ignored. And Italians, a previously almost voiceless population having found a forum for themselves, were taking advantage of that opportunity.[22]

Packaging the News

As more letters continued to express appreciation for what the *Evening Ledger* was providing, their contributors appeared to be unaware that the information was carefully controlled by Italian military authorities. If only vaguely cognizant of that aspect of the dispatches reaching them, it did not bother them very much, for news even laundered by censors was preferable to not receiving word from the front. And that it arrived in their own language could only validate what they were reading. But with prefatory praise by local editors of the role of Italy in the war, it also stood in welcome contrast to the preoccupation with violence and crime that often marked newspaper coverage of life within the Italian colony.

In his appraisal of news from the Italian front, Mark Thompson describes the "system of lies" by which reporters kept two accounts, one for publication and another as a more private record of events in defiance of controls imposed by authorities. Luigi Barzini, a highly respected journalist, was the "chief fraudster" whose distortions angered soldiers who knew the truth to be different than what was being reported. Under censorship intended to prevent information from reaching the enemy, he practiced a prowar form of journalism. What was lacking in accuracy, Barzini embellished with exaggerated prose that made him the most favored journalist of the supreme command until he began to agonize over losses in the Tenth Battle of the Isonzo. But even that crisis of conscience remained more of a private matter than one that freed him to reveal the deception in which he had willingly engaged. With censorship impeding correspondents on all fronts, a compromise, somewhat similar to what has come to be known as "embedded journalism," allowed limited access to information provided by official bulletins but not the freedom to report what was actually seen. And as soldiers on furlough expressed views that could be condemned as defeatist, journalists accepted what was necessary in order to gain access to information. While sometimes transforming the press into "a parallel ministry of information, propaganda and intelligence," Thompson's "closed loop," as he labels the scheme, fostered the "arrogance, hatred of criticism, brutal treatment of the troops, and a zero-sum attitude in relations with government."[23]

The U.S. Congress imposed a similar policy by passage of the Trading with the Enemy Act, approved on October 6, 1917, as part of the emergency war powers deemed necessary to protect Americans from foreign influences. It prohibited the dissemination of any news item or comment pertaining to the United States, or by any nation engaged in the war, or referring to American policies or international relations, written in any foreign language, without a translation into English being submitted by the publisher to the postmaster at the place of publication. The translation had to be made under oath and accompanied by a statement that it had been filed along with the name of the post office where it had been done. Any publication that failed to meet such requirements could not be submitted to the mails and further distribution was deemed unlawful. Any false statement in the required affidavit amounted to perjury by the applicant. As articles written in Italian appeared in the *Evening Ledger*, accompanied by an ominous caveat that they had met these requirements, "the first casualty of war" was being abetted by the sanitization provided by the American version of the "system of lies."

The packaging of news, however, was not practiced by the government alone but also by newspapers in their editorial policies. With sympathy for the Allies long before the United States entered the war, news reporting, editorials, and vivid cartoons often offered strong support for the cause of Italy. An almost bloodthirsty editorial page image in the *Evening Public Ledger* in May 1918, one of numerous others like it, illustrates the point. After the war, it could be openly admitted that "the war period, particularly the year 1918, was filled with propaganda. At times it required a nice distinction to ascertain just what was news and what represented press agenting of war activities." But despite local newspapers being eager participants in such practices, the same writer ignored their role in his indictment.[24] (See Figure 5.1.)

If Philadelphia's newspapers had found it expedient to compromise coverage of news from the Italian front, it became even more necessary after

FIGURE 5.1 Coming up. (*Evening Public Ledger* [May 25, 1917].)

American troops reached the Western Front. With the need to comply with government regulation, as well as to maintain morale on the home front, the *Evening Ledger* and other newspapers were only too willing to join in the patriotic spirit that pervaded the city. And even after the war, it remained neither apparent nor admissible to state what was quite evident. In 1922, the "official" account, prepared for the Philadelphia War History Committee, claimed that local newspapers had reported the war with none of the distortion, half-truths, or misuse of journalism that afflicted counterparts in other nations but had only upheld "the best traditions of the Fourth Estate." Doing more than mere duty, they had stood staunchly behind the men overseas and carried a banner into the foremost rank of zealous patriotism by faithfully portraying state, civic, and military efforts. With the exception of the *Tageblatt*, the "single alien and seditious voice," forced out of existence and its editor jailed for being "the propaganda mouth of rabid socialism," even German-language newspapers "spoke the common thought of patriotism," making "a positive stand for America and American arms." The author praised the press for voluntarily stifling the very breath of journalism—suppressing its inherent instinct, purpose, and right to pursue criticism that might have discouraged its own citizens and comforted the enemy. Acting as their own censors in military and all other matters, Philadelphia's newspapers "marched as truly and courageously against the enemy hordes as those columns of khaki that baptized France and Flanders with American blood."[25]

With the end of the war, newspaper coverage shifted to issues related to the complicated difficulties facing Italy that waited to be settled, such as the "just aspirations" of Italy in regard to Fiume and the Adriatic Coast soon to be taken up in discussion by diplomats in April 1919. While the *Evening Public Ledger* continued to use war-related news to reach Italian readers, it also reported more routine events—engagements, marriages, deaths, and crime—both in English and sometimes Italian. But while expanding in bilingualism, larger events remained the focus of its use of their language. When an article in Italian reported the resumption of steamship service between Philadelphia and the ports of Genoa and Naples by the Societá Italiana di Navigazione Italia America in July, it reasserted the worth of Italians as readers. When it continued to report such news as the arrival of the Italian battleship, the *Conte di Cavour* in October, it reaffirmed the value of their presence as citizens of Philadelphia.[26]

If the demands of war had led to the abandonment of critical impulses and freedom supposedly enjoyed by the press in a democratic society, it brought more favorable consequences for the reporting of immigrant life in the city. In contrast to the focus on a colorful, sometimes exotic foreign colony, and often darker aspects of violence and crime among Italians, the expectation that young men of all backgrounds would serve in the military forces of the United States opened a new window. And local newspapers, especially after the United States entered the war, would begin to describe an important new phase of immigrant life that reflected the growing assimilation of the citizens of Little Italy. It would be found in episodes of military life, from recruitment and conscription, indoctrination at training camp, and engagement on battlefields, but most of all by the appearance of names in a most sanguine measure of assimilation, the casualty lists of wounded, missing, and dead, a subject that will be taken up at a later point.

Images of War

With the entry of the United States into the war in the spring of 1917, Little Italy expanded the parameters of the previous two years to embrace its citizens as Americans. It was not just Italy's war nor that of England and France any longer but now America's war as well. If it were to end in victory, it depended on support for a war being waged far away, along with the mobilization of military and civilian personnel to conduct a successful campaign, and the conviction that it was a just cause, indeed one even ordained by a Supreme Being. It also required the dissemination and control of information that would "sell" the war to the American people. While various strategies, instruments, and operations would serve this need, the daily press remained at the core of the task.

Beyond routine coverage, newspapers provided articles in which scholars offered analysis for readers who sought to go beyond the details of battlefield maneuvers. In January 1915, Professor William Roscoe Thayer, America's foremost Italianist, diligently described Italy's precarious position against her former partners of the Triple Alliance in a Sunday edition of the *Public Ledger*. Shortly afterward, Professor George B. McClellan, of Princeton University, the son of the famed U.S. Civil War general, who would later serve as a lieutenant with the U.S. Army in the Meuse-Argonne campaign, offered a three-part series, ardently supportive of Italy, which explored war issues in the *Public Ledger* in the spring and summer of 1915. Harvey M. Watts, not only a poet and science writer but another Italophile, offered his vigorous defense of the Italian territorial claims as another version of "manifest destiny" in March 1915. The journalist/historian Frank J. Simonds perceptively analyzed the situation facing Italy on entering the war that anticipated events of later years. Guglielmo Ferrero, one of Italy's foremost intellectuals, in a four-part series in February and March 1915, explored the implications that alternative outcomes of the war could have for Italy and Germany. And Professor Saladino Vincenzo Di Santo, a native of Palombaro in the Chieti Province, who had earned three degrees, become a specialist on Machiavelli, and taught Romance Languages at the University of Pennsylvania, described how his reading of history had inspired a love of war.[27]

With the war remaining the leading topic of international news during the period of American neutrality, newer forms of graphic representation gained popularity among the public. The highly creative work of imaginative cartoonists became regular features in editorial and opinion sections. And beyond pen and pencil drawings, the increasing use of the camera, with a full page of pictures in weekend editions, offered more vivid images of the war. Photography drew attention to real and sham battle scenes, earlier of foreign armies, later of doughboys; smiling recruits on their way to training centers, unaware of what awaited them; laborers in factories or shipyards; volunteers in medical garb; solicitors of relief funds; political leaders of belligerent nations; and children in military uniforms. It included images of gigantic new artillery weapons, powerful dreadnoughts on the water, and fleet planes, all capable of wreaking death and destruction upon the enemy. It displayed the ruins of pillaged and devastated villages of Belgium and France; the spires of defiled churches in which worship was now denied; and the empty shells of houses that could no longer offer shelter. It captured the dogs, horses, and mules who unconsciously shared not only the tasks but also the dangers of war with their human companions. It portrayed forlorn warriors occupying water-soaked and rat-infested trenches, hiking snow-covered trails of higher peaks, and donning the face masks that falsely promised protection from gas attacks. It revealed the wounded awaiting medical aid and relief from battle and unburied dead lying on roads. While wartime photography reached new levels of technical accomplishment, the "pictorial section" placed a gallery of renewed failure of its human subjects before the eyes of readers. From the cerebral musings of scholars to the puckish sketches by graphic artists to the stark images of photographs, newspapers, the devices that brought the war to the public, reduced the distance between battlefield and home front. Newspapers offered an increasingly important resource in the arsenal that shocked senses and galvanized sentiments. And despite articles that sometimes clarified Germany's interests, the inclination to favor the Allies included strong sympathy for Italy. It would also serve the need to mobilize civilians and to dress them in the uniforms of an expeditionary army when that time came.

Among efforts to reach the public, the motion picture had also emerged as a popular means of transmitting news of the war. Along with the images being presented, the movie house, with its darkness, was a setting that more convincingly brought the battlefield into the imaginations of audiences than newspapers could to readers. As America remained mired in neutrality, news-reels, focused on the devastation that war brought, had already chosen sides. In their struggle to win support, the governments of belligerent nations had seized the opportunity to sponsor blatantly partisan films. And while news films showing conditions on the Italian front had been featured since Italy's entry into the war, they gained popularity as the struggle approached decisive moments. In September 1917, as Cadorna's forces awaited defeat at Caporetto, a new film, *The Italian Battlefront*, appeared on the screen at the Garrick The-atre. Described as an official war film photographed by the cinematographic division of the Italian army, it featured scenes of mountain-climbing Alpini, the movement of artillery, ice-covered trenches, the surrender of Austrians, and the capture of Gorizia. It was not the splendor of the photography, or the astonish-ing close range of action, or its historical value, however, but the reaction from an audience of "submerged Carusos and undeveloped Tetrazzinis of the city" that was most newsworthy. "The way that they rose to the occasion was, to the descendant of a northern breed, simply stunning," wrote one reporter. Noting that the exhibition of the film began at 2:15, and the applause at 2:16, he main-tained that "an Italian-filled auditorium on opening nights would insure a riot of reclame for almost anything." But while men, women, and children in the audience "clapped and stamped and boiled over" at every scene, they exploded with "a fervor that was as funny as it was touching and tremendous" when Cadorna came on the screen. For Italians, it was a long-awaited opportunity to applaud heroes of their homeland, not only on the battlefield against the foe but on the venue of an "uptown" theater. It also gave them credibility as worthy Allies after America joined them in war. And perhaps even more important, it elevated them as fellow citizens within the often inhospitable environment of Philadelphia.[28] (See Figure 5.2.)

In another article, newspaper coverage shifted to a vignette presented in *The Italian Battlefront*, which featured "one of the greatest boy heroes of the Euro-pean war," Aurelio Baruzzi, a 19-year-old sublieutenant, who, with four other men, had captured more than 200 Austrians along with a large cache of arms and ammunition during the battle for Gorizia. The enemy had not only faced the ignominy of surrender but the embarrassment of having been duped into believing that Baruzzi had led a much larger force. Another article called atten-tion to Cadorna, the only military head of any of the belligerent nations who had remained in command from the beginning of the war and was even more noteworthy as the son of a heroic figure of the Italian Risorgimento. Anticipating

NOTHING CAN
STOP THEM!
THEY ARE
WINNING
THE WAR!
EVERY DAY
RECORDS
NEW VICTORIES!

See Them in Action!

The Royal Italian
Government's Own
Official War Pic-
tures.

American Tour, Direction
of William Moore Patch.

"The Italian
Battlefront"

Authentic—Official—Exclusive

GARRICK
2.15—Twice Daily—8.15

ITALIA IRRESISTIBLE

FIGURE 5.2 *The Italian Battlefront* (film). (*Evening Ledger* [September 8, 1917].)

the capture of Trieste, the same item noted the debt that Italy owed to father and son in acquiring "Italia Irredenta." But while Baruzzi's accomplishment endured, Cadorna's reputation would soon suffer a total reversal, although Italian movie house patrons could still revel in both cases for the moment.[29]

By September 1918, with the Allies nearing final victory, *Italy's Flaming Front*, an added attraction to a Tom Mix cowboy film, brought excited Italians to the Victoria Theatre in Center City. After a week, the highly promoted film, which claimed to have cost the lives of 2 of 10 photographers in filming its action, moved to the Alhambra Theatre in South Philadelphia. In other cities, Italian American organizations reportedly urged members to see and promote the film in every way possible. In Des Moines, Iowa, a circular, printed in Italian, saturated the Italian district with praise for the film. When it played at a theater decorated with flags of Italy and the other Allies, it was claimed, perhaps with exaggeration, that nearly all of the city's 6,000 Italian residents had turned out to see the film. Hundreds of theater patrons in El Paso, Texas, reportedly regarded it as the greatest film ever shown in their city. Describing it as "a truly great and wonderful picture," a journalist in Ogden, Utah, who judged it to be far superior to other propaganda films, declared that its scenes of Alpine combat made all other forms of fighting seem like "child's play." For some critics, it was nothing less than the best war film yet made. And Italian moviegoers even claimed to recognize in some scenes the faces of soldiers who had only recently been residents of the cities and towns where the film was being shown.[30]

While the most important question that can be asked about such films is what impact did they have, particularly on the views of other Americans toward Italians, an answer is not easily reached. But a comment that appeared in *Our Navy*, a magazine that served one branch of the nation's armed forces, showed that viewing *Italy's Flaming Front* could be muted by other factors: "Took in an official Italian war picture last month called 'Italy's Flaming Front.' It was a great picture and carried us right to Italy and the Alps. To make the local color more realistic we sat right between two wops who had been eating garlic for dinner."[31]

While *Our Navy* usually projected a more favorable judgment of Italy's military capabilities, its humor in this case had regressed into a familiar perception of Italians that almost spoke for itself. But a light-hearted item found in the gossip column of a Philadelphia newspaper as *Italy's Flaming Front* appeared on local screens offered a more compelling assessment: "Isn't it brain-taxing the way you have to calculate these days, so that you can be sure to have enough nickels left over for tomorrow . . . because sometimes there are pictures that you just have to see, and it seems wrong to miss any war films."[32]

While newsreels, documentaries, and feature films focusing on the Italian front represented only a small part of a vast repertoire that played in theaters, the dramatic depiction of warfare enjoyed popularity well after the war had ended. In December 1918, when *Under Four Flags*, a Committee of Public Information film, which included scenes of the fighting on the Piave and Monte Grappa, opened at the Stanley Theatre, long-waiting lines of patrons seeking to get in showed that Philadelphians were still quite willing to find nickels to spend at the box office. While newspapers and movie houses provided extensive coverage and memorable images throughout the war, it was never more than a vicarious experience for the public. But a delegation of Italians in search of aid from the U.S. government would place Italy's struggle on a more personal level before the American people in the spring of 1917.

6

The Italian War Commission

Seeking American Aid

W hen the United States entered the war as a partner of the Allies, it did not solve the problems that such an alliance would entail. When it finally occurred, it provoked immense demonstrations in England and France. The American flag, alongside the Union Jack at the British House of Parliament in London and the French tricolor at the National Assembly at Palais Bourbon in Paris, was widely visible in the capital cities of two major Allies. It did not happen, however, in Rome, where the Stars and Stripes remained conspicuously absent from public display, and the Italian government, while expressing relief and welcome, limited itself to formal but restrained gestures of appreciation to its American counterpart. While an informally offered explanation was that no American flags were available in the Italian capital, another even more implausible view maintained that Italians did not express their satisfaction in such a manner and that any overt demonstration was likely to invite counterdemonstrations. But Italy's political leaders also held a prevailing skepticism about American motives and interests in entering the war. While England and France had shared affinities with the United States, reflected in the recent demonstrations, Italy retained a more hesitant and ambiguous attitude about its relationship to its new ally. Seeking to clarify matters, Ambassador Page, the most strategically placed American observer of the Italian scene, noted that the other Allies had already sent commissions to Washington with the purpose of bolstering the war effort of their own nations. It was not until the Italian press demanded a similar initiative that Italy would send its own commission seeking to gain material aid and strengthen the relationship with the United States. But for the huge immigrant population of such cities as Philadelphia, it would do even more during its brief stay in the United States. In sharp contrast to the cautious response in Rome to America's entry into the war, the exuberant reception for the War Mission would become a decisive moment that redefined Little Italy and indeed the presence of all Italians in Philadelphia. It would also facilitate the widening portal through which many young Italians would pass while going off to war as recruits of the U.S. Army.[1]

When Mayor Thomas B. Smith and city officials met with the French diplomatic mission in Washington to discuss arrangements for its reception in Philadelphia in April 1917, they reported that some 15,000 Italians were also expected to take part in the program. Beyond the present occasion for the French, it provided an opportunity to initiate plans for a similar program for Italians in the following month. On the same day, the Italian government announced that it intended to send two missions with officials of a similar rank as delegations of the other Allies to the United States. With the Great War casting the United States for the first time in its history as the provider of aid to other nations, as Italy took its place in the queue among them, the stage was also being set for international diplomacy to take to the streets of American cities.[2]

Arriving on a special train provided by the State Department, the Italian War Commission, escorted by two cavalry units of the U.S. Army, passed through Washington, gaily decorated in its honor in late May 1917. Italy had sent a group of business, political, and scientific luminaries that included, among other officials, Ferdinando of Savoy, the prince of Udine and the king's own cousin; Francesco Saverio Nitti, a future prime minister; and Senator Guglielmo Marconi, the widely respected inventor of the wireless. While their main task was to place before officials in Washington Italy's great need for coal and the tonnage to transport it, the delegation would deliver a more ambiguous message about the role of American troops. The official position, stated by an unidentified member, which would be widely repeated, was that "Italy has all the man-power she needs, and the American soldiers should be sent to the battle front in France." But the same delegate also observed: "We would, of course, welcome American soldiers on the Italian front if your government saw fit to send them," before reiterating the plea for economic assistance. With greater confidence in the likelihood of receiving material aid, the mission was pursuing a more cautious strategy on troops.[3]

With news important enough to warrant coverage in their own language, Philadelphia's Italians followed the arrival of the War Mission, but the paucity of information did not fully reveal the complex challenge facing it. While diplomatic tact prevented openly asking that American troops be deployed, Italy, having already incurred tremendous losses of manpower, was undoubtedly willing to accept them. But recognizing what had long attracted Americans as tourists, the Italian delegation could only express that need as a metaphorical postscript to its official position, namely that the "Italian kitchen" would be left open.[4]

Diplomacy on the Streets of Philadelphia

Meanwhile, C.C.A. Baldi and other *prominenti* had drafted a program with a "monster parade" of 75,000 marchers as the main event, along with an anticipated purse of $50,000 in donations from local residents to be donated to the Red Cross, to serve as incentives for the Italian War Mission to include Philadelphia on its itinerary. As it had the second largest Italian population of any American city, intensely loyal to their adopted country but still having "a soft spot in their hearts for old Italy," Baldi contended that the agenda would stimulate their interest in the war and cement more firmly the relationship between the United States and Italy.[5]

More than making it merely another public celebration, Baldi, their major spokesperson, had recognized the opportunity to affirm the place of Italians in the city, while renewing the bonds between Little Italy and Mother Italy. At the same time, it provided the mayor and other leaders with their own moment to resuscitate the esteem that Philadelphians since colonial times had held for Italy as the embodiment of a great culture and to consolidate their own political positions among Italian voters. With its vast Italian colony, city officials could not allow the diplomatic mission to come so near without coaxing it to participate in some kind of program in the urban center that contained so much historical significance for any entente between Italy and America, while also strengthening the agenda of the visitors.

Mayor Smith put the impending visit more firmly into the perspective of what it would mean to the city of Philadelphia. After praising the Italian visitors as representing "the best blood and the best brain of modern Italy," he too turned to our own Italian citizens who, along with their "fine qualities," had demonstrated loyalty to their new country "by taking up arms in the service of the United States and thousands more [who] will help when the industrial mobilization begins." Like Baldi's testimony, the mayor's comments indicated a shift in emphasis, which would become clearer in the days ahead, from simply being a reception for the dignitaries of the Italian War Mission to also being a celebration of the presence of the Italian colony in the city.[6]

But as the mayor's efforts to organize an official program began to stall, Italian leaders launched their own plans with a preliminary meeting that resembled a veritable "Who's Who" of the immigrant community. Before an estimated 600 eager participants at the Italian Beneficial Hall on South 8th Street, Giuseppe Gentile, acting Italian consul, calling for the contribution of money to the families of soldiers who had sacrificed their lives, exclaimed, "Let there not be a long flow of oratory, but let there be action," and the audience roared its endorsement. After Baldi reportedly drew five $100 bills from his wallet, evoking cheers from enthusiastic onlookers, other donors lined up to contribute cash, write a check, or place a gold watch and chain on the speakers' table. Within an hour, more than $2,000 had been donated to the purse that the Italian War Mission was expected to carry back to Italy for the benefit of widows and orphans. And almost as a reward for their "outburst of patriotism and enthusiasm," an announcement confirmed that the Italian War Mission would include a brief stop in Philadelphia as it passed on its way back from New York City to Washington in early June.[7]

As Philadelphia's Italians prepared to welcome their much-anticipated guests, the visitors clearly knew gaining material assistance from Washington would depend upon convincing the American government of their common interests. In an interview shortly after arriving, Nitti, the scholarly economist, sought to reach this understanding by declaring that Italy had entered the war for the same reasons as the United States. Moreover, despite great military disadvantages, his country had chosen to oppose Germany for the benefit of all nations and the good of humanity and civilization. He similarly maintained that the mission was not seeking anything for Italy alone but to bolster the military undertaking shared by all the Allies.[8]

Beyond negotiating with the U.S. government, the outcome of the Italian War Mission would also be facilitated by the reaction of the American public. And by the time discussions in Washington ended, listed among the destinations chosen by the State Department with large Italian populations who could extend highly enthusiastic support were such cities as New Orleans, Saint Louis, Chicago, Pittsburgh, New York, and Philadelphia. But despite the presence of a member of the royal family with the delegation, it was Marconi, with his celebrity status, who had emerged as the most popular attraction. If the success of the mission rested partly on convincing Americans that the two nations had common interests, he was more equipped than any other member to assume that task. In a message prepared for the *Evening Ledger*, which could only win favor among local residents, Marconi declared that the Liberty Bell had a strong attraction for Italians who, like Americans, were "a liberty-loving people," before adding: "We also want to pay a tribute of love and respect to our fellow Italians in Philadelphia who have done so much to aid the city in its march of progress."[9]

With the balance of its previous loan nearly exhausted, the Italian War Mission sought additional aid that would raise the total of borrowed money to $700,000,000. After several days of meetings, American negotiators proposed a new loan of $100,000,000 to supplement the aid that Italy had already received. While Italy would not receive what it had hoped for at this point, it would secure a total of $760,000,000 in another year. With funds generated by the sale of Liberty Bonds to American subscribers, Italy would be enabled to purchase more arms and ammunition from manufacturers in the United States. The Italian War Mission, as it embarked on its "good will" tour, could help its cause by ingratiating itself to prospective buyers of bonds. In some sense, the Italians were here, as the United States prepared to enter the war, promoting their own nation's part in the struggle with increased profit for American industry.[10]

But other tools of persuasion would plead Italy's cause. During the brief moment that the Italian War Mission was in the United States, new books, reviewed on the same day in a local newspaper, offered highly favorable perspectives on Italy. In *Greater Italy*, William Kay Wallace, a scholar and diplomat who would later serve as a member of the American delegation to the Paris Peace Conference, examined the political, social, and moral revolution that was shaping modern Italy. Full of praise for Italy and its people for having transformed petty states into a new nation, he saw their accomplishments as examples of great political progress in the nineteenth century. It not only had inspired the Serbs, Bulgarians, and Romanians in their struggle for national sovereignty but had been endorsed by President Wilson in his discussion of the principles on which peace must be built. In Wallace's view, Italy, tired of merely acting as a curator of historical antiquities, had begun pursuit of a future that justified the annexation of the Trentino and Trieste. In *Italy at War and the Allies in the West*, E. Alexander Powell, a journalist who had been with the Italian army, sought to end the ignorance of Americans on the difficult conditions under which Italy had waged a war against militarism and autocracy. While both books offered an understanding of a distant war, they also prepared readers to greet the Italian War Mission in their own city.[11]

In anticipation of the Italian War Mission, the editorial pages of local newspapers expressed similarly strong support for Italy. Under the gracious title of "Our Debt to Italy," the *Evening Ledger* reminded readers that "every time we say 'America' we speak the eloquent tongue of Rome. Every time we trace the life of civilized America to its source, it is the glorious heir of Italy, the pioneer of modern science and culture that must furnish the background of our thoughts. An Italian found our new world. An Italian named it." Both relating America's debt to the eminent guests who would soon arrive and, particularly, the wreath laying at the Columbus monument in Fairmount Park, which would symbolize the historic link between Italy and the United States, noted the carnival atmosphere with which "our own Italians" would receive the envoys, before repeating the pantheon of names—from Columbus to Cadorna—by which the reception would honor "immortal Italy." Meanwhile, Donato Cugino, chastising residents for not displaying Italy's flag alongside the other Allies, wrote that outside of the various "Little Italies" of the city, one would think that Italy was not in the war at all. Asserting that if Italy had not joined the Allies, the war would have already ended in a German victory, Cugino implored: "Wake up, American citizens, to the serious business before us all. Don't fail to fly the Italian emblem with the flags of the rest of our Allies, for that flag deserves more than a good many of you think." While both editorialist and letter writer may have exaggerated, their ringing endorsements reflected the receptivity with which the city prepared to meet the Italian War Mission.[12]

By early June, although the final plans of an official reception by the City of Philadelphia remained uncertain, there was no doubt about the enthusiasm of the Italian colony. Despite the expectation that the Italian War Mission would make not more than a visit of five hours, organizers announced their intention to obtain some kind of donation from each of the city's Italians, now estimated to be a population of 150,000. The members of various societies had undertaken a house-to-house effort to canvas Italian neighborhoods in search of contributions. While reports claimed a generous response from laborers offering their "bit," which presumably meant cash, women donating rings and other jewelry, and even children "shaking their banks and making contributions from penny boards," the actual results remained uncertain. As immigrant benefactors gained public attention, Baldi once again spoke for them: "We have every hope of raising the fund for the Italian Red Cross. Italians throughout Philadelphia are stirred to deep enthusiasm by the proposed visit of the war mission to this city. . . . We have a certain pride that our compatriots on the firing line in Italy know that the Italians of liberty-loving Philadelphia are not delinquent in the matter of lending succor to their countrymen in the stress of this great war."[13]

But Baldi was probably wrong in one important respect. If the reservists who had reported for duty in 1915 thought about Philadelphia's Italians at all, they must have been wondering when their conationals whom they had left behind might be coming to join them. With many of them now being greeted by the Selective Service System of the United States, if those who had ignored the earlier summons of their native land ever believed that they had escaped the ordeal of the Italian front, they would very soon find themselves on the Western Front. And for them, the impending celebration would provide only a momentary distraction before they discovered the reality of war. Meanwhile, spurred by expectation, a general euphoria, evident throughout the community, had taken root among Philadelphia's Italians. When Baldi again met with Mayor Smith and former Ambassador William Potter to coordinate activities, he found the anticipated program was expected to be as large as any previous reception accorded to a foreign delegation. As great numbers of Italians attending other meetings pledged sums of money in support of the Red Cross, they confirmed the likelihood of success. And further resonating with the mood of the community, on June 4, the traditional day of celebration of the Statuto, the constitution of the kingdom, a lodge of the Sons of Italy sent a message to King Victor Emmanuel III "interpreting the wishes of 30,000 members . . . in the State of Pennsylvania" and expressing admiration of "the work of the gallant soldiers fighting in the Carso" with the wish "for prompt and complete victory for the vindication of the rights of justice and civilization."[14]

Convinced that the city deserved a longer visit from the mission, a group of prominent Italians announced their intention to call upon Secretary of State Robert Lansing to propose that the event be extended to at least 24 hours. Giuseppe Donato, a well-known sculptor who had emerged as a spokesperson, objected to the planned three days to be spent in New York, a place of lesser significance, while Philadelphia, the most historical city in the nation, would be granted only a few hours. He argued that Philadelphia as the shrine of world liberty meant more to his countrymen than any other city, especially with the story of the Declaration of Independence being retold on every battlefront in Europe and whole races of men only beginning to glimpse its real meaning. As Baldi had done, Donato cited the accomplishments of local Italians who after imbibing "the principles of real republican government in the shadow of the world's finest monuments to democracy" were playing an important part in the development of their city by entering fields of art and the professions. Speaking as an artist, he stated that the members of the Italian War Mission should see what Italians of the area were doing to aid the uplift of humanity. Philadelphia, as the birthplace of liberty and center of the arts, he contended, required more than five hours to grasp its significance.[15]

The agenda of the Italian War Mission, meanwhile, also continued to unfold with the announcement that General Emilio Guglielmotti, its military attaché, would remain in the United States after his colleagues had returned to Italy, partly in an attempt to resolve a major issue—the status of reservists who had not answered the earlier call. While it was expected that the Italian Parliament would soon consider a proposal to grant a general amnesty, Guglielmotti would have the authority to solve cases on an individual basis. Along with recruits who would be able to return without penalties, punishments would be dropped for men who had committed crimes in Italy. With an estimated 300,000 Italians eligible for military service living in the United States, men with dependents would be allowed to remain if they were employed in agriculture or willing to serve under the American flag but not as members of exclusively Italian regiments. Such concerns indicated that Italy had not forgotten its negligent reservists and that its delegation had come for more than material aid from Washington.[16]

While Philadelphia's Italian leaders further nurtured their plans for celebration, Donato, the sculptor, offered an impassioned plea describing what would be found by expanding the occasion from the more familiar historic sites of the city to include Little Italy as a destination:

> The Italian colony of this city reflects the enterprise and progress of Philadelphia Italians. It shows what real liberty has done for an alien people. We have in Little Italy banks, restaurants and stores which compare favorably with those in long-settled sections of the city. In the faces of our school children is reflected the fire of American ideals and patriotism. We want the distinguished visitors from Italy to see these things so that they may take a real message back to the people of Italy. The visit of the Italian mission would hardly be complete if it failed to visit Little Italy and see what Italy is doing for America.[17]

By shaping Little Italy into an experience that conveyed for its own residents and the visitors what immigrant life meant in America, while also reaffirming the enduring linkage between the country of origin and city of adoption, Donato had sculpted an artistic image comparable to any other work in his studio.

Beyond what Donato had urged, preparations for the visit of the Italian War Mission were evolving in other ways. Almost daily newspaper accounts reported that the fund-raising effort for the Italian Red Cross had reached $18,000 by the end of the first week of June. Solicitors were continuing their door-to-door push in Little Italy, along with a special effort to reach all professionals and businessmen in the community. Representatives of the Federated Societies, meeting at the office of *L'Opinione*, voted to contribute another $250 and urged all member organizations to make similar donations. While still negotiating with Prince Ferdinando, the special committee had also placed its request before Secretary of State Lansing to allow the visit of the Italian War Mission to be extended to a full day.[18]

While the prominenti of Little Italy viewed the upcoming visit as unique in the lifetime of the community, enterprising merchants seized on the event more as a commercial opportunity. Recognizing that patriotism needed banners, they sought to accommodate the needs of Philadelphians who planned to join in the celebration. In early June, a newspaper advertisement offered the flag of Italy ranging from a 12- by 18-inch version at $0.20 up to a five- by eight-foot version at $3.50. One could buy a set of the smaller flags in silk for any three Allied nations, mounted on black staffs with gilt spearheads for $2.50 or any seven nations in one-foot by one-and-a-half-foot cotton standards for $3.50. The automobile owner could find brackets holding three or five flags as well as suitable silk flags for all of the nations. A notice boldly asserted: "Now is the time to buy a flag." If manufacturers of weapons could find profit by providing the means of killing other human beings on battlefields, purveyors of another kind could sell flags to cheering crowds who endorsed the same cause on sidewalks of the home front.[19]

Unlike merchants who saw an opportunity to make money, Philip Cotumaccio, a 12-year-old North Philadelphian, made a more honorable proposal. In a carefully composed letter to the *Evening Ledger*'s columnist Tom Daly, the young artist offered his own painting of Venice to be sold for the benefit of the Italian Red Cross fund. Reproducing Cotumaccio's proposal in his column, Daly, whose dialect humor often poked fun at Italians, mentioned his own contribution of $1, then called on other readers to give what they could, "even if it be a few pennies," toward a fund to purchase the painting. In his own manner, Cotumaccio, too young to serve in the military and too poor to give money, reflected the growing enthusiasm as the day of visit by the Italian War Mission approached.[20]

Italian community leaders, echoing a sense of gravity that they shared with a young artist, increased their calls for an expanded celebration. Two days before the scheduled date of arrival of the Italian War Mission, another committee of Italians, led by Donato, again called upon Mayor Smith to ask for his support. While Smith was said to be ready to extend the widest hospitality, even better news could be released. The State Department had agreed to extend the program to a full day that would culminate in a "mammoth parade." Donato summed up reaction to the announcement: "Enthusiasm is growing daily in 'Little Italy' over the proposed visit of the mission to Philadelphia. Italians, young and old, are rejoicing over the prospect of seeing these great men of their native land."[21]

With the basic format in place, after almost nightly meetings at the Beneficial Hall to polish details, Mayor Smith promised, "We shall do all we can to make the visit of the Italian envoys memorable." But with the effort of the mayor's office lagging, the burden on Italian leaders had increased. In their most recent meeting, with an additional $10,000 pledged, the total for the Red Cross Fund had climbed to over $60,000. Father Terlizzi reported that a special collection on the previous Sunday at Our Lady of Good Counsel had brought $731 more, with some parishioners, who could not give cash, donating rings, bracelets, and other jewelry. Italian workers at the Snellenberg clothing factory had contributed $144. The Sons of Italy donated $7,199, the largest sum for any group, and Frank Roma, the well-known banker, subscribed $500. Although Italians were meeting the needs of the situation, time was running out. The Italian War Mission had already begun its tour with a reception given by U.S. Army Reserve officers at Fort McPherson, Georgia, where 400 German prisoners of war watched the proceedings with interest. In order to reach success, Philadelphia would have to offer its own memorable attractions for the visitors.[22]

In mid-June, the *Evening Ledger*, reporting that the Italian community had met its financial goals, declared: "Little Italy is preparing to give the Italian envoys a royal reception next Wednesday, and with its usual generosity is preparing something more than cheers. Its Red Cross fund is expected to leap above the $50,000 by the middle of next week." Despite being less than what had already been reported as collected, the amount surpassed expectations. And in contrast to a mayor's desultory efforts, the prominenti had mobilized their resources and energies into what would be "something more than cheers."[23]

With Italian efforts gaining approval across the city, a "society page" writer coyly warned: "Do not be surprised if a charming young girl with dark flashing eyes and carmine cheeks approaches you today and attempts to pin a flag or some such patriotic emblem on your coat." Advising that if it were not already being worn another would soon be offered, the writer rhetorically asked: "Perhaps as these same small Italian girls are many of them so ravishingly pretty, you would like to buy an emblem from each of them." It referred, of course, to another facet of the Italian Red Cross drive. Meanwhile, some 18 Italian motion picture owners had agreed to donate a day's receipts to the cause. Whether by the allure of young women or the largesse of movie house proprietors, the widening campaign was also erasing boundaries that had separated Little Italy and its people from the rest of the city.[24]

Using newer tools to stimulate interest, the *Evening Ledger*, in the vanguard of photojournalism, increased its depiction of training camps, battlefield scenes, and military leaders. Under a banner reading, "Exclusive Photographs of the Great New Italian Offensive against the Austrians," its illustrated section showed Italian soldiers in their trenches east of Gorizia; an Austrian counterattack with gas as Italians fell back to their second-line trench positions; Italian artillerymen hauling their great guns in the Julian Alps; Italian artillery officers conferring to determine the proper range for their guns; Italian howitzers on the road to Trieste; Italian sharpshooters lying prone on a hillside taking aim at the enemy; and a heroic portrait of Cadorna as "The Captor of Gorizia." With the approaching visit of the Italian envoys, such coverage could only encourage more attention to the event.[25]

Capturing the anticipation sweeping through Italian neighborhoods, the local press, increasing coverage even more, now reported: "Elaborate plans for entertaining the distinguished mission from Rome are being made by the 150,000 Italian residents of the city, whose colonies already have blossomed with the national colors of Italy." As preparations continued, teams of girls were still canvasing for donations to the Italian Red Cross fund, with more than $8,000 reportedly collected on one day. Every Italian business in the city was said to be closing for the entire day of the visit. Baldi and other leaders were scheduled to address Italian tailors at Snellenberg's shops on behalf of the Red Cross drive. And young Philip Cotumaccio's painting of Venice and the $10.50 it had gained in bids were both being donated to the Italian Red Cross. But even more was taking place, as a war that would ask more concerted action of the people of Italy if it were to end in victory was bringing an immigrant aggregate into a more cohesive stage in its history in a city far removed from the scene of the actual conflict.[26]

When the Italian War Mission finally arrived on June 20, coming from Pittsburgh instead of New York City, at 11:00 A.M. rather than at 9:00 A.M., its revised plans also called for a visit of a day and a half. It was immediately engulfed by what the *Evening Ledger* described as "an overwhelming expression of Philadelphia's devotion to the cause of world democracy." On the next morning, *The Inquirer* offered a similar appraisal: "In such an uproar of jubilation as Philadelphia has not seen for many a year, the city—and first, foremost and peculiarly its Italian citizenry and residents—paid yesterday its respects to the Italian war mission now visiting here." The *Evening Ledger* noted that among the thousands gathered at the Broad Street Station, Italians "contributed all of the fine warmth and splendid emotion of their nationality to Philadelphia's greeting to their countrymen." Inside the station, a reception committee, composed of Mayor Smith, former Ambassador Potter, the sculptor Donato, and

Cavaliere Baldi welcomed the guests. After Marquis Luigi Borsarelli di Rifreddo, the undersecretary for foreign affairs, the easily recognizable Marconi,
wearing a white Italian navy uniform, was the second to leave the train. As the
delegation approached the exit to Market Street, an immense crowd, vigorously waving American and Italian flags, roared its greeting, "and from the
throats of thousands of dark skinned Italians rose the cry, 'Viva l'Italia.'"[27]

Escorted by local officials, prominenti of Little Italy, the State Fencibles,
the quasi-official honor guard of the mayor and city councils, a company of
U.S. Marines, mounted policemen, and plainclothes detectives, the Italian
War Mission passed city hall and turned south on Broad Street. Marching with
the motorcade, a police band saluted the visitors and entertained the throng
along the route. With spectators jamming windows and perched on other vantage points, a continuous ovation, sufficient to have "gratified the vanity of a
Roman conqueror," enveloped the parade. Along with thousands of schoolgirls
in white dresses waving the tricolor of Italy, laborers, mill operators, drug-
gists, clerks, lawyers, and physicians represented all stations of Italian life in
Philadelphia. In his official greeting, Mayor Smith proclaimed America's two
principal reasons for being grateful to Italy. The first involved the hundreds of
young American students, recognizing that no other country provided as great
a font of artistic treasure, who were drawn to "eternal Rome" to study art every
year. Smith's second reason, even more pertinent for the moment, involved the
multitude of humble, strong, and sober workers that Italy had sent to raise the
economy of America by constructing railroads, digging canals, cultivating des-
erts and forests, and transforming swamps into florid gardens with products
from their native lands. As Smith shifted his praise to the immigrant population that had enthusiastically joined in the reception, the celebration began to
honor Philadelphia's Italians as much as it did Italy's envoys.[28]

The *Evening Ledger*'s Italian version, recognizing a more subtle nuance of
the event, declared that the union between Italians and Americans that had
its "baptism" by the prior reception in Washington now received its "confir-
mation" in Philadelphia. Against the contention that Italy had acted with
treachery in breaking from the Central Powers, the delegation established a
"communione di sentimenti" between Italy and the United States. The reception in Philadelphia, reflecting immigrant sensibilities, afforded a cordial
welcome to the Italian War Mission but reciprocally brought the greetings of
a homeland—"always remembered, never forgotten, in the faithful conduct
of duties toward an adopted country."[29]

If the public had come to see any particular member of the mission, it
was Marconi. Along the short distance from the train station to the Ritz-

Carlton Hotel, voices from crowded sidewalks shouted greetings to the famous inventor. When the mission reached its destination, where a large police squad again forced open a lane through a blocked entrance, eager spectators attempted to break through the protection to embrace him. A young Italian woman who approached Marconi with the hope of kissing him, pushed back by a policeman, gestured her fingertips in salute. As the dignitaries disappeared from view, quickly sequestered by a private luncheon, the solidly packed throng, estimated by police to be between 50,000 and 75,000 people, facing the hotel on Broad Street, and stretching from Chestnut Street to Spruce Street began chanting for Marconi. And when a band began playing "Garibaldi's March," another hoarse roar reached an even greater crescendo. But when Marconi did not appear, several Italians entered the hotel to ask if he would address the people outside. *The Inquirer* reported: "One man of determination brought about spontaneously the most colorful and thrilling feature of the public welcome to the Italian Mission yesterday." Disappointed at the infrequent appearance of a face in a distant upper-floor window, waving to greet the cheers below, Michael Casaccio, a well-known Walnut Street tailor, entered the hotel to urge delegates to appear on a low balcony just above the sidewalk. When asked, "Whom do you represent?" Casaccio replied, "No one, but those people want to see you." With his reply, the intrepid tailor had succeeded. After a few moments, members of the Italian War Mission emerged on the balcony, where they were greeted by more applause and cries of "Viva l'Italia," "Viva gli Stati Uniti," and "Viva Cadorna." As they removed their hats and bowed in response, Marconi, "almost all American because of his long residence in this country," appeared to best understand what was happening but did not speak to the crowd below. Instead, Borsarelli delivered "a fervid eulogy," extolling the king, especially for his presence at the front, and Italy's other war heroes. As he ended his remarks, Borsarelli thanked Casaccio for the opportunity to greet Philadelphia.[30]

It had been an auspicious beginning but clouded by less pleasant realities, especially the threat of disruption by anarchists, a fear that had entered minds long before the arrival of the War Mission. A letter, purportedly signed by an "Anarchist" promising to use dynamite, had gained attention from the police who took precautions to protect the visitors. After Captain James Tate, chief of detectives, read the message at roll call in bureau headquarters, local detectives and agents of the Secret Service formed a protective cordon around the Italian visitors as admirers, unaware of any danger, followed closely and cheered. But at another end of the spectrum, detectives arrested an alleged pickpocket and her young daughter after observing their attempts to open the handbags of women spectators. From possible anarchist violence to the actual work of pickpockets providing cause for excitement, the main attraction remained the visitors from Italy.[31]

The exuberance of Philadelphia's Italians, however, also threatened to disrupt the celebration. With the delegates secluded at the hotel luncheon, a massive throng marched to Fairmount Park, where an estimated 10,000 members of the Sons of Italy awaited the resumption of more public ceremonies. When the dignitaries' motorcade, stopping only to allow the placing of wreaths at the Washington monument at the Green Street entrance to the park and the Lincoln statue on East River Drive, brought them to the Columbus Monument, a chorus of 2,000 voices greeted them. As the front ranks of the crowd rushed toward the approaching vehicles, mounted policemen and club-wielding patrolmen sought to maintain order but still several altercations occurred. Once calm had been restored, the delegates paid tribute to Christopher Columbus and Giuseppe Verdi and received the money collected for the relief of war victims and a medal for Cadorna. Despite a momentary disturbance, the occasion had been salvaged by a community united for the moment.[32]

The Sons of Italy, the largest and most powerful Italian fraternal organization, was well suited for the task of organizing the program. Founded in 1905, Philadelphia residents made up about half of its 20,000 members in Pennsylvania. By taking the initiative, it had assumed the strategic center in the ongoing struggle among factions within the immigrant community. Giuseppe Di Silvestro, acting as master of ceremonies for the day, could aptly be described as "the leading spirit in the organization, the main purpose of which is to care for immigrant Italians and to see to it that they are naturalized in as short a space of time after their arrival here as the law permits." Such characterization obscured the dilemma of an organization and leadership caught in the contradictory agenda of trying to facilitate material well-being and adjustment for immigrants and their families while urging them to retain their identity and cohesion as Italians. But ceremonies that honored the presence of visitors from Italy, acknowledged the contributions of Italians to America, and affirmed the military and political alliance of Italy and the United States also provided the occasion to brush aside such ambiguities and anomalies.[33]

The extensive attention accorded by press and public to the War Mission emphatically reinforced what it represented for the city but especially for its Italian population. In addition to coverage by news articles, op-ed pages were given over to Italy and its people. In the *Evening Ledger*, a large cartoon depicted William Penn, the city's Quaker founder, greeting a Roman centurion, on whose shield was inscribed the words "Italian War Commission," while three articles, seeking to capture aspects of the moment, graced its editorial section. Under the heading of "Welcome, Italians," a brief but solemn message declared: "We greet Italy's illustrious representatives as allies, and as something more than allies. It needed no war to cement the friendship of Americans for the liberty-loving, enthusiastic and industrious Italian race." But beyond the new alliance, the analysis saluted the many immigrants who had chosen to stay in America and could be counted as "among the most loyal and valuable of her citizens." It concluded: "In this city, where citizens of Italian birth are so well liked, are so indispensable a part of us, the Italian envoys are assured in every section of the most cordial and warm-hearted greeting." A quarter of a century after the lynching of Italians in New Orleans had disrupted relations between Italy and the United States and threatened the security of immigrants in 1891, the *Evening Ledger* sought to extinguish any lingering damage. And one could ask if "Welcome, Italians," the widely visible slogan on banners throughout the city, was meant more as a greeting to the Italian envoys or to the immigrants who had made their home in Philadelphia.[34]

Adjacent to the editorial, Tom Daly provided another parody in which an Italian barber, speaking broken English described a baseball game between teams representing the Malatesta macaroni factory and the Unione e Fratellanza. In the final inning, after both "Pasquale Scarpa" and "Tony Torquato" come to bat with bases filled, and after reading a note delivered by a boy on the field, strike out on three pitches. Joe Piccirelli, despite receiving the same message, hits a home run to win the game. When Joe admits that his inability to read prevented him from understanding the note, his teammates tell him that it came with the threat: "Eef you hit da ball, you are dead man! Black Hand." The storyteller-barber then reveals: "No, my frand, eet ees not da real Blacka Hand at all, but jus' som' of does fallows een da crowd dat was bettin deir money on da Malatesta Macaroni Factory for ween da game." After another home run on the following day, "eet was longest home run dat annybody deed evra mak' een da gama baseball," the slugging Joe abandons both baseball and America: "For da nexta day he gat on boarda sheep an' sail for Italy an' nobody ees nevva see heem here no more." Despite his irreverent portrayals, Daly's poetic tribute to Columbus on the same day, as well as his close friendships with Italians, indicated that he too had for the moment joined into the celebration.[35]

In a more serious item, Henry T. Craven, proclaiming its linkage with ancient Rome, argued that modern Italy, despite having a ruling monarch, was actually a republic. But whether as tourists who mainly saw a museum of antiquities and art or as "stay-at-homes" living in the midst of immigrants from a once backward and impoverished society, most Americans were unable to recognize the indisputable progress of Italy "rushing forward in the march of civilization." While praising recent immigration from Naples (presumably referring to the provinces of Southern Italy), he concluded: "For purposes of civilization we are all in essence Roman citizens in Rome's new struggle against barbarism." Having reconstructed history to serve the new alliance, Craven's convoluted analysis had met the expectations of nationalistic Italians as well as the visions of "simpatici" Americans. It was part of newspaper coverage that was still finding the virtues of a recently acquired battlefield ally whose people were now partners in what had become a struggle of civilization against barbarity. Whether as news, editorial, or feature, it also afforded the opportunity to rediscover and redefine Italians who as immigrants had become neighbors and fellow citizens of Philadelphia.[36]

At the formal dinner at the Bellevue-Stratford Hotel provided by the mayor and city council later in the evening, speakers paid tribute to Italian contributions to Philadelphia and America while a hidden recording rang the long-silenced sounds of the Liberty Bell. When the most eagerly awaited voice, that of Marconi, who was resplendent in his naval uniform, declared: "We fight together for liberty and humanity," his captivated listeners delivered the loudest and longest ovation of the evening. But beyond the sound of a sacred bell or words of a celebrated inventor, the night still belonged to the Italians of the city. As one observer described the scene: "The wistful-eyed bootblack, flaunting a hatband of red, white and green as wide as a sash and hanging longingly around the hotel entrance, and the Italian consul both had a part in it. So did the pretty dark-eyed girls leaning from the boxes, chattering softly together in Italian." But the evening took a more poignant turn when the final oration became muffled under the sound of voices rising from the streets. An unimaginative policeman might have quickly stopped the chant, declared one newspaper, before one of the envoys raised his hand and quietly said, "It is the song of Garibaldi." And Philadelphia sat silent as "Italian voices, strong and sweet and fervent . . . of the men who clean our streets and shine our shoes rose and fell and died away," as they chanted: "We go, farewell; we go to victory; Perhaps to return; if not, to die gloriously for Italy and for victory."[37]

The banquet was the overture for more dramatic scenes on the following day. In the morning, another motorcade swept past cheering spectators waving American and Italian flags as the Italian War Mission passed along Chestnut Street on its way to Independence Hall. Near the entrance to the most celebrated site of America's most historic city, as the envoys paused to pay homage at the statue of George Washington, they encountered Mary Trapizzani and her four-year-old daughter, Elizabeth, and three-year-old son,

John, one wearing the national colors of Italy, the other of the United States, members of a family from South Philadelphia. Marconi embraced and kissed the two children, who then handed their flags to him, as the crowd raised another great cheer. Inside the hall, the main speaker, Judge Norris S. Barratt, president judge of the Court of Common Pleas, praised Italy for its contributions throughout history; promised American support in the present struggle; and proclaimed the Italian nation as a democracy. As Mayor Smith escorted the members of the mission to the bell and began to explain its history, one of them declared in distinct English, "Yes, we Italians know."[38] (See Figure 6.1.)

Outside the historic hall, the party again halted in Independence Square, but this time to honor a Philadelphia Italian. In a brief ceremony, Consul Gentile, on behalf of King Victor Emmanuel III, bestowed a silver medal to Gaetano and Cristina Del Gatto, residents of South Philadelphia, in recognition of the valor of their 22-year-old son, Luigi, who had died on the Italian front in September 1916. Both parents wore clothing expressive of deep mourning. As the medal was placed on the hand of the grieving mother, she lifted her veil and, with tears streaming from her eyes, kissed the token of memory to her son. Each member of the mission placed his ceremonial kiss on the parents. From a place where Thomas Jefferson, James Madison, and Benjamin Franklin once stood, an immigrant father, in a trembling voice and native language, urged his countrymen to take up arms for Italy and to die, as his son had, if necessary, for the cause of liberty. With testimony to a young Philadelphian who had left his home on South 8th Street to die on the distant Carso, the scene at Independence Hall concluded.[39]

The reaction of other Philadelphians, whether to the distinguished emissaries or the city's own immigrants, was less discernible. But disdain could again be glimpsed from the predictably snide comment that Tom Daly slipped into his column for the day. Of a delegation that included an eminent scholar, a statesman, and a scientist, he could only declare that the Italians who had passed silently by his office window had been unnoticed because they had no music—"The idea of two or more Italians in motion without music!" Like the earlier parody of the baseball game, his "good-natured" comment, fatuously indifferent to the sorrow with which the program at Independence Hall had ended, revived the "opera buffa" perspective that even a more empathic newspaper still too often permitted on its pages.[40]

Leaving the hallowed hall, the Italian War Mission made its way to a comparably significant shrine of American commerce, the John Wanamaker Department Store on Market Street, where two members of the smartly uniformed John Wanamaker Cadets, an organization of youthful employees of

FIGURE 6.1 The Italian War Commission is greeted by two children, Elizabeth and John Trapizzani, dressed in Italian and American colors, at Independence Hall. Along with their mother, the scene also shows Baron Luigi Borsarelli Di Rifreddo, an unidentified police officer, and Mayor Thomas B. Smith. (*Evening Ledger* [June 21, 1917].)

the city's most famous retail emporium, presented more flags to their guests. Having paid homage to American business, the envoys made their way to the Manufacturers Club for a farewell luncheon. At its entrance, another mother and child, the most efficacious device for such tasks, again gained the attention of the Italian dignitaries. When 11-year-old Anna Maria Dell'Olivastro offered a bouquet of roses, Marconi bowed and kissed her on both cheeks, as the chagrined girl blushed and rushed back to her mother.[41]

As his reception by the public repeatedly confirmed, the charismatic Marconi, with his partly Scotch Irish ancestry, fluent command of English, and enormous popularity, was better suited to play his role than any other person Italy could have sent. But his message took on greater significance when he assessed the current situation at the luncheon at the Manufacturers Club. While security demanded that details not be released to the public, he predicted that recent innovations would soon make submarine warfare more difficult for Germany. As for further developments in wireless technology, he had adapted the system for use by airplanes and submarines, but everything else remained impractical at the present time. He offered a more definite analysis of Italy's part in the war. From an army of 250,000 with few reserves, it had grown to a well-supplied force of over 4,000,000 men. Asked about America's role in Italy, Marconi demurred before suggesting that it was more likely to be used to reinforce France, despite that nation having enough men at the front to not only hold its own but carry out offensives. As for the British, he believed that they had all the men and ammunition they needed, as well as troops that had not been used at the front. Marconi's view of the future provided a fitting message for the occasion.[42]

As the Italian War Mission moved on to the Reading Terminal, where an estimated 15,000 persons had assembled, city detectives and Secret Service men were again required to force open a path to the train. With enthusiasm as great as at their arrival, "The roof of the shed fairly shook with the roar after roar of applause which was given when the mission headed by the tall Marconi appeared." From the rear platform of the last car, they blew kisses, "after the manner of their nationality," a gesture that Mayor Smith awkwardly reciprocated as the train pulled away, "while the crowd laughed and cheered alternately with delight." And unlike the chaos in the park on the preceding day, the visit to Philadelphia came to a more dignified close.[43]

As festivities ended, Philadelphia's Italians found more reason for celebration with news that Cadorna's new offensive in the Asiago Plateau had regained much of the bitterly contested Monte Ortigara and taken nearly 1,000 Austrian prisoners. With ground forces advancing against resistance in sectors of difficult terrain, air squadrons supported heavy artillery bombardment upon a rapidly retreating foe. The timely news from the battlefield increased the confidence with which the War Mission had sought aid from a new ally by its efforts in faraway American cities.[44]

Shortly after the departure of the War Mission, Adalberto Caporale reported the views of Francesco Nitti by an interview conducted while other members had been at Independence Hall. As a former minister of agriculture, industry, and commerce and native of Basilicata who had sought the development of Southern Italy, Nitti occupied an especially strategic vantage point. Along with his great admiration for a country that he was visiting for the first time, he noted that the intervention of the United States, while widely acclaimed throughout Italy, was particularly appreciated in the South, from where the great majority of the 3,000,000 Italians in America had emigrated. With relatives abroad, small villages had been swept by elation upon learning that America would send an army to join the fight against a common enemy. Nitti emphasized that it was in the regions of Southern Italy where America was known and loved more than anywhere else and the immense moral and material value of the new ally was most keenly received. He looked forward to a postwar period in which Italy, widely opened as a marketplace for American-made products, would enter a partnership in which the United States would assume the kind of position that Germany had once held in the Italian economy. Above all else, the massive number of returned emigrants with an "undying remembrance of the country where they had lived and worked" held the promise of a new era of development for Italy and prosperity for America.[45]

Proclaiming a desire for a peace that would end the war, the Italian War Mission had actually sought a pact that would strengthen the likelihood of victory. And beyond financial assistance for Italy, it hoped to broaden America's role in the war. But the focus had shifted away from distinguished visitors who lingered a mere day and a half to the immigrants of humbler status who had chosen to make Philadelphia their permanent home. On Columbus Day each October, when they marched through the streets to the statue of the explorer in Fairmount Park, the city's Italians isolated themselves from other Philadelphians. The festive events that greeted the War Commission took on a more inclusive character when dignitaries and local leaders saluted the Italian colony itself. They not only paid tribute to the newer life of Italians as Philadelphians but welcomed their presence in the city. And while still being identified by speakers and journalists as "Italians," they were becoming "Philadelphia's Italians," tantamount to being Italian Americans. And beneath all the ceremony, diplomatic negotiations were strengthening the imminent recruitment of its younger men into military life as Americans. Along with the appointment of Italy's military attaché, Guglielmotti, who would remain in Washington seeking to settle the status of Italians of military age, the Selective Service Act would convert reluctant reservists into inductees of the American army. And for them, cheering on the streets of Philadelphia would soon be replaced by the spilling of their blood on the battlefields of France.[46]

While the War Mission, reaching its next destination, made a special pilgrimage to Staten Island where Garibaldi, the most famous hero of the Risorgimento, had once lived and worked, Philadelphia's Italians were remembering a more personal hero. In a "clean-as-wax" kitchen in a row home on South 8th Street, neighbors and friends gathered to see the silver medal that had been awarded to the parents of Luigi Del Gatto. His mother could only say, "I grieve for my Luigi for wasn't he the big one of the family?" Her pain would not remain hers alone but would soon be shared by other parents and families in her neighborhood and city. Mother Del Gatto prophetically added: "I have his picture in the album, and when I am alone in the house I take the picture in my hand and kiss it—kiss it the same as a thousand American mothers would kiss the pictures of their boys if they were killed by the enemy." Along with others who would in time face a similar grief, this sorrowful mother announced: "I have decided to keep the medal and picture together in one place. We are going to place them in a drawer and keep it locked. The key to the drawer will be worn around my neck." For the Del Gattos and other immigrant families, the memory of their own immortalized martyrs would prevail over the exploits of Garibaldi.[47]

Postscript: Crisis and Community

In autumn 1917, three months after the War Mission had placed its plea for increased aid before the U.S. government, Italy's need would not only take on far greater urgency but elicit further response from Philadelphia's Italians. When combined Austrian and German forces broke through Italian defenses in the Twelfth Battle of the Isonzo, an entire nation, with its army reeling on the brink of defeat, struggled to survive. As news of the unfolding disaster reached Philadelphia, local Italians, having only recently celebrated the greatness of their native land, shifted their support from donating to relief agencies to more directly engaging themselves in the war. If Little Italy's citizens had once hesitated to answer its call, these "heirs of Garibaldi" now heard that cry for help. In late October, more than 1,000 of them, awakened by the *disfatta* at Caporetto, converged at the Italian consulate seeking passage to

Italy in order to join its army. It would, however, be in vain as the lack of any available transoceanic transport prevented them from being accommodated. But if Italy could not receive them, America would. In early November, as their homeland suffered through the darkest chapter of the war, and further reports of its troops in retreat reached Philadelphia, some 60 Italians reported to recruiting offices in the city seeking to enlist in the U.S. Army.[48]

Philadelphia's Italians were not alone in their rush to aid their beleaguered country, as executives of William Cramp and Sons, Chester Shipbuilding, American International, New York Ship, and other local maritime construction firms, as well as Cambria Steel, U.S. Steel, and several more shipping-related producers met with federal officials in Washington to formulate plans to expedite construction of vessels intended to alleviate the critical shortage of food, munitions, and other materials needed in Italy. Although the crisis in Italy was given as the incentive for governmental and industrial leaders, their planning also anticipated the challenge that would soon be facing American shipping in meeting its own military and mercantile needs.[49]

With news that Prime Minister Vittorio Emanuele Orlando had wired Cadorna with the message: "Italians, profiting by their country's invasion, have composed their internal dissensions, enhancing their energies and unshakeable determination"; a similar spirit swept through the immigrant community. In early November, representatives of 250 Italian organizations held another mass meeting at a hall on South Broad Street, under the auspices of the Italian Reconstruction Committee, to begin formulating further plans of assistance for Italy.[50]

And then in an eerie interlude, residents of the Italian colony, who claimed to have witnessed an occurrence that augured the outcome of the war, provided other Philadelphians with a reminder of the folk beliefs that still held sway among them. On October 31, during Halloween night, when the moon appeared to project the outline of a bright cross to puzzled observers who sought to understand it, some Italians, linking it to the cross of Constantine, declared that it was an omen that Cadorna would stand fast against the advancing Austrian and German forces. Unfortunately, neither the diminishing strength of the Italian army, nor the Allies who hoped to meet the enemy offensive, nor any supernatural intervention had been able to prevent defeat at Caporetto. But when the *Evening Ledger* responded with: "Instead of a despairing Italy, there may be a determined Italy," the new spirit, resolved to stand firm until final victory, that seemed to be emerging in Rome, Milan, and Turin, was found in Philadelphia's Italian colony as well.[51]

A week after the cross in the moon's glow brought an omen to Little Italy, Francis De Caria, a 28-year-old Italian-born medical student at the University of Pennsylvania, offered a more earthbound assessment of the war in a letter to the *Evening Ledger*. Objecting to the view that recent events had brought his country to the verge of a separate peace, the situation, while depressing, was not by any means demoralizing: "For a defeated Italy—however disheartened, however disappointed, however mutilated—the national spirit will emerge from the chaos just as irresistible and as strong as ever." De Caria believed that the people of Italy, never having been conquered in their long history, would draw new strength from the heroic tenacity, perseverance, and sacrifice of their ancestors: "No, the dead have not died in vain, and not for one instant will the Italian people lose faith in its army and its chief. . . . The discontent and distress are to be buried by the irresistible, formidable avalanche of vengeance, which is now powerfully arising from the immense height of increased patriotism of the whole nation."[52]

While a steadfast young man might be expected to exaggerate the readiness of his nation and its people to recover from military disaster, De Caria's expectation of what the future would bring was not far from what would happen. Despite his continued faith in Cadorna who was being relieved of his command at almost precisely that moment, De Caria had sensed the resilience that was about to reverse the fortunes of war. During the next year, under new leadership and with reinforcements from the other Allies, Italy would not only survive but turn the tide against an old enemy. De Caria had well captured the view of local Italians who believed that Italy would prevail. While able to cheer from the safety of America, the opportunity for immigrants to serve their besieged homeland, as Italy relaxed authority over its tardy reservists, had passed. But the war in Europe had become America's war as well. With Washington sending out its own summons, Little Italy would discover that it had far more than the 3,000 reservists who had met Italy's call to be concerned about—and Philadelphia's Italians would answer in far greater numbers.

7

Recruiting Immigrants and Other Americans

Holy Cross cemetery in Yeadon, Pennsylvania, is a place where etched reminders reconstruct much of the history of Philadelphia's Italians. Among its many gravestones, one stands out not only as a marker of the burial site of the members of several families but as a monument to an almost forgotten chapter of that story. Across the front of the tall central headstone, the family name "Iannelli" remains visible; alongside the main inscription, the names of several of its deceased members are found. An almost full-length statue of a uniformed soldier, holding his rifle in a resting position, flanked by a similarly imposing saint holding the infant Jesus on one side and an archangel on the other give this iconic scene an imposing and memorable character. The passage of time has worn the front of the soldier's brim completely off, making him appear to be wearing a fireman's helmet of a bygone era rather than the distinctive hat of the American Expeditionary Force. But while reflecting the profound bereavement and grief of the family whose name it bears, it is a monument that goes beyond that original intention. For it also provides an indelible reminder of a time when young men, many of whom had arrived in America only a few years earlier, instead of awakening to an "American dream," found themselves facing the nightmare of trench warfare on the Western Front. Private Vincent Iannelli, the Philadelphia-born son of Vincenzo and Gemma Iannelli, lived on South 8th Street, before dying in France at the age of 23 on October 10, 1918. (See Figure 7.1.)

FIGURE 7.1 Iannelli's Grave. (Photo taken by Richard Juliani [October 2018].)

With entry into the war in 1915, Italy's demand that its reservists in the United States report to meet their military obligation did not produce an exhaustive response. Estimates of the number of Italians who were subject to the call reached as high as 30,000 for the Philadelphia Consular District but only about 3,000 reported and embarked for Italy. While local newspapers paid much attention to men who lined up in the streets before consular offices and made their way to the docks to board ships returning to their native land in the summer and autumn months, many of them in Philadelphia and elsewhere chose to ignore that summons. After all, some men could freely admit that they had migrated, at least partly, to avoid military service. But for eligible reservists, such action made them deserters in the judgment of

Italian authorities. For those who already were American citizens, whether by birth or naturalization, along with those who now sought citizenship, while it momentarily deferred their military life, they would soon enough find themselves subject to conscription after the U.S. government enacted its Selective Service System. And those who hoped to avoid any call to the colors, whether from a country of birth or adoption by remaining as resident aliens, would become the center of a fierce debate over their status and obligations. While some of them could plead, or at least pretend, that they were confused by the ambiguity of their situation, many others, including men who were as committed to lofty nationalistic ideals as other Americans, chose to enlist in some branch of military service. For them, it offered the opportunity to escape the often unrewarding options of civilian life.

The military experience of many young Italians began with the news that Mexican rebels under Pancho Villa had crossed the border and raided the town of Columbus, New Mexico, in March 1916. Within a week, President Wilson ordered an expeditionary force of nearly 5,000 soldiers, commanded by Major John J. Pershing, to pursue the capture of Villa. Despite Pershing's claims of success, the short-lived Mexican "punitive expedition," which lasted only until June, neither caught Villa nor ended the border raids. And while a relatively small number of regular army troops had moved deeply into Mexico, the 110,000 National Guardsmen, stationed along the border, served more as a show of force than for engagement against any enemy. A military historian wrote: "If the Pennsylvania Guardsmen dreamed of following Pershing's Expeditionary Force into the heart of old Mexico after the wily Villa, they were doomed to disappointment." By January 1917, almost all American troops had been withdrawn from Mexico.[1]

The expedition, however, provided an opportunity for an 11-month rehearsal for what would transpire in Europe. After the futile pursuit of Villa had ended, the War Department, with lessons learned from what was happening on the Western Front, began preparing its troops on the Chihuahuan Desert, using periods of seeming inactivity to introduce the use of hand grenades and trench warfare. And for the first time in American history, it also put recently formed units, mainly, if not entirely, made up of members of Italian birth or descent into the field of battle. In early February 1917, a foreign military officer, who had seen the armies of the major powers in action, extolled Pershing's forces: "Without doubt it is the finest fighting machine in the world." Although only about 12,000 men, he added: "On this globe there is no army of its size to compare with this little army of Americans. They are equipped to perfection. Not a buckle on a mule's harness is lacking." The same observer also noted the more intangible character of the men themselves in his litany of praise: "And with it is the spirit of the American soldier. What it is I cannot say, but it is there. In the swing of their bodies and the set of their shoulders I could see it." Despite these attributes, Pershing's first contingent was clearly not large enough to meet the formidable enemy force waiting in Europe.[2]

Unlike the Japanese attack on Pearl Harbor, which brought the United States into World War II, the decision to enter the Great War in the spring of 1917 was not provoked by any direct act of aggression. While much of the nation may have held strong sympathies with the Triple Entente, many Americans, particularly those of German and Irish origins, and citizens who simply opposed war as a solution to international disputes, were less eager to abandon neutrality. But if there were any incident that served as a "tipping point," the discovery of the Zimmerman Telegram may have served that function. Its message, sent by Arthur Zimmerman, the foreign secretary of Germany, to his ambassador in Mexico, revealed a plan that proposed, along with the resumption of submarine warfare, a military alliance between the two nations. In return for Mexican support, Germany promised to restore Arizona, New Mexico, and Texas, the previously lost territories, to Mexico as its rightful patrimony. It also intended to divert American interest and support away from the war in Europe to a possible conflict on its own southwestern border. Intercepted and decoded by British agents, the revelation of the secret plan, along with renewed German submarine activity against ships on the open seas, swayed public opinion in America toward the Triple Entente.

When President Wilson secured from Congress a declaration of war on April 6, 1917, it ushered the Great War into a new chapter. With the armed forces of both sides nearing exhaustion, the anticipated arrival of a vast army of Americans, more than delivering a decisive blow on the battlefield, threatened to further discourage the already sagging morale of the enemy. In Italy, the news from America was met with great favor but with a measure of uncertainty as well. Italian officers, largely drawn from regions of the North, had fewer ties with the United States than soldiers of lower ranks recruited from Southern Italy, where most emigration to North America had originated. And although the U.S. government, having declared war on Germany but not Austria, did not initially appear to show much interest in Italy's war, by 1918, especially with the enrollment of immigrant reservists into Italy's army, America came "to loom almost unnaturally large in the Italian eye."[3]

The declaration of war by the United States, by which the Triple Entente became the Western Allies, came as no surprise. As sympathy for England and France steadily gained momentum, the decision, even before Congress acted, had become almost inevitable. It was apparent from the support for Italian reservists when they answered their government's call in 1915. It was expressed in relief efforts on behalf of civilians in Belgium and Poland. It was reflected in warm receptions given to visiting military and political figures of France and England. It was affirmed by volunteers who enlisted in the Canadian armed forces. An emergent spirit of patriotism was manifested, sometimes in regrettable incidents, in the hostile reaction to critics of the war. But despite the depth of prowar sentiment, the United States, when it finally came, was not well prepared to wage war. While England had seen a deluge of men seeking to enlist in 1914, America's entry produced a far lower number of volunteers in the spring of 1917. And enthusiasm for war was not easily converted into prowess in combat. The recruitment of an army of sufficient size and trained for combat would not be accomplished quickly but take more than a year. Many men, with their indoctrination at newly established cantonments proving to be inadequate, would require further training after reaching France. And many of them would only learn under enemy fire just how deficient their preparation for warfare had been.

During the course of the war, Philadelphians would be spread across the entire range of military service. They joined the ranks of the U.S. Marines; served on ships of the U.S. Navy; and flew as aviators in the fledgling air corps. But the great majority of local men found themselves in the ground forces of the U.S. Army, which they would enter through voluntary enlistment, the draft, and the conversion of National Guard units.[4]

As early military preparations unfolded, civilians in Philadelphia displayed their support for the coming entry of the United States into the war. In late March, a throng of residents, estimated to be nearly 200,000 strong, answered the call of the mayor and Chamber of Commerce to show their loyalty by marching to a rally at Independence Square. Coming from all neighborhoods and most surrounding communities, with delegations representing major industries, the huge crowd listened to music and speeches throughout the day. Defying the contention that ethnic diversity divided the American people, Germans and Austrians joined fellow workers of other backgrounds in a contingent from Midvale Steel. And as Philadelphians rallied, foreign support for American intervention came. Leon Bourgeois, former prime minister of France and now a member of its Senate, saluted the rally as a "world event" that demonstrated that the ancient friendship between his own nation and the United States had been "recemented in a common resistance against the monstrous German intent at throttling that which all free men throughout the world hold dearer than their lives." And 70-year-old Ricciotti

Garibaldi, son of the hero of the Italian Risorgimento, offered his services to the United States in war against Germany "anywhere in Europe" in a cable that reaffirmed the bond between Italy and America.[5]

With the patriotism being expressed on the streets of Philadelphia, the contrast between diversity and divisiveness reasserted itself. In his oration at the rally at Independence Square, former Pennsylvania governor Edwin S. Stuart raised the issue of the loyalty of aliens: "While those who come to our shores should have a fond remembrance of their native country, they are here to become a part of this nation and, when after thoughtful consideration, they have assumed the duties and accepted the rights of American citizenship, then in any issue arising between the United States and any foreign country their absolute allegiance and loyalty must be given without reservation to the land of their adoption." By such remarks, the buildup toward war was being fused with the question of the identity and affiliation of the foreign born. And while apprehension would eventually focus on enemy aliens, it also touched immigrants with origins in nations that would be among America's allies in the war. As Methodist bishop Joseph F. Berry reminded the foreign born: "An American is not necessarily one who was born in the Republic. He may have been born here, or in England or France or Germany or Russia or Italy, or in some other land, provided he gives his love for his adopted country the first place and lifts the Stars and Stripes above every other flag which flutters in the breezes." But beyond the self-perception and behavior of civilians, the question became even more critical when it pertained to the motivation and intentions of potential recruits for the armed forces.[6]

Aliens in Khaki: The Italian American Soldier

As the United States moved closer to war, the need for an adequate body of armed forces increased in urgency. By April 1917, with Pennsylvania leading all states in the number of voluntary enlistments, Philadelphia ranked third behind only New York and Chicago among cities. But it was already clear that recruitment would not meet what the new National Army would require if and when the United States entered the war. On the same day as another rally to encourage enlistment in Philadelphia, the U.S. House of Representatives overwhelmingly voted in favor of a selective draft over a hybrid system that would have given priority to a volunteer army before shifting to conscription. The result, highly cheered by House members, placed recruitment on a more promising system, favored by President Wilson, recommended by the War Department, and expected to be fully approved by Congress.[7]

With voluntary enlistments proving to be insufficient, the demand for manpower brought passage of the Selective Service Act of May 1917. Two days after House approval, the Senate, despite an attempt by Senator Robert La Follette of Wisconsin to submit the question to a national referendum, approved its version of legislation for a draft system. On May 7, the War Department, supported by a proclamation by Wilson, ordered the new system to be set into motion. While a joint House and Senate Committee still had to resolve such details as the draft age limits before final approval, the main issue had now become how to implement the new law as quickly as possible and get men into uniform and trained for action in Europe. But while a token force soon would be sent, it would be another year before a sizable deployment of troops would occur.[8]

As Congress negotiated the final version, the new system of military mobilization ignited controversy. The first estimate, based on the male population between 21 and 30 years of age in the Federal Census of 1910, set the number of men in Pennsylvania who would be required to register at 873,000 and in Philadelphia at 171,800. From the projected figures, Pennsylvania would provide one-twelfth of the new National Army being created. Unlike the draft during the Civil War, a strict prohibition would prevent the hiring of substitutes. While all men within the specified age span were asked to register, exemptions for reasons of physical health and employment in defense industries would be allowed. Although no exemption would be granted for marriage, married men with dependents, already excused from service in the National Guard, would be dispensed from the draft by local boards whose decisions would determine the outcomes of appeals. The legislation also anticipated the need for subsequent increments until the necessary complement had been reached. With the bill awaiting final approval, the issues of fair quotas, the grounds for exemptions, the failure of men to register, and the actual operation of local boards remained sources of contention.[9]

On May 18, President Wilson signed the final version of the bill enacting the Selective Service Act of 1917. Seventeen days later, men began registering for the draft. After physically unfit men and those exempted for other reasons were weeded out, the "first 500,000" would begin training before being sent to reinforce Major General John J. Pershing's regulars who were expected to have already carried "the starry flag to the front of the French battle line." It was an optimistic expectation, blind to the actual difficulties of the tasks lying ahead. But the designation of Pershing as commander of the newly created force had, at least, resolved one issue. Another announcement declared that the persistent offer of former president Teddy Roosevelt to raise a volunteer army could be dismissed "for very good military reasons," and the War Department could begin to accelerate the machinery of mobilization.[10]

In his proclamation to the public, Wilson not only attempted to explain the operation of the Selective Service System but to persuade the American people of the underlying wisdom of the plan. Fearing that the program would not be fully accepted, he declared: "The nation needs all men; but it needs each man, not in the field that will most please him, but in the endeavor that will best serve the common good. . . . To this end Congress has provided that the nation shall be organized for war by selection and that each man shall be classified for service in the place to which it shall best serve the common good to call him." Placing his argument into a broader perspective, Wilson added: "The significance of this cannot be overstated. It is a new thing in our history and a landmark in our progress." And investing the moment with even loftier meaning, it was a date "destined to be remembered as one of the most conspicuous moments in our history . . . nothing less than the day upon which the manhood of the country shall step forward in one solemn rank in defense of the ideals to which this nation is consecrated."[11]

Despite Wilson's exhortation, such important details as the conditions for which exemptions would be granted remained unanswered. About a month after enactment of the bill, when the War Department submitted its plan to the president, it only provided for the organization of personnel and the course through which petitions for exemptions would be moved. Other than vague references to physical tests, the particular grounds for exemptions and whether quotas would be based on the size of a state, county, or voting precinct had not been decided. It was a formula that not only failed to resolve disagreements that had already arisen but was certain to generate new issues.[12]

While relying on the draft as the primary means of recruitment, the mobilization of a military force far greater than the nation had ever previously needed would call upon two other sources of manpower—the continuation of voluntary enlistments and the federalization of National Guard units—but each presented problems. Although the regular army had increased from 100,000 to 250,000, the National Guard from 150,000 to 260,000, and the Marine Corps from 17,000 to 30,000, and along with other branches of the service having reached more than 500,000 men altogether over the past three months, it had not been enough. With voluntary enlistments producing a steady but insufficient volume of recruits, the War Department introduced more ambitious strategies. In Philadelphia, in late June 1917, a weeklong celebration of military life sought the enlistment of 670 men as the local contribution to a national effort to reach 70,000 recruits for the regular army—as well as 2,000 others for the National Guard. On the first day, an airplane circling overhead dropped copies of President Wilson's recent proclamation on enlistment, while another shower of leaflets was launched from William Penn's statue on top of the Philadelphia City Hall. The "bombs," as they were termed, seemed to hit their intended targets. By 4:00 P.M., with 35 men signed up for the army and 50 more for the National Guard, the effort appeared to be heading toward its intended goal.[13]

The terms of enlistment, as listed on the leaflets, represented an important aspect of the recruitment drive. Unmarried men between 18 and 40 years of age would be obliged to serve for the duration of the war. Men with relevant skills would be accepted for the quartermaster, engineer, and signal corps. Minimum pay was $30 a month, with all living expenses and clothing included. Opportunities for promotion were described as being excellent. With existing treaties prohibiting their conscription, other inducements specifically encouraged the foreign born to enlist. While expected to be able to speak English, they did not need to know how to read or write it, although it was not clear by whom or how this determination would be made. Even more important, neither citizenship nor first papers were required. As the door became slightly opened, the War Department would soon report that the 9,659,382 men who registered for the draft included some 1,239,865 from countries other than Germany. With such men required to register but not to be drafted, military recruitment sought to tap into that vast pool of aliens as the knotty matter of the treaties that had protected them were now set to the side as aliens had been persuaded to enlist on their own. From early indications, the drive for new recruits, which included several natives of Italy, had even achieved some success among Philadelphia's Italians.[14]

The program that unfolded during the week sought to persuade native-born Americans and immigrants to find their way to recruiting tents on the sidewalk in front of the Union League on Broad Street and other locations of the city. On Tuesday of recruitment week, a massive parade of regular army units, patriotic organizations, and military bands, led by a former colonel of the Confederacy now engaged in securing volunteers for the army that he had once fought against, marched through Center City. Regularly scheduled band concerts at midday before the Union League and in the evening at City Hall Plaza entertained and inspired. Meanwhile, "recruiting parties," made up of regular army and National Guard members, scoured neighborhoods and factories in search of candidates for "hometown" regiments that were expected to be formed. The presence of National Guardsmen, who could not be deployed for duty outside of the country without being federalized, suggested the widely anticipated reorganization, already underway, that would remove that restriction.[15]

The events of subsequent days offered further attractions to young Philadelphians. Adopting the methods of advertising, as if trying to sell a household product, the program gained the attention of potential recruits by slogans and jingles: "Enlist now! Your president calls you! The army wants you! The country needs you! Come on, you loyal Americans, and let's help free the world that our children may live in peace." But when the War Department announced that only 6,299, some 63,701 less than the goal of 70,000 for the nation, had enlisted, the numbers told a more sobering tale. While "Army Recruitment Week" had entertained crowds on city streets, it fell far short of its primary aim of recruiting men for military service.[16]

By June 30, the announcement that the recruiting drive had not succeeded confirmed the need for an earlier introduction of Selective Service than had been previously intended. Despite a spurt of enlistments in late June and early July, military authorities had overestimated the willingness of civilians to place themselves on the path to combat. With even the opportunity of commissioned rank proving to be less popular than anticipated, its refusal astonished more confirmed military minds. When applications to officer training camp fell far below expected levels, an artillery captain in charge of recruiting in Philadelphia declared: "The lack of interest on the part of Pennsylvania's youth is beyond belief." Despite the inspired slogans of "200 Men a Day" and "Philadelphians for Philadelphia Regiments," the efforts of National Guard recruiters were also falling far below expectations. Contrary to the earlier plan of an all-volunteer force, it was now obvious that recruitment had to come from other sources.[17]

Anticipating that its initial muster would not be sufficient, the Selective Service Act had authorized subsequent calls for registration in order to reach the desired levels of manpower. The first call of all men between 21 and 31 years of age to determine their eligibility for military service was scheduled for June 5, 1917. But one year later, the second call was issued for men who had reached 21 years of age after June 5, 1917, to begin on June 5, 1918, with a supplemental registration held on August 24, 1918, for men who became 21 after June 5, 1918. A third call for men from 18 through 45 years of age was held on September 12, 1918. On its eve, the final call before the end of the war was estimated to reach 13,000,000 for the entire nation. While expected to generate a new quota for Philadelphia of 256,000, the actual registration for the city was projected to exceed it by another 20,000 men. From the first call until the termination of the Selective Service program in March 1919, some 440,555 Philadelphians registered, among a grand total of 24,000,000 for the nation. Of that number of local registrants, some 53,127 men would be inducted for military service. With its effectiveness, in late September 1918, even before the war ended, the U.S. Army was able to close its recruiting office on Arch Street, where some 20,000 volunteers of 38,000 applicants had been accepted for military service.[18]

The recruitment of men through Selective Service, however, was never a matter of numbers alone. The sometimes-enthusiastic rituals of farewell, mixed with tears, could not hide the fact that these men were being inducted into an army that would soon be in combat. In Philadelphia, a draft official, seeking to temper the pain of separation along with the thinly veiled reluctance of many men who had been summoned, with an appropriately patriotic gloss, declared that it was "a dual blow for democracy and a headache for the Kaiser." While such words may have gladdened the hearts of politicians who did not have to answer the call, they also reflected the need to rationalize underlying realities. On the eve of the final registration, an editorial, under the portentous title of "The Seal of Liberty," intoned: "The covenant with liberty which thirteen million registrants will make tomorrow will be virtually identical in spirit with a voluntary pledge." As it solemnly canonized inductees, while also laying out the rules and procedures by which they must abide, the message concluded that the registration should not become complicated by such issues: "It will be the simple and superb ratification of the compact which the members of a democracy have made with one another for the preservation of their inalienable rights." But such vigorous rhetoric easily lent itself to the suspicion that it was also meant to rebut an increasing wariness with the draft and weariness with the war itself.[19]

As the draft began building a military force, answers to other matters had to be found. While federal officials lacked authority to establish new National Guard units, which only the states could do, they could raise their size to the full war strength of 150 members in a company thus also increasing the total number of men available for military duty. With its broadened agenda, the new army was expected to consist of a million soldiers, with about 528,000 draftees, 293,000 regulars, and an indefinite aggregate of National Guardsmen, depending upon the number and size of units in each state. As Pennsylvanians waited for an announcement by Secretary of War Newton D. Baker, it was expected that the federalization of the National Guard would come sometime between June 15 and July 15. While the shortage of equipment was seen as the principal obstacle, it was believed that the National Guard would be well trained and prepared for further action before the draft reached full operation.[20]

Despite lingering issues, supporters praised efforts to build the army. An editorial in the *Evening Ledger* declared: "Everywhere there is an eagerness to answer the call of duty, as evidenced by the spontaneous rejoicing in the four Pennsylvania National Guard regiments yesterday when it was learned that they were to be mobilized for foreign service next month. These guardsmen are as fit as any regulars, having been hardened to service on the border." But such optimism too easily converted anticipation into the desired outcome.[21]

Among other problems, the status of aliens remained unresolved. The recently enacted legislation did not exempt men of foreign origins but required them, within prescribed age limits, to register with the local board. While aliens who had filed their first papers for citizenship could be inducted, other foreign-born men who had not indicated any intention to become American citizens were not eligible to be drafted even if they were registered. Italians, in particular, were protected by the Treaty of Commerce and Navigation between the United States and Italy, ratified in 1871, which provided that "the citizens of each of the high contracting parties shall be exempt in their respective territories from compulsory military service, either on land or sea, in the regular forces, or in the national guard, or in the militia." This treaty was not only unequivocal on the matter but still recognized as members of the U.S. House of Representatives deliberated manpower needs in the summer of 1917. If the large population of Italians and other immigrants was to become a source of recruitment without abrogating a still binding agreement, some way of circumventing these considerations had to be found.[22]

With passage of the draft act (Selective Service Act), aliens became a more inviting target of criticism by ordinary citizens as well as politicians. In a letter to a Philadelphia newspaper in May 1917, an angry reader objected, saying that it was unfair "to allow unnaturalized foreigners of military age to reap a harvest in factories while our men are being slaughtered on the battlefield." With the expectation of the United States soon fighting alongside England, France, Russia, and Italy for self-preservation and in defense of humanity and liberty, he asked, "Why should our boys give their lives and the sons of these lands remain here in peace?" Calling for a census of foreigners, he urged that enemy aliens be put to work on roads and other public projects under the supervision of our reserves and home guards and that citizens of our allies be "sent home to serve under their own colors." The foreign born, he concluded, having abandoned lands of oppression to gain their livelihood in our country, should join Americans in defeating German and Austrian autocracy and in establishing democracy.[23]

On June 5, 1917, the first National Registration Day, Philadelphians responded in massive numbers to their new obligation. At the top of a page in the *Evening Ledger*, a banner proclaimed: "Patriotic Landslide Sweeps Philadelphia as Its Sons Rush to Register." In Italian districts, where "a healthy spirit of patriotism" prevailed, large crowds gathered at registration sites even before they had opened and remained until noon, while interpreters helped to expedite matters. At most locations, Italians, including many not yet naturalized, expressed hopes of obtaining first papers in time to join in the struggle ahead. In many sections, more than half of the eligible residents were registered before noon; in one division of the Second Ward, some 150 men had registered by noon, with a similar volume in other divisions. In the largely Italian Third Precinct of the Third Ward of South Philadelphia, it was noted that "out of 125 eligibles sixty had registered at 10 A.M." And in a similar rush on the other side of the Delaware River, "An encouraging phase of the Camden situation is the splendid manner in which aliens are coming forward." Such depictions reflected the wishful projections by observers caught up in the illusion of patriotism that reached even into the press rooms of major newspapers.[24]

When final results were tallied, some 174,898 aliens from countries not at war with the United States and 12,670 natives of enemy nations were among the 830,507 men who had registered in Pennsylvania. Many Italians, within the vast population of immigrants working in mines and factories throughout the state, were among the registrants. While their leaders had long urged them to seek American citizenship and to learn the English language in order to find employment, that well-intentioned advice brought them even closer to eligibility for military service.[25]

Almost immediately, some members of the Senate, charging that quotas for Northern states had been increased in order to relieve the South of the burden of providing manpower for the new National Army, challenged apportionment procedures. They asserted that population figures for Northern cities had been multiplied three or four times their actual size while being reduced for the South. Senator Atlee Pomerene, an Ohio Democrat, pointed out that past estimates of Canton had usually placed its population at about 80,000, but the Selective Service System reported 177,000 residents. Along with demanding clarification from the Census Bureau, the size of the alien population as well as its obligations were added to the debate. Senators Frank B. Brandegee, a Connecticut Republican, and Henry Cabot Lodge, a Massachusetts Republican, objected to the inclusion of aliens exempt from military service (as high as 20 percent in Northern states while usually less than 1 percent in Southern states) in determining quotas. Arguing that aliens were able to reap benefits from the war without suffering inconvenience, Senator Porter J. McCumber, a North Dakota Republican, asked if the State Department would seek to modify any treaty with an Allied nation to allow their subjects to become eligible for military service. While debate would end with more inclusive conscription of aliens, the claim that Northern manpower had disproportionately carried the burden of military service would be reiterated throughout and even after the war.[26]

With inflated quotas and excessive selection from Northern states entwined with alien obligations, the question of draft evasion also emerged. Throughout the war, the government, press, and public shared a concern over the draft dodger, or "slacker" as he was popularly known, an internal enemy who had to be tracked down and held responsible for his dereliction. With the growing patriotism in the country, newspapers that previously identified doughty volunteers presenting themselves at recruiting stations, and not much later on induction lists, shifted to publishing the names of absentees suspected of being "slackers."

In Philadelphia, with Mayor Smith empowered to nominate candidates for 40 district boards who would be formally appointed by the governor, and with boundaries based on existing voting wards, registration would take place at police headquarters in each district. Against political leaders who expected to be involved, the mayor appointed a blue-ribbon group of clergy, physicians, educators, and businessmen to oversee the system. But only a week after registration began, government authorities, convinced that many eligible men had not registered, sought more effective ways of enforcing the law. Federal agents, concerned with the possible issuing of bogus registration cards, launched a comprehensive plan to find men who had sought to escape their obligation. Calling on "loyal citizens" to become police informants, confidentiality was promised to anyone providing information. As early figures were announced, officials were being warned that any attempt to protect friends could bring a prison sentence. Local boards were asked to provide lists of men who had registered in order to enable the police to search for others who had not reported. Two hundred plainclothes officers, under Captain of Detectives James Tate, began combing the tenderloin district where nonregistrants were believed to be hiding. The police were authorized to bring suspected offenders to district stations, ensuring their names would be turned over to Frank L. Garbarino, the local director of the U.S. Department of Justice, for further investigation. Meanwhile, aliens who had not understood their obligation were being encouraged by the clergy of "foreign churches" to voluntarily report themselves and seek information on how they still might register.[27]

Some 15,414 Italian-born men registered in Philadelphia. After one all but unreadable listing, more legible records begin with Pasquale Abanese [*sic*], a 25-year-old laborer, from the town of Campagna in the province of Salerno, who had declared his intention to become naturalized as an American citizen, before ending with Dominick W. Zurzolo, a 30-year-old native of Messina who worked as a barber at the Reading Terminal shop of the Roma brothers. Combined with registrations for seven counties—Delaware, Montgomery, Chester, and Bucks in Pennsylvania and Camden, Gloucester, and Burlington nearby in New Jersey—the number of men born in Italy who were issued cards climbed to 22,263. The large population of Italians in Scranton, Wilkes-Barre, and other communities throughout Pennsylvania further increased the number of eligible inductees.[28]

In Philadelphia, the Second, Third, and Fourth Draft Districts were densely populated areas of Italian settlement. The Second District ran from Broad Street on the west across South Philadelphia to the Delaware River and from Christian Street on its northern edge down to Ellsworth on the south then dipped for a short distance at Passyunk until it reached Wharton, which became its southern border. The more regular Third District ran east from Broad Street to the river as its northern border and followed Christian Street as its southern extremity. The Fourth District included a panhandle, between Fitzwater and Christian Streets, that jutted into Little Italy. With large concentrations of Italian registrants, these neighborhoods would carry a special burden of sacrifice when casualty reports began arriving from the Western Front.

In early July 1917, President Wilson clarified the "gigantic machinery" by which the Selective Service System would assemble the new army. Defining the classes of registrants eligible for exemptions, he noted that few men would be summarily excused from military service and that others would be permitted to place appeals before tribunals whose decisions would be protected by safeguards against unfairness and widely transparent before the public. While failing to describe the lottery that would come in a later edict, the gist of Wilson's message was found in the eagerly awaited categories of exemption. They included workers in industries necessary to the military or national interest; men with wives, children, parents, or a brother or sister dependent solely upon them for support; members of religious sects whose creed forbade bearing arms; divinity students and ordained ministers; legislative, judicial, or executive officers of the federal government or states of the union; men already in the army or navy; aliens who had not filed first citizenship papers; subjects of Germany; workers in armories, arsenals and navy yards; pilots and mariners in the merchant marine; convicted felons and the morally deficient. With the decree being almost as much about the officials who would judge the appeals as it was about their procedures, the public had to be reassured about the arbiters and criteria of the process. But Wilson's final remarks offered only noble sentiments: "Our armies at the front will be strengthened and sustained if they be composed of men free from any sense of injustice in their mode of selection, and they will be inspired to loftier efforts in behalf of a country in which the citizens called upon to perform high public functions perform them with justice, fearlessness and impartiality."[29]

The implementation of conscription, however, brought further problems. In Philadelphia, when the first eligible name was drawn and summoned for physical examination, the prospective inductee promptly filed a claim for exemption. In his implausible tale, after registering on June 5, Charles Arey, a Center City resident, had gone home, only to be told by his father that he was too old to be drafted. After examining family records in a bible, he claimed to have discovered that he was more than 31 years of age, older than he had previously thought. When he returned to the registration office to demand return of his registration card, his request was refused. On June 20, with his number announced at the top of the list, his case, remanded for final disposition to Provost General Enoch H. Crowder in Washington, provided an inauspicious start for the Selective Service System.[30]

While Italians and other aliens who had filed their "first papers" or declarations of intention to be naturalized, along with immigrants who had already become American citizens, entered into military life, the question of what should be done about the thousands of other men throughout the state and nation who had not yet initiated the process remained unanswered. With passage of the Selective Service Act, one concern had been how aliens might use their status to avoid being inducted. By early July, federal officials claimed that clever aliens who had waited until after June 5, the first date of registration, to apply for their declarations of intention were using their presumptive citizenship to dismiss enlistment demands by their native countries; but when called by draft officials in the United States, the same persons, concealing their initial efforts toward naturalization, were seeking exemptions as foreign citizens. Without having carefully considered the matter, Francis Fisher Kane, federal attorney for the Eastern District of Pennsylvania, believed that the filing of a declaration of intention should not change the status of an immigrant as far as citizenship was concerned. Other officials referred to court opinions that had ruled a declaration of intention was merely a notice of future action but did not confer citizenship in itself. Any person who filed a declaration of intention had obtained a document that would allow him to proceed with or abandon the process and hence remain an alien until a court issued the final decree of citizenship.[31]

By July 1917, with the status of aliens still unsettled, few political leaders could escape from the necessity, or perhaps expediency, of placing their views before the public. Writing in the *Public Ledger*, J. Hampton Moore (who would serve 14 years in the U.S. House of Representatives before being elected mayor of Philadelphia) addressed a reader's question, "Must the Alien Fight for Us?" While treaty restrictions limited Congress from finding an answer, foreign governments, he maintained, had the right to recruit for their own armies, but aliens could not be compelled to return and serve in their own countries. But Moore also asked why Americans were being forced to leave their homes to defend other countries whose subjects were permitted to remain in peace and safety to gain jobs and wages in the United States. More than a rhetorical question, Moore argued that draft legislation had failed to deal with a matter that generated great ill feeling among native-born and naturalized citizens in America.

Throughout the summer of 1917, the military obligations of aliens remained a controversial issue. While officials sought to assuage the public, some politicians used the opportunity to reinforce hostility toward exempted aliens. Ordinary citizens, as another Philadelphian in his letter to a newspaper, also expressed their outrage: "What is the status of aliens in this present conflict? Are they to stand by as spectators in this great arena of war and look on with cold indifference while young American blood is being shed? Are we to fight and die to make this country a safe place for the aliens to live in?" The writer, of course, answered his own question: "Such a thing looks like a super burden thrown upon the American citizen." In his view, America protected the rights of thousands of aliens who lived here, acquired fortunes, earned a living wage, enjoyed the same rights as citizens, but when asked to defend these rights, they seemed to "vanish, never to be seen until America has once more been made safe for them." As for treaties exempting them from military service, the writer merely asked: "But in a true sense of the word are they aliens?" He once again had an answer: "People leaving their mother country and making their homes here should be considered as having expatriated themselves and transferred their undivided allegiance to America." Mirroring the concerns of many Americans, he recommended granting "de facto" citizenship to resident aliens, which was, in fact, the solution that public authorities were moving toward and military service would implement.[32]

As government officials sought to address the inequities of the selection process, protest of a different kind—by opponents and resisters to the draft—posed another threat. Joseph D. Cannon, a Socialist labor organizer, testifying before the Senate Military Affairs Committee, argued that if America sought to establish democracy in Germany it should not establish autocracy at home. He pointedly noted: "Conscription is against every ideal for which our forefathers fought. Prices will soar, strikes will be called, riots will result and blood will run in the streets." Another witness, reading a letter from Samuel Gompers, president of the American Federation of Labor, declared that organized labor "stands solidly against it." A pacifist similarly opposed the proposed legislation before the committee summarily dismissed his testimony, allowed only as a courtesy but not to be taken too seriously. Unable to ignore warnings, federal authorities made plans to deal with rioting on the streets of New York and other cities. Despite reminders of the draft riots during the Civil War and uncertainty about the plans of the Industrial Workers of the World, such fears proved to be largely groundless as prowar sentiment increased its hold over America.[33]

When Secretary Baker finally drew the numbers that determined who would be called by the Selective Service System on July 20, the *Evening Ledger* proclaimed: "America today drafted her youth to join the battle against Kaiserism," before even more dramatically adding "American history is written here." But another item, nearly buried by bulletins and baseball scores, reported that Arcona S. Mario, inverting his actual name, a barber who lived with his brother on Pierce Street in South Philadelphia, whose father and sister were still in Italy, was not an American citizen but an Italian subject and therefore not eligible to be summoned by the draft. Despite its brevity, it also confirmed that the alien question remained unresolved.[34]

In July, Senator George E. Chamberlain, an Oregon Democrat and chairman of the Senate Military Affairs Committee, introduced a resolution that allowed the drafting of aliens from countries at war with Germany but exempted natives of any nation with a treaty prohibiting it. At almost the same moment, Representative Edwin Y. Webb, a North Carolina Democrat and chairman of the House Judiciary Committee, offered a bill, believed to have administration support, authorizing the deportation of draft age aliens to their home countries. A day later, diplomatic negotiations were reported to be seeking the permission of Allied nations to allow the drafting of their citizens. Meanwhile, Senator McCumber placed another resolution before the Senate Foreign Relations Committee about drafting aliens and deporting them if they refused to serve. With the War Department having already approved the plan, the State Department, noting provisions of existing treaties, objected that it would place Americans living abroad at risk of being conscripted by foreign governments. Meanwhile, with news that President Wilson favored the McCumber bill, it was hoped that other countries would agree to nullification of prior agreements and allow conscription of their subjects, as legislators argued that laws should supersede treaties.[35]

The large population of Italians, estimated to be as high as 300,000, living in a haven of diplomatic immunity from which neither the United States nor Italy could dislodge them, provided a principal target for these efforts. As Congress contemplated legislative alternatives, negotiations being conducted with the Italian Embassy in Washington sought an endorsement of the Chamberlain strategy, permitting the drafting of aliens if their own government did not object to the provision. Despite prior agreement by Great Britain and France, both with far smaller numbers of draft age men living in the United States, Italy's unexpected rejection of the proposal forced a search for another solution. While Congress was expected to expedite action on a bill sponsored by Representative John L. Burnett, an Alabama Democrat and chairman of the House Immigration Committee, that would simply send "alien slackers" back to their native lands, Italy's decision remained to be better understood. But with that beleaguered nation desperately in need of manpower for its front line and hoping that its sons would return to join the struggle, the easy answer may have been the correct one: Italy still wanted these men in its own army rather than in American uniforms.[36]

From the first phase of selection, the draft system proved to be more difficult than anticipated. By early August, more than three-fourths of all men being called up across the nation had asked for exemptions. The failure to generate a sufficient number of recruits was further complicated by the likelihood that quotas for Philadelphia's 51 draft districts would be revised. But the alien issue remained at the center of the problem. With the great number of men of foreign birth required to register but exempted by their status as aliens included in determining its demographic base, the quota for the city as a whole had been set far too high.[37]

With the widespread reluctance of men, whether native born or alien, to submit themselves to conscription, local draft boards were being "driven to drastic measures" to fill their quotas. On one day in August, of the 60 percent of 1,000 men who had passed their physical examinations, some 50 percent expressed their intention, mainly on the basis of being married and having children, to seek exemptions. Meanwhile, officials, stating that they would be successful if they were able to draft one man of every four being examined, declared war on "married slackers." Mindful of aliens in their midst, one board member, with a view shared by others, bluntly announced that none of them in his district would be exempted. With more than 70 percent of 3,200 registrants being aliens, while dismissing legal considerations, he argued: "To exempt them is not fair to the American-born boy. It would mean that to fill our quota of 253 we would have to call on a very large per cent of all the Americans in the district." The spokesperson for another district, however, noting the law was very clear on the matter, maintained that an exemption could not be denied to any alien who sought one. With officials in sharp disagreement, the matter remained unresolved.[38]

The inclusion of aliens in determining the quota for a district all but ensured an unacceptable outcome. In neighborhoods with high concentrations of immigrants, their right to claim exemptions had greatly increased the likelihood of native-born Americans being selected for military service. In the view of one newspaper, "Philadelphia's draft machinery continued to creak and groan," with many married men, as well as aliens, seeking exemptions, creating a near crisis. But while other officials called for a solution that would force aliens into military service, Governor Martin G. Brumbaugh urged a return to voluntarily enlistment. Edward F. Swift, chairman of the Eighth District in Center City captured the gist of the issue: "Under the law an alien can claim exemption from the National Army. That is his legal right, but not his moral right . . . the big sturdy fellows who have fled from the tyranny of European governments should stand up like men and share the responsibilities of the country that protects them and gives them the opportunity to better their condition in life. It is cowardly for these men to lag behind in the present crisis and force American-born youths to do their fighting." Proposing that all single aliens be required to take physical examinations, Swift's argument brought them another step closer to induction. But he went even further by adding an ultimatum: "If they do not think enough of this country to step forward and aid in the work of protecting it they ought to go back to their former homes." While hoping that Congress would soon deny exemptions to such men, Swift urged local boards to increase their efforts. Facing a struggle that allowed no toleration for slackers, he concluded: "The alien has had his taste of Kaiserism and ought to be willing to make some sacrifices in the struggle to overthrow it."[39]

While difficult to see how immigrants from Allied nations had tasted kaiserism, other local officials held a similar view. With the large alien population in the Second and Third Districts of South Philadelphia, every American-born registrant appeared likely to be drafted in order to fill their quotas. Being an American meant being penalized. And the system unfairly punished single men or those married but without children. Dr. John H. Remig, a member of the Third District Board, gave evidence of what was feared. Of 143 men examined on one day, some 67 of them were exempted as aliens, leaving 76 native-born men, of whom 29 were rejected for reasons of physical health, with 47 accepted for military service. Of that number, more than half claimed exemptions on other grounds, which if granted would yield only 22 men of the original 143 called up, hardly sufficient for the proposed National Army. The answer appeared to depend on tightening exemptions granted to citizens while also finding a way to draw upon the large alien population.[40]

The early fears of officials, however, had been largely unwarranted. On August 8, aided by more resolute examiners, the yield of recruits shot upward, as 40 boards in Philadelphia reported that more than 700 men had met physical qualifications, an increase of 200 over the previous day. After two more days, with reduced exemptions for married men, all records had been exceeded by the results. Some 1,400 men of the 2,400, or 60 percent of all who had been examined were accepted. While still facing a flood of exemption requests, the local board awaited further instructions from Washington. But willingness to grant exemptions had also begun to shift against married men without children, especially those with wives who were capable of working and unlikely to meet financial hardship by the loss of their husbands' wages. And for the moment, attention had shifted away from the question of whether aliens should be exempt.[41]

With figures released in early August, the earlier charge of unfairness against native-born men had seemingly been refuted. For the Second Draft District, based at the 7th and Carpenter Streets police station, some 20 names of the 22 men accepted for military service, out of 27 examined in all, were unmistakably of Italian origin. With that result being partly due to the inclusion of aliens, a newspaper observed that "virtually all of these men proved to be of sturdy stock and passed the doctors with flying colors." While the summons to Italian reservists in 1915 may have missed the "imboscati," the Selective Service System was not as likely to overlook slackers, even within the alien population. And almost immediately these early inductees would find themselves on their way to Camp Meade in Maryland, a harbinger of what awaited Italian-born residents and Americans of Italian origin.[42]

Resisters: Aliens before the Courts

Another cloud soon cast a shadow over prospects of the draft with charges that the Workmen's Circle, a Socialist organization of mainly Jewish membership, meeting at its headquarters at 505 Reed Street, had instructed aliens on how to claim exemptions. According to a newspaper account, the Federal Bureau of Investigation had begun investigating whether aliens living in the

"the Ghetto and Italian sections" of the First and Second Districts, who had already been granted exemptions, could be reexamined. Federal Attorney Kane declared that if charges that men were being "coached" were true, arrests would be made. While draft officials found "evidence" in the reappearance of too many men, who after previously expressing their willingness to serve, sought exemptions from their boards, the figures for each district suggested some reason for the charge. In the First District, with a quota of 467 men for the first draft, some 5,060 had registered, the names of 600 had been drawn, 300 had been examined, but only 22 men were selected for military service. In the Second District, with a quota of 368 men, more than 4,000 had registered, with 2,600 aliens of draft age, but a similarly steep decline had yielded only 60 men for induction. Any possible contributor to such attrition invited the attention of federal authorities.[43]

Among several persons suspected of aiding aliens in seeking exemptions, Emanuel Kline, a notary, made his services available at the Workmen's Circle office every night. He was a Socialist, who had advertised in *The People's Press*, a newspaper that had recently lost mailing rights because of its opposition to the draft. His message had read: "Are you going to claim exemption? If so, see Emanuel Kline, Notary Public, at 1114 South 5th Street, who has had many years' experience in drawing up legal papers." (When he registered with the Second District Board of the Selective Service in September 1918, the 35-year-old Kline was a self-employed real estate and insurance agent.) In an interview with a reporter, while admitting to being a Socialist, Kline denied that he had ever advised men on how to obtain exemptions: "I never coached anybody on how to answer questions of the exemption boards and I never will. I would be crazy to do so." Jacob Weinman, manager of the Workmen's Circle, similarly maintained that his office merely assisted "poor foreigners in this section" who came with stories about their own poverty or of family members dependent upon them, before adding: "But we positively do not instruct or coach the men." By providing the aid of notaries to aliens without funds, the local Workmen's Circle was only doing what its branches in other cities did.[44]

Chairman Swift, of the Eighth District Board, asked for an investigation by the Department of Justice of what he believed to be an organized effort among aliens to evade military service. After 60 men, among 66 accepted from 80 examined by his board, sought exemptions, Swift was convinced that opponents of the draft had been influencing the process. After questioning candidates, he claimed to know the identity of a "downtown physician" who was "coaching the aliens and doing everything possible to interfere with the draft machinery," whose name he intended to give to federal agents. As for the registrants, despite their claims, Swift promised that few of them would win exemptions but soon find themselves on their way to Camp Meade. And for others, he added: "In our district but few of the aliens signified a desire to evade service when they registered. Why they have changed their minds since then is a matter for the Department of Justice to determine."[45]

Within a few days, another local official, Daniel J. Connelly, secretary of the Fifth District Board, made similar charges against an unidentified notary in his section of the city. Asking for an investigation, he declared: "We have had trouble enough with the aliens without being subjected to the influences of disloyal notaries." A recent event had encouraged his charges. Two aliens who had indicated their intention to serve in the army when they reported for physical examinations had returned on the following day with exemption affidavits. Under questioning, the men said that they had been advised to file their claims by the notary. Connelly described how the local board persuaded them to accept induction: "We have explained to the aliens that they have a legal but no moral right to claim exception and through the medium of diplomacy and common sense have been able to win them over to our cause. We have informed them that they are part of America; that they are sharing our joys and privileges and in return must be willing to share our responsibilities." Having already reached a first quota of 268 recruits, with plans to continue examining men in the future, Connelly sought to assure the public that aliens would not be allowed to escape military obligations.[46]

Some local boards, however, had too eagerly pursued their objectives. Assistant U.S. Federal Attorney T. Henry Walnut advised the Eighth District Board that its overly aggressive rejection of petitions from aliens had to be discontinued. But Chairman Swift, with 2,000 aliens among 4,500 registered men, as well as too many slackers in his judgment, sought a reduction of the quota for the district. While Walnut agreed that too many "deserters" were failing to answer the call, he appealed to citizens to assist his citywide effort to round them up.[47]

As local boards sought to certify as many men as possible, dissenting voices objected. In a letter to a local newspaper, a "naturalized citizen," who believed that aliens should not be drafted, pointed out that they did not have the privileges of citizens. They could not hold government offices; they could not get licenses for certain kinds of businesses; and lacking the right to vote, they had no voice in selecting the government. He argued: "To conscript foreigners would be taxation without representation of the worst form." And with laws preventing most aliens of draft age from becoming naturalized, he asked: "Why should we compel foreigners to execute a governmental function (military) when they have no voice in the government?" He ended with a simple exhortation: "Let us be reasonable." The legal merit of his argument would soon be tested.[48]

The Federal District Court took up the status of aliens when five Russian Jews and two Italians applied for exemptions in September 1917. Judge Oliver B. Dickinson would hear the case. On behalf of the Russian Jews, attorney John N. Landberg asked for a writ of habeas corpus on the grounds that local draft boards had basically misinterpreted the law as it pertained to aliens. Representing the Italians, Francis Rawle and Joseph W. Henderson argued that the 1871 treaty with Italy exempted citizens of either nation from any draft while in the other country, and if it did not hold in this case, then it represented a breach of faith by the United States. But Federal Attorney Walnut contended that the Selective Service Act gave Congress at a time of emergency the right to abrogate any treaty, thus negating any relevance for the present case. Despite ongoing diplomatic negotiations, the matter was now under the jurisdiction of the court. And while the plea of the Russians rested on different grounds than that of the Italians, their cases would be heard and decided together.[49]

While relatively few details can be discerned about the plaintiffs, Giovanni Troiani of Marcus Hook, being held in the Delaware County jail for having defied Local Board Number 4 of Media by refusing to report when called, would be identified as the principal defendant in the official record of the case. A bemused newspaper account described the other Italian plaintiff: "There is one man in Camp Meade who is in uniform and doesn't intend to stay there if he can help it." He was Francesco Pasquini, a 21-year-old brickyard laborer and resident of nearby Chester, Pennsylvania, who, after having registered and passed his physical examination, had claimed an exemption as an alien who had not sought naturalization. When the local board rejected his claim as being too late, Pasquini was ordered to begin basic training. While the case of the Italians was believed to have merit because it was based on an existing treaty, the five Russians were in a more precarious situation, partly because of who was serving as their counsel.[50]

While the pleas of the plaintiffs had been joined together, the attorneys representing them could hardly have been further apart. Rawle was not only the scion of one of the oldest and most prominent families in Philadelphia but a distinguished scholar, an overseer of Harvard University, and a founder and former president of the American Bar Association. Henderson, while not of quite the same lineage as Rawle, was a recent Harvard Law School graduate and partner in the firm of Rawle and Henderson. Beyond serving as legal counsel to the Italian consulate, their practice was willing to take on unpopular causes.

In sharp contrast to both of them, Landberg, as an attorney and public figure, brought potential liabilities to the courtroom. He was a Russian-born Jew, who was not only ready to defend controversial clients but had run as a Socialist candidate for political office. It could not ingratiate him to a judge who would preside over a naturalization court at a military base only a few months later.[51]

The greater implications of the petitions of the two Italians and five Russian Jews pertained to possible consequences for hundreds, or even thousands, of aliens who could raise similar objections. A newspaper account noted: "Drafting of Italian citizens into the new National Army, in many cases by force and in violation of treaty rights between the United States and Italy, has reached the stage of diplomatic procedure." With the Italian ambassador taking up the matter with State Department and military officials, hundreds of Italians from Philadelphia alone had purportedly been sent to Camp Meade against their will. Italian authorities, insisting that insufficient shipping had prevented these men from meeting military service in their native land, retained the hope of being able to recruit them into their own army.[52]

In his initial response to the petitions, Judge Dickinson, refusing to grant the writ of habeas corpus that would have dismissed the charges against the plaintiffs, declared that his court did not have jurisdiction to decide the constitutionality of the Selective Service. When Landberg immediately announced that he would seek an injunction on behalf of his clients, it threatened to tie up the certification power of all local and district draft boards as well as training operations in the camps. The situation for the Italians, meanwhile, had become further complicated by reports that Italian consular agents had admitted to having instructed Italian citizens that they were exempt from the draft and could legally resist efforts to force them to serve. And Henderson had apparently informed the District Appeal Boards that Italian citizens could not be drafted as their treaty rights excluded them. Further complicating matters, state officials had charged the Italian consulate with interference with the movement of draftees to training camps by informing men in Philadelphia and Scranton that they had not needed to answer the call. When Dickinson announced that he would reconsider the case, he intended to reach a decision after consultation with colleagues that would reflect the opinion of the entire Circuit Court of Appeals.[53]

With Judge Dickinson's decision to defer action, part of the matter shifted to other quarters. After Federal Attorney Walnut asked for a ruling, the provost general's office in Washington issued an order that allowed aliens to file again for exemptions if local draft boards decided that they had initially failed to do so out of ignorance but not if their claims had already been rejected. It further prohibited appeals boards from reconsidering such cases. But the ruling did not cover the present case, which still awaited action from Dickinson. Rawle and Henderson, on behalf of the Italian consulate, predicted that some 20 violations had to be taken up by the State Department, which would be forced to transmit orders to military authorities to exempt all aliens as well as for camp commanders to release all such men being involuntarily held in violation of their treaty rights. Meanwhile, Walnut had been instructed that men arrested for violating draft procedures were to be sent to the "nearest military post," which with the refusal of local recruiting stations and the navy yard to accept them would be Camp Meade.[54]

After more than two weeks of consideration, Judge Dickinson rendered a ruling essentially the same as his earlier view that federal courts had no jurisdiction to review decisions of draft boards, thus rejecting the suits by the aliens who had sought exemptions as well as establishing a precedent against such petitions. By rejecting the case of the Italians, his judgment that military authorities alone determined the eligibility of aliens also dismissed the relevance of the 1871 treaty between Italy and the United States. Rawle had unsuccessfully argued that his clients were not "slackers" but seeking to return to Italy in order to serve their native country. Landberg had attempted to defend his clients on the grounds that by not even filing their first papers for naturalization, they were not subject to the draft by the very terms of the legislation. But with habeas corpus dismissed as a mere technical question, the main issue remained how far the courts could invade the domain of military authority. And for Judge Dickinson, the right that the people had granted Congress to declare war and maintain armies was "a master power to be exercised without the hampering influence of any one." Since the call to the colors fell within that "master power," it alone should provide the required system and tribunals to adjudicate related questions that may arise. Omitting any explicit reference to aliens who had not filed for naturalization, Dickinson deemed it "lawful, but fitting" that military tribunals had exclusive jurisdiction in determining exemptions. But some aspects about the outcome remained questionable. On one hand, the decision reversed the provision of President Wilson's proclamation of July 2, setting up the appeals system in which the draft boards themselves, not military courts, were clearly designated to serve as the tribunals. Even more fundamentally, Dickinson's decision had not only revoked the terms of a historic treaty but vitiated the power of the State Department in such matters.[55]

Judge Dickinson's opinion reflected the spirit of the moment sweeping across the nation. On the same day as his decision, Congress considered another joint minute resolution, just prior to a long adjournment, proposing new diplomatic negotiations with Allied nations seeking permission to draft aliens who had been previously exempted. The aim was to reach a "showdown" with men who had neither enlisted here nor answered the appeals of their own native countries to return for military service. Although further considerations would postpone action until December, the enthusiasm supporting the resolution showed that the war against the "alien slacker" had been declared by all branches of the government.[56]

The effort to pass legislation that would enable the drafting of aliens was now being even more imaginatively advanced. In early September, U.S. Representative Stephen G. Porter, a Pittsburgh Republican, introduced a bill to extend provisions of the draft by allowing aliens, particularly those men with origins in enemy countries, to enlist into what would become an "American Foreign Legion." While intending to place drafted foreigners into units by nationality, except where such action was prohibited by an existing treaty, the act would not apply until the respective government formally agreed to allow the drafting of its citizens into the armed forces of the United States. Porter declared that his bill would only require the consent of the Allied powers, with whom negotiations were said to be underway, to "do away with the tedious delays of diplomatic intercourse." Meanwhile, the State Department was offering assurances to members of the Military Affairs Committee of the House of Representatives that all questions of international diplomacy would be resolved in time for Congress to enact a bill to draft eligible foreigners. A few days later, when the Senate announced that it would adjourn after another three weeks, the alien draft resolution was among the items that had been approved during the session. Although awaiting action by the House, no delay in passage was expected.[57]

From National Guard to National Army

The reorganization of the National Guard provided the third major source of recruitment for the new National Army. Its roots were found in the "Associators," the militia organized by Benjamin Franklin to defend the colony against the threat of invasion by French and Spanish pirates in 1747. In 1755, with growing hostility from the French and Indians on the western frontier, the Pennsylvania Assembly passed the Militia Act, which authorized the formation of volunteer units. In 1757, another act made service mandatory for all males between 17 and 45 years of age. In 1858, the state legislature restored the volunteer status of the state militia. It was officially renamed as the National Guard of Pennsylvania (NGP) in 1870. From colonial years to the Spanish-American War

FIGURE 7.2 Company A of the Third Regiment of the Pennsylvania National Guard, whose many Italians made it the "Italian Brigade," marches to a local armory in June 1916. Under Sergeant Frank Attanasio as their commanding officer, James Baldino, Charles Cianfrani, Victor Cippolone, Victor Bonovolto, "Kid" Missolina, Angelo Maturo, Joseph Leopoldo, and J. Parri also served as members of the unit. (*Evening Ledger* [June 23, 1916].)

of 1898, its units had not only commendably served the nation but provided young men with the opportunity for military experience. With the coming of World War I, the NGP would enter a new era.[58]

The National Defense Act of June 1916, federalizing the National Guard, consolidated the First, Second and Third Regiments of the First Infantry Brigade of Pennsylvania, with headquarters at Philadelphia armories, under the authority of the U.S. Army. (Company A of the Third Regiment, with a large number of Italians in its ranks, had already earned the title of Philadelphia's "Italian Brigade.") With the proclamation of war in spring of 1917, officers at local armories "seething with activity" despite serious shortages of men declared: "a new Fourth of July" for the NGP. While details of commissions and physical examinations remained to be determined, assignment to a "concentration camp" (as such sites were unfortunately designated at the time) and further training at Fort Hancock, near Augusta, Georgia, was expected to come within a few days.[59] (See Figure 7.2.)

With almost all personnel having reported for duty, Colonel Hamilton D. Turner, commanding officer of the Second Regiment of Pennsylvania, the first unit to be federalized, described his men as anxious to leave for France as soon as they could be fully equipped. But "marching orders" required not the legs of more men, as much as the hooves of 900 more horses to bring Turner's cavalry unit to the maximum strength of 1,100 mounts and place it on a "war footing." With preparations underway, the adjutant general's office notified the War Department that some 16,953 officers and men of the NGP, a figure that did not include previously mobilized units, had entered federal ranks on July 15. It comprised headquarters, sanitary, signal, supply, engineer, artillery, infantry, and cavalry units. Their selection as the first National Guard contingent to follow regular troops overseas, as a result of their service on the Mexican border that required only temporary federalization, made them permanent units of the U.S. Army. Relieved of its traditional duty to protect domestic sites, the NGP had become eligible for overseas deployment. But the future remained an uncertain part of the formula needed to raise American forces to the necessary strength to wage war on the Western Front.[60]

After being absorbed into the regular army, speculation also persisted on whether the National Guard faced permanent dissolution. With officers recommissioned at similar levels, except for men at the highest rank, who had to be appointed by the president, its recruiting stations would be closed and such activities taken over by regular army offices. And with former members on their way to camps where they would be trained before being sent to France, the National Guard itself was expected to pass out of existence. When the last 75,745 members were called into active service, it had provided approximately 400,000 men for intensive training, which included trench digging, the use of mortars and hand grenades, and bayonet drills. But even after being reshuffled into the National Army, local units sought to retain their identity as part of the NGP rather than accept the official taxonomy. On August 16, when the War Department announced its assigned numbers for units of the National Army, it designated the newly created 79th Division as being for men from Southern Pennsylvania. And for former National Guard units, it identified the 28th Infantry Division as being for the state of Pennsylvania. Both designations would remain of paramount importance during the Great War. But with mobilization now completed and plans for some of its more trained units to be in Europe by winter, followed by others in the spring, the events of August left no doubt that the former National Guard would soon find itself alongside the regular army in combat. Assuming a new role as part of the expeditionary force, the "Keystone Division" would soon face some of the bloodiest action of any American troops on the Western Front.[61]

As the war brought Italians and Americans together in military service, National Guard units became another part of the process. In August 1917, Italian consul Gentile visited the encampment of the Military Training Corps in suburban Lansdowne, ostensibly to witness a demonstration of the new "trickling" method of advancing under fire introduced to trench warfare by

ITALO-PHILADELPHIA GUARDSMEN ON REVIEW

FIGURE 7.3   Colonel George E. Kemp, regiment commander, Charles C. A. Baldi, titular head of Philadelphia's Italian community, and other "prominenti" inspect Company A of the Third Regiment of the Pennsylvania National Guard, said to be "composed almost entirely of young men whose ancestors came from the land of Garibaldi and Victor Emmanuel," at camp in Lansdowne in September 1917. (*Evening Ledger* [September 6, 1917].)

the British. But the composition of the troops stationed at the site suggested another reason, which became more apparent when he addressed them. As Gentile declared that America's entry into the war had not only cemented the bonds of friendship between Italy and the United States but served the cause of democracy and humanity throughout the world, a large number of young Italians were among his listeners. For them, the training grounds of army life would become another venue of assimilation. Although for immigrants and sons of immigrants, who found themselves alongside other Americans, the experience would become transformative; their unit retained enough presence of "foreigners" to be recognized by its ethnicity. In September, a caption under a newspaper photograph of "Italo-Philadelphia Guardsmen on Review" showing Company A of the Third Pennsylvania Infantry at the camp at Lansdowne, declared that it was "composed almost entirely of young men whose ancestors came from the land of Garibaldi and Victor Emmanuel." And with a delegation of civilians, headed by C.C.A. Baldi, almost appearing as if they were standing in review of Little Italy's own army, it provided a remarkable scene.[62] (See Figure 7.3.)

Training the Italian American Soldier

From Camp Meade to France

Philadelphia, like other major cities, would not allow its men—whether they were voluntary enlistments, National Guardsmen, or draftees— to leave for training camps and eventually the Western Front without a proper send-off. But more than a simple farewell, such events also demonstrated the conviction that every citizen had to do his or her own part; meet his or her particular obligations; and make his or her own contribution to the war effort. The celebration that saluted departing troops expressed that sense of duty. And while many men already in uniform or soon to don their uniforms marched in a parade, civilian spectators on city sidewalks enthusiastically shared in the scene. In Philadelphia, recruiting efforts had been accompanied by significant demonstrations, but they would be greatly overshadowed by what came now. It was also the beginning of a massive show of public support that would last through the months ahead and be expressed even after triumphant troops had returned home at the end of the war.

"Where Do We Go from Here?"

In late August, Philadelphia officials announced that the program being planned to honor men who would soon be departing was expected to surpass anything that the city had ever seen. On the eve of the Draft Parade, a newspaper assessed what was being anticipated: "No army that has ever marched forth to battle in all the red history of war carried with it the memory of a more inspiring farewell than will be accorded by Philadelphia to those of her sons selected for the new National Army." Along with the thousands to whom "the honors of the draft have fallen," who would march on Broad Street, half of the city's population were expected to form "a human court of honor from Diamond Street to Wharton, through which the recruits will pass," as it all was so deftly phrased. It included flags flying from every building and window as well as brass bands in the streets and church bells ringing overhead—and "the mighty cheers that will go up to express the city's respect and admiration for the men who have been labeled by the Government as fit to be its champions in the cause of democracy." The newspaper preview was not merely an exercise in the marketing of patriotism but also an instruction manual for participants.[1]

An attempt to involve spectators in singing provided an especially innovative aspect of the agenda. An official of the Philadelphia Community Music Association had proposed distributing song sheets to enable the crowd of onlookers to join the marching men in voicing "the familiar tunes that are dear to Americans." With a fervent sense of patriotism, she declared: "Only by song can the emotions of all people be fused into a compact national organism." And if that premise were not sufficient, this champion of the martial virtues of music quoted Major General J. Franklin Bell's widely circulated adage: "A singing man is a fighting man." But the spiritual power of her proposal held its greatest potential influence: "So let's all sing on Saturday. Everybody will sing and we will all catch the fire from one more latent source of power which only needs recognition and a channel for expression to sweep us all upward and onward"—and somehow presumably to victory over Germany.[2]

Newspaper coverage, vibrating between reporting and promoting, spread details of the parade over the pages of various editions. The event began with a 21-gun salute, actually explosives ignited from City Hall Tower, heard miles away, beneath overcast skies that had brought the threat of rain but would not dampen the spirit of the huge crowd that alternated ringing cheers with awed silence. Despite foreboding weather, the undaunted marchers, according to one account, "who before so many days will face shot and shell and all the tortures that the savage ingenuity of the Prussian hordes can devise thought little of the rain that fell at times during their march." But the approbation of the national cause as well as the indictment of the enemy continued: "The people for whom they will fight to preserve democratic ideals seemed to feel that it was the least they could do to bear the showers to pay tribute to these men selected to crush autocracy."[3]

A massive formation of about 50,000 enlisted men, National Guardsmen, and draftees, many still in civilian clothes, swept down Broad Street, before an estimated crowd of half a million spectators, taking about five hours to complete the march. On both sides between Arch Street and city hall, aging, almost venerated, veterans of the Civil War, seated on chairs as guests of honor, vigorously greeted the most recent recruits and bestowed their special benediction to the present cause. And as a local newspaper saluted these "hoary veterans who were mere boys when this country was threatened with destruction as a result of internal strife," including many who had falsified their age in order to join in the struggle to preserve the Union, it suggested that the new recruits had probably done the same thing. Whether by the presence of old Yankees of an earlier war or the homage paid by press and public to new Yankees who would soon go off to another war, it was part of the sacred rite of civic religion unfolding on this day.[4]

After a great hush as the crowd waited in respectful silence, Mayor Smith, as grand marshal, accompanied by U.S. Army brigadier general William G. Price Jr., led a platoon of mounted city policemen, at the head of the grand procession. In the first division, some 6,000 sailors, Marines, infantry and cavalry men, field hospital, and other troops followed. Despite the solemnity of the occasion, the float carrying members of a bakery company leavened not only dough but spectators with a syncopated routine as men rapidly kneaded while keeping time to the music of "Where Do We Go from Here?" being played by a trailing band. As they handed the dough to comrades in khaki uniforms, white aprons, and bakers' caps, who passed it on to other mates who placed it in ovens, the bakers broke the austerity of the crowd. But with the approach of the hospital unit, whose men carried stretchers folded for a long march, the mood became more somber as spectators uttered their hope that "there would be very little for these lads to do." And such was their innocent perception of what the war would hold.[5]

Members of the British Recruiting Commission, recently arrived in Philadelphia, made up the second division of the parade. The Caledonian Bagpipe Band, Scottish Highlanders in kilts, noncommissioned men with a banner that read "Brothers in Arms," and officers carried British and American flags. They were the first British troops to march on Philadelphia streets since General William Howe had occupied the city, some 150 years earlier, in September 1777, but more widely welcomed than on that previous occasion. The third division of the parade provided the platform for city council members to wave at constituents and for the lions of local industry—Baldwin Locomotive, Remington Arms, and Eddystone Ammunition with floats displaying military ordnance, of undoubtedly high cost to taxpayers and great profit to producers—promoting their claims as defenders of democratic ideals.

Politicians and weapons manufacturers appeared to comfortably enjoy being together. The fourth division, consisting of "independent military organizations," contained old soldiers of past wars as well as underage cadets being groomed to serve in future ones. Within its ranks, along with the United Spanish War Veterans came the innocent youths of the Snellenberg Department Store Cadet Corps, the Saint Francis de Sales Battalion, the Saint Francis Xavier Boys' Battalion, and other paramilitary organizations.[6]

Beyond anything else, the fifth division, composed of 51 sections of draftees, the newest recruits of the National Army, with all other units serving mainly as their escorts, represented what the Draft Parade was about. With great candor, *The Inquirer* opined: "For the first time in half a generation, Philadelphia had a glimpse of its sons going forth to war. It watched them, awkward, unsure of themselves, trying their manful best to march like trained soldiers, most of them painfully self-conscious and all of them subtly aware of something new and unknown in their experience." Vignettes from the street revealed the tacit interaction between ambivalent conscripts, untested in their capabilities but compelled to answer their country's call, and their more propitious relatives. Two women patiently waited until they saw a familiar face among the marchers. As they waved their handkerchiefs, he smiled back at them, too far away to exchange words. And then the younger woman, turning to her companion, was overheard: "Well, it's his chance. Maybe it will make a man of him." To which her companion replied, "I shouldn't wonder," in a manner said to be not hopeful, but nothing more. A curious reporter could only add: "Maybe they were mother and sister; maybe mother and wife." In contrast to the chagrined women, an aged, white-bearded father, proudly recognizing his son among the troops, exclaimed over the crowd: "There is my boy!" Almost in reply, a policeman standing nearby pointed at the recruits and declared: "There goes my boy, too." And the two men clasped each other's hand and wept silently for several minutes. Such scenes unfolded throughout the day. But while martial music had aroused patriotism, "it was the popular tunes of lively rhythm that stirred the onlookers to the greatest enthusiasm." And if soldiers still harbored any doubts and needed to be reminded, as bands played "Where Do We Go from Here?" the favorite among all the songs, the crowd promptly shouted one word in response—"France!"[7]

The four remaining divisions provided an anticlimactic potpourri of home defense organizations, Masonic lodges, and other groups, ending with the South Philadelphia Civic Association, gratuitously endorsing proceedings that might have better served the overly patient public by their absence from the parade. Their presence emphatically underscored the belief, just beginning to take root, but greatly nurtured in future months, that everyone, including the youngest children, had a role to play in winning the war. It was an element of self-consciousness, often lacking in past wars, that would become a more defining attribute of the home front in modern times. But the day had also been marked by a naivete that reflected how little was really known, or how unrealistic were the perceptions of buoyant spectators, about what these men in the streets would face upon reaching the front lines—and how many of them would never return.[8]

While the great Draft Parade was intended to reflect civic pride and support for the troops, it also sought to mobilize the home front in the war effort. But integrating a diverse population is seldom accomplished by public spectacle. And the men who marched in the streets on this day would not share the same meaning of the parade. For many Italians, the 20th of September remained a more meaningful holiday than the 4th of July. The encounter at Aspromonte still meant more to them than the encampment at Valley Forge. Giuseppe Garibaldi was a more significant historical icon than George Washington. But these immigrants from Abruzzi, Basilicata, Campania, Calabria, Apulia, or Sicily who had flooded into Philadelphia in recent years, many not entirely literate in the language and accustomed to the ways of a new country, would soon discover after being summoned by the U.S. Army that they still had much farther to march if they were to more fully become Americans.

Camp Meade: Making Good Soldiers—and Americans

With the large detachment of men taking part in such events as the Draft Parade, the mobilization of the new National Army had reached another level. Some 343,500 young Americans from across the country had already bid farewell to their families and started on a journey that within a year or less would reach the Western Front. Among them, Philadelphia's first contingent of drafted men, largely selected by three local boards in West Philadelphia, boarded railroad cars bound for the newly opened Camp Meade in Admiral, Maryland.[9] (See Figure 8.1.)

As early arrivals reached Camp Meade, their reception vividly captured the moment, while auguring what would follow in later days. A "chunky little fellow," who had been a traveling salesman, swinging a suitcase, was the first off the train. An officer, about five feet, six inches tall, with keen gray eyes, wearing the two stars of a major general on his shoulders, stepped forward in

"CAMP MEADE SPECIAL" LEAVING BALTIMORE AND OHIO STATION

FIGURE 8.1 "Camp Meade Special," leaving the Baltimore and Ohio Station. (*Evening Ledger* [September 22, 1917].)

a lithe and agile movement to meet him. Extending his hand in a warm and hearty manner, he introduced himself: "I am Major-General Kuhn, the commandant of this camp," before quickly adding: "I am glad to welcome you as the first selected man to this camp. I extend my welcome to you and to all the men with you. I hope that you will like the place and I am sure that you are going to help us to make you a good soldier." With his eyes fixed on Major General Joseph E. Kuhn, the traveling salesman replied: "Thank you sir. I am glad to be here and am sure everybody on this train is glad to be here. We all want to be good soldiers." As their arrival unfolded, eager but confused draftees smiled while the band played familiar tunes. When it reached "Where Do We Go from Here?" military police ushered them into columns for their march to barracks about a mile and a quarter away—as well as to their uncertain future as the "good soldiers" that their spokesperson had claimed for them. They would soon be followed by many more men like themselves.[10]

If any of the new recruits thought that Camp Meade would provide an easy introduction to military life, Kuhn quickly disabused them of their presumption. Born in Leavenworth, Kansas, in 1864, he had attended the United States Military Academy, graduating first in his class in 1885. During the early years of his military career, he served with various engineer units before returning to West Point as an instructor of civil and military engineering from 1889 to 1894. After duty in the Spanish-American War in which he earned the temporary rank of major, Kuhn went back to his alma mater as commander of the engineering company, chairman of the Department of Practical Military Engineering, and a member of the Academic Board for the next three years. In 1904, promoted to the rank of major, Kuhn commanded an engineer battalion in the Philippines. After serving as an observer in Japan and Germany for two years, his authoritative report on military maneuvers in Manchuria during the Russo-Japanese War was used as a textbook and reference work at the Army War College. For the next several years, he held appointments as a military engineer, including a brief period in which he served as district engineer for the river, harbor, and fortification works at Philadelphia in 1912–1913. At the outbreak of World War I, Kuhn was neither a stranger to Germany nor unfamiliar with its military organization and operations. Between June and September 1906, he had attended German army maneuvers, where he reportedly engaged the kaiser in conversation on strategy and tactics. Returning to Germany with the U.S. Military Mission from December 1914 to March 1915, he was promoted to colonel and assigned as military attaché to the American Embassy in Berlin, where he remained until December 1916. Attached to Imperial General Headquarters, he frequently visited German lines on both the Western and the Eastern Fronts. More knowledgeable about German military methods than any other officer in the U.S. Army, Kuhn was believed to have been forced by authorities in Berlin to leave the battlefronts. In January 1917, promoted to brigadier general, he was appointed as president of the Army War College and member of the general staff. In August, elevated to major general, he assumed command of the 79th Division at the time of its organization at Camp Meade. With a reputation making him more valuable as a leader of combat troops than in any capacity at a training cantonment, Kuhn had entered, like the men under his command, an ineluctable path toward the Western Front.[11]

If Kuhn's formidable record did not convey to the men under him what was expected of them, his words confirmed his determination for what lay ahead. As belligerent nations wearied of war and talk of peace resurfaced, officers, charged with preparing men for combat, contended that such distractions threatened to undermine morale. One of them bluntly declared that "nothing could be more harmful, for the average American is unable to put any heart and spirit into army training unless there is a prospect of real fighting." In defiance of hopes emerging on all sides, the anonymous jingoist continued: "As there is no immediate prospect of peace, the friends of America ought to end the discussion, for not until the peace talk ends, will we be able to win the hearty cooperation of the men who are able to do the fighting." Although Kuhn shared the perspective of "Si vis pacem, para bellum" (If you want peace, prepare for war), he was more circumspect on the immediate situation. While the war would go on with America playing a major part, it had to be better understood if American participation was to help bring hostilities to an end. Kuhn declared: "Every man who enters this camp must become imbued with this idea and devote his entire time to the effort of putting himself in such shape that he can do his best when called upon to act." While it was believed that he would soon be asked to join Pershing in the field, Kuhn would remain at the cantonment for several more months until the 79th Division was called to France.[12]

As the United States prepared for war, it was clear that the success of mobilization would depend not only on what happened in military drills but on gaining the support and consent of its civilian population. In the spring of 1917, newspapers described an enthusiastic cohort of inductees, eager to embrace the life of the "good soldier," who found wholesome fun at training camp. But one apprehensive Philadelphian, arriving at Camp Meade in September, expressed his concerns in the first of a series of letters to family and friends that became a regular feature of the *Evening Ledger*. Signed only by "Bob," its writer described his fear that he would look "like a hobo within three days unless my olive drab arrives." Anticipating the adjustment that he would have to make, "Bob" said he intended "to do as I am told and say little." Unlike the fine-looking chaps who were sure to do things to the kaiser, he was far more cautious. Noting that some of the boys were laughing or trying to sing or whistle, he declared: "But I don't know why unless they were trying to drown out the band." Finding the scene to be, in his own words, "colorless," he summed up his feelings: "Personally, I felt a bit awkward and embarrassed as I stood in line while the general and the others in his party surveyed us." But "Bob" was not alone in his uncertainty about the future; he was perhaps only more candid about what they all knew or feared and chose to deny. And as he adjusted to camp life, his letters invited the empathy of readers.[13]

Shortly after the opening of Camp Meade, other men like "Bob"—sons of Little Italy who had not responded to or were not eligible for the conscription order of the Italian government two years earlier—found themselves facing the call to colors of the United States. As Selective Service filled the needs of the armed forces, it provided them with an opportunity to find a role in the war effort as well as an important avenue for Americanization. When the first contingent left South Philadelphia at 7:30 A.M. on September 22, some 250 men, mostly Italians, selected by Local District 2 of the draft board would march from the 7th and Carpenter Streets police headquarters to the Baltimore and Ohio Station at 24th and Chestnut Streets. Relatives and friends had gathered on the streets to observe a vigil during the previous night. In the morning, a police detachment sought to maintain control over a crowd of nearly 1,000 persons as the men began their departure. C.C.A. Baldi, ever conspicuous on such occasions, other prominenti of the Italian colony seeking to share in the glory, and draft board officials, presumably to ensure that no one would get "lost," took positions at the head of the induct-ees, followed by a police band and honor guard, as the procession made its way to the depot where a train would take them to Camp Meade.[14]

A few hours later, "a great wave of enthusiasm" engulfed "Little Penn," the unofficial name given to Camp Meade, as nearly 600 "singing, shouting and cheering draftees" from the draft boards of Local Districts 2, 3, and 35 of South Philadelphia reached their destination. Greeted by the same band, playing a scrappy two-step, that had met earlier arrivals, the men and boys from "downtown" hopped off the train. While "pals swung into step as the strains of the band music wafted over the sand hills," the impromptu celebration welcomed them, leading a newspaperman to observe: "All doubt about the draftees becoming willing soldiers in the army of Uncle Sam was dispelled as the South Philadelphians detrained. A more happy and enthusi-astic crowd of men have not been seen in Dixieland since Civil War days."[15]

A few moments after their arrival, Colonel A. E. Saxton ordered the men to begin the short march from the train station to Camp Meade. The boys from the draft board of Local District 2 were given the dubious honor of leading their fellow inductees as they abandoned the security and comfort of civilian life for the uncertainties and dangers of military adventure. As a dozen or so Italian youths shouted, "Get in the lead, Salvo," Salvatore Ponzo, a short, but sturdily built, unemployed 25-year-old plasterer, born in Bronte in the Catania Province of Sicily, who had left his home on South 7th Street, obeyed their order. Although a native of Italy, Ponzo was said to like Uncle Sam well enough to loudly boast that he was willing to go to France, even if he had to go alone. After another South Philadelphian, Morris Goldman, led the second group, Tony Grassi, born in Castelluccio Valmaggiore in the Foggia Province of Apulia and now a tailor at A. B. Kirschbaum and resident of South Mildred Street, stepped to the head of the third contingent. As they reached Camp Meade, they were cheered by workers constructing barracks, and as the marchers neared the Philadelphia section of the camp, bedlam broke loose. And for a brief moment, military discipline was forgotten in welcoming these newcomers. Over the next 11 days, a flotilla of trains would arrive, bringing the vanguard of draftees for the National Army that would carry America into war.

As Philadelphia's Italians joined the war of an adopted country, newspapers extolled their special qualities. In October 1917, a caption under a photograph described John Aloysius Festa as a "young Philadelphian" who lived on McKean Street before resigning as secretary of a corporation to enter military life at Camp Meade. He was 24 years old, born in Cerno al Volturno in the Campobasso Province of the Abruzzi, an American citizen by virtue of his father's naturalization, and employed as an accountant at both the office of Molino and Farina [*sic*] on Federal Street and an automobile dealer, Thornton Fuller, at 24th and Bainbridge Streets. The human interest of such stories of men in uniform, ranging from the mundane to the highly dramatic, provided momentary distraction from the carnage that waited on the battlefield.[16]

While Congress and the courts sought to clarify the draft status of aliens, military authorities began attempting to integrate recruits who widely differed in how Americanized they already had become—and, most important, in their knowledge of English. In early October 1917, almost immediately after their arrival at Camp Meade, General Kuhn announced that hundreds of Italians and other immigrant soldiers would be removed from active units and left behind when the time came for the 79th Division to sail for France because of their inability to understand commands given in English. Within the 314th Infantry Regiment, with 900 men from mining regions of Pennsylvania and other areas "thickly populated with foreigners," some 34 of the 148 members of one company were reportedly unable to speak English. With officers convinced that fighting efficiency would be impaired by language deficiencies, the men would be assigned to "training units" where they would be taught the fundamentals of English and other matters essential to preparing them for combat at a later time.[17]

If Italians posed a problem to higher command, a more receptive attitude was being nurtured at the lower ranks. When "Bob," the young Philadelphian, who had worried about his appearance on his arrival, again wrote to his mother about conditions at Camp Meade, he declared that the longer he remained in the National Army the more convinced he became that it was "a real democratic institution." He firmly believed that the caste system described by novelists and other writers had been "so completely booted out of military life that not a trace remains." As he described members of the 315th Regiment, mainly from his own hometown, this tolerant young observer, without hostility or condescension, wrote: "We have a big bunch of Italians in our regiment and it is quite a problem to handle the men who don't understand English. Those who have but little knowledge of the language are being placed in the kitchen and under the careful guidance of the cooks and will probably learn to master the language in a short time." While previously enthusiastic over camp food, "Bob" now praised the "spaghetti, Italian style" coming out of that kitchen. His appreciation of their food may have made it easier for him to include Italians in his discussion of democracy within the military setting.[18]

Less than a month later, having become better acquainted with Italians, "Bob" provided more details on them in another letter to his mother. He described the widespread unhappiness resulting from the transfer of about 5,000 Pennsylvanians, including "hundreds of boys from the old town," to camps in the South, which had left the "dandy Fifteenth" (his abbreviated term for the 315th Regiment) as "nothing but a skeleton of a regiment, for every company has been stripped." Among "a bunch of new arrivals" enabling the regiment to resume recreational activities that made camp life enjoyable, "Bob" praised the 40 Italians, assigned to the 154th Depot Brigade, who had organized some sort of Italian society only 48 hours after reaching Camp Meade. With remarkable empathy, he noted that beyond being probably the first of its kind within the new National Army, it proved that "the sons of Italy who have made Philadelphia their home are awake to the needs of the army."[19]

"Bob" identified Nicola da Dario, from Fulton Street in South Philadelphia, who would become president of the new Italian society. Born in Italy and not yet an American citizen, he had waived exemption to join the army. With so many Italians in the depot brigade, da Dario explained the need to organize them: "Many of our men cannot speak English any too well and nobody can teach them so well as their own people. And these men get very lonesome unless they have their kind of amusement, so we have decided to provide it for them. The membership will be restricted to Italians, and when we get things going a genuine Italian concert will be given."[20]

Praising his new Italian friends for their military ability, "Bob" described the depot brigade as an organization that served the regiment much like a training brigade did. Its men were being groomed as replacements to fill the ranks wherever they were needed in all branches of the army. It was "all to the good" because the Italians—"who seem to monopolize honors, are taking to the work like ducklings to fresh water"—were not only adjusting well but contributing to the success of "Philadelphia's own."[21]

"Bob" found lighter aspects in their tensions with the Irish that had been carried over from civilian life. He wrote of John di Santo, of South 9th Street, a South Philadelphian with "a keen sense of humor," who explained the appointment of First Sergeant Conway as their drill instructor by pointing out that it was necessary for Italians to have an Irish boss. But when "Bob" suggested that 1 Irishman and 40 Italians made a good fighting combination, di Santo replied, "Justa nough Irish. And more spoil it." "Bob" added that di Santo, although not yet an American citizen, was a good soldier who would do well. He cited two others, Vito Dianno of Reading and Joseph Smeriglio of South 7th Street, as organizers among the Italians.[22]

"Bob" strongly praised another Italian, not from Philadelphia but from Washington, about a month later, when he wrote: "Dear Mother, I find it almost an impossibility to pen you a letter without discussing a few of the camp notables; in fact, the human side of the cantonment is all that is interesting, and today I shall introduce you to John Eopolucci, who admits that he is the happiest man at Little Penn." Relaying a powerful tale from his new friend, "Bob" claimed that Eopolucci was elated to join the 312th Machine Gun Battalion, "the Statesmen's Suicide Club," because it gave him the opportunity to avenge the death of a brother. After asking drafted officials to place him in a machine gun unit, 22-year-old John Eopolucci claimed to have been told that it was up to staff officers to do so. When he later learned that men from Washington were being assigned to "suicide clubs," he arrived at the camp as a happy man, eager to carry one of the heavy machine guns into combat with the 79th Division. "Bob" quoted Eopolucci: "I shall avenge the death of my brother and will make a few Huns pay dearly for his murder. They may get me, but I shall get a few before they reach me." While the drama of the Eopolucci brothers, a Verdi opera on the Western Front, had captured "Bob's" imagination, it seemed like braggadocio being told by one young soldier to a more impressionable listener. "Bob," moreover, had confused the names of the two brothers. John Eopolucci died while serving as a gunman on the *Aztec*, an armed merchant vessel sunk by a German submarine on April 1, 1917, one day before President Wilson asked Congress for a declaration of war. A few days later, a newspaper offered a tribute, "In Memory of John E. Iopolucci of Washington, D.C., the first American killed in the line of duty in the war with Germany."[23]

"Bob's" letters were usually addressed to his mother but sometimes to a friend or his sister, as in January 1918 when he described the men of his own Company L of the 315th Infantry as being a bit more advanced than other units while going about their work with genuine enthusiasm. He also portrayed their ethnic diversity: "It is a cosmopolitan bunch, too, for on the rolls are 142 Americans, seven Russians, seven Austrians, one Greek, nine Italians, three Germans, one Pole, one Hungarian, one Armenian and last, but not least, two gentlemen who were born in Ireland." Among the Germans was one who had served two years in the kaiser's army, but recently earned a promotion at Camp Meade, and whom "Bob" judged to be "a mighty good corporal." He described an "Arabian," born in Ramallah, about nine miles outside of Jerusalem, "perhaps the only native of that country at Little Penn," who was a member of the 304th Engineers. With parents, two brothers, and three sisters living in the Holy City, Misleh Jacob, having obtained his first citizenship papers, was "anxious to become a full-fledged American."[24]

As "Bob's" letters to his mother signed by "your dutiful soldier son" became less frequent, he paid glowing tribute to "war correspondents" met at Camp Meade. In his final message, he described preparations in the use of gas masks in a letter to his sister Betty in late June 1918. In his portrayal of camp life, he had not only described his own contact with foreign-born soldiers but introduced them as Americans in the making to readers in Philadelphia. Unlike the generals who found their language deficiencies to be sufficient cause to relegate them to "training units," "Bob," an Anglo-American, far removed from Italians and other "foreigners" in his civilian life, had consistently depicted them in exemplary terms.[25]

An important caveat, however, remains necessary. Reading "Bob's" sketches from Camp Meade at face value, they provide a candid glimpse of daily life. But was there ever really a "Bob," a recruit who composed these letters to his family and friends? Or was it a tool of propaganda intended to persuade civilian readers? With discrepancies such as his confusion over the Eopolucci brothers undermining credibility, the authenticity of "Bob's" letters as well as their writer becomes dubious. Perhaps his messages were another effort by a government agency or an editorial staff of a newspaper to gain support for military objectives, at a time when voices of antiwar opposition could still be heard. And given the restrictions that would be imposed on reporting from the camp, it becomes even more likely that "Bob" was, in fact, a contrived device, most likely of the Committee of Public Information, designed to project favorable images of military life to families and friends of men called to duty.[26]

"We'll Bring Back the Kaiser's Moustache!"

By January 1918, new orders requiring newspapermen in uniform to submit their writing to censors greatly increased military control over the flow of information. It did not affect accredited correspondents in daily contact with commanding officers and already under their control, the "embedded" reporters of their time, but writers who, having become soldiers themselves, were expected to distance themselves from further journalistic activities. By forbidding payment for their writing, the directive sought to prevent disclosure of military information. But shortly before the edict, another Philadelphian, at Camp Hancock, the tent camp housing the 28th Division near Augusta,

Georgia, would write of the unity emerging among descendants of veterans of both sides of the Civil War. Inspired by a crowded service at a nearby Episcopalian church on Christmas Day, 1917, where men of the North were now ready to fight alongside their brothers of the South, he declared: "Surely that is a test of unity. I felt then that there is no longer a North or South, but there is only one America." That unity would soon be tested in France.[27]

In early 1918, in contrast to more favorable assessments, the provost general's office reported that only about one-third of men of draft age in Pennsylvania were physically fit and qualified for military service. Over 800,000 men in the state had registered; local boards had called slightly more than 300,000; and a little more than 100,000 had been certified for duty. While almost 26,000 had failed to appear, they could not all be considered slackers, as some had enlisted without notifying their boards, moved to other districts, or died. Although claims for exemptions by Pennsylvanians actually fell well below the national average, a higher percentage of such decisions were awarded in the state. Of almost 132,000 men who sought to be excused from service, exemptions had been granted to over 114,000, or 86.6 percent, of them. Perhaps of greater interest, slightly more than 176,000 aliens had registered in the state, a little more than 98,000 of whom were citizens of Allied nations. Of more than 68,000 aliens called by draft boards, just over 14,000 had been accepted for military duty. With their eligibility yet to be been determined, the manpower needs of the U.S. Army also remained unresolved.[28]

The flow of recruits from Philadelphia to Camp Meade, which had begun in September 1917, continued into the next year. On February 6, 1918, a contingent of 800 men, largely from northern sections of the city, left North Philadelphia Station, as part of the final quota of the first draft in a now familiar scene of mixed laughter and tears. Young Men's and Young Women's Christian Associations' (YMCA and YWCA) workers, passing through the crowd, distributed woolen sweaters, caps, and wristlets to inductees. One young man shouted from the train, "We'll bring back the Kaiser's moustache!" to his mother whose laughter at her son's jest covered her anguish. After another 20 men, having marched together from Germantown under a police escort, boarded their railcar, moistened eyes and flowing tears replaced smiles before the train ground into motion at 9:25 A.M. Some 800 more men from central and southern districts of the city would leave from the Baltimore and Ohio Station at 24th and Chestnut Streets in the early evening with yet another group of an unspecified number due to depart on the following morning as replacements for Camp Meade men who had been belatedly rejected or reassigned to other training bases. With 1,600 draftees leaving on this day, one week later, nearly 300 more recruits completed the city quota, after various deficiencies and rejections of earlier men had further pared the ranks. The mounting totals of local recruits strengthened charges that cities and states of the North were contributing more than their share of manpower to the National Army.[29]

Despite repeated claims that the "last quotas" of the first draft had left Philadelphia, departures continued in the spring of 1918. In early April, some 261 draftees boarded another special train at North Philadelphia Station, completing the contingent of 600 local "boys" on their way to Camp Meade. Accompanied by relatives and friends, a squad of 18 men marched up Broad Street behind a band in a more organized procession. Unlike most others who waited until their draft numbers were called, two brothers, one a Stetson Hat Company factory worker and the other a patternmaker at the Link-Belt Engineering Company, had petitioned to enter the army together, both anxious to "take a crack" at the kaiser. As the train pulled away, the crowd on the platform saluted its passengers by singing "The Star-Spangled Banner" in "a rousing burst of patriotic enthusiasm." And as on previous occasions, with tears shed and cheers raised, apprehensions rose as civilians bade farewell to departing men with hopes for a quick and certain victory.[30]

As more recruits reached Camp Meade, they too would quickly be turned into American soldiers. While some of them would remain behind in depot brigades composed of men deemed unfit for overseas duty, others adjusted for what lay ahead in France. Capturing one aspect of their training, General Kuhn described the "most military and properly executed salute that he had ever seen at Camp Meade" in early April 1918. He was referring to the gesture of Private Felice Petrini, a 27-year-old baker from Giulianova in the Teramo Province of Abruzzi, before becoming a resident in the Italian enclave in suburban Ardmore and now a member of Company F of the 304th Ammunition Train of the 79th Division. While Petrini had mastered some preliminary duties of military life, he would become more American, naturalized by the special court in May before more fully demonstrating his new allegiance, along with other Italians, in the Meuse-Argonne campaign on the Western Front during the closing weeks of the war.[31]

9

Turning Aliens into Citizens

As military authorities directed efforts at cantonments where basic training prepared recruits for the Western Front, Congress remained preoccupied with finding a solution to the problems of how to induct aliens, capture slackers, and allow no able-bodied male to avoid army service. With hearings by committees of both chambers, a series of legislative proposals, refined by amendments and disputed by opponents, tested the resilience of legislators, while reflecting the demands of a public aroused by the urgency of mobilization. House efforts had begun with a bill that would allow the drafting of aliens for work on farms, in factories, or at other forms of home service; the deportation or exclusion of others who refused to be conscripted; and the banning of naturalization for anyone who sought exemption, proposed in August 1917. Meanwhile, the Senate, considering legislation that would require consent before any draftee could be sent to Europe, demonstrated that the prospect of combat was no more welcome by native-born recruits than it was to aliens. Confirming that reluctance, the Justice Department reported that hundreds of registrants, especially in larger cities, had provided false addresses, along with misleading information on nonexistent bridges, vacant lots, streets, and factories, before disappearing into hiding and leaving diminished prospects of ever being found. But legislation to induct aliens also faced the need to find some means of negating any existing treaty that forbade the conscription of foreign nationals. Such efforts would bring Congress into conflict with the White House and State Department.[1]

Enemy and Friendly Aliens

While the war had forced America to seek, as it never previously had to do, an understanding of its own demographic and cultural diversity, the alien problem remained a stumbling block. Approaching the final stage, the registering of "enemy aliens," particularly men with German origins, still occupied the attention of authorities. In February 1918, Philadelphia joined the rest of the nation in an ambitious effort aimed at German males, 14 years of age and older, who had been not been naturalized. With assurances that they would be received in "a courteous and friendly manner," all aliens were required to register at police stations, where each person was expected to present "four unmounted photographs of himself, not larger than 3 by 3 inches, on thin paper, with light background." The penalty for failing to register was imprisonment.[2]

The response of Germans, however, revealed not only their reaction to the required registration but the unwholesome position to which the U.S. government had committed itself. In Philadelphia, where about 6,000 men who were still subjects of Germany were expected to register, a newspaper declared: "With scarcely an exception they gave the impression of being loyal Americans who were 'sore' at the turn of fate which had kept them from being fully naturalized before the war broke out." When registration opened at the police station at 65th Street and Woodland Avenue in West Philadelphia at 8:00 A.M. on February 4, among the five men already waiting, four of them wore Liberty Bond buttons and three other men who soon joined the scene wore a Red Cross button that read, "A heart and a dollar are all you need." Within an hour, four more men had arrived. One man, "who did not in the least look like a German," reportedly asked a police officer to kick him off the front steps and into the snow. When asked why, he was said to reply: "Because I'm ashamed of myself. I've lived here for years and no one imagines that I am not an American citizen. But, as a matter of fact, I never took out citizenship papers. I'm so ashamed of myself I don't want to look anybody in the face." After registering, he repeated his request to be kicked into the snow, adding that it would do him good. A 70-year-old registrant, who wore a Liberty Bond button in his lapel, sobbed as he entered the police station escorted by his already naturalized son. He did not object to being required to register, but, having already taken out his first naturalization papers, he was described as disconsolate over being identified as an "enemy." Similar scenes were reported at police stations throughout the city.[3]

These men were not subversives, terrorists, or threats to the safety of other Americans or security of the United States but permanent residents who had embraced life in America without citizenship when it had not been necessary to do so. Having now become required by law, they now registered as "enemy aliens." For citizens of "friendly nations" who faced induction into military service, the expectation that they secure citizenship was far less harrowing but similarly imposed. The odd result was the convergence of "friendly aliens" and "enemy aliens" in pursuit of naturalization. As registration opened for them, some 200 Germans, Austrians, and Italians, seeking to file applications for citizenship, thronged the Federal Building in Philadelphia. But while Italians, after the usual waiting period, were allowed to submit petitions for naturalization, Germans and Austrians, receiving only their first papers, or declarations of intention, were forced to wait until the war had ended before final papers would be issued.[4]

In September 1917, one month after the introduction of the alien slacker bill in the House of Representatives, the Senate approved its version of a similar act. Frustrated by the slow pace of action after authorizing the president to reach a diplomatic agreement, the Senate sought to enact its own legislation. With several senators declaring that they were tired of waiting, an unexpected voice vote met little opposition. Meanwhile, the initial proposal in the House of Representatives had been unexpectedly blocked by one member without any explanation. While supporters in the House regrouped for another attempt, the Senate's successful effort had modified earlier proposals by permitting the drafting of "enemy aliens" for noncombat forms of labor such as in agriculture and public works. But opposing members of the Senate still asked how American citizens residing overseas could be protected against conscription by foreign governments. Summarily dismissing such concerns, Senator Henry Cabot Lodge retorted: "It is within the power of any of our allies to give us the authority to apply the selective draft or to withhold it. If they consent, that is a diplomatic settlement; if they refuse, nothing can be done."[5]

With the alien slacker bill passed by the Senate but stalled in the House, momentum shifted to a possible solution reached by diplomatic negotiations. In late September, Secretary of State Lansing, testifying before the House Committee on Military Affairs, contended that enactment of legislation would prove embarrassing to the nation. Clarifying his position, he pointed out that Mexico could take similar action in reprisal by impressing Americans living in its territory and forcing them to take part in the revolutions in which that country was constantly involved. Turning to possible effects on immigration, it could also create a labor shortage in states where large numbers of aliens worked in the manufacture of war supplies. With his objections suggesting that Congress had not been fully attentive to the possible consequences of the proposed bill, Lansing had presented a convincing argument.[6]

On the following day, with the State Department expected to reach agreement with several countries before the second draft quota was called, the committee postponed any further action. Although Lansing had convinced members that diplomacy was preferable, legislative efforts had not entirely died. Representative Burnett, a persistent proponent of congressional action, immediately announced that he would continue to seek passage of such a bill despite opposition from the State Department. One month later, a final effort to secure approval, or at least get the House to "go on record," failed due to the absence of a quorum.[7]

Writing in the *Evening Ledger*, J. Hampton Moore argued that Burnett's intention had been to reach a "showdown" with aliens who had neither enlisted for military service in the United States nor answered the call to return home for duty in their native countries. But by being called to a vote near the hour of adjournment for the House session, the measure, despite being less drastic than other proposals, had been "bowled out" by opponents who had succeeded in delaying further action until the next term of Congress. Noting fears that passage of the bill might encourage a foreign nation to retaliate, Moore pointed out that the German Reichstag was considering the enactment of a similar law that could lead to the induction of American residents into the army of that country. The House debate closed with a reminder that the impressing of American seamen by England had been among the causes of the War of 1812.[8]

Although debate had started with the preference given to aliens who had not been called to duty, as Moore noted, it involved immigrants for whom repatriation could bring some form of punishment or even death in war. But by including aliens in determining quotas, the necessity of drafting nearly every native-born registrant brought a travesty upon patriotism by enabling foreign workers to replace Americans who had gone off to do the fighting. The activities of the Industrial Workers of the World in areas of the nation where workingmen were needed to take the place of conscripted men further aggravated the situation. Above all else, with the serious shortage of labor facing mine operators, manufacturers, farmers, and other employers in the war economy, Moore concluded, the military implications of hiring foreign workers required action by Congress in its next session.[9]

Early in 1918, Giovanni Preziosi, sociologist, former priest, and immigration expert, interpreted the issue from a very different point of view. With about 220,000 of the 750,000 Italian reservists living abroad answering the summons issued by the Italian government, about half of them had returned from other European countries. About 120,000 of the much larger migration of 620,000 in the Americas had reported for military duty, which left about

500,000 men who had ignored the order. Preziosi believed that the principal reason for the lower number of reservists returning from America was that many of them had been naturalized as Americans without bothering to renounce their Italian citizenship. But among other factors making repatriation difficult, many men would have had to bring their families back to Italy as the meager subsidy provided by the Italian government was not sufficient to support them overseas. In addition, transportation was inadequate for bringing their families with them to Italy; and no assurances had been given that anyone would be allowed to migrate again after the war. These circumstances increased the probability that more Italians would serve in the American army than in their native country. Despite the attention given to reservists who had answered the call, as Preziosi noted, a much larger number had become "defaulters or deserters" in the eyes of the Italian government by choosing to stay in America. Without being able to recognize still unfolding implications, they had also placed themselves more fully on the path of Americanization.[10]

At almost the same moment as Preziosi's scholarly analysis was being published, the Sons of Italy, indirectly confirming part of his argument, proudly displayed its recognition of Italians who had made the choice to remain in America. Above the entrance of its bank at 7th and Christian Streets, two service flags, with 900 stars on one and 700 stars on the other, waved in honor of the 1,600 members from Pennsylvania claimed to be in the U.S. Army. Some 400 were said to be at Camp Meade while the rest were in training camps in southern states. Although not entirely successful in persuading reservists to return to Italy in 1915, the OSIA had turned its efforts to recognizing the presence of Italians in the armed forces of the United States.[11]

In February 1918, when Congress resumed consideration of its alien slacker bill, the *New York Tribune*, leading the opposition, charged that it was an unwise attempt to rush legislation that interfered with existing or pending treaties, especially alongside the more promising efforts of the State Department. The proposed plan, moreover, would not only radically alter the status of subjects of cobelligerent nations but weaken the comity supposed to prevail among friendly nations. Recalling the right to exemption granted to Allied aliens, the penalty of deportation and denial of any further opportunity to seek American citizenship would go too far in the wrong direction. Citing the existing reciprocity with England and Canada that allowed the option of drafting or returning a reluctant recruit to his own country, a similar agreement was urged for other nations. And if any nation did not approve of such an arrangement, it remained important to preserve the status quo in regard to enforced service. The *Tribune* asked: "What would it profit us, for instance, to deport tens of thousands of Italians simply because they objected to being drafted? We need labor. Every man who works in a war industry helps to win the war. We should only injure ourselves economically by deporting able-bodied aliens who are willing to work, although they may not be willing to fight." With the House bill resting on the premise that it would entail returning reluctant recruits to unreceptive homelands, the more practical solution would be to allow them to remain and bolster our own labor supply.[12]

In late February, deliberation unexpectedly halted when the House appeared to drop further consideration of the alien slacker bill because the draft would not be calling up any more men until May or June, thus negating the need for immediate action. With the opportunity for a diplomatic solution having returned, Lansing, shortly afterward, announced that France and Italy had agreed to a bill, similar to a recently negotiated treaty with Great Britain and Canada, compelling military service of subjects of cobelligerent nations, which was expected to be quickly enacted. But on the following day, despite Lansing's objections, the House, by a vote of 344–21, approved Burnett's earlier bill that authorized immediate deportation; prohibited aliens who claimed exemptions from any future chance of citizenship; and provided for their drafting for agricultural or manufacturing work. The administration still opposed the bill on the familiar grounds that it would embarrass the government and jeopardize efforts to negotiate a treaty with cobelligerent nations that would allow conscription of their citizens. But even if enacted, the lack of available ships also made it impossible to deport any appreciable number of them in the near future. While the administration and Congress had pursued alternative courses, pitting diplomatic negotiation against a more unilateral legislative approach, the House bill, if approved, would hold unforeseen implications for postwar immigration policy.[13]

With opposition continuing, the *New York Tribune* again argued that the proposed bill negated not only existing treaties with Italy and Serbia but pending treaties with Great Britain and Canada. Seeking to avoid the "vicious principle" that would justify the seizure of Americans by other governments, it called for temporary agreements to settle the issue in a manner that would "make for harmony and eliminate friction." It also argued that the House bill had ignored manpower needs: "The alien who works here helps to win the war as well as the man who goes abroad and fights. We ought to take no chances on deporting men whom our allies do not need and whom they will not make actual use of at the front." But with legislation stalled, aliens remained unlikely to be called by the next draft that was expected to take place in the summer.[14]

As the House bill reached the Foreign Relations Committee of the upper chamber, Senator William J. Stone, chairman of the committee, refrained from making any decisions while waiting for results from the State Department. Despite calls for action from supporters of legislation, efforts appeared to be languishing. In June, Congressman John Jacob Rogers, a Massachusetts Republican, claiming that 1,000,000 aliens were being allowed to evade the draft, blamed the State Department for the impasse. In his view, the Burnett Bill, stalled in the Senate, was now as dead as an earlier bill that had been approved in the previous September. With the blocked legislation, Secretary Lansing, after cautious efforts by the State Department, abruptly withdrew from further consideration proposed treaties with Great Britain and Canada. Declaring "Here the story stops," Congressman Rogers now asked, "How long is the alien slacker to escape?" Although they were calling for renewed efforts to reach agreement with other nations, it was already too late. In late August, when Representative George Edmonds, a Philadelphia Republican, proposed a new bill that would punish resisters by denying citizenship to them at any time in the future, it too failed to gain approval. Although discussion continued, the "alien slacker" had become a moot issue. And the broader question, the legal status of aliens, would not be taken up again until peace had been restored, when "Burnett Bill" would no longer refer to legislation intended to conscript them but to proposals to reduce the volume and control the origins of immigrants.[15]

Naturalizing Aliens

For many public officials, the uncertain allegiance of the alien population, however, remained a threat to America's security. When Philadelphia's public schools reopened in September 1918, their evening programs offered special classes designed to meet the needs of foreign-born adults. Meeting three nights a week at 14 schools in neighborhoods with heavy concentrations of immigrants, the curriculum included instruction in the use of English and preparation for naturalization. With forms provided by the U.S. Bureau of Naturalization, teachers showed how to apply for citizenship, while a written manual, distributed without cost, enabled students to prepare themselves. Examiners visited classes to offer further advice on how to become an American citizen. With such methods complementing efforts to assimilate alien soldiers in military camps, the multifaceted Americanization program would continue to operate well beyond the end of the war, guided by the premise that, whether to wage war for the nation or to secure personal prosperity and well-being, the foreign born had to become more American.[16]

With the passage of the Alien Naturalization Act of May 9, 1918, establishing the special courts that would provide citizenship for alien recruits, authorities still struggled with the dual problem of recruitment and assimilation while the voluntary enlistment of men eager to become citizens attracted widespread public approval. In May 1918, Hugo A. Ricci and Armando Tunon Ricci, brothers from South Philadelphia, achieved a moment of acclaim when the *Evening Public Ledger* reported that they had not only entered military service but been naturalized as American citizens. According to a caption under photos of the two young Italians, Hugo had joined the aviation corps in the previous December, before becoming stationed with the 224th aero squadron in France, while Armando, a senior at the School of Industrial Art, was already at Camp Belvoir, Virginia, with a regiment of engineers. But their story went well beyond this scant information. Hugo, born in 1892, and Armando, in 1895, both in Venafro in Campobasso Province, had immigrated with their parents, another brother, and two sisters to Philadelphia in August 1900. Hugo worked as a tailor and Armando attended the Philadelphia Museum and School of Industrial Art when they registered for the draft on June 5, 1917. But Hugo, rather than waiting to be called, enlisted in the army in December 1917 and served one year before being discharged. Armando enlisted in February 1918 and remained in the service until October 1919. Hugo's petition for citizenship in February 1919, based on his honorable discharge, was filed under the Act of May, 1918. But the subsequent filing of a later petition suggested that provisions made by Congress on behalf of alien soldiers, despite newspaper acclaim, did not always reach their intended results.[17]

While recruitment of foreign-born men had faltered, the Americanization of aliens who entered the military, whether as volunteers or draftees, proceeded on its own course. On reaching camp, while discovering that their basic training included a broader indoctrination than their more American mates would need, Italian recruits would not be asked to fully abandon their prior identity. In May 1918, preparations were also underway for a celebration of the third anniversary of Italy's entry into the war by the display of colors at Camp Meade. Hundreds of Italians, a majority of them from Pennsylvania, who had been praised by officers as excellent soldiers, were expected to participate in the event. Two days later, news from Camp Meade, with the naturalization court scheduled for the coming week, claimed that aliens from many nations were elated at being able to go to war as citizens of the United States. Somehow American citizenship had gained the power to make war more palatable.[18]

The naturalization courts were convened not only at Camp Meade but also at Camp Crane in Allentown, Pennsylvania, and Camp Dix in Wrightstown, New Jersey. Before May had ended, some 10,000 new recruits had arrived in one week, many of them aliens who would gain American citizenship during their basic training at Camp Meade, requiring that naturalization proceedings be extended. With great attention being given to this departure from the routine of military life, soldiers of foreign birth were reported as being very enthusiastic to learn that by gaining citizenship they would be able to fight for their adopted nation as well as their land of birth when they finally arrived "over there." Their mood was typified by the Italians, more than two-thirds of the 364 applicants at a naturalization court at Camp Dix, who rose and gave a "mighty cheer" in response to the summons of the presiding judge. Similarly, when the U.S. District Court of Baltimore moved to Camp Meade for the first naturalization proceedings in early June, among the 1,500 immigrants from various nations, a majority of them were Italians who came from industrial centers across the state of Pennsylvania but also from the foreign quarters of Philadelphia, Baltimore, and Washington, DC. But if secular ceremonies had not provided enough sanction, sacred intercessions also blessed proceedings. Some 22 Catholic priests heard confessions at Camp Meade before a Mass celebrated by Cardinal James Gibbons, the archbishop of Baltimore and preeminent member of the Catholic hierarchy, while priests distributed Communion to as many as 5,000 soldiers. Brushing aside barriers to induction, indoctrination, and inclusion, the event offered the comfort of a common faith. It was a fitting rite in the political liturgy of Camp Meade, inspiring erstwhile foreigners now clad in uniforms that made them American soldiers spiritually prepared to face the enemy in battle.[19]

By September, the naturalization court gained an expanded role in its third session at Camp Meade, when about 1,500 aliens swore allegiance to their new country and "thus be clothed with citizenship in the land of their adoption and for which they are willing and anxious to fight in this war against autocracy." Under recent legislation, local draft boards could now send aliens who had expressed a desire to be naturalized to a camp where citizenship, which remained a necessary condition for overseas deployment, could be conferred. With more recruits coming from cities, the number of aliens was also increasing. And with naturalization proceedings having been introduced to camps, the wide diversity of their origins now included Germans, Austrians, and Turks who would become American citizens before being sent to face their former countrymen in battle. With the number for all groups far exceeding the previous session, Italians again provided the largest contingent of new citizens. And military camps had become not only training bases but important centers where "aliens in khaki" were transformed into naturalized Americans.[20]

While the main objective for the naturalization of alien soldiers was to allow them to be sent overseas, other concerns encouraged its necessity. In the minds of apprehensive Americans, Europe was a place where radical ideologies had been conceived, widely spread, and still held root. In September 1918, such fears inspired a campaign at Camp Lee in Petersburg, Virginia, to combat propaganda "especially designed to break the spirit and morale of Italian soldiers in the American army." It also alleged that Germans had used Socialist literature to persuade many Italian draftees that they were being sacrificed for the cause of American capitalism. Reverend Ottavio B. Neyroz, a prominent Presbyterian pastor of an Italian congregation in Schenectady, New York, and secretary of the YMCA, recruited to defuse suspected propaganda, stated: "We have launched a drive against this insidious effort to discourage our Italians and will keep at the task until our men serving under the colors of America are made to understand that they are fighting for a righteous cause and that they must contribute in full measure to its success." Claiming that there were 3,000,000 Italian men in the United States, he asserted: "It is safe to say that every fifth man wearing the olive drab uniform of Uncle Sam is either a native of Italy or of Italian extraction. Today we have more than 300,000 Italians serving the colors, and all the discontent among these men can be traced directly to German propaganda." Having not indicated the source of his information, the number could be disputed but not the general thrust of his contention. Neyroz had made a point that other observers had neglected to mention—an enormous number of foreign-born soldiers as well as American-born men of foreign ancestry were in uniform. And every session of the naturalization courts in the camps reaffirmed the presence of Italians among them. Fittingly, Neyroz had delivered his message on the same day that 1,000 more Italian inductees passed through their own naturalization proceedings in ceremonies at Camp Lee.[21]

The implications of Neyroz's remarks went even further for Philadelphia's Italians. While he claimed to have written 750 letters over three weeks to families of men at Camp Lee, incorporating points by President Wilson and others in his attempt to counteract German propaganda, it had not been enough. With about 5,000 Italians at the camp, and at least 90 percent of them from Pennsylvania, he noted that "Philadelphia, which has one of the largest colonies in America, is represented at this camp by more than 800 Italians." He called for mass meetings in Philadelphia and other cities with large Italian populations at which "representative citizens" could set forth the real aims of America and tell Italians of the benefits that would come as a result of the defeat of Germany. But Philadelphia's Italians were well aware that the Central Powers included Germany as an ally of the Austro-Hungarian Empire, an older enemy with which their native country had been at war for two years before the United States had entered. And they had long-accepted their obligations toward their country of adoption, whether by their men in uniform or the support of Little Italy as a home front.[22]

Meanwhile, Philadelphia newspapers, portraying the diversity of the nation at war, offered personal sketches of such men in military service. Under an *Evening Public Ledger* photo, readers became acquainted with Lieutenant Joseph A. Pessolano, an acting captain of the 346th Field Artillery, in training at Fort Lewis, Washington, who was somewhat different from most of the "boys" in his neighborhood. Born in 1889, the son of Nicholas and Katherine Pessolano of Fitzwater Street in South Philadelphia, Pessolano was a medical school graduate and physician when he entered the service in April 1917. Reaching France in July 1918, he would serve at Base Hospital 47 at Beaune in Côte d'Or before being discharged nearly a year later. While not a typical son of the neighborhoods of Little Italy neither was he entirely unique. Pessolano and others like him, as the Sons of Italy had sought to represent by their service flags, embodied another kind of Italian American who posed no threat, needed no indoctrination, and had already become as well integrated as any other American.[23]

10

Italy—The Forgotten Ally

Only a few months after the Italian War Mission came to the United States, not only to affirm a new alliance but to secure financial and military aid, Italy would find itself on the brink of defeat. If Cadorna's forces had once held any advantage, it was for a war of short duration, before a serious shortage of artillery, ammunition, and other supplies would arise. And while Italy faced the task of integrating natives of different regions who spoke their own dialects, the Austro-Hungarian Empire had already consolidated the peoples of several incipient nations into a relatively efficient army. Despite these conditions, if Cadorna was able to wage a swift campaign, Italy could prevail in the struggle. But it was not meant to be.

From the outset, the geography of the war gave the Austro-Hungarian army a strategic advantage that began with the territorial salient penetrating Italy between Lombardy and the Veneto almost to the city of Verona. The landscape—with rivers that had to be crossed, bridges that had to be built, plains that had to be occupied, trenches that had to be defended, heights that had to be scaled, and passes that had to be protected—similarly favored them. Along nearly 500 miles from the Stelvio Pass to the Adriatic Coast, Hapsburg forces, entrenched in higher positions of mountainous areas, which were easier to defend and served as vantage points to observe troop movements and gun placements, held a nearly impregnable line. It reproduced the arteries through which Goths and Huns had attacked, before pillaging, plundering, and devastating Italy in the past, but now another enemy threatened. Forced to begin from highly exposed positions, to pass with great vulnerability across open plains, and to climb under withering fire from above, the Italians faced an enemy with a long history of having defeated them. As it had long been, it remained, in Trevelyan's words, a "pistol held to the head of Italy."

From Disaster to Victory

Instead of the quick Italian victory that had been hoped for at its beginning, the war stretched over the next three and a half years. Although waged more widely, the Twelve Battles of the Isonzo, numbered by the Austrians to attest to the repeated failures of the Italians, became a main focus. Unlike the Western Front, where epic battles continued for months, attacks and counterattacks in the Isonzo sector lasted only a few days or weeks before ceasing then being resumed. With every attempt to advance, Italian troops moved into more vulnerable positions that left them highly exposed to enemy fire, until it became a war of attrition, with the main question being: Which side would wither, despair, collapse, and surrender before the enemy did? But with raids and skirmishes in which men died nearly every day, the campaign on the Isonzo, renewed by major offensives with huge losses from casualties, capture, and disease but only meager gains of precarious positions, had raged almost continuously from June 1915 through October 1917.

In late October 1917, with both armies drained of material resources and morale, having reached the "breaking point," the Twelfth Battle of the Isonzo etched the disaster at Caporetto onto the pages of history. The Austro-Hungarian army, reinforced by 7 German divisions, 35 divisions in all, breaching a point that Napoleon had warned in an earlier war was vulnerable to attack by Austria, overwhelmed Italian lines. Infiltration and lightning-speed maneuvers penetrated Cadorna's poorly deployed and confused defenses. Convinced that the war was over, Italians abandoned their weapons and wandered off; despite scattered resistance in places that never fell and equipped with ineffective gas masks, many of them surrendered. In a few days, the combined Austro-German forces regained territory that had taken Italian troops 11 battles over two and a half years to win. But by allowing much of the Italian army to escape, fall back, and regroup, the offensive had also fatally overextended itself.

With Cadorna forced into "retirement" and replaced as supreme commander by General Armando Diaz, a Neapolitan who was almost the antithesis of his predecessor, Italy began its journey toward recovery. In late November, with the Italians holding a shortened, more easily secured line, the Austro-Germans, hoping to deliver the final blow before support from the Allies could arrive, renewed the offensive in the First Battle of the Piave. Field Marshal Franz Conrad von Hötzendorf, confidently advising his troops, asserted that the Italians holding Monte Grappa were "like men hanging by their fingers to a window sill. All we have to do is to cut off their fingers and they will fall down." But against enemy aspirations of launching the final action of the war, the Italians held their positions on the mountains and west bank of the river. By January, with the Austro-Germans forced to suspend the campaign, the Italians had begun to regain belief that the war could still be won.

The aftermath of Caporetto, despite the ignominious defeat that had been inflicted, became a turning point for Italy. During early 1918, Catholics, Socialists, and pacifists, long-opposed to the war, united in support for it, while workers reached unexpected levels of production of war-related materials in the factories of Northern Italian cities. In June, with newly arrived British, French, and Czech units and aided both by rains that brought raging floods that destroyed the pontoon bridges of the enemy and by effective air support for ground troops, the reorganized Italians turned the Second Battle of the Piave into a disaster for the enemy. But Diaz, by a strategy of isolating and swiftly counterattacking in infiltrating thrusts, had also devised the solution against the tactics that had devastated Italian defenses at Caporetto. By their success on the Asiago Plain in the Battle of the Solstice, the Italians, against an opposition that had only recently threatened to capture Venice, placed themselves on the road to final victory and began to erase the stigma of Caporetto.

Austrian military officials saw their failure as the beginning of the end, and the significance of the Italian victory was also noticed in America. Simeon Strunsky, the Russian-born, Jewish editor of the *New York Evening Post*, asserted that the blow that destroyed German hopes and became the turning point of the war had not occurred on the Marne in France but at the Piave in Italy. While Italy had been expected by the German general staff, as well as many Allied leaders, to follow Serbia, Russia, and Romania in falling before Teutonic military power by collapsing at the Piave as it had on the Isonzo, it gained a decisive victory. And while the spirit of the Italian people had been expected to break, as it nearly had during the previous autumn, forcing Italy out of the war, it was renewed. But at the very least, Italy would have had to draw upon the support of French troops, which General Ferdinand Foch, Supreme Commander of Allied forces, could hardly afford to remove from the Western Front without seriously weakening his troops. Instead, "it fell to Italy, the weakest of the Allies, to shatter the entire German scheme of victory."[1]

The American Role in Italy: Unfulfilled Promises

In early April 1918, Secretary of War Baker, meeting with General Diaz at the Italian front, then with King Victor Emmanuel III, Prime Minister Orlando, and other officials in Venice and Rome, praised the shared aims of the two nations and expressed the admiration of Americans for the army and the people of Italy. It was not what Italians wanted or needed to hear with the defeat at Caporetto still fresh in their minds. And even worse, at the end of the month, Baker would assert that large quotas of Americans were desperately needed in order to fill the greatly depleted ranks of Allied forces on the Western Front. But the necessity to which he had alluded, at least for the moment, appeared to allow for the inclusion of help for Italy. In the following month, when Baker, speaking at an observance of the third anniversary of Italy's entry into the war, announced that American infantry, machine gun, and artillery units would soon be "shoulder to shoulder with the Italians on their front line," his largely Italian audience resounded with enthusiastic cheering and applause at the Metropolitan Opera House in New York City. Accepting an American flag from a local organization, Baker spoke of the pleasure that would come when he placed the banner in the hands of the first American contingent leaving for deployment on the Italian front along with his regret at not being privileged to see it "break to the breezes on the Alpine frontier."[2]

But precisely at the moment Secretary Baker made his promises, American support of Italy was becoming more symbolic than real. As part of a nationwide observance of "Italian Flag Day," President Wilson had ordered the Italian tricolor to be flown from federal buildings, while the State Department issued similar instructions to embassies and consulates. And as Austro-Hungary prepared to launch a new offensive on the Italian front, Wilson delivered a special message to Italian Americans that left them buoyed by the illusion that the United States was finally coming to Italy's aid. In Philadelphia, Father Tommaso Terlizzi, pastor of Our Lady of Good Counsel, organized a local celebration. Residents were urged to display the Italian flag from their windows, and numerous fraternal, civic, and religious organizations assembled on Christian Street to begin a march to the Society for Italian Immigrants at 10th and Bainbridge Streets for a program of patriotic speeches to be delivered in Italian and English by Consul General Poccardi and other dignitaries of the community. The *Evening Public Ledger* declared: "No Italian who feels the beat of any patriotic ideal in the fibers of his heart can afford to miss participating in the occasion of this evening which offers the promise of a great step toward a better attitude on the part of Italians in this chosen land." But like the hopes and expectations of military aid to Italy, the event in Philadelphia rested upon a chimera in which flags became more important than troops.[3]

In June, Secretary Baker notified General Pershing that only one regiment from his command would be authorized for deployment on the Italian front. Contrary to Baker's promises in New York City, the American presence was limited to the training of pilots in Foggia who would fly not in Italian skies but above French fields; two small detachments of naval pilots at Bolsena near Rome and Porto Corsini near Ravenna that would see only scant action; several contingents of ambulance and medical aid volunteers; and one infantry regiment that arrived far too late to be of any real impact. Baker's misleading words to Italians in Rome and New York City had been a part of a broader agenda of disingenuous gestures by the American government that left only unfulfilled expectations for a disappointed ally.

The U.S. Army Ambulance Service

Despite repeated requests from Prime Minister Orlando and persistent hopes of the Italian people that reinforcements would soon arrive, not more than about 6,000 Americans would serve in Italy. But even before the United States entered the war, some Americans had already volunteered to serve as ambulance drivers with the Italian army. They represented a small vanguard of the U.S. Army Ambulance Service, which would eventually serve alongside the 332nd Infantry Regiment of Ohio in the final days of the war on the Italian front. While the fuller narrative of American participation in Italy goes beyond the parameters of the present work, and is well told elsewhere, the presence of men from Philadelphia's Little Italy deserves some attention. And while Philadelphians and other Americans found their greatest role in Italy in their work with the ambulance corps, it also provided the opportunity for local Italians to find their way back to their ancestral land.[4]

With congressional authorization for the expansion of military forces, in late May 1917, the Medical Enlisted Reserve Corps began engaging volunteers at its temporary central office at the Cooper Battalion Hall at 23rd and Christian Streets in South Philadelphia. By early June, the renamed U.S. Army Ambulance Service opened operations at Camp Crane, on the former fairgrounds of Allentown, Pennsylvania. In April 1918, after a year sometimes disrupted by controversy, local officials, presenting Italian and American banners along with the recently minted emblem of the corps, honored the 30 sections of the "Italian contingent" designated for duty on the Italian front. Among some 76 Philadelphia Italians teaching their language to other recruits, G. Theodoricus Maioriello, an attorney, had closed his office in the Real Estate Trust Building on Broad Street and set aside a promising career to join the U.S. Army Ambulance Service as an interpreter despite linguistic skills that had not yet been fully developed. But other Italians used the naturalization proceedings to affirm their newly acquired allegiance. In one incident, as some 200 men of various origins became citizens, an Italian petitioner, overcome with emotion, rushed up to kiss an American flag that draped the judge's bench. And when a delegation of 500 members of the Sons of Italy presented an Italian flag to the corps, Private Carlo Bianchi carried the banner in the ceremony. On the anniversary of Italy's entry into the war, Italians from Germantown awarded their 300 recently naturalized brethren a "talking machine," invented by a member of the delegation and reputed to produce matchless sound. The main orator of the day reminded them that they would soon be fighting for the United States as well as for the sovereignty of their former country. While the *Evening Public Ledger* reported that the contingent would soon be leaving for Italy, *La Libera Parola* added that most of them were Italians. A day or so later, a photograph of these men flanking their benefactors in anticipation of their imminent return to a cherished homeland appeared in the *Evening Public Ledger*. Within a few more days, some 2,000 recruits yelled themselves hoarse watching boxing matches in the recreation hall on their final night together. On the next day, the "Italian contingent," marching before commanding officers, left Camp Crane for a more dangerous venue in which their mettle would be tested.[5]

The full record of the U.S. Army Ambulance Service could only be measured after the war had ended. Of the 30 sections sent to Italy, 15 of them would be reassigned to France, probably their covertly intended destination from the beginning, almost immediately after their arrival at Genoa. Serving in the Piave and Isonzo areas, Italian American members of the remaining units quickly gained the attention of community leaders in Philadelphia. Disregarding military protocols, Giuseppe Di Silvestro, a founder of the Sons of Italy as well as the editor and publisher of *La Libera Parola*, sought a promotion for Maioriello, the aspiring interpreter, from the rank of private to a commissioned officer in a letter to Lieutenant Colonel Clarence P. Franklin, commanding officer of the ambulance corps in early June 1918. Reprinted on the front page of *La Libera Parola*, Franklin's reply, after explaining what made the promotion unlikely at the moment, described the enthusiastic reception, "literally on a bed of flowers," that had been given on the arrival of the ambulance service as well as "the cordial relations between us and Italians of all classes and ranks." Shifting to another matter, Franklin wrote that the flag that had been presented earlier at Camp Crane was now being displayed at the new base and that he had told the Italian war minister and other officials in Rome about it. With benign exaggeration, he declared that Philadelphia "loomed very large on the Italian map and in the Italian mind." Noting the many photographs taken of the banner, Franklin promised to send one to Di Silvestro, claiming that it was the first Italian flag from America being flown in Italy before more obscurely adding that he had made it a point "to give the honor to Philadelphia Society." His final remark, which he asked Di Silvestro to convey to the members of the Sons of Italy, was less equivocal: "Tell them that the many Italians from Philadelphia with us are doing good service and giving you all at home a good record and making a good record with your fellow countrymen over here." The message had to be warmly received by readers of *La Libera Parola*.[6]

But with promises of a large contingent of combat troops being sent to Italy remaining unfulfilled, Franklin's words about Philadelphia Italians held even more truth than he had expressed, as the nearly forgotten reservists who had answered the call of their homeland three years earlier now found themselves in the thick of action as the war reached its decisive moment. In a September letter reprinted in *La Libera Parola*, Corporal Antonio D'Alessandro, a machine gunner in an infantry regiment, vividly described his experiences in day and night fighting on the Piave. The Italians, finding the strength of "lions," had successfully defended "our beloved Italy" against a "barbaric and cowardly enemy" who sought to destroy it, but they found its closed doors held only with the strength of iron. Although claiming to be outnumbered five-to-one, but holding to win or die as their only thought, D'Alessandro averred, "We have avenged Caporetto"—making the plains of the Piave and Monte Grappa the tomb of the Central Powers. Despite the rhetoric of a message that reflected military censorship, it probably served to assuage the anguish that had sprouted on the docks at the scenes of departing ships and lingered among the families that reservists had left in Philadelphia.[7]

Philly Boys in an Ancestral Land

Despite its gravity, the news reaching Philadelphia was sometimes trivialized on a newspaper "society page," almost in denial of what the war really brought, as the scions of more privileged families lost their lives in the conflict. Under a regular feature, "Just Gossip about People," the reporting of the arrival of the ambulance corps in Italy had focused on a theatrical production that its members had been performing rather than on its service to wounded men. But after noting it had been the first American unit to reach Italy, a columnist, implicitly demeaning the mission, wrote: "I think it's interesting to hear about things like this, don't you? When I hear I'll tell you about that, too, because there are lots of boys from here with the ambulance over there, and some time I may hear something about somebody you know." The banal encapsulation, in sharp contrast to what was actually being accomplished, revealed how media coverage could denigrate the work and demean the men themselves. Along with stage actors, vaudeville performers, socialites, and other figures who had become the fodder of such coverage by the American press, even the men of the ambulance service could be turned into "gossip," as if war itself could be reduced to simply another society event at which to be seen.[8]

The letters and postcards of cousins Charles M. and G. Theodoricus Maioriello, who had lived in the same household on Federal Street at the time of their enlistment, published in *La Libera Parola*, portrayed a scene very different from any gossip column. Charles (also known as Carlo), a cashier in the Sons of Italy bank on Christian Street, offered his highly favorable impressions of Italy in September 1918. After complaining, despite denying that he was doing so, about the failure to receive replies to previous mail, Maioriello wrote that he had been in France for only three weeks before being redeployed with the American military mission to Italy. He found it difficult to describe the reactions of Italians who were both demoralized by the defeat at Caporetto and convinced that the war would end when Americans reached the front lines and who asked when the rest were coming. Agreeing with them, he believed that the work of the ambulance corps was only the first piece of the American effort. Describing what its volunteers had accomplished, he had particular praise for the "courage and cold blood" of American women volunteers as ambulance drivers. While partly accounting for the reception of troops who found cities bedecked in banners and flowers thrown before them, the Italians were also aware of what American soldiers were accomplishing in France. Having reached what he regarded as "the beginning of the end," Maioriello turned to the condition of the enemy. Commenting on a recent air attack that revealed the scarcity of their munitions, he sarcastically noted that instead of real bombs what they were dropping had the strength of a "sardine can," striking two nearby houses without inflicting any damage. But Maioriello had also finally earned the praise of the newspaper's editor for his newly acquired fluency in Italian, despite never having received any formal training in the language. While the compliment came with a measure of exaggeration, it also implied Italy's effect on a prodigal son.[9]

A month later, Maioriello, in the same newspaper, introduced what he regarded as a noble letter by two young sisters showing the soul and sentiments of Italians toward American troops. Natives not of the war zone but of Capri, the two writers extolled the "paladin crusaders" of America who had crossed the ocean to join in heart and effort with the valiant but long-suffering soldiers of Italy. Maioriello, greatly moved by their words, had gained permission from the military censor to have it published in America. He also found friends from Philadelphia serving with the ambulance corps who were elated with the opportunity to see the land of their parents. His message, which could have described an encounter with tourists in peacetime rather than volunteers in a war, showed that not even the horror of battle could obliterate the meaning, or perhaps even enhanced it, of being in a place that had so often been described with affection. And while other Americans could not leave fast enough, Italian American soldiers lingered in the land of their ancestors. In January 1919, Maioriello, writing in English on a postcard with an image of the Piazza Unità d'Italia, simply declared: "I am stationed in Padova, fine old city. Best wishes." He had obviously joined in on the postcard craze that had swept through the ranks of American troops overseas. Meanwhile, writing from Vipacco in Austria later in the same month, his cousin, Theodoricus Maioriello and 11 other soldiers had received the War Merit Cross, recently introduced by the Italian government in recognition of valor during the final offensive. While pleased by the recent honor but no longer content at being away, he expressed his desire to return home.[10]

By spring 1919, with whatever lure Italy once held having been exhausted, Philadelphia's Italian Americans, like other American soldiers, yearned to be back on more familiar streets. It was cleverly expressed in a fantasy written by Harold Speakman, a former member of the 332nd Infantry Regiment, set in the far-off year of 1940, in which General Pershing, sitting in his library and reading a history of the Great War, is asked by his grandson, "Grandpa, what became of the American regiment that was sent to Italy?" Springing to his feet, the long-retired general replies: "Great heavens, child, I'm glad that you reminded me of that! They must still be in Italy!" Charles Maioriello's brief message, on a postcard depicting the piazzale at the train station in Bologna, carried his wish to return home: "It seems that it will be a long time before I return to good old Philly." While the editor, when these words appeared in his newspaper, called attention to a soldier's impatience, underlying the explicit query of if and when they would ever see home again seemed to be the sentiment that even these men, having "done" Italy, were now done with Italy. While sons of Italy in some sense, they had married America and were now eager to see their bride again. But it would not come soon enough for them. In another postcard from Padua, Maioriello declared: "We are anxiously waiting for our orders to return, but they have not yet come. Within a short time, all the American troops will be returning to America . . . but I must go to France." And by December, when Maioriello, identified as "Carlo" as he became more Italian once again, attended a Sons of Italy banquet honoring Major General Guglielmotti, with the remaining men discharged, life in Little Italy was returning to normal.[11]

Theodoricus Maioriello was not the only Philadelphia Italian to return home officially recognized as a hero. Renato Di Lauro, another recipient of the Italian Merit Cross, was a native of Casoli in Chieti Province of the Abruzzi, who had immigrated in October 1906 at the age of 13. After being rejected by the U.S. Navy, he enlisted in the ambulance service in April 1918, became a citizen of the United States at Camp Crane in May, and was sent to Italy as a member of Section 529 in June. After the war ended, *La Libera Parola* reported Di Lauro (either forgetting Maioriello or redefining him as an "Italian American") as the only Italian in the American army to be awarded the Merit Cross by the Italian government. Urging every Italian resident in the city to share in the pride, the paper's editor accused C.C.A. Baldi, who had failed to report Di Lauro's accomplishment in his own newspaper, of being a German. But the slander of a rival journalist did not diminish the recognition being given to Di Lauro.[12]

Other men could not be acclaimed as heroes on their return to America, because they would not come home at all—at least not alive. One of them, Gino Protevi, had emigrated as an 11-year-old with his parents and siblings from Livorno (Leghorn) in August 1902. Despite declaring Atlantic City as their intended destination, the Protevi family took up residence in Philadelphia. In 1907, Gino, a 16-year-old student at the William Welsh School in South Philadelphia, won a scholarship to attend the Pennsylvania Academy of Fine Arts, where he would study sculpture. But he also pursued the field of music, an interest shared with other members of his family. In the federal census of 1910, the 19-year-old Gino was living in a large extended household on South 12th Street in South Philadelphia. With three members listed as musicians, it was a family for which music was a serious pursuit and Gino himself would soon follow, along with his work in art. By the summer of 1915, he was performing as the featured cello soloist with the recently formed Meyer Davis Orchestra at the Malvern Hotel in Bar Harbor, Maine, with his future about to be greatly altered. With America's entry into the war, Gino, together with his younger brother, John, registered for the Selective Service on June 5, 1917. On that day,

Gino listed himself as a musician and a naturalized citizen of the United States, while John had only completed his declaration of intention. In another year, in May 1918, they reported together to Camp Crane as members of the U.S. Army Ambulance Service. While John would survive the war, Gino would not.[13]

In August, Gino Protevi, with Section 559, made up largely of men from Purdue University in Indiana, moved up to forward posts at the front, where they encountered little enemy activity, except for an occasional Austrian plane seeking to bring down an Italian observation balloon. With the Italian breakthrough at Vittorio Veneto, Section 559 stretched from the mountains down toward the enemy line on the plains and became engaged throughout the day and night extracting wounded men from the field of action. But while Protevi escaped the dangers of actual warfare, he was not able to avoid a disease, probably influenza, of the sort that took more American lives than the fighting would in Europe. In January 1919, both the *Evening Public Ledger* and *La Libera Parola* reported that Gino Protevi, a sculptor with a studio at 2548 South 17th Street, had died of pneumonia while serving as an interpreter for the ambulance corps in Italy on December 22 of the previous year. Beyond his studies in sculpture at the Pennsylvania Academy of Fine Arts, the obituaries described him as an accomplished cellist, a passionate lover of string instruments, and a member of numerous orchestras.[14]

The news of Protevi's death took an unexpected turn about six months later with an official report, which appeared in the *Evening Public Ledger*, that he had recently returned to duty despite the previous account of his death. But Protevi had died, and his body would remain at the Staglieno Cemetery, the famed burial place of Genoa, for almost three years before it was removed for interment in the United States. In June 1921, another notice invited relatives, friends, and members of La Vittoria Lodge of the Sons of Italy to join in mourning the death of Private Gino Protevi, U.S.A.A.C., 27 years old, at a funeral mass at Saint Monica's Church, before a military burial at Holy Cross cemetery in Yeadon. A few days later, *La Libera Parola* reported that Lieutenant Colonel Franklin, Captain Adolfo Caruso, the former U.S. military attaché in Italy and second in command of the ambulance corps, and other comrades of Protevi, had participated in the funeral. With his parents wishing for him to be buried in the city where he had lived, his body arrived on June 25 at the house in South Philadelphia where they grieved his loss. On the following day, his family and friends bade farewell to him. Protevi might have become a successful sculptor or musician; instead, he died as a soldier in the land from which he had once come. Placed to rest in a cemetery just outside of Philadelphia, he was buried in the earth that had become his country. Poignantly marking his experience, his tombstone, under his name, would carry the words "Italian Front," probably the only one so inscribed, which can still be read today.[15]

While the hazardous duty of the ambulance corps had seen some men lose their lives, the only American infantry regiment to reach the Italian front was far more fortunate. When Lieutenant Carl Hugo Trik, who described Italy as "the land of the flea and the home of the knave," returned home on the *Duca d'Aosta* at the port of New York, he related the unique record of his unit to a newspaper reporter in April 1919. Giving his home address as being on Queen Lane in the Germantown section of the city, he was a member of the 332nd Infantry Regiment, made up mainly of draftees from Ohio and Western Pennsylvania. Intended to increase the morale of a nearly defeated nation as well as to deceive the enemy into believing that it was the vanguard of a vast force, consisting mainly of Italian Americans, his regiment would leave a curious legacy during its one month in action. Recalling that "the enemy always ran," Trik declared: "we didn't seeing much fighting," with most of their time spent in chasing the Austrians. Meeting resistance at the Tagliamento River on the war's final day, the imminent cease-fire brought the necessity to gain and hold as much land as possible. But contact with the enemy would last only 15 minutes during which one man died and three others were wounded. On the next day, despite crossing the river and covering much ground, they found themselves 30 miles behind Italian cavalry whose rapid movement made it impossible to even maintain communications. Noting the great number of prisoners who were glad to have been released from combat, Trik ended his account of American efforts in Italy.[16]

Assessing the American role on the Italian front remains a daunting task. Although not decisive for the outcome, the aviators, ambulance units, and an infantry regiment that only briefly faced enemy guns all earned the gratitude of the Italian people. On another level, these confident, sometimes impious, young men, and even some women, had facilitated the impact of modernity on Italy by bringing their popular culture to an old, somewhat intransigent society. As they absorbed the architecture of antiquity and the art of the Renaissance as well as the appetite slaking value of polenta, American personnel introduced baseball, jazz, children's playgrounds, and chewing gum into Italian life. While not an exchange equal in cultural value, it was mutually transformative. A Philadelphia newspaper particularly applauded the "Tonys, Pasquales and Giuseppes" who, reaching the land of their fathers, had performed a valuable service for Allied unity: "Happily bilingual, they can not only converse with their co-workers, but solve many perplexing problems for the solely English-speaking 'doughboy.'" Although much less serious than the linguistic barriers in France, the editorial noted Italian words that were easily misunderstood when forced into presumed English equivalents. Despite the exaggerated belief that one-half of American troops in Italy were of Italian birth or parentage, they had, nevertheless, helped bring the two nations together: "A stranger in a strange land will exchange a dictionary for a pal who is also an enthusiastic interpreter any day." But such news served to redefine their presence and nurture peace on the streets of Philadelphia as well.[17]

They Who Served

While Italian reservists who had returned from America played a role on the Italian front, it was not enough for some critics. In 1918, a journalist, writing in *Il Corriere della Sera*, demanded that Italians hiding in the immigrant colonies of American cities be conscripted for military service in Italy. He proposed a propaganda campaign to show them how they would benefit from the increased power and prestige of a victorious Italy. But he also suggested the possibility of enabling them to enlist in the American army or employing them in strategic defense industry labor. Without such measures being taken, and especially if reservists who had not returned were granted amnesty, the likelihood of difficulties between men who had served and those who had evaded their obligation would become great in the postwar period. But while the *renitenti*, the reluctant reservists who ignored the summons from Rome, would remain an often revisited issue in Italy, their response to military obligations would preclude friction and contention among them in Philadelphia.[1]

Although it is almost inevitable, or at least expedient, to refer to "Philadelphia's Italians" as if they comprised a monolithic population of singular character, it is also misleading. Wherever they settled, "Italians" were not immediately, fully, and uniformly transformed into Americans but redistributed along a trajectory of assimilation that left them at differing points in personal identity, legal status, and motivations. Recent immigrants, who remained more highly Italian in their sense of self, citizenship, and readiness to act, could hardly

FIGURE 11.1 James Giordano, a 15-year-old who had run away from his home in South Philadelphia to become possibly the youngest member of the U.S. Army, died after being accidentally shot while at a camp in Syracuse, New York, in September 1917. (*Evening Ledger* [September 17, 1917].)

do anything else but answer Italy's call to return as reservists for military duty. But other men, already wavering in how they saw themselves, and perhaps seeking to avoid any obligations, were predisposed to wait until such questions would be answered for them. And of another biographical and historical generation, "Italians," in a more diluted sense, born and bred as Americans, faced no dilemma as they waited for their government in Washington, not Rome, to summon them.

Italians and Italian Americans, who had heard the chant, "Where do we go from here?" in Philadelphia and other locations of an adopted nation, would give the same answer as other Americans—waging their war on the battlefields of France and Belgium. They would fight at Château-Thierry in July, Saint-Mihiel in September, and the Meuse-Argonne offensive of September–October—against a resolute but retreating enemy. And following the Armistice, when Americans marched for the first time in history on German soil, Philadelphia Italians had played an important part on every step of the path. Disregarding the nuances of assimilation, a German officer, writing in a diary found on the battlefield, would use an especially appropriate term in confirming this basic truth: "Only a few of the troops are of pure American origin; the majority are of German, Dutch, and Italian parentage. But these semi-Americans—almost all of whom were born in America and never have been in Europe—fully feel themselves to be true-born sons of their country." Whether as immigrants or American-born sons of immigrant families, they remained among those peoples still trying to find their place in

American society. And although naturalization while in uniform was an attempt to resolve that issue, their military service, despite being heroic, would leave their quest less than fully answered.[2] (See Figure 11.1.)

The First to Die

While the complete record of Italian and Italian American soldiers who served in the National Army is difficult to delineate, newspaper coverage, often focusing on the experiences of local soldiers, showed that they had begun to pay the ultimate price for their military adventure, even before leaving for any foreign battlefield. The first Philadelphia Italian to die as an American soldier, James Giordano, had been recently promoted to corporal in a machine gun company of the 16th Infantry Regiment. While playing cards, he was fatally wounded by an accidental shot from a revolver being carelessly handled by a soldier in another tent, which tore through adjacent canvas before striking the back of its victim at a camp near Syracuse, New York. Immediately brought to a nearby hospital, Giordano declared before dying that he had no idea how the accident occurred and implicated no one as an assailant. Further details made his case even more poignant. According to his grief-stricken brother, Giordano had run away from his family on Montrose Street on Decoration Day, seeking to fulfill his aspiration "to fight for the Red, White and Blue." In a letter received on the morning of the tragedy, he had written that he was well. Newspaper accounts also pointed out that Giordano, having not yet reached his 15th birthday, was probably the youngest member of the U.S. Army. While his death, at an age that should have precluded enlistment, was not the first casualty of the war for the immigrant colony, as men who had returned to Italy to serve in the Italian army had already died, it would be followed by many others as members of America's armed forces.

The earliest reporting about Philadelphia soldiers overseas sought the special angle that provided human interest—such as the 10 University of Pennsylvania students who had already died in the war by February 1918. In April, another article reported the death of Frank De Flavia, one of the first Philadelphia Italians to die in France, a 20-year-old railroad repair specialist with the 19th Engineers Regiment who had drowned in the Loire River. With a great need for workers skilled in railway maintenance who could facilitate the transport of troops, recruiters found an abundant supply of them in Philadelphia. One of seven children of a South 9th Street family, De Flavia had attended the James Wilson Public School before enlisting the previous April. His death presaged the many noncombat casualties resulting from illness and accident that would occur during the war. Searching for the "human" side also brought attention to Dominic, Alex, and Joseph Ferraiolo of Tasker Street, three "brothers in service," being trained in different camps in July 1918. Their experience would be shared with other families who provided several sons for military service.[3]

During the early months of American participation, the U.S. War Department, seeking to prevent the dissemination of information that might have value to the enemy or a negative impact on the civilian population, prohibited publication of casualty lists. By the autumn of 1917, however, it had begun to release lists of names and hometowns, which would be "denatured" in the following spring by withholding information on hometowns, despite objections that it might be confusing for families seeking news. But as addresses were included, dropped, and then restored, the names, ranks, and hometowns of men who had been wounded, killed, or were missing in action gradually appeared in newspapers throughout the nation. In April, citing it to be a matter in the public interest, the *Evening Public Ledger,* with approval of the Committee on Public Information, asked readers for assistance in identifying names on the casualty lists who might be men from Philadelphia or elsewhere in Pennsylvania, New Jersey, and Delaware. But having reached the public, the lists also prompted concern that the information could provide opportunities for "legal leeches" to exploit the families of men being identified. A patriotically inspired response defended publication of the lists by incongruously declaring that "blood is the price of salvation." A more pragmatic approach argued that the lists had brought the war home while urging the public to do its part by buying Liberty Bonds. But with the release of information becoming permitted by the army, the Marine Corps momentarily hesitated (although some names had probably been included with army personnel) to reveal losses before a new policy was introduced at the end of the month.[4]

The Casualty Lists: Sketches of the Heroes

By May, with more American troops reaching the battlefield, the *Evening Public Ledger* was publishing a daily casualty list, eventually accompanied by a collage of small photographs of men reported as wounded, killed, or missing in action. In August, another notice invited families to provide information that would allow more detailed profiles of the men. While apparently already using personal letters sent by soldiers to family and friends, the *Evening Public Ledger* introduced "Sketches of the Heroes," a feature that would remain on its pages until well after the war ended. Tempering the pride that came with listing the names of men who had recently enlisted or been drafted, the casualty lists along with the personal details of the "sketches" provided a steady reminder of the price being paid by Philadelphia's sons. And for Italians and other soldiers with immigrant backgrounds, lives that had been crushed on the battlefield could now become names mangled by misspelling in a hometown newspaper.[5]

The first Philadelphia Italian who died in combat on the Western Front appeared almost incidentally in a newspaper article on the first Liberty Loan drive at Camp Meade that praised two soldiers, trained at that base, who had done much more for their country than buy bonds. The first soldier, identified as "Girolone Viscusi, of Philadelphia," came to Camp Meade in November 1917 before going to France with the 10th Company of the 154th Depot Brigade in the following January. Assigned as a replacement to Company D of the 168th Regiment of the Iowa National Guard, he died after being struck by a shell on April 12 at Village Negre while on the road to Alsace-Lorraine. Conscious for only a short time after being hit, Viscusi reportedly bade farewell and quietly died with little suffering. He was buried with other American soldiers in the cemetery of the town then known as Baccarat. Viscusi would be remembered in the regimental history published after the war as being a foreigner by birth, an Italian "who made it a point to show everyone that his heart and soul were in the fight," before sadly adding that "all missed his presence, both as a soldier and a comrade."[6]

In later weeks, more Italians followed Viscusi onto casualty lists enlarged by a backlog of previously unreported cases. Their names lyrically resonated alongside fellow Philadelphians in a roll call that testified to the loyalty of Italian Americans. In early May, the name of William Charles Viti, son of an Italian-born father and an Irish American mother, appeared. Although severely wounded, he would recover, return home, and live until the age of 92. By July, more Italian names, Ludovici, Cimino, Sabatino, Mezzanotte, Piccoli, Di Sciascio, Blotto, Viola, Curione, and Giuliani, from South Philadelphia, Germantown, Mount Airy, Ardmore, and Ambler, appeared. And far from any battlefield, Germantown's Italians, in a community where "the greatest patriotism manifests itself this year," celebrated Independence Day by unfurling an immense American flag, then a service banner with an extraordinary 125 stars, at Holy Rosary Church in recognition of the sacrifices being made by sons "serving the nation."[7]

Some Italians who found their way as soldiers to the Western Front had immigrated without establishing any family or permanent residences in Philadelphia. Official reports of the War Department could only identify them as being from Italy or by some incorrectly spelled location in their native country. In July, names appearing on the lists included F. Di Cresco, simply of Italy, Antonio Lozzi of Veto Reto, Anachetto Bononni of Ovindoli, Joseph Masciocca of Pisbo, Tommaso Scima of Lesandro De Roca, and Angelo Zitto of Spella. Who were these men, where were they from, what news about them, if any at all, ever reached family and friends in Italy? While Ovindoli can be recognized in the province of L'Aquila, and Spella was likely to have been Spello, many such places remained poorly identified throughout the war.

In August, the names of men from the Philadelphia area that appeared on the growing casualty lists included Cozzie, Di Pietro, Gallo, Graziani, Berenato, Britti, Pritta, Parione, Pacione, Cerasoli, Gerasoli, Geonnotti, Cappuzza, Apostolico, Durando, Zullo, Durando, Calabrese, Schiavo, Di Salvo, Lupu, Coppola, Lhyona, Scioli, Santangelo, De Stefano, Mattia, Ricuelli, Caramanna, Juliano, Zhorella, Calabrese, Liberatore, Turco, D'Alessandro, Amato, Anao, Parrotti, Fecca, Del Fonso, Bruno, Lucente, Spirito, Copolla, Malandra, Malandria, Mogavero, Caveritta, Simons, Berardini, Camerota, Turco, Lizzi, Filippeni, Viola, Merola, Aradia, Romano, Palencia, Ruggiere, Di Luzio, Parrotti, Di Cicco, Monzo, Perry, Tartaglia, Avilla, Chicone, and Petri. Many of them were from South Philadelphia, but they were also from West Philadelphia, Germantown, Manayunk, Conhohocken, Jenkintown, Chester, Eddystone, Norristown, Ardmore, and Berwyn. While still confusing for military authorities and newspapers, and the names were often obviously misspelled but recognizably Italian, other information revealed more about those listed. They had mothers or both parents who lived in Italy. They had brothers who were in the Italian army. They were barbers, tailors, paper hangers, laborers, pressmen, boilermakers, and cinema projectionists. Some men had enlisted as soon as they could while others waited for their numbers to be called by the draft. Some had served with the NGP on the Mexican border before their reorganized units were sent to France. The battles of the Marne and Vesle would be especially costly for them. Many of them would suffer the gas attacks inflicted by the enemy. From mid-July on, casualties rapidly increased with a major offensive, although many would not be reported until much later. The official messages from the War Department or letters written by men who had served with them reported that they had been killed in action, or died from wounds, or were severely or slightly wounded, or died from disease or accidental causes, or were missing in action. And newspaper photos offered haunting images of young men whose lives had been ended by the war to end all wars.

Some men expressed their thoughts and concerns in letters to relatives and friends at home, but others would not leave any personal testimony to their ordeal. Private Sabatino Lizzi, trained at Camp Meade and Camp Hancock before being shipped to France, wrote to his family on Federal Street that he was enthusiastic about army life. With three younger brothers waiting to be drafted, he would later be reported as missing in action. Private Dominic Di Cieco, a laborer at the Philadelphia Naval Shipyard and naturalized eight years earlier, was lost in combat four months after being drafted into the army. Private Arthur Perry (with an already Anglicized name) of West Philadelphia had enlisted at the age of 19 in 1917. After serving with the NGP, he went overseas with the 109th Infantry Regiment in May. In his final letter, Perry said that he was getting along fine but asked his father for "some real smokes" as he found French tobacco to be awful. Two weeks later, he was missing in action.

Some streets in South Philadelphia appeared destined to carry an especially costly burden of the war. In early August, Private John Gerasoli, of South Hicks Street, had been reported as missing in action. At almost the same time, Private Frank Calabrese had written to his four brothers and two sisters on the same street that he had found the countryside so quiet that it was hard to believe that a war was going on, and just a few days later he was reported as missing in action. Private Gaetano Di Salvo was a tailor who lived a few blocks away from both Gerasoli and Calabrese on South Hicks Street; he was in the United States only four years, still unable to speak a word of English, or so they said, and a veteran of the Italian campaign in Tripoli with the army in which his brother still served. In his final letter to his family, Di Salvo wrote that he was well, but he too was soon missing in action. Before the month ended, Private Julio Merola, another resident of South Hicks Street, was reported as wounded. But with other families on nearby streets—Christian Street, Federal Street, and others—suffering similar loss and sorrow, Little Italy appeared to have gone to war against Germany. And in a sense, indeed it had.

Among many men, wherever they lived, who encountered similar fates, Adamo Parrotti had worked at the New York Shipbuilding Company in Camden before enlisting and being trained at Gettysburg in July 1917. Private Parrotti, a member of Company I of the Ninth Infantry, was among the first American soldiers to reach France. Within a few days, he had been wounded. Writing from a base hospital, he informed his sister in Philadelphia that he was recovering from slight injuries. Three weeks later, a War Department telegram declared him to have been severely wounded, possibly after having returned to combat, before reporting his death. Private Joseph Tartaglia, who lived on Christian Street, was drafted in April and stationed near an unnamed large city in France, when he wrote to his family two months later about the fine treatment by the French who were providing nightly entertainment for American soldiers. By August, Tartaglia was missing in action.

As a new cast reprised the drama of the Western Front, Philadelphia Italians became even more conspicuous on casualty lists in September. The names now included Felliso, Bougi, Cercone, Sfrattone, Palacio, Caville, Spototo, Tassoni, Verna, Chicone, Ciccone, Inverso, Trafficante, Stotto, Basile, Roselli, Di Martino, Mammala, Di Paolo, Bomente, Conicello, Volpe, Gallena, De Stefano, Bruno, Crocco, Aiello, Acosta, Dominick, Corradino, Pichezzi, Gianotti, Belli, Di Bernardino, Di Fabio, Contraciano, Cellucci, Scardellette, Sasso, Familiare, Di Gregorio, and Ardizzi. Some men who had previously been reported as missing—Juliano, Calabrese, DiCicco, Lyhona, and Zullo—were prisoners of war. Others who had been listed as missing—such as Louis Chicone—were reported as killed in action. Some had migrated from Italy only a few years before the war. They lived in South Philadelphia but also in West Philadelphia, Roxborough, Conshohocken, Chester, Eddystone, and such New Jersey places as Vineland and Wildwood. They were volunteers and draftees. Many had not been naturalized as American citizens before entering the army. Some of them had served in Pershing's foray on the Mexican border. They too endured gas attacks while in the trenches.

As their comrades in earlier months, they wrote with bravado to their families at home of their adventures in France. Private Enrico Monzo declared that "Dutchmen ran like sheep when we got after them." Peter J. Verna, only 19 years old, who had lost one eye in the fighting as American troops crossed the Vesle River, had written in a letter that his parents received on July 29: "We've got the Germans down and they're going to stay down." He was recovering from wounds and expected to be sent home soon. Private Louis Chicone lived almost directly across Christian Street from Tartaglia. Using the alias of Tom Sheridan, a South Philadelphia pugilist, he had boxed in local arenas. But now like his brother who had died in military service on the Mexican border, he too lost the fight of his life when he was reported killed in action. Whether with loss or survival, extraordinary heroism was often a part of their experiences. After Private Luigi Mammala, a resident of Tioga in civilian life, took up an exposed position 50 yards away from his own line and downed a German sniper who had already killed or wounded several Americans, he would be awarded a special citation for bravery.

Among many brothers and sons who died, one case, graphically captured by side by side photographs of Alfred and Alec [sic] Volpe, on the casualty list, revealed the short span of time within which tragedy could afflict the same household. On September 14, the *Evening Public Ledger* reported that both a letter to a friend and information received from the Red Cross had brought news of the death of Corporal Alfred V. Volpe, 25 years old, of Company C of the 30th Infantry, in combat near Mezy-sur-Seine on July 15. Before entering the service, he had been a familiar face to many Philadelphians as the operator of a newspaper and magazine stand at 16th and Market Streets, one of the busiest intersections in Center City. Drafted in October 1917, Volpe had begun his basic training at Camp Meade. Transferred for further training at Camp Greene in North Carolina, he was quickly promoted to the rank of corporal and then to sergeant before being shipped overseas in April 1918. The first newspaper notice of his death briefly mentioned that his brother, Alexander, a machine gunner, was also in France. Another telegram from the War Department to their brother Angelo at home on McKean Street in South Philadelphia reported that Private Alexander Volpe, 23 years old, had met a similar fate in action along the Marne as French and American troops counterattacked on July 18. With the entry of the United States into the war, he had left a position with the Alan Wood Iron and Steel Company to enlist in the army, before sailing with the first American troops to reach France in early December 1917. A younger brother, Joseph, who had registered for the draft during the previous week, was at home waiting to be called into the army. When he became employed at the factory in Conshohocken, Alexander had left his brothers at the newsstand where they had worked together. Their oldest brother, Angelo, having founded the Philadelphia Boot Black Supply Company on North 15th Street, expected his brothers to join him in business after the war. But now the only partnership was found in the grim pair of photographs of two brothers who had lost their lives three days apart that appeared in the *Evening Public Ledger* on September 20.

The saga of the Volpe brothers held another unanticipated twist in its final chapter. On October 5, Angelo Volpe received a postcard from his brother Alfred who, after having been reported missing, then as killed, wrote that he was a prisoner in an undisclosed German camp and getting along as well as could be expected. The card had been routed through Geneva, Switzerland, thus delaying its delivery. On November 20, the most recent list of casualties confirmed that Alfred V. Volpe of Conshohocken, Pennsylvania, previously reported as killed in action, was a prisoner of war. It perhaps also meant that two Volpe brothers would someday soon be operating the Philadelphia Boot Black Supply Company.[8]

While each of these cases carried its own kind of pathos, some of them could be reconstructed in greater detail. Private James (Jerry) Crocco of South Delhi Street in South Philadelphia had worked with his father as a tile setter before being drafted in November 1917 and assigned to the Fourth Infantry Regiment. In his final letter to his parents, dated July 12, 1918, he wrote: "I am too busy killing Germans to write much of a letter. I have set my heart on getting at least 250 before I come back to the good old U.S.A., and if the good work continues that won't take me so very long. I have lost count of those to date, but I have a pretty good idea and anyway I expect to go over the mark that I have set."

But Crocco's plan would not be fulfilled. In action along the Vesle River, separated from his fellow soldiers and surrounded by the enemy, he died in combat on August 1. Another member of his company described Crocco's final moments in a letter to his parents: "Jerry was always in front and over-anxious to get to the Boches. We had a mixup with the Germans and he must have been cut off from the rest of us. We missed him and later we found his body with several Germans lying near. I guess that tells the story better than I could write."9

Such vignettes did not always end tragically. After 19-year-old Samuel Geonotti, of Carpenter Street, of Company B of the 110th Infantry, was reported as missing in action, at Château-Thierry on July 15, his parents had given him up as dead. But information from the American Red Cross and the War Department later revealed that he had been captured and was being held by the Germans in a prisoner of war camp.

By September, messages carried anticipations of the war's end. Private Joseph Di Gregorio, a native of Gessopalena in the Abruzzi, wrote to his parents on Annin Street that the French people idolized the men of the old First and Third Regiments of the Pennsylvania National Guard and that Pershing had promised to send them home first but that the war would probably go on through the next year. After enlisting in June 1917, then being sent to France with Company B, 110th Infantry Regiment of the 28th Division, Di Gregorio had suffered a severe wound to his leg. (His more fortunate younger brother, Dominic, would make seven trips across the Atlantic as a member of a transport crew of the U.S. Navy without being wounded.)

By October, as the great influenza epidemic eased in Philadelphia, its sons continued to face the perils of a far-off war. And on the casualty lists, names that brought grief to its Italian families appeared and even reappeared as the ranks of the dead, wounded, and missing swelled further—Biaselle, Uzzardo, Del Vacco, Fiocca, Bruno, Biondi, Caramanna, Ferranti, Familiare, Thorella, Viola, Gihotte, Volpe, Fiora, Giordano, Malandra, Migliaccio, Rizzo, Giannipietro, Tartaglio, Lucente, Fanelto, Colletta, Rizzi, Cortelli, Nasuti, Pelleschi, Trotta, Acosta, Perry, Cambarto, Scutti, Di Marcio, Ambrosia, Leuzziio, De Stefano, Rieri, Visletti, Constantine, Marcantili, Mammala, Muccigrosso, Grande, Di Tullio, Cugini, Fecca, Franco, Pritta, D'Agostino, Neoselli, Mosero, Mariana, Proffetta, Giannantonio, Trafficante, Salvatore, Di Pietro, Cerrato, Sammartino,

D'Agostino, Capaldi, Coco, Bocalo, Crumasta, Pardini, Zerlo, Carella, Liberto, Matteo, Colio, Costa, and Giampietro—with no less valor than what had been reported before. While still being largely from South Philadelphia, other men came from Kensington, Edge Hill, Conshohocken, Chester, Ambler, Norristown, and Pottsville but also nearby Camden, Vineland, and Bridgeton in New Jersey. They worked as pavers, cement finishers, tailors, and bankers. Many of them had served in the Third Regiment of the NGP before being reassigned to units of the National Army in the summer of 1917. As before, some of them had parents and siblings still in Italy. As the month drew closer to its end with quarantines being lifted and schools and churches announcing that they would begin to reopen with the influenza epidemic finally seeming to be under control, Philadelphia's Italians along with the rest of the city's population resumed normal life. They could also celebrate the advance of Italian troops under General Armando Diaz that was underway in the war where their brothers and cousins were still fighting.

In their letters to family and friends, Italian American soldiers continued to recount combat experiences. Writing to his brother on Gerritt Street, Private Frederick Familiare, who would lose his sight in one eye, along with some teeth, and injure his shoulder, described his harrowing encounter with the enemy: "Well, I suppose that you heard what the American boys did to the Germans. My, but we certainly did give it to those Dutchmen. We handed them a lacing that Berlin will remember for a lifetime or more. I got one boche with my bayonet before a shrapnel shell got me. When I stuck him, he began to yell 'Kamerad, Kamerad,' but who in the world wants a German for a comrade? He will not do any more talking on this earth."

Grim stories with unexpected favorable endings often reached anxious families. Private Angelo Malandra had enlisted in the Pennsylvania National Guard at the age of 17 in August 1917. He was subsequently assigned to Company K of the 110th Infantry of the National Army when it was being organized at Camp Hancock, then sent to France in May 1918. After being wounded in action in August, he wrote to his mother at their home on Wilder Street of his appreciation of a popular song "I Don't Want to Get Well," before adding: "It's like heaven here in the hospital, compared to the hell of the trenches. Ice cream, cake, fruit, cleanliness and quiet. The nurses sure are good to us. I went along fine during the fighting in July and up to the 22nd of August, when a machine gun got me in the ankle at the crossing of the Ourcq. One of the boys picked me up and hustled me to a dressing station. I am rapidly recovering and hope to have another shot at Heinie soon" (the Ourcq is a tributary of the Marne). Although leaving it unclear how serious his wounds were, Malandra's letter, with its praise for the military hospital where he was being treated, reflected the effort of a loving son seeking to allay the apprehension of his worried mother. Although Malandra may have gotten his wish to return to battle, with his name reappearing on the casualty list in another two months, his luck also held out as he survived and returned home at the end of the war.

In contrast to men with families, some Italians who served in France had lived in Philadelphia in ways that reflected the transiency of immigrant workers as well as their lingering ties to Italy. Private Joseph D'Agostino, who had no relatives in the United States but had two brothers serving in the Italian army, had been a boarder at a home in North Philadelphia prior to showing up as a member of Company H, 110th Infantry, reported on an October casualty list as having been wounded in the previous July. The October lists further revealed the ways that wars take lives. Private Sebastiano Uzzardo, who came from Carpenter Street to Company H of the 109th Infantry, would be wounded by machine-gun fire in heavy fighting in the last week of August. Quinto Paradini, of South 9th Street, who had entered military service in March 1918 and trained in the field artillery at Camp Meade, would die in a battlefield accident when a defective safety clip failed on a hand grenade that he was trying to throw and it prematurely exploded.

Private John S. Costa, whose work made him unlike most other men, had been a trader for a banking firm in Philadelphia. After voluntarily enlisting, he was assigned to the 316th Infantry Regiment and sent to France in late June. Costa, in a letter to his mother at home on South 58th Street in West Philadelphia, vividly described his response to being wounded: "At first I thought I was killed, then that I was fatally wounded. It was the shock from the explosion of the shell near me, however, for by the time that I got over being dazed I found that while painful, my wounds were not dangerous." But he assured his mother that he was receiving excellent care and treatment, before adding: "War is sure hell . . . that old general, Sherman, was a wise guy and had the thing sized up in great shape. I won't be sorry when it's all over." Despite shrapnel wounds to his head and leg, Costa wrote that he had "got off easy," before expressing his sorrow for other Philadelphians: "They will never see the City Hall again." His words succinctly revealed the widely shared fear of men facing mortality far from home.

As the war reached its final days, the casualty lists and anecdotes that accompanied them often revealed the character of men on the battlefield. William J. Bandiere, the first son born in America of an immigrant family from Pennapiedmonte in Chieti Province, a member of Company F, of the

Fourth Infantry, gave a matter-of-fact account of his experiences in a letter to an older brother in West Philadelphia: "We are shock troops, and if the others can't start or stop them, then it is up to us." Only 17 when he enlisted in April 1917, Bandiere was wounded twice in two major drives against the enemy a year and a half later. His version of the Marne campaign, in which he casually described his own wounding; the death of friends; the absence of artillery support; the lack of food; and his exhaustion reflected the outlook of a young soldier who had matured quickly under the hardships and misfortunes of war: "Our division turned the trick on the Huns at the Marne. We boys were right in it. I lost a few friends in that gain. I, myself, landed in a base hospital, but I'm feeling great now. We sure did drive the poor Huns back. We went so fast that our artillery could not keep up with us. Prisoners were coming in by the thousands. We just kept after them; in fact, we did not have time to sleep or eat."[10]

By November 1918, with Germany preparing to accept defeat, the casualty lists continued to mount—identifying men who would never return, would come back wounded, were still missing somewhere on a battlefield, or were known to be prisoners of war. But their names reflected more of what had happened in previous months than what was bringing the war to its closing days. And young men who had enjoyed earlier years in Philadelphia remained conspicuously recognizable, however misunderstood and misspelled by military authorities on the rosters of war—Gazzara, Cavallo, Tulli, Fornaci, Rizzo, Checcio, Dominick, Lo Sasso, Gramasta, Antonio, Triboletti, Marabella, Festini, Siravo, Giangreco, Cincotta, Diego, Causerana, Pelliconi, Cavaretta, Biferno, Passanto, Patane, Massetti, Melchiore, Martelli, Pascuallo, Fandasia, Angelucia, Cucinotta, Ventura, Ventrone, Cinco, Pertricino, Phillipi, Martini, Spoto, Cammarata, Di Vito, Picone, Palasone, Cancillera, Dolio, De Santo, Giuffrida, Donofrio, Falacci, Fattinnazi, Spinnalli, Belezza, Di Placido, Loro, Trombetta, Aloi, Cincotta, Bertillini, Antonnucci, Polito, Battista, Pallogruto, Di Pietro, Curato, Jannacone, Tobasco, Tureco, Valerio, Bianchino, Monaco, Donato, Musicante, Marino, Pasquola, Mucci, Catono, Maturo, Volgoni, Di Stefano, Scorza, Donatelli, Sgro, Schiave, Bruno, Moffa, Caposole, Salino, Pinnacchia, D'Aracangelo, Romanelli, Gabriele, D'Aulerio, Sallotti, Juliano, Dessanio, Ricciardelli, Domenico, Porrecca, Petri, Canio, Farracca, Pantalono, Garafolo, Marietta, Stiffanell, Bundy, Pagilla, Carmelo, Rossal, Martino, Vurcio, and Iadevaia.[11]

As in previous months, while many of these casualties had lived in South Philadelphia, they also came from West Philadelphia, North Philadelphia, Tioga, Chestnut Hill, Manayunk, Norristown, Willow Grove, Chester, and Camden. But South Philadelphia again suffered losses of boys from nearby blocks, who had lived "just down the street" from one another before the war. Private Philip Checcio of South Clarion Street had been gassed, while Corporal Joseph Passanto, who had lived one block to the east on the same street, had died of disease, as had Private John Gazzara of nearby Watkins Street. Private Leonard Massetti of Wilder Street had been wounded and so had Private Antonio Pantalono from a few blocks away on the same thoroughfare. Corporal Louis Moffa of Kater Street died of his wounds, while Private Michael Ricciardelli, who had lived only a block away, was missing in action. Private Neil Cusato and Private Charles D. Martino, both of South Juniper Street, had been wounded. And Private Pietro Polito, from the seemingly ill-fated South Hicks Street had been killed in action. Casualties had also revisited Catharine, Carpenter, Ellsworth, Montrose, Annin, Ritner, Clymer, Delhi, Watkins, Tasker, Federal, 7th, 8th, 9th, and 10th Streets where boys once played but now had been remade into avenues of grief. In row houses on tightly packed corridors, immigrant families, still holding powerful folk beliefs of traditional culture, could easily believe as they learned of casualties clustered close by that "la forza del destino" (destiny) was wiping out their entire neighborhood.

In Little Italy West, rooted around the church of their national parish, Saint Donato at 65th and Callowhill Streets, immigrant families similarly feared what the war had done to their young men. Privates Louis Lo Sasso, of North 64th Street, previously reported as wounded, and Dominick Country, of Vine Street, were now prisoners of war in Germany; Private Carlo Triboletti of Callowhill Street and Private Joseph Sgro of North 59th Street had been wounded; Corporal Frank J. Marabella of Callowhill Street was missing in action; Corporal Chester J. Cincotta of North 63rd Street had been gassed; Private Basilio Causerana, who lived with his brother on Vine Street, had died of spinal meningitis; and the recently married Sergeant Michael C. Ventura, of North 64th Street had been killed in action. All of them were "neighborhood boys," but some would never see it again.

Only a year earlier, a prophetic photograph in the *Evening Ledger*, showing Father Pietro Michetti, pastor of Saint Donato's, blessing a group of soldiers who were members of his parish, projected the bond uniting religion and military life. As their priest sought the intervention of a higher power to protect them, he offered the belief and conviction of a just cause while their intent faces reflected the seriousness of a religious ceremony as well as their apprehension to the violence that awaited them. In another year, several of them would be found among the names of the casualty lists. Private Louis Lo Sasso had been severely wounded; Privates Frank Contri, Daniel Celucci, and Antonio Gaudiosi were missing in action. They were now among the men

MEMBERS OF COMPANY L, SIXTH REGIMENT, RECEIVE PRIEST'S BLESSING

The Rev. Pietro Michetti, of St. Donato Church, Sixty-fifth and Callow-hill streets, officiated at holy communion late yesterday for the lads from his church who have enlisted. In the picture are Sergeant William A. Mieles, Sergeant Nicholas Teti, Corporal Frank M. Panichelli, Corporal Frank J. Marabell and Privates Joseph Amorosi, James Bassano, Frank Bonk, Charles Bonner, Dominick Contri, Frank Contri, Dominick Coladonato, Daniel Cellucci, Edward Di Bono, Philip Di Fabio, Joseph Di Donato, Philip Calabrese, Louis Sasso, Antonio Gaudiosi, Jr., Ralph Di Camillo and Mark Sabatino.

FIGURE 11.2 Father Pietro Michetti, pastor of Saint Donato's in West Philadelphia, blesses members of Company L of the Sixth Regiment—Sergeant William A. Mieles, Sergeant Nicholas Teti, Corporal Frank M. Panichelli, Corporal Frank J. Marshall, and Privates Joseph Amorosi, James Bassano, Frank Bonk, Charles Bonner, Dominic Contri, Frank Contri, Dominic Coladonato, Daniel Cellucci, Edward Di Bona, Philip Di Fabio, Joseph Di Donato, Philip Calabrese, Louis Sasso, Antonio Gaudiosi Jr., Ralph Di Camillo, and Mark Sabatino—in July 1917. (*Evening Ledger* [July 31, 1917].)

who were, as their fellow West Philadelphian had put it, unlikely to see city hall again. The fate of the rest of "the lads from his church who had enlisted" remained unknown.[12] (See Figure 11.2.)

The casualties reported in the November lists held a familiar array of occupations—laborers, carpenters, musicians as always, such personal services as barbers and tailors, but also hatmakers and silk workers, occupations for which Italian immigrants had provided so many skillful eyes and hands. It was not only neighborhoods that felt their wounds and deaths but such industrial giants as the Stetson Hat Company, the Reading Railroad, the Midvale Steel Company, and the Victor Talking Machine Company. Several men had worked at the Victor factory in Camden, the largest phonograph producer in the world and the studio where Enrico Caruso had recorded his spirited "Over There," which they themselves would hear and answer.

The letters that men sent home often carried more welcome news. While still depicting details of recent exploits, their words sometimes included what they were anticipating on their return. Corporal Horace L. N. Fornaci, of Company M, 314th Infantry Regiment, severely wounded in heavy fighting west of the Meuse River, revealed his hopes to his Irish American wife whom he had married just before sailing for France:

> I went over the top with my rosary and yours and mother's pictures in that little locket. I have the bullet the doctor took out of my leg as a souvenir, and I am ready for a dance anytime if you were here. Now don't worry about me and continue to pray as I am doing. I am fine; just be patriotic and patient and don't forget to prepare a good Christmas dinner for me when Kaiser Bill salutes Uncle Sam and says, "I am finished." The nurses are certainly nice to the boys, and they often work until late at night to make the soldiers happy. The nurse in our ward is a beautiful singer and entertains us even when she is working.[13]

Not every soldier's ordeal would end as favorably as Fornaci's tale. Corporal Philip Checcio of Clarion Street had first been gassed then returned to the front where he became a victim of shell shock. With great candor, he revealed the gravity of his condition. After being removed from active military duty, he tended a garden in a recuperation facility in Paris. Claiming to be doing well "outside of a bad case of shattered nerves," his self-assessment, beyond raising the question of how well he actually understood his own situation, was a form of suffering that would become only too familiar among veterans of the war.

Many soldiers had suffered as a result of the haste and frequency with which they had been returned to combat. Eager to serve when the war began, Private Joseph Sgro, a 24-year-old barber who lived with his parents on North 59th Street in West Philadelphia, tried to enlist three times but had been rejected because of physical conditions. Finally drafted in April 1918, rushed to France a few months later, and assigned to Company C of the 108th Machine Gun Battalion, he was wounded in early September. After being treated at a first aid station, Sgro returned to the firing line, where he too became shell shocked. And Sgro, like Checcio and others who had survived the ordeal of combat, would be another victim of post-traumatic stress.

For some men, such as Private Joseph A. Salino, the war pursued them even more in what were supposed to have been safer havens away from the battlefield. After being wounded in action near the Marne River, Salino, a member of the 30th Machine Gun Company, was undergoing surgery at the precise moment that a German plane attacked the base hospital, striking the unlucky patient with bomb fragments. A friend wrote to Salino's mother that "he had a remarkable escape from death and is now on the road to recovery."

The letters from the front revealed the costs of the war in many different ways. When a friend wrote of 26-year-old Sergeant Michael C. Ventura, formerly of 408 North 64th Street in West Philadelphia, then of Company D, 314th Infantry Regiment, before being killed in action in late September, he described him as "the best man in the regiment." Perhaps Ventura's young wife already knew that.

Beyond the grief of a young widow, the magnitude of loss for a family could be even greater. In a paroxysm of praise that newspapers make of horrific events in wartime, the *Evening Public Ledger* routinely featured any family that suffered several losses. In November, it focused on the Antonucci brothers, all of Italian birth, who had lived on Master Street in West Philadelphia when called by the draft. Although eligible to ask for exemptions as aliens, the three young men accepted induction and reached France with the great buildup of American troops in July 1918. Three months later, Privates Mattia Antonucci and Joseph Antonucci were missing in action and Private Frank Antonucci had been wounded. While hope remained that the two brothers would be found with the evacuation of prisoner of war camps, the shared suffering only increased pain for their family at home.

Under more ambiguous circumstances, Private Joseph Reitz, of Company H of the 315th Regiment, previously wounded in September, returned to action in the Meuse-Argonne and Aisne-Marne campaigns and died from wounds received in the bitter fighting at Montfaucon on November 6, five days before the Armistice. When he registered on the National Draft Day in June 1917, he listed his residence with his mother and stepfather at Tioga Street and employment as a spinner at Dobson Mills at 8th and Somerset Streets in North Philadelphia. Trained at Camp Meade, he sailed for France in July of the next year. The news of his death (which was not published until March 1919) reported him, as "born in this country of an Italian family." Although unable to bestow an Italian surname on him, his stepfather had evidently inducted Reitz into an Italian household and identity.

Private Frank Mirarchi, who had lived with his mother on Kater Street, provided perhaps the saddest instance among many unfortunate cases. Having migrated from Italy as a 10-year-old child, he attempted to enlist in the army when he was only 17, a year too soon to meet the legal requirement. But his robust physical appearance allowed the recruiting officer to be a bit careless, maybe deliberately so, in inquiring about his age and enabled Mirarchi to join the former Third Regiment of the NGP. At Fort Hancock, he was transferred to the 58th Infantry Regiment, which had been organized at Gettysburg in 1917. His regiment would see action at Aisne-Marne, Saint-Mihiel,

Meuse-Argonne, Champagne, and Lorraine. Having two uncles who served with the Italian army during the war without incurring the slightest injury, the men in Mirarchi's family had seemingly avoided the dangers of war. But the young nephew would prove to be an extraordinarily tragic exception. About an hour before the Armistice ended the war on the Western Front, Private Mirarchi became one of the last casualties of the American armed forces, one of three Philadelphians who died on that day.[14]

Delayed, Uncertain, and Tragic News—and Controversy

With the war winding down, letters often brought comforting news that a son or brother previously reported as missing or dead was recovering in a base hospital. When the *Evening Public Ledger* reported that the families of two local soldiers, after being informed of their deaths, had received mail that indicated they were alive, it carried hope to other families about the fate of their own sons. Military authorities were now also able to begin identifying men who had been in German prisoner of war camps and would soon be released. But a labyrinth of contradictory telegrams, letters from comrades, and other communications often left families uncertain whether someone had been killed, only wounded, or was about to be released from captivity, with the consoling word of one day easily erased by a later message. And families in Philadelphia could only wait as uncertainty unfolded on their doorsteps.[15]

By early December 1918, with the war over, the casualty lists, nearing the end of their usefulness, became a subject of controversy. When Secretary of War Baker was called to testify before the Military Affairs Committee of the U.S. Senate, some members sought to determine why only slightly over 100,000 names had been released when casualties had been officially reported to have reached 262,693. The gap revealed why the lists would continue to reach the press and the public, often with greater numbers than before, in the months ahead.[16]

As the year entered its final month, despite being relegated to back pages, the lists obdurately reflected the tragedy of war. On December 2, the first day of the month for which casualties were reported, the names of another seven Italians from Philadelphia appeared, three as killed in action, one other as wounded, and three more as among the missing. As names climbed, they could be sometimes interspersed by more modest numbers. On December 9, the honor roll contained 26 Philadelphians, with 13 of them being of Italian origin, either killed, wounded, or among the missing. Between December 11 and December 26, the lists ranged from 12 to 23 names of Italian or Italian American men. Accompanying photos and sketches included one, two, or even more men who had appeared on the list of another day. As cases continued to be reported, Christmas of 1918 became indelibly sad for Italian families in Philadelphia.

The profile—the streets and neighborhoods from which the men came; their occupations; and other family details—of the December cases remained similar to preceding months. As before, they had left their tools at tailoring shops, construction sites, railroad yards, cigarette factories, ammunition and weapons plants, and shipyards of the "workshop of the world" and donned the khaki of the American Expeditionary Force. Many of them had gone from work that had been difficult, dirty, and dangerous to an adventure that rendered them wounded, dead on the battlefield or from an accident or disease, or missing in action. They had abandoned challenges of the sidewalks of South Philadelphia or other neighborhoods for the more perilous trenches of the Argonne Forest, the Marne, and Saint-Mihiel. And while some men were Americans by birth, others were immigrants, even aliens, who answered the call to serve in the armed forces of the United States. And although being justly claimed by one deserving regiment, all of these men had earned the right to be called "Philadelphia's Own."

Within the tapestry woven of poignant fibers, the news reaching their families often corrected erroneous reports previously received. The sequel could contain greatly welcomed or the most dreaded of notifications. Soldiers who had been reported as dead were now being discovered as very much alive but recuperating in base hospitals. Other men who had long been counted as missing in action had been found in prisoner of war camps in Germany. Soldiers who had been reported as severely wounded were now known to have suffered only minor injuries.

The unraveling of Italian names by an Anglo-American press corps could still leave confusion before being sorted out. Photos appearing with casualty lists included a tragic trifecta of Privates Anthony De Luca, as wounded; G. L. Ruffo, as missing; and Tony Trico, as died on December 4. But along with the photo listing G. L. Ruffo as missing, the honor roll for the same day, with a slightly changed surname, included Private Giuseppe L. Buffo of Earp Street as among the "Missing." In the more detailed "Sketches of the Heroes" after being introduced as Private Giuseppe L. Buffo, of Company G, 61st Infantry Regiment, he became Private Russo through the rest of the article. But Ruffo, Buffo, or Russo had written, in a letter dated September 22 to his sister, that after taking part in the flattening of the Saint-Mihiel salient he was anxious to get back into the fighting. Nothing further would arrive from him before he was officially reported as missing on October 14. He had left another sister and his parents in Italy, when he came to the United States about eight years earlier, and had worked as a roofer, before being drafted into military service about a year earlier. Whether as Ruffo, Buffo, and Russo, his elusive surname illustrated the challenge of identifying men of foreign origin, even when other details could be found, and obscured the recognition that they had earned.

The misinterpreting of names aggravated the ties of immigrant life to war experiences. On the same day as the prior fiasco, Private Anthony De Luca, was reported, under his photo, as wounded. The accompanying biographical sketch noted that he was enjoying Red Cross programs and other amusements of a nearby town while recuperating, but unaware that his own mother had died, giving their address on Earp Street, near the "Buffo" residence, in error for one of them. De Luca, now 20 years old, had left Italy with his parents five years earlier and worked as a tailor before enlisting. But his case also showed that these men were not necessarily returning to entirely joyful circumstances, without their own sorrows, with the end of the war.

A more complicated transnational life could be sometimes easily told without the ambiguities of elusive names. Private Theofile J. Risso, 24 years old, of Company K, 316th Infantry, a native-born Philadelphian, lived on Spruce Street in West Philadelphia but had been sent for his early education to Italy. After graduating from secondary school, he had returned to Philadelphia in 1915. While working as an electrician at the Hog Island shipyard, he was called into the service, and after about one month in training at Camp Meade sailed for France. During the fighting of early November, Private Risso was killed in action.

The sketches of other men provided further, sometimes fuller, pictures of overseas experiences. Private Joseph Chicano, of Hall Street, another 24-year-old Philadelphian and member of a machine gun company of the 30th Infantry Regiment, was wounded in his right thigh and lost an eye in heavy fighting in July. First being captured, then left for dead, he spent four days and nights with nothing to eat or drink before being recovered by American troops and brought to a base hospital. A later report on Chicano's ordeal added that while lying wounded in a trench, a German officer unsuccessfully attempted to obtain information by pointing a revolver at his chest, before his rescue by American infantrymen. By December, he had returned to the United States and was among some 700 men recuperating at a military hospital in Cape May, New Jersey. In a similar episode, Private Joseph Fiocca, of North 40th Street in West Philadelphia, a member of the 11th Infantry Regiment, while trying to enable two wounded comrades to reach a first aid station, became the victim of a nearby explosion in which shell fragments killed both companions and fractured his spine as well. Fiocca and other Philadelphians would soon be bound for New

York as passengers on the hospital ship *Mercy*. But as Christmas approached, another soldier, Private Vincenzo Perna, would not return with the wounded or healed. A member of Company B, 60th Infantry, missing since mid-October, he had written in his last letter to a sister at their home on West Stella Street in North Philadelphia of his plan to visit their mother as soon as the "big fuss" was over. Perna died in action on the day that he had been first reported as among the missing.[17]

In December 1918, nagged by uncertainty over sons and brothers in uniform, other families faced the added agony of conflicting messages. Marino Venturella, also identified as Marino Venturaglia, was among the many names on the casualty lists of that month. Drafted in October 1917, trained at Camp Meade and later Camp Gordon, and sent to France as a horse wagon driver in the following April, Venturella was reported as wounded and missing. He informed his sister, with whom he lived on Mountain Street in South Philadelphia, in a letter in October 1918, that he was recovering in a hospital. In early December, an official telegram declared him as missing. While protesting that the War Department had made a mistake that would soon be corrected, his family desperately held on to its belief. Italian families were not alone but part of a much wider spectrum. It was Anglo-Saxon; it was Teutonic; it was Slavic; it was Celtic; it was also African American, although mainly hidden, as if black soldiers were not as much a part of it. But they too were there. And it was overwhelmingly Pennsylvanian.

Some Italians provided a colorful, almost theatrical, performance, as they often did in civilian life, such as in the saga of Private John Pessagno, a former chef at the Bellevue Stratford Hotel. The details, provided by a friend who had received the news of Pessagno's fate, stretched the imagination. The Falstaff-like Pessagno (who became "Passagno" in a newspaper account) was five feet, one inch in height and had a waist of 60 inches. He was a 30-year-old native of Genoa who had lived in Philadelphia for several years. After being rejected by several branches of the armed forces including the ambulance corps and deemed physically unfit by the Selective Service, Pessagno had convinced his draft board to send him to physicians who could reconsider his suitability for military service. At Camp Lee, he was able to meet every test and be accepted. Assigned to Company C, 145th Infantry, Pessagno sailed for France in June 1918. When his unit joined Allied forces in Belgium, Pessagno entered combat. During the final week of the war, he took part in an attack against a strong German position from which only a captain and 10 other men returned. Pessagno, who had made a heroic effort to become a soldier, was among the fallen men whose luck had run out.

The "Sketches of the Heroes" often emphasized the special circumstances of citizenship and nationality reflected by service to the United States. Private Pasquale Guida, 25 years old, a resident of South 11th Street, had immigrated to Philadelphia in 1911 and worked as a carpenter before being drafted in September 1917. Having recently received his citizenship papers as a new American before sailing for France, Guida died from pneumonia during the influenza epidemic in early October 1918. Similarly, Private Luigi Aloise, 24 years old, immigrated in 1915 and lived on Girard Avenue in West Philadelphia. Since he had not been naturalized as an American citizen, Aloise was not subject to the Selective Service Act but had not filed a claim for an exemption while working at the ammunition plant at Eddystone; he accepted the call as an inductee in autumn of 1917. After basic training at Camp Meade, he left for France with the 315th Infantry in the summer of 1918. In December, he was reported as having been wounded in the leg on September 25. A couple of days later, the casualty list included Private Lorenzo Rionaldi, who had lived with his sister on West Logan Street in Germantown for about six years before being inducted and becoming a member of Company A, First Infantry. A War Department telegram stated that he had been severely wounded in action on November 7. He was "another native Italian who willingly responded to a draft call and fought side by side with America's own on the battlefields of France." While notices were easily enhanced by hyperbole, they informed readers that Italians, some only recently naturalized, were serving their new country. It was, or should have been, an important piece of information for Americans who feared the immigrant masses.

By late December, corrections of previous casualty lists had become common. Two days before Christmas, Private Antonio A. Angiolillo, of West Manayunk, first reported as killed, had been found to be severely wounded but alive—good news for parents who had persistently held to their belief that he had survived. On the day before Christmas, Mattia Antonucci, earlier listed as missing, was reported as being treated for wounds in a base hospital. He had been acclaimed in a newspaper account with his brothers, one missing and the other wounded, for their dedication only one month earlier.[18]

The corrections became anachronistic as the fog of war continued to lift. On December 24, Private Antonio Cocozza, a 24-year-old member of Company I, 145th Infantry, appeared on the list among the severely wounded. But he had already reached the United States nearly a month earlier for medical treatment at Camp Dix, before returning home on Catharine Street, with much to tell of his recent experiences. Although the first in his company to capture an enemy soldier, he did not receive the reward promised by his captain who would be killed in the same fighting. Cocozza had been in charge of two Germans, and after passing them cigarettes, one prisoner suddenly grabbed and tossed a hand grenade, killing another American, before Cocozza killed the German with his bayonet. Wounded on September 28, the third day of action in the Argonne Forest, when an explosive bullet shattered his arm, Cocozza had gone over the top six times in the Alsace before the final campaign. Hardened by battle, he had become convinced that one month of training in France was equal to six months in the United States.[19]

As 1918 drew to a close, Private Michael Mastropolito, quoted in a vignette alongside a casualty list, probably spoke for most men on what they had shared whether in combat or not. Enlisting in July 1917, he was with the reconstituted Third Regiment of the NGP when it was shipped overseas as part of the regular army 10 months later. Having boxed as a civilian as "Andy Rivers," he would fight in friendly exhibitions in France. But after being severely injured in training near Verdun, he never reached the battlefield. As he recuperated in a hospital, his comrades in Company F, of the 110th Infantry, went into action and only a few survived. Returning to the United States, Mastropolito was sent to a base hospital in Lakewood, New Jersey, in late November. On a 10-day furlough with his family on South 13th Street for Christmas 1918, the fortunate South Philadelphian declared: "Notwithstanding that I am a fighter, I say that war is hell, and I got all of it I need. . . . Home looks mighty good to me."

As Christmas approached with 15,000 soldiers being released each day, and a rate of 30,000 anticipated in the near future, an increasing number of men saw their dream of returning home being fulfilled. Although the War Department had announced that some 824,000 men already in the United States were scheduled for discharge, an increase of over 200,000 over the previous week, they were being "separated" from service rather than fully discharged. The inconclusive process left many families impatient to see their soldier sons and brothers safely return home again. As demobilization continued, the War Department released new casualty lists, with nearly 50,000 more names added during a 10-day interval in mid-December. On the final day of the year, a now familiar story played out when the casualty list identified six more Philadelphia Italians—Privates Harry Coraluzzi of Baynton Street, Panteleone Fulginetti of Kater Street, Pasquale De Carlo of Fernon Street, Gaetano Di Salvo of South Hicks Street, Giuseppe Coroni of Washburn Street, and Giuseppe Paolucci of Manton Street—among the wounded. While a bittersweet year saw the Armistice restore peace, it had also brought immense sorrow for the families of soldiers who would not return.[20]

The list of casualties reported on New Year's Day 1919, with the fewest cases since early summer, encouraged a sense that the worst had finally passed. By the end of the month, while the dwindling lists, with photographs of smiling faces of young soldiers who were dead, wounded, or missing, were no longer being published, news of casualties still reached the public. After migrating from Italy, Private Daniel Lovisi had lived in the household of his sister on Market Street in West Philadelphia before being inducted in the previous April and sent to France in July. In action with Company K, 316th Infantry, he was wounded by machine-gun fire in early September before returning to the front where he was struck a second time two months later. Naturalized as an American citizen during his military service, his two brothers had answered the call of Italy's army. The conjunction of immigration and war that separated brothers by distance and military experience, unprecedented in history, had become common for Italian families.

On January 7, the reduced report of casualties did not lessen the tragedy for the family of Nicola Pelliociotta, 28 years old, of Carpenter Street, who died from wounds received in battle. He had left employment with the National Biscuit Company to enlist in the army. After training at Camp Greene, he went to France with the advance guard of the American Expeditionary Force. As she received news of his death, his mother collapsed with the grief that had become too familiar for her. She had now lost her third son to the war. Two other sons, members of the Italian army, had previously died on that front, and another one had been captured in "the big drive that almost put the Italians out of the war." Few families had to carry the heavy burden that fell upon the Pelliociottas— from the Isonzo to the Marne, from Caporetto to the Argonne Forest—with now their third son who would "give his life in the cause of freedom."[21]

Nearly two months after the end of war, the Iannelli family of South Juniper Street remained uncertain about the fate of their son. Private Michael Iannelli, a 25-year-old native of Alberona in the province of Foggia, employed as a hatmaker at the John B. Stetson Company, had been inducted in July 1918 before being sent almost immediately overseas. On the day after Christmas, the War Department informed his parents that their son had died of wounds received in action. When his name appeared in the casualty list published on January 3, his distraught parents held on to the hope that it was a matter of mistaken identity, as other cases that had been reported. His mother pointed out that his name had been misspelled and the home address was incorrect. In his last two letters, dated December 9 and December 12, which had arrived a day or so before Christmas, he had written not only that he was well and having a fine time but that he expected to be home shortly after the new year began, without mentioning any wounds. On January 4, a photo in the *Evening Public Ledger* with a caption declaring him to be dead seemingly confirmed the official report. Subsequent events would show not only that the information had been erroneous but that a mother's intuition had been correct.[22]

Decorated Heroes of the War

As "Sketches of the Heroes" faded as a regular feature, Philadelphia's Italians could be found in other articles that depicted heroic deeds. On January 20, when the *Evening Public Ledger* acknowledged 20 soldiers who had received various military honors, Private Giuseppe Spadafora was listed as the recipient of the Distinguished Service Cross, the second highest decoration given by the U.S. Army. He was born on October 26, 1890, and as a young man left both his mother and his wife, Rosalia, in the town of Maletto, at the foot of Mount Etna in the Sicilian province of Catania, and migrated as a farm laborer on the steamer *Stampalia*, which arrived at the port of New York in early December 1913. He had given the name of a cousin in North Philadelphia who would be awaiting him in his new location. He was in good health, at five feet, three inches tall, the same height for each of the 30 newcomers recorded on his page of the ship passenger list by an indifferent official at Ellis Island. Spadafora also bore a visible scar on his left cheek. But in November 1917, his life changed even more with his induction to the U.S. Army, followed by training at Camp Meade and deployment to France, where heroism came almost immediately as the 79th Division entered combat. His citation formally read "for extraordinary heroism in action while serving with Headquarters Company, 315th Infantry Regiment, 79th Division, A.E.F., near Montfaucon, France, 29 September 1918. Private Spadafora was helping remove wounded men from a dressing station to a place of greater safety, when an enemy bombardment began. He forced four German prisoners to assist him and repeatedly entered the heavily shelled area, bringing out wounded men." After returning home, he would find a more peaceful life. When he registered for another draft as World War II began, Spadafora listed his residence at West Harold Street in North Philadelphia; his height as five feet, nine inches tall, a more likely measure than the ship passenger list had given; his weight as 254 pounds; and that he still bore a scar on his cheek. A millwright at the Budd Manufacturing plant, he could only place an "X" for his signature. At his death in April 1965, probably few mourners at Saint Mary of the Eternal Church and Holy Sepulchre Cemetery were aware that they were bidding farewell to a hero of the Great War.[23]

Spadafora was not the only Philadelphia Italian to earn the Distinguished Service Cross. Three days before Spadafora's heroic actions, Private Giacomo Masciarelli performed his own act of valor. Born on March 31, 1891, in Roccascalegna in the Chieti Province of the Abruzzi, he had arrived at the port of Philadelphia on the *Taormina* in late July 1910. He was a laborer residing at an address on Frankford Avenue when he filed his declaration of intention to become a citizen in December 1915. By the time that he registered for the draft in June 1917, Masciarelli had become a plumber's assistant with the United Gas Improvement Company, the main provider of heat for city homes and businesses. Of medium build at five feet, six inches tall, with brown eyes and black hair, and still unmarried, the athletic Masciarelli shipped to France, where he competed as a swimmer in friendly events against other units. But his greatest accomplishment came on the field of battle when he "displayed extraordinary heroism in action while serving with Company L, 315th Infantry Regiment, 79th Division, A.E.F., near Malancourt, France, 26 September 1918." In the words of his award, he "alone charged a machine-gun nest, which was holding up the advance of his platoon. With a flanking fire, he killed one member of the crew and caused the rest to surrender. His prisoners consisted of one noncommissioned officer and seven privates." In late May 1919, when Masciarelli returned with 1,631 other men, including 400 members of the 315th, on the transport ship *Dakotan*, and was enthusiastically greeted as "Philadelphia's Own," he sought to put aside his own experience. With his decoration tucked away in a pocket, Masciarelli denied that he had done anything deserving of special recognition, but a fellow soldier would relate his dramatic story to awaiting reporters. Despite being a hero, he remained an alien; after he submitted his petition for naturalization on June 5, exactly two years after his draft registration, he received final approval enabling him to become a citizen two months later.[24]

In the final days of the war, two other Italian-born Philadelphians earned the Distinguished Service Cross for their conduct under fire. Although little else is known about him, Private Joseph Falacchi, born on November 26, 1888, had lived on South 10th Street in South Philadelphia. But what more is known deserves remembering. On November 5, 1918, Falacchi and two other men of Company C, 316th Infantry Regiment, 79th Division, occupied a small shell hole on Hill 378 of the front line near Verdun, with a detachment of another 15 men in a crater a few yards to their right. After about 60 Germans crept through the lines on the foggy morning, outflanked the Americans in the larger shell hole, disarmed them, and ordered them to stand fast, Falacchi with his companions opened fire, killing six of the enemy, routing

188 | CHAPTER 11

the others, and rescuing his comrades. His extraordinary action would not be formally recognized until he received his Distinguished Service Cross in January 1929. Quietly living out the rest of his life until his death at the age of 75, Falacchi was buried with military honors at the Beverly National Cemetery in New Jersey in June 1964.[25]

Private Americo Di Pasquale, of North Taney Street in North Philadelphia, posthumously received the Distinguished Service Cross for his actions on the last day of the war. Born on October 15, 1893, he had arrived as a 16-year-old immigrant on the *Celtic* at the port of New York in April 1910. Seven years later, he stood only five feet, four inches tall, weighed 140 pounds, and worked as a machinist at Midvale Steel when he registered for the draft on June 5, 1917. In another year, as a member of Company G, 315th Infantry Regiment, 79th Division, Di Pasquale was well suited for the task for which he would be awarded a medal but lose his life. Volunteering to cross fields under artillery shell and machine-gun barrage, he had maintained contact between units before being struck by enemy fire. The official history of the 79th Division, noting that the final hours of fighting had been costly, listed him among the men who died in action or from wounds received on the day of the Armistice. His citation gave the name of his father in the town of Introdacqua in the province of L'Aquila in the Abruzzi as his next of kin, indicating that he had been without any other family member in Philadelphia. But the record also identified Miss Ruth Mary Shaw as a "friend" at an "emergency address" not far from where he lived, suggesting that she was more than just a "friend." And in his petition for naturalization in June 1918, just before his deployment to France, he asked that his remarkably emblematic name be changed to "Harry Patty," revealing a desire to be more American than citizenship alone would confer. Such details, even a century later, sketch a life filled with aspirations that would end not happily in Philadelphia but in death on the final day of the war and in burial at the Meuse-Argonne American Cemetery in Romagne, France.[26]

Private Antonio Aiello of Company A, Fourth Machine Gun Battalion, Second Division, was the first Italian-born Philadelphian to earn the Distinguished Service Cross. His citation revealed that near Vierzy, France, on July 19, 1918, he "left the safety of the trench, advanced nearly a hundred yards in the open under heavy artillery fire, and carried back to safety a severely wounded marine." Although one source states that he lived on Dipon Street at the time of his enlistment, there is no such street in Philadelphia. Little else is known about Antonio Aiello, who was indistinguishable from several immigrants with the same name. But only one of them, who served from May 23,

1917, to May 15, 1919, lies buried, as Anthony Aiello, in Arlington National Cemetery, perhaps, in some sense, as the unknown soldier of Little Italy.[27]

The bravery exemplified by these men is difficult to adequately capture. The stilted wording of official citations falls short of their actions. Along with those mentioned from Philadelphia, Private Joseph T. Angelo, also won the Distinguished Service Cross. He was a resident of Camden, New Jersey, the nearby city that even though it lies in a different state is close enough, directly across on the banks of the Delaware River, to almost be another neighborhood of Philadelphia. In action near Cheppy, France, on September 18, 1918, Private Angelo rescued his commanding officer, of Headquarters Company, First Brigade of the Tank Corps, by running under heavy fire within 40 meters of German guns and then carrying the wounded officer to a shell hole where they stayed for more than an hour, except to come out twice to give orders himself, until being rescued. Eloquent words, attributed to Pershing, perhaps came close to suggesting what such courage implied:

> When Napoleon found a brave man he acclaimed him a hero and placed on his breast a medal. The man was a hero and the envy of his companions. Today a voice greater than that speaks to me from 3000 miles away, the mighty voices of 100,000,000 people peal forth their share of victory, carrying shrill music to our souls of the extraordinary brave of action for the end of time. Your name is written on the pages of history, for you have faced death and been not afraid.
>
> Be brave and cool in peace as you have been in war, and remember thousands have slaved to support you before the enemy, and thousands have died and never received the reward that you now receive. I thank you.[28]

While wary of the hagiographic accounts provided with citations for medal winners, such testimony can be neither entirely ignored nor easily dismissed. The criteria invoked in awarding such honors were stringent, but the information serves only as a starting point in searching for greater detail about these men and their encounters on the battlefield as well as their lives away from it. And if the heroism of these remembered men—Spadafora, Masciarelli, Falacchi, Di Pasquale, Aiello, and Angelo—cannot be denied, the record of hundreds, perhaps thousands of more anonymous immigrant soldiers who did not receive honorific recognition should not be forgotten.

But some of them were. Esterino Angelo Crudele, born in Isernia in 1888, had migrated to the United States at the age of 17 in March 1906. By the time of his registration on National Draft Day in June 1917, as an unmarried printer living on Wharton Street and the sole support of his mother (still in Italy), he had filed his declaration of intention to be naturalized as a citizen. Drafted into the U.S. Army in October, Crudele, along with other Italians of the 315th Infantry Regiment, swore their allegiance as new Americans in the following month in ceremonies at Camp Meade. In June 1918, visiting on furlough to Philadelphia, he enthusiastically spoke of military life and informed friends of his imminent departure, possibly for Italy, with the 315th Infantry Regiment. In July, the recently promoted corporal Crudele left with his regiment, believed to be made up almost entirely of Italians, for Europe, with Italy expected by some of them to be their likely destination. But far more diversely composed and not destined for their homelands, many of the newly minted "Americans" of the 315th Infantry, as well other men, deployed to the Western Front would lose their lives in the costly struggle ahead. Crudele would be among them.[29]

On September 26, Crudele, with his fellow soldiers of Company A along with the rest of the regiment, went "over the top," advancing into "no man's land." The official history of the regiment describes what awaited them in the action at Montfaucon and Nantillois: "That night we dug in on Hill 274, and as the rain poured down on us, so did the shells of the Boche. The night of September 28, 1918, can never be erased from the minds of the men who were there; words can never describe it, nor is the mind imaginative enough to conceive it. On September 29, 1918, at daybreak we attacked the woods for the third time but met with no better success, as nothing living could face the German machine gun fire or hide from the German artillery." On the next day, as Company A, relieved by replacement troops, sought a safer position under heavy enemy fire, Crudele was severely wounded. After nearly a month of medical treatment, he died on October 27.[30]

Unlike most casualties, his death would go unnoticed by local newspapers, until *La Libera Parola*, under a moving banner, "La Morte Di Un Eroe," belatedly reported that Esterino Crudele, a much-liked member of the Sons of Italy, fighting with the American army, had lost his life in action in France. A later article, describing him as a young man of mild manner and good spirit, noted that he had left a large number of grieving relatives and friends, in both Isernia and Philadelphia. His body would be returned, along with about 46,000 other fallen members of the American Expeditionary Force, for burial. At his gravesite at Holy Cross Cemetery in Yeadon, Pennsylvania, an inscription, still visible a century later, reads: "Corp Co A 315th Inf 79th Div Killed In Action Argonne Forest." While later records show the Esterino Crudele VFW Post 3094 as being located on Passyunk Avenue in South Philadelphia, it has now disappeared, if it ever existed. Although almost entirely forgotten in Philadelphia, he would be remembered elsewhere. Crudele's name, along with those of his boyhood friends who had lost their lives on the Piave and Isonzo, can be found inscribed in the memorial columns of the Park of Remembrance of Isernia, his place of birth, in mute testimony to another immigrant who brought honor to Italy while serving in the army of the United States.[31]

Waging War on the Home Front

Women, Children, and Others

Throughout the course of the war, another kind of effort, far away from the battlefields of the Marne or the Isonzo, was being waged in Philadelphia and other American cities. On the home front, a complex, sometimes overlapping campaign entailed protecting the nation against espionage and sabotage by enemy agents, raising funds to finance the war, staging public events to promote patriotism and unity, and providing aid for domestic and overseas victims of the war. When Italy entered the war in 1915, Little Italy became a home front two years before other communities of the United States did. It would evolve from a setting of apprehension, then to mobilization of its men summoned to war, and finally to a network of agencies of civilian support. As the rest of America joined in similar efforts, the service of women should not be overlooked. A misguided perception of their role in immigrant life tends to find them only as homemakers within the family and household and to depict them as nurturers of "needy" men, but it omits them from the larger narrative of the war. It is a seriously flawed vision. While they would not carry weapons or face the enemy on the battlefield, immigrant women and their American-born daughters shared in the ordeal and offered their own contributions but remain a neglected dimension of the full story of the home front.

Women from Italy—Women in Italy

Several factors not only encouraged but shaped the role of Philadelphia's Italian women in their support of the war effort. First, the personal accounts and experiences of distinguished visitors from Italy provided models of inspiration and conduct. Despite an intended audience of middle- and upper-class women of more fully American backgrounds, their message also reached Italian women, whatever their social rank, within the local population. In June 1918, Countess Lisi Cipriani, a Tuscan native who had earned a Ph.D. at the University of Chicago, declared that women in Italy had heroically taken their place "side by side with the men," particularly in munitions factories, where they could be found partly or wholly operating every department. Anticipating what her listeners hoped to hear, she added that such service guaranteed the granting of the right to vote at the end of the war. In October, another writer of mixed Tuscan and American ancestry, Amy Bernardy, after three years as the only woman ever officially appointed as an observer at the front, and now an attaché of the Italian government, claimed before an eager audience that Austrian forces with bombing attacks deliberately targeting schools and hospitals had committed atrocities against civilians and children in Italy. And even after the war had ended, Countess Maria Loschi, a journalist from Rome who had served as a nurse at the front, reiterated the "bonus" message that the spirit of Italian women had been so great as to make it very likely that their service would produce more civil and property rights than they had ever known before. While such informants as Cipriani, Bernardy, and Loschi had not come as impartial witnesses but as propaganda agents for the Italian government, they had brought an undeniably compelling message to Philadelphia's women.[1]

Along with the testimony of elegant and articulate visitors, local newspapers also described the efforts of Italy's women. In the early days of the war in June 1915, women volunteered to operate the tramway cars of Rome, thus freeing men for service at the front. In the next year, some of them, who had been made widows or penniless by the war "in which their loved ones have been fighting," were said to be using yarn sent by Philadelphia women to knit socks and mittens for troops at the front, under the supervision of Mrs. Page, wife of the American envoy in Rome. In July, Ambassador Page himself claimed that "social life" had ceased in the Eternal City and the rest of the nation as Italian women devoted themselves entirely to the task of aiding their soldiers and relieving the needs of military and civilian victims of the war. At another level of social class and lifestyle, by June 1917, Italy's War Department reported the hiring of more than 72,000 women, with many of them working in munitions factories, along with several thousand others digging trenches along the Austrian front. The Department of Railroads and Transportation, meanwhile, announced the hiring of 500 women as clerks and 9,300 women as cleaners or gatekeepers on the rail lines. And with the war approaching a decisive moment, a special cable brought news of Arditi forces in counterattacks, while Italian women, ignoring heavy bombardment overhead, cheerfully sang in nearby fields in their attempt to sustain military morale. But events in Italy easily resonated with what lay ahead for women in other places. A local writer, after surveying what had been transpiring in various nations, asked, "Will women—American women, English women, Italians and French ones—return to their homes when peace comes?" The anonymous journalist's emphatic answer was: "Europe, after three years and a half of watching war, says no." It also was a message with immediate meaning for Philadelphia's Italian women.[2]

The increasing use of photographic images, portraying the war by vivid scenes of women and girls mobilized into war-related activities, with special meaning for their counterparts overseas, appeared in newspapers in Philadelphia and elsewhere in America. In an early scene of the home front, a group of smiling Italian Girl Scouts is shown seeking a contribution from a similarly amused soldier in Rome. In a full-page picture, in the *Day Book,* a Chicago newspaper published by the Scripps syndicate, under a heading announcing "Women of Italy Get Ready for War!" a female instructor teaches the "art of warfare," or how to handle rifles and shoot straight, to other women at the artillery grounds at Milan so that they can defend their homes from enemy attack. A photograph in a Washington, DC, newspaper depicts the meaning of "German kultur," by showing Italian women, allegedly captured in the previous year, digging trenches for the defense of Austrian troops. Another picture in the same newspaper shows Italian women and children getting their first look at British reinforcements marching toward engagement against the enemy in Italy "where they are so sorely needed." An image in the *New York Tribune* portrays Italian women digging trenches for the defense of their own troops at an unspecified area of the front. And in Philadelphia's *Evening Public Ledger,* yet another photograph presents Italian women, with faces and garb not much different from counterparts in immigrant colonies across America, pausing at their laborious task of preparing trenches behind the battle line, with an inappropriately jocular caption declaring: "Now they're digging trenches, those women, and we men scarcely know what to look for next . . . but to all appearances they seem to be making a good job of it." While the smiling expressions of women engaged in ostensibly war-related tasks might betray such photographs as not being authentic scenes but contrived devices of propaganda, readers in America remained likely to find some empathy for their sisters in distant places.[3]

Women at Work

In Philadelphia and other American cities, Italian women, almost from the beginning of the war, would join, as they had in their native land, in the effort to produce materials for the troops at the front. Long before President Wilson and the U.S. Congress committed the nation to the conflict, business leaders recognized the prospects for commercial profit by providing the means by which the armies of other lands could destroy one another. By October 1915, under the lure of orders reportedly reaching as high as $30,000,000 showered upon local manufacturers by agents of the Allies, the hiring of an army of factory hands, which included men, women, and children, producing arms and ammunition had already transformed Bridgeport, Connecticut, from a city engaged in "peaceful arts and industries" to "a zealous and energetic handservant of Mars." In place of corsets, sewing machines, baby carriages, phonographs, and typewriters, they now rushed to fill orders for shells and cartridge cases, machine guns, rifles, and other small arms. At employment bureaus to which job seekers flocked from other parts of the country, efforts were being made to weed out applicants of German, Austrian, and Hungarian origins, with preferences given to workers with backgrounds in neutral or Allied countries. The colorful description of what was happening in Bridgeport, which could be compared in the volume of its industrial production to Essen, Germany, was not unique but provided a template that soon easily applied to cities elsewhere in the United States. It also delivered an unprecedented spectrum of opportunities for women.[4]

While employment records of local industries for these years are not widely accessible, sporadic events showed the presence of women in new areas of work. Glimpses of Italian women employed in war-related industries can be found throughout the war, but such opportunities often held their own risks, which could easily turn tragic. When an explosion devastated the Eddystone Ammunition factory, a subsidiary of the Baldwin Locomotive Company, on the banks of the Delaware River, only four days after the United States entered the war in early April 1917, Italian men and women were listed among the dead and injured. Among workers in critical condition at the local armory, one victim could be described only as "an unidentified Italian woman." With remains mutilated beyond recognition, some 55 unidentified bodies would be buried in a mass grave in the nearby Chester Rural Cemetery. After it was first feared to have been the result of enemy sabotage, later investigation found that the explosion was an industrial accident, but the victims, including many who commuted daily from Philadelphia, could be widely regarded as the first civilian martyrs of the war.[5]

By August, it was apparent that the opening of employment to women did not provide enough workers to meet the demand of a wartime economy. While an official of the Women's Division for National Preparedness maintained that, against an oversupply in previous years, women had begun not only to take the place of men but to command similar wages as men since the war had started, the needs of labor in local industries had grown so great that efforts were being taken to recruit workers from other states. But New Jersey and other nearby places, which faced similar shortages in their own factories, were unable to provide much assistance. With the failure to find adequately prepared workers, at least one trade school, where girls and women could be trained for gainful employment, had been established in North Philadelphia. Such conditions provided opportunities to all women—whether native-born Americans, the foreign born, or the daughters of immigrant parents.[6]

The diligence demonstrated by Italian women and girls, along with their willingness to work in unwholesome conditions, as their men long had, confirmed their usefulness as workers in agriculture and industry. But along with the sacrifices entailed, such work also provided opportunities for increased personal gain. As fruit pickers in blueberry fields, the "more expert Italian women," long a staple presence in farming areas of Pennsylvania and New Jersey, paid at a rate of $0.06 a quart, could earn as much as $5.00 a day in the summer months of 1917. Even more noteworthy, in another year, the Budd Manufacturing Company, a major producer of metal parts for automobiles and other vehicles, would express a preference for Polish and Italian women in a newspaper ad seeking workers "able to do heavy work" at its factory in North Philadelphia.[7]

From ragpicker to field-worker and factory laborer; from store clerk and office assistant, earners of modest wages, to the doyens of a more affluent and leisure class, the women of Philadelphia's Little Italy comprised a far more diversely stratified—and assimilated—population than what might be expected by the cruder vision of outside observers. And for Italian woman at the more privileged level of their own hierarchy, their activities in support of Italian and American efforts reflected the system of economic and social class differences that had arisen among them, while simultaneously serving to further affirm and validate it. Yet, outside of that population, despite a great sensitivity to the needs of Italy at war, whether to armies at the front or families left behind, on the part of wealthy and prominent "American" women, those programs, efforts, and activities almost always excluded any representation or participation by Italian women. While exclusion also provided some incentive, initiative, and an organizational model that could be emulated within the immigrant colony, such undertakings only occasionally crossed over from one community to the other.

Women without Men

In some sense, the contribution of Italian women to the war effort, along with their anguish, began when they stood on the docks as their men boarded ships as reservists answering the call issued by the Italian government. But newspaper accounts greatly differed in what they saw and described. When the *Ancona* departed in March 1915, a writer for *The Inquirer* reported that "into the eyes of the women came tears which could not be brushed away." At a similar scene in June, an *Evening Ledger* reporter wrote: "There were no weeping women, no sorrowful faces. The sunny-browed young men who sailed laughed because they were happy to be on their way to service for their Italia." A few days later, *The Inquirer*, at the sailing of the *Canopic* of the White Star line, described an almost identical scene in which, despite the tears of some men leaving wives, mothers, sweethearts, children, and friends, most of them appeared to be happy at the expectation of bearing arms for their mother country. In what may have been the most pathetic vignette, as another contingent boarded the *Ancona* in July, although many "assumed an air of bravado," the reservists who sensed the seriousness of the situation included a father, surrounded by his five children, who broke down completely and had to be "assisted" up the gangplank. As such scenes were repeated at subsequent departures, while men feared what awaited them on the battlefield, women harbored great apprehensions at the prospect of life without men. And in August, if it remained less visible to any reader, *The Inquirer* emphatically added in a subheading, "As men depart hundreds of women and children lose their means of support."[8]

Within the context of the departure of reservists for Italy, the reaction of women, being left behind to wait out the war within the confines of an immigrant colony, had assumed an even broader dimension. They undoubtedly would have preferred that their husbands and sons stay with them over any patriotic sentiment for Italy's cause, even if they became more stoic as they recognized the inevitability of obligation. If the departure of reservists carried significance, the response of women on the docks must not be overlooked—for their sentiments contained not only their uncertainty over what the future held for them but an unprecedented shift in immigration history. Their lives were changing. Beyond the immediate pain of separation from a loved one, they had to fear the long-term possibility of poverty and isolation. Italian women sensed that they would have to find new roles with the absence of their husbands. Reversing a pattern of men without women that had long-characterized immigration, the war had created precisely the opposite circumstance.

The anguish suffered by women, abandoned by men taken away by the call to arms, however, would range from the seriocomic to genuinely tragic. While newspaper coverage focused on the latter aspects of war, an occasional item offered a glimpse of another facet of separation, grievous enough for whom it directly touched but amusing for less involved readers. In August 1918, a young woman asked the advice columnist of the *Evening Public Ledger* for help in finding her boyfriend:

> I am in love with a young man who is now in the Italian army and I haven't heard from him for five months. He left one year ago to fight for our native home, and as I know the Americans are always kind to those in their country I am sure you will help me. I haven't his address, as I lost it some time ago, and maybe he's angry that I have not answered his letter; but I cannot write, as I do not know where to write. I know you will help me. Tell me where I could find it. I know his name, but that is all, as he has no friends left in America.

As with the letters of "Bob" from Camp Meade, the authenticity of the case can be questioned, but its possibility cannot be dismissed. Whether as ruse or actuality, Juliet's search for Romeo suggested that absent soldiers created various kinds of sorrow for those left behind on the home front.[9]

If any doubt existed on the gravity of separation, it would be sadly confirmed by the tragic saga in November 1917 of Angelina Miele Bertolino, a 16-year-old wife who attempted suicide because life without her recently drafted husband, Frank Bertolino, had become worse than death. A newspaper compassionately commented that if Angelina had been born into another environment, she might have sold Liberty Bonds, made brave speeches, marched in patriotic parades, and been able to declare, "I give my man to his country." But while Angelina knew little about patriotism, she harbored a profound love for her husband. Two weeks after his departure for Camp Meade, the distraught wife reached the breaking point at their home on Washington Avenue. When she did not appear for breakfast, her brother-in-law went looking and found her unconscious in a bedroom, along with a half-emptied bottle of pills. At a nearby hospital, while the early prognosis was that she would survive, no further record can be found of her in later years. But in one of the many vicissitudes of the war, Frank Bertolino, a pianist at Verdi Hall on Christian Street when he was drafted, would return from the war, eventually remarry, and work as an organist and hotel musician before his death in 1952.[10]

Women in War Relief Efforts

With Italy's declaration of war, as public attention turned to local initiatives to provide relief to needy families, Italian women, bringing their own enthusiasm and energy, were finding new but still limited opportunities in civic life. In May 1915, under the aegis of the War Relief Fund, a committee of Italians, with headquarters on South 10th Street, claiming to have already collected $3,000 of its goal of $50,000, called for a mass meeting at the Musical Fund Hall. Not to be outdone in concern, the Sons of Italy announced plans to raise $100,000 for a similar purpose. With C.C.A. Baldi at its helm, the Italian Federation, a coalition of organizations, declared its intention to provide an aid program. In early June, 18 teams, each composed of five young men and five young women, began selling flags on Philadelphia streets on "Italian Flag Day," seeking to raise $25,000 to be sent to the pope for distribution among families in Italy. A few days later, a more elaborate plan, with more than 200 Italian girls seeking contributions, anticipated even greater results. Within a couple of weeks, about $3,000 was reported to have been collected, but much more was expected to be raised when the dire need of local families became better known. In the same month, marchers bearing Italian and American banners followed the Gaetano Roselli band to Lyric Hall at 6th and Christian Streets for a program sponsored by the Italian Federation. With Baldi, E. V. Nardi, Poccardi, and other community leaders in attendance, participants were provided a special supper of "the principal dish . . . the traditional spaghetti" and entertained by Ferruccio Giannini, the popular local tenor, singing his own composition, "A Trento e Trieste." In October, Baldi and other leaders would replace the annual Columbus Day parade with a mass meeting to announce a new plan "to raise funds for the suffering Italians across the sea and to relieve distress here." All funds previously collected for a proposed hospital and a school for instruction of English would be diverted to war relief. By their participation, Italian wives and mothers, abandoning kitchen and other domestic fetters, were gradually embracing obligations that presaged even greater transformation for themselves as well as for other women in the future.[11]

Alongside efforts within the immigrant community, Philadelphians of loftier backgrounds also responded to Italy's need. But despite sharing similar objectives, the two campaigns would exist in parallel universes, generally remaining separate from one another. Since its founding in late October 1914, the Emergency Aid Committee, often identified in press coverage as "an organization of society women," had mounted a campaign to provide assistance to sufferers of the war in Europe. In newspaper accounts of its work, the names of "proper Philadelphians"—Wanamaker, Cassatt, Biddle, Lippincott, and others—conspicuously appeared. Although events sometimes seemed to be more a "social" happening with lists of "prominent persons present" being published in local newspapers, the effort energetically raised money and supplies for overseas distribution and supported the work of the American Red Cross in Europe. Reacting initially to the needs of Belgium, the Emergency Aid Committee, after establishing a Home Relief Section in December, turned its attention to the distress and destitution of local residents who were "indirect victims of the war." In March 1915, it delineated a new district, which included in particular the "Italian section" of the city, for the relief of poor families in the foreign quarter. A few weeks later, in April, it enabled the Martella family, husband and wife and their seven children, evicted by a constable from their home on South Mole Street over a $42 rental debt, to find housing, clothing, furniture, and "other accessories that made life bearable" at another location. By May, however, Emergency Aid announced that suspension of the work of its Home Relief Section had become necessary, although it would continue to devote itself to war relief in Europe.[12]

Despite a nearly ceaseless agenda of bridge parties, lectures, films, concerts, auctions, luncheons, teas, and receptions for celebrated visitors, to which the press accorded lavish attention, Emergency Aid, through its pretentiously labeled *Comitato pro Italia*, gathered comparatively little money to alleviate suffering in Italy. In July 1917, published figures showed that of the $2,000,000 that Emergency Aid had raised for home and foreign relief, its Italian committee had collected a modest total of slightly more than $33,000, which paled into insignificance alongside more than $300,000 intended for Belgium and $580,000 for France. But material deficit was further aggravated by the exclusivity of human capital. In the final year of the war, the Emergency Aid Committee, adopting the slogan "Italians to the aid of Italy," attempted to organize 25 younger Italian-born men as volunteers, working three hours in weekly sessions, to make and prepare bandages, pillows, and other medical supplies to be shipped to hospitals in the battle zone. While providing Italian youths with "an opportunity for patriotic service," it relieved members of Emergency Aid of "a great deal of arduous labor." In a somewhat patronizing manner, the director of the program declared: "If more Italian young men care to join us, we shall welcome them, for there is much to be done and this offers an excellent opportunity for patriotic service of Italian-Americans to their brother Italians, our allies in arms." But while capable of occasionally introducing an innovative initiative, Emergency Aid, ignoring a more obvious pool of potential volunteers, did not enlist women from the Italian community within its ranks. And while repeatedly claiming to be the only committee on the East Coast that was working for the relief of Italy and seeking to gather and send clothing and medical supplies to troops at the Italian front, the Italian War Relief Committee (IWRC) remained far more concerned with bombing threats to the artistic patrimony of Venice than to needy residents of Philadelphia's Italian neighborhoods. With the founders and members of Emergency Aid drawn from upper-class families and their attention turned entirely to relief efforts in Europe, and with boundaries that excluded the participation of women with foreign backgrounds, if Italians were to find assistance for women and children left behind by the departure of reservists for service in the Italian army and later as doughboys in the American army, they would learn during the course of the war that they had to do it themselves.[13]

Within the immigrant community, the *Official* Italian War Relief Committee, as another effort identified itself, after more than $5,000 of a sought-after goal of $100,000 was collected in June, initially carried the promise of success, before wading into the controversy brought about by City Solicitor Michael J. Ryan's recommendation to arrest departing reservists for abandoning their families. The answer had provoked angry responses within the Italian colony. Against the contention that enforcement applied to reservists of all belligerent nations, residents of Little Italy, stirred by what they regarded as discrimination directed against them alone, asked, "Why single out Italians?" But Ryan, insisting that it would be legal to arrest men as "deserters" unless they provided assurance that their departure would not lead to their families becoming public charges, urged that the matter be taken up by the district attorney whose office had jurisdiction in such matters.[14]

Recognizing that it would affect their own people more than any other group, community leaders met to support the Italian Federation for Relief in an effort to raise funds that would enable families to avoid becoming dependent upon public assistance. C.C.A. Baldi, promising that responsible businessmen in the colony would provide a monetary bond if necessary, expressed his belief that local Italians would gladly support needy families of reservists. Insisting that the situation had been anticipated, he declared that the plan for assistance would now have to be even more quickly implemented. But Carlo D. Nardi (now identified as Charles D. Nardi), editor of *L'Opinione*, suggested that reservists could take their families back to Italy, claiming that many already had, while those families who chose to remain would be well cared for. Going almost unnoticed, however, was that the proposed relief scheme asked the community, despite its meager resources, to indirectly help finance the war itself.

Meanwhile, Baldi and other community leaders argued that Italian reservists, except for one unhappy husband seeking to divorce his wife, were not abandoning their families but bringing them back to Italy, where the government provided support while men were at the front and pensions in the event of their death. But if any cases of destitution did exist, they would be taken care of by the Federation of Italian Societies. Baldi explained: "You will find that those left on the dock are not wives and children, but fathers, mothers, sisters, brothers and even friends, who are no way dependent upon them." It was an opinion intended to defuse the charge that the city would have to assume the care of the affected families. But offering a solution to a problem that they claimed did not exist, the prominenti proposed to raise an emergency fund of $10,000 for cases brought to the attention of the federation. Similarly, the IWRC, as well as the newly organized General Committee on Italian Civic Mobilization, berated the "bad judgment" of fathers who had left their families in answering the call. With such contradictions afflicting organizations seeking to pursue relief activities, their troubles had only just begun.[15]

Within two days, another decision, backed by "influential members of the community," revealed a plan to reorganize the IWRC after its failure to have accomplished any meaningful results. With the promise that "new life is to be put into the activities of the body," it was hoped that any further obstacles to being able to amass a large fund in support of its work would be avoided. And despite the indictment of the previous effort, Baldi's incumbent role as treasurer, which had to be ratified by a vote at the next meeting, remained a foregone conclusion. Against earlier allegations, Baldi emphatically asserted that cases of destitution would not be remanded to any city agency but be assigned to mutual aid societies of which nearly all reservists were members. As more men gathered for departure, Italian leaders remained concerned with Solicitor Ryan's view that reservists were subject to arrest unless they had made arrangements for the care of their families. After another week, while newspaper coverage described the expected role of the prominenti, the choice of new officers and the means of raising funds to conduct its welfare program remained issues for the IWRC.[16]

After several meetings in the following days, the reorganized IWRC released details of an agenda that included concerts, lectures, lawn fetes, and other activities to generate funds for a program that strongly resembled the work of the women of Emergency Aid. With each member pledging a weekly contribution of $5, it also announced the intention to conduct a census of the entire Italian population of the city to determine a weekly or monthly assessment that would be recorded under the donor's name and sent to the king of Italy at the end of the war. It was an overly ambitious plan that rested on an unrealistic foundation in view of the financial limitations of most Italian families in Philadelphia. As another "final call" was issued for reservists to report to the consulate before being classified as deserters, the IWRC continued to proclaim assurances that families would be protected from penury resulting from their absence. At the end of August, the committee, reporting $3,000 in recent donations, called for partitioning the city and suburbs into 26 sections for the further collection of funds, which would now be shared with the Italian Red Cross. Almost daily newspaper accounts giving further details of the plan continued until early September. But inexplicably, with the cessation of newspaper coverage of its activities at this point, the *Official* Italian Welfare Relief Committee, abruptly disappeared as an agency of the Italian community. In late September, when another IWRC, meeting for the first time, received a telegram from Mrs. Page offering support from her office in Rome, it was as a section of the Emergency Aid Committee with Consul Pocardi and Baldi as the only Italian members of the newly formed group. And it appeared that the responsibility for relief for destitute families had been relocated from the community itself to the "society" women of the city.[17]

If the plight of impoverished Italians seemed to have been mitigated, it would vividly reappear in the presence of Teresa Seata, a 102-year-old woman who roamed the streets of South Philadelphia crying, "ho tanto fame—pane . . . pane!" in a desperate search for food. When she reached the door of the Moyamensing Soup Society on a cold morning in January 1916, where crowds of hungry supplicants gathered nearly every day, two volunteer workers were unable to understand her words. Their names, Wilcox and Stoneman, which revealed their distinctly American backgrounds, reflected the cultural gulf that impeded the well-intended work of their agency. But 14-year-old Tony Capobianco, reputed to be the "terror of Little Italy," graciously served as an interpreter, easily translating the woman's plea, "I am so hungry—bread . . . bread!" After receiving a handout of soup and bread, Seata, who routinely made her living by picking rags, returned to the one room apartment she shared with Angelina Casanta, her housemate, who was said to be "only" 97 years old.[18]

Beyond the wail of an elderly beggar, other women abandoned by husbands who had gone to join the fighting in Italy, whose small savings had already melted away, revealed their fear that they too would soon be left in poverty and isolation. But while the soup kitchen sought to feed the poor, the response exposed broader aspects of the situation—women helping women; impoverished Italian women helping one another; Anglo-American women providing aid to Italian and other immigrant families; and Italian women seeking their own adjustment to life in America. While military experience would soon begin to reshape immigrant men into Americans, women burdened by the less transparent exigencies of the home front would enter their own trajectory of assimilation. And beneath all else, their plight implicitly asked whether assimilation for women would take the same course as it did for men.

In the months that followed the almost operatic case of the ragpicker who cried for bread, with the threat of wider distress brought on by the departure of husbands called away as reservists, other Italian women entered their own struggle. In contrast to the highly emotional scenes that occurred as reservists left the port of Philadelphia, they would more calmly take up the task of providing support for the struggle in which first Italy and then the United States would be engaged. Some efforts would be conducted by the Stella d'Italia, founded as the Italian Ladies' Mutual Beneficial Association in August 1897, which had become the most prestigious such organization by the early years of the new century. With Italy's entrance into the war in 1915, its attention had shifted from relief for the victims of earthquakes to the needs of wounded soldiers, widows, and orphans in the homeland as well as the wives and children of reservists in Philadelphia. Some efforts sought to bring together the higher echelon of the Italian colony with upper-class Americans. In February 1917, the plans of a group calling itself the Circolo Italiano anticipated the participation of members of the Italian Emergency Aid Committee at a grand ball at Horticultural Hall in Fairmount Park intended to raise money for the Italian Red Cross. But other programs, falling short of such expectations, had become increasingly more restricted, events mainly or entirely for Italians, without the presence of guests from the Anglo-American population—or vice versa. In January 1918, the organizing committee announced that the proceeds from the annual ball of the Stella d'Italia would be sent directly to Queen Elena of Italy as a donation to benefit the sufferers of the war in the homeland. The publicity given to the largesse of the organization also revealed the women—Louisa Lombardi, Katie M. Laury, Julia Calderoni, Elizabeth Malatesta Kennedy, and others—emerging as leaders in the community.[19]

By early 1917, with Italy's military and domestic needs becoming more acute, Philadelphia's Italian women were making even more dramatic personal sacrifices in support of their homeland. In February, Emergency Aid announced that, along with more than 4,000 local women ready to take up the work of preparing hospital supplies, the "Italian Society" (without any further clarification) had offered the services of 200 members already experienced in such work. Four months later, in June, when the Italian War Commission arrived in search of aid, according to newspaper accounts, married women donated wedding rings and other items of jewelry while teams of girls sought cash contributions in door-to-door canvasing of neighborhoods. And after another few months, when Philadelphia's Italians celebrated Columbus Day, with Baldi once again imploring an audience in Fairmount Park to remember the men at the front and to aid the war for democracy by subscribing to the

Liberty Loan, some 50 girls attired in uniforms of Red Cross nurses collected donations for the benefit of the widows and orphans of Italian soldiers.

Women and the Liberty Loan

While modestly supporting six national loans (*Prestiti Nazionali*) through which Italy sought to finance its war expenses from 1915 to 1918, Philadelphia's Italians contributed far more greatly to the Liberty Loan drives of the American government. A division for the various foreign-born groups had been first established during the second drive, but it was not effectively organized until the third drive in the spring of 1918. With legislation authorizing the third Liberty Loan enacted by Congress in April, the leadership of the Italian community, seeking to reach $1,000,000 in subscriptions, launched its own efforts under the slogan: "Every Italian resident of Philadelphia a Liberty Bond holder." The first stage of the campaign was marked by extravagant pledges of financial support ranging from $25,000 to $75,000 by some of its most prominent members and organizations. Within a week, as the drive turned into a competition among immigrant groups, the executive committee of the Italian program claimed that it had already amassed a total of $500,000 in bonds. At the end of the opening month, the Italian women's subdivision, headed by Concetta Branca Lippi, the wife of a well-known pharmacist, was praised for "unusual success among women of that nationality," after reporting the sale of $30,000 among residents of South Philadelphia, with 90 percent coming from the purchase of $50 bonds.[20] (See Figure 12.1.)

But Italian women, besides their energy as workers and solicitors, had other talents to offer as well. In April 1918, Euphemia and Dusolina Giannini would sing patriotic songs and operatic arias at an outdoor rally for the third Liberty Loan at 12th and Wharton Streets in the heart of Little Italy. The two young sisters, along with their father, Ferruccio Giannini, the famed local tenor and impresario, frequently appeared together with other family members at such events.[21] (See Figure 12.2.)

While not all of the young women of the Italian colony were as vocally gifted as the Giannini sisters, their appreciation of music could still become a part of their service on the home front. One group of about 50 of them, already commended as "amazingly energetic and thorough Italian girls" for raising large sums in the Liberty Loan drive, reorganized by the Circolo Italiano under Mrs. Lippi, sought to provide musical instruments from mouth harps to violins and pianos along with records and phonographs as gifts for men leaving for overseas duty. And from headquarters on South Broad Street,

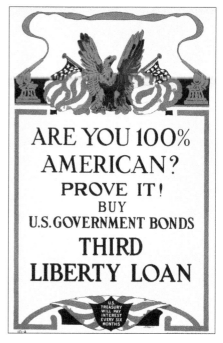

FIGURE 12.1A Liberty Loan Poster, #1, "Buy U.S. Government Bonds." (Courtesy of the Library of Congress.)

FIGURE 12.1B Liberty Loan Poster, #2, "Are You 100% American?" (Courtesy of the Library of Congress.)

the recently formed Italian Music Unit also planned dances and other entertainment programs in support of programming at the recreation center of the Fourth Naval District. Whether world-class performers or merely admirers who recognized the power of music, young Italian women were offering their time and energy in support of the war effort and to ease the apprehensions of recruits who were preparing to fight.[22]

But they sometimes took on even more challenging responsibilities. Mary Sabatini, who claimed to have at least 40 male relatives serving in the Italian and American armies, found employment as a volunteer translator of letters dealing with war activities in the Personal Service Bureau of the city of Philadelphia. With an uncle killed on the Western Front, as well as a cousin captured and a brother-in-law suffering the loss of an arm on the Italian front, the young Mrs. Sabatini became an outspoken advocate for the purchase of Liberty Bonds: "I can't understand why people who have loads and loads of money don't invest more and more of it in bonds. We have to whip the Huns and we can't stop until we do. . . . The men can do the fighting,

FIGURE 12.2 Euphemia and Dusolina Giannini. (*Evening Public Ledger* ([April 29, 1918].)

SING FOR LIBERTY LOAN

but we women can help by giving and giving and giving. We must, yes, we must whip the Hun"[23] (See Figure 12.3.)

The performances of the Giannini sisters, the testimony of Sabatini, and the fervor of the young members of the Circolo, caught up in the momentum of the third Liberty Loan drive, reflected a deeper transition taking root within the Italian community. Despite kin serving in the Italian and American armed forces, the primary allegiance of Italian women, as expressed by Sabatini's reference to "my country," was ineluctably shifting to the United States. As their spouses, brothers, and sweethearts were being indoctrinated by more formal programs of Americanization in military camps, these women were also being reconditioned under less formal but similarly powerful forces of acculturation on the home front. Full of enthusiasm for life in America and eager to be more American than their parents, they were migrating toward a newly emerging consciousness and loyalty as Americans. It would become even more fully manifested in subsequent events.

When the fourth Liberty Loan campaign was launched in late September 1918, an even greater effort than in previous drives was aimed at the immigrant populations of Philadelphia. Some 500,000 appeals for subscription printed in various languages distributed through 25 committees of the foreign language division initiated the effort. On October 11, dubbed as "Preparation Day," about 300 squads of loan workers, behind a town crier dressed in a Continental Army uniform, accompanied by a Boy Scout carrying an American flag, a member of the Home Defense Reserve, a "Four Minute Man," and a man or woman solicitor, proceeded along the city's most populous streets. At each corner of the foreign districts of the city, the town crier used the language of its residents to urge the purchase of bonds. And in Little Italy, the town crier, clad in quintessentially patriotic American garb, spoke the vocabulary

FIGURE 12.3 Mary Sabatini. (*Evening Public Ledger* [April 29, 1918].)

of Dante Aligheri, Giuseppe Mazzini, and the immigrant masses.[24]

While newspaper coverage had not identified the Four Minute Man who accompanied the town crier into Little Italy, he could have been either Eugene V. Alessandroni or John Di Silvestro. Both men were among the lawyers, bankers, and businessmen recruited by the U.S. government's Committee on Public Information to wage war in a civilian "army" by delivering brief speeches about America's place in the war in movie houses, at workplaces, on street corners, and at other public venues. They were not only stalwarts of Little Italy but bilingual sentinels of loyalty, uniquely equipped to address Italian audiences. It also was a moment at which Italian American women nearly assumed the role with the prospect that the ranks of the Four Minute Men might be opened across gender lines. In late September, the directors of Philadelphia's Four Minute organization, as a result of successful performances in previous drives, proposed "tryouts" for nearly 100 women who sought to join the program as speakers. But while continuing to engage in public oratory on behalf of the campaign, the applicants were never formally invited to become Four Minute Women. Such aspirations, however, were made even more remarkable by their coincidence with the moment that the worldwide influenza epidemic, more lethal in Philadelphia than almost anywhere else, was reaching its peak in local deaths.[25]

Despite the ongoing health crisis, the Italian women's committee, still directed by Mrs. Lippi, prepared an agenda of educational work and fundraising intended to increase bond subscriptions in South Philadelphia. For Italians and other "foreign" groups, however, the Liberty Loan drives had been designed not solely for raising money to finance the war but also as a way of reaffirming and demonstrating their loyalty as Americans. At almost the same time as the women inaugurated their new program, Philadelphia's "Americanized Italians" gathered, with similar events being held simultanously in other cities, organized by the Roman Legion of America, an affiliate of the Committee on Public Information, for a mass meeting at Independence Square. Directed by John Di Silvestro, the chairman of the local branch of the legion, several thousand members of the Sons of Italy and other Italians listened to

ITALIAN SECTION OF WOMEN LOAN WORKERS OF SOUTH PHILADELPHIA

FIGURE 12.4 South Philadelphia volunteers for the third Liberty Loan drive. *Bottom row*: Adelina Baldino, Christine Camerotta, Elvira Cavalieri, Elizabeth Scarpa, Lena Falcone, and Bessie Giuliana; *second row*: Marie Mazzei, Katherine Gagliardi, Gina d'Angiolelli, Elvira Scarpa, Mrs. Andrew F. Lippi (chairperson), Jennie De Carlo, Elsie Cavalieri, and Rose Arino; *third row*: Rose Rossi, Elsie Di Nardo, Anna Teti, Dionisia Revelli, Arturo Andrioni, Millie Baldino, Maria Cavalieri, Carolina Teti, and Olga De Luca; *top row*: Nellie Rossi, Rose Giurado, Maria Costa, Julia Palumba, Rose Camarona, Antonietta Cirino, Florita De Dominicis, Amelia Donato, and Adelina Damiani. (*Evening Public Ledger* [May 10, 1919].)

Italian and English speakers who included William Potter, the former American envoy in Rome; Pennsylvania congressmen George S. Graham; Captain Arturo Zampaglione, a much decorated member of the Sardinian Grenadiers who had lost an arm in the fighting for Gorizia; Pietro Solari, a distinguished visiting journalist; and Gaetano Poccardi, the Italian consul in Philadelphia. For Italians, the Liberty Loan drive now preempted the traditional celebration of Italy's Independence Day on September 20, the historic date that nationalist forces, breaching the Porta Pia in Rome, had defeated the army of the Papal States in 1870. But for others, the occasion capped the success of the appeal. And when a tabulation of all Liberty Loan drives was later reported, with Italians listed among the 19 groups of "loyal Americans of other nationalities" who purchased a staggering sum of $83,000,000 in bonds, some $33,000,000 coming in the highly successful fourth campaign, Philadelphia's Italian women could justly take pride in their own efforts.[26] (See Figure 12.4.)

Promoting Patriotism: Celebrities, Soldiers, and Children

While women diligently participated in fund-raising efforts, such celebrities as Mary Pickford, Charlie Chaplin, Douglas Fairbanks, and Enrico Caruso more often stole the limelight in highly publicized performances before massive crowds. But like the women, other less prominent persons calling for the purchase of bonds, particularly some very ordinary soldiers, also contributed to the campaigns. In April 1918, under a plan initiated by General Kuhn at Camp Meade, Vincenzo Di Leonardo, a member of the 315th Infantry, although unable to write and without relatives in America, appealed to Italian workers at the Stetson Hat Company in Philadelphia. In a message transcribed by his sergeant, Di Leonardo implored former colleagues to buy Liberty Bonds in support of Italy and the United States, contending that both nations were waging war for the same democratic ideals, as well as for "the many sons of Italy who are fighting side by side with their American brothers." Private Di Leonardo, born in Pianella in the Abruzzi region, who lived in North Philadelphia before entering military service, would see combat alongside those "brothers" in the Meuse and Argonne campaigns. In a similarly public letter released in early May, John M. Carrozzino, a native of Altomonte in Cosenza Province and a barber in South Philadelphia before becoming a member of the 315th Infantry, called upon his fellow Italians to remain steadfast in their loyalty to their adopted country by supporting the Liberty Bond campaign. Unlike Di Leonardo, Private Carrozzino, reassigned to a depot brigade, would not go overseas but remain in the United States before being discharged at Camp Dix at the end of the war. Beneath the irony of Italians enjoining other Italians to be patriotic Americans, the contrived nature of such appeals must be recognized. Rather than spontaneous gestures by their "writers," these invented tools represented an attempt to finance war by the selling of patriotism.[27]

But if local soldiers had a place in generating support for the financing of war, the presentation of even more exotic foreign troops before the American public held greater promise. Although soldiers from other nations had been brought to the United States since the opening of the war, their potential value was still being exploited in its final days. In early October 1918, a contingent of 90 Alpini and 90 Bersaglieri veterans of the Italian front, along with a regiment of musicians drawn from the Royal Sardinian Grenadiers, arrived at New York City as part of planned appearances in several cities in support of the ongoing Liberty Loan campaign. Despite hopes of city officials and community leaders that Philadelphia would be included among its destinations, the visit, along with almost all public events, would be canceled

FIGURE 12.5 Guido Pologruto—A four-year-old "enthusiastic patriot" in uniform salutes. The little soldier lived at 609 Washington Avenue. (*Evening Public Ledger* [December 19, 1918].)

by the deadly influenza epidemic that ravaged private and civic life in the city during the autumn of 1918.[28]

Another weapon of manipulating sentiment and support, in some ways an extension of the role that women had played, also surfaced on the domestic front—the children of the community. Since the beginning of the war, younger Philadelphians, sometimes shown kissing the Liberty Bell in Independence Hall, had been depicted in patriotic moments by newspaper coverage. In April 1918, a photograph showed Joseph Petti, only 22 months old, described as being a Liberty Loan "booster" with more than $20,000 in subscriptions to his credit. Its caption, identifying his father as a plant manager at A. B. Kirschbaum, one of the largest clothing manufacturers of the city, indicated that workers were the actual buyers. Despite his bewildered and forlorn expression as "the youngster makes his personal plea to the employees," this device encouraged further support for the bond campaign. In May, another portrait displayed the precociously pensive Amerigo Palumbo, the 13-year-old son of a well-known leader of the Italian colony, as the winner of a Liberty Loan contest among pupils at the Campbell School, who had obtained subscriptions of more than $13,000. And if little Joe or teenage Amerigo were not enough, the smiling, four-year-old Guido Pologruto, in an army uniform, as "an enthusiastic patriot, ever ready to salute his superior officer," even more smartly supported the war in December.[29] (See Figure 12.5.)

The use of such graphic representations was meant not only to persuade the reading public to act but to show how far foreign children had come in becoming more American themselves. In one image of the celebration of Flag Day in June 1917, not long after the United States entered the war, attended largely by children of Italian and Jewish families, an orchestra of boy musi-

FIGURE 12.6 The boy musicians of the Campbell-Lyons School orchestra, with Marie Giudice as the Goddess of Liberty, offer a program of patriotic music to enliven Flag Day in June 1917. (*Evening Ledger* [June 14, 1917].)

cians is primed to begin a program of patriotic music at the Campbell School, at 8th and Fitzwater Streets in South Philadelphia. With Martin Schonberg identified as the orchestra leader, Maria Giudice, holding a large American flag, stands above the musicians as the "Goddess of Liberty." While her deification suggests her Americanization as well, another photograph, which appeared on the same day, with a caption that read, "What Once Was 'Little Italy' Is 'Young America' Now," showing a large crowd of children, many holding American flags, made the meaning of the occasion even more explicit. Both scenes show children of Italian families eager to celebrate but also ready to become Americans, at least in the view of a Philadelphia newspaper. Throughout the war, Philadelphia's children would be cast in cameo performances as flower-bearing acolytes on ceremonial occasions or as miniature soldiers garbed in uniform, whose devotion to the presumed virtues of the American or Allied cause was meant to inspire adults to emulate them. In the case of Italians and other "foreign" youngsters, the implicit meaning of such representation was also intended to convince other Americans that the children of immigrant families were being swept into loyalty as the newest Americans.[30] (See Figure 12.6.)

On the eve of the concluding battles of the Western Front, Philadelphia's Italians again enacted their own symbolic efforts in the war being waged on the home front. In September, Italians gathered at 8th and Montrose Streets after a mock hanging of Kaiser "Bill" to contribute money and drive a nail into his coffin during the fourth Liberty Loan drive. After the noise of hammers drowned out the meager sound of a small band of musicians, the event concluded with the body of the kaiser being removed for burial to a chorus of boos and hisses from an enthusiastic crowd of about 1,000 participants. While no casualties from enemy bullets or artillery shells resulted from the mock warfare, the enormous toll of the influenza epidemic continued to convert neighborhoods into zones of affliction somewhat akin to what European cities and towns had endured for the past four years.[31]

"Le Donne Hanno Sempre Aiutato"

For Philadelphia's Italian wives and mothers, like women of all backgrounds, the war was a difficult reality that had provided opportunity and tragedy. But its greatest weight came in its impact on their relationship to the men in their lives. At its outset, they had tearfully bade farewell to reservists going off to fight for Italy with their own hearts heavy with apprehension. Two years later, after the United States entered the war, when National Registration Day summoned men to present themselves as candidates of another army, women had risen early on that morning to remind sons, husbands, and brothers of their duty and even to accompany them to registration sites. In some cases, they came, accompanied by children, to offer themselves as visible proof of being dependents who might preclude conscription of their men. Italian women were undoubtedly among them. And at its end, after the long, uncertain wait, they welcomed husbands and sons home or grieved for those who would not return. Rather than their lives unfolding in some kind of social vacuum, they were caught in the vortex of a shortage of men available for industrial employment; a growing suffragist movement; the protests of a vocal pacifist faction; the frenzy of wartime patriotism; and the power struggles of leaders seeking control over the immigrant community. At a more personal level, it included a domestic life disturbed by the separation of family members called to military service and the pressures imposed by increasing calls for the loyalty of "foreign" residents. They had to respond to all of it. As various stages of the Liberty Loan drives progressed, women in general succeeded

FIGURE 12.7 "Le Donne Hanno Sempre Aiutato." (*La Libera Parola* [April 19, 1919].)

in becoming essential participants in the campaign, while encouraging the broader mobilization of all Americans in support of the war. But they also entered employment in the newer defense industries while reaching higher levels in more traditional work. Their contributions served as a scaffold for further emancipation in gender-related roles and a conduit for assimilation as ethnic Americans. It presupposed an even greater role that Italian American women, indeed all American women, would play in a future war.

Although not widely visible to the outside community, the efforts of the women of Little Italy were vividly and succinctly recognized by *La Libera Parola* at the beginning of the fifth Liberty Loan (or the Victory Loan) drive in April 1919. Calling on readers to subscribe to the new campaign, a full-page poster proclaimed: "Le Donne Hanno Sempre Aiutato—Che Iddio le Benedisce" (Women have always helped—may God bless them). Intended as a tribute to Philadelphia's Italian women for their service to the war effort, it reflected the customary chivalry of a traditional culture, perhaps already rendered obsolete by what they had accomplished. (See Figure 12.7.)

Making It Through—and Coming Home

Oh! boy the minute the battle is over,
Oh! boy the minute the foe is dead;
I'll put my uniform away, and move to Philadelphia,
And spend the rest of my life in bed.

Irving Berlin,
"Oh, How I Hate to Get Up in the Morning" (1918)

O n a cold morning in late January 1919, Antonio Felice, a 39-year-old Italian immigrant, wearing the uniform of an American soldier, stood on the corner of Pulaski Avenue and West Queen Lane in the heart of Germantown. As he walked from one corner to another, grinding out patriotic tunes on a hand organ, a crowd showered him with coins in appreciation of his impromptu concert. But if the tale he told was true, they had much more for which to be thankful. Felice, who lived on Salter Street in South Philadelphia, claimed that, with the declaration of war by the United States nearly two years earlier, he enlisted in the army, then after training at Gettysburg left for France with a small contingent that preceded Pershing's command in April 1917. He continued his story: As a member of Company G, Fourth Infantry, he would see action at Verdun, the Second Battle of the Marne and Château-Thierry, before being gassed; when he returned home, his face showed the scars of the poisonous vapors that had ended his days of combat. As a musician capable of playing several different instruments, he said: "I did not wait for my Uncle Sammy to get me a job. . . . But I must work, so I got the organ, and now I am making plenty of money." The crowd, noticing the two gold stripes on his sleeves, applauded his performance, while he grinned and played on. And when he paused to answer such questions as, How many Germans had he killed? Felice replied, "Not many. Only eight or nine, I think." It was a reversal of what occurred a half-century earlier when veterans of the Union army, many of them maimed by the war, sought to displace newly arrived Italians as street musicians. Italians who had gone to fight on the Western Front were now coming home.[1]

"Some Guys Are Born Lucky"—and Some Were Not

As the men who had "made it through" began to arrive home, they carried a wide range of memories and attitudes about their recent experience. Along with those haunted by sadness over comrades in arms who had not come back with them, other men returned with almost irreverent disregard for what they had encountered. At the end of it all, Private Anthony Matera, of Company I, 316th Infantry, as he wrote to his sister in anticipation of his return, claimed that he was "peeved" at having passed through the entire war "without a scratch," leaving him unable to wear the gold stripes awarded to the wounded. Describing himself as the "luckiest courier in the United States service," he related his story:

> The Germans nearly got me at the Argonne, at St. Mihiel and again at Verdun, but always I was just a little too quick for them. Once they shot my motorcycle under me; again I was within a few feet of a shell when it exploded and in the Argonne drive they shot down one of my companions. But they never touched me, and I'm coming back soon, I expect, in better physical shape than I went away. Gosh, ain't it the dickens to come all the way over here, go through the big drives and then come home without a wound stripe.[2]

After telling how one of his friends had been hit in the arm by shrapnel and another by a sniper's bullet, Matera declared that "some guys are born lucky." But underneath his lighthearted sarcasm, this fortunate soldier was probably hiding his own pain over the physical suffering as well as the loss of his fellow soldiers that he had witnessed.

For men like Matera who had "made it through," the celebration of their return from the war involved much more than informal concerts on city streets. It also entailed parades by men who were now among the lucky ones marching on Market Street where, as Private John S. Costa had put it, they could see city hall again. It included citywide celebrations such as when General Armando Diaz, the supreme commander of Italy's army, was honored with a grand reception by the Italian immigrant community and city as a whole. But the most satisfying events for many soldiers had to be those more private moments when they crossed a familiar threshold and reentered the embrace of family and friends. The case of another musician provided a pre-view of that encounter. After enlisting in May 1918, Private Alfred Setaro, son of Giovanni Setaro, a well-known harpist, had been a member of the regimental band of the 316th Infantry. Transferred to the ranks, he was severely wounded in the Argonne Forest. On February 12, 1919, he arrived at the port of New York, assigned for further medical treatment at Camp Merritt in New Jersey. His widowed mother and family on Catharine Street eagerly anticipated welcoming him home, with rooms lavishly decorated by Italian and American flags and a specially prepared feast of his favorite foods—an understandable reception by an Italian family. And similarly suitable for a family of musicians, his thoughtful mother had arranged for a band to perform for the occasion. But Private Setaro's return would be delayed. Without knowing the extent of his wounds, his family had received news that he was unable to walk. But this family saga would have a happy ending. In March, released from the hospital and discharged from the army, Setaro returned home for the festivities that his family had planned. He would go on to pursue his own career as an organist in later years.[3]

By the time Setaro reached New York on his way home, the return of all the men had become a serious personal and public issue. In addition to reporting on the homecoming of those men who were arriving, newspapers carried stories of men who longed to be home. Private Marion Luciani, after being wounded twice, wrote from a hospital to his sister in West Philadelphia that "France is a beautiful country, but there is no country on earth that can equal the United States, and it will be the happiest day in my life when I can get back in old Philly again." Meanwhile, local officials had become increasingly critical when men belonging to families of constituents had not been given priority on earlier ships bringing the troops back to the United States. Mayor Charles H. Ellis of Camden, angrily declaring that the treatment of soldiers, languishing in a rest camp, no longer part of an army of occupation, and anxious to get home, was "shameful and outrageous," promised to take up the matter with the governor of the state and officials in Washington. In early April, the War Department announced that some 1,535,471 of the 3,670, 888 officers and men in the service at the time of the Armistice had been discharged, with 573,474 of them having left France, 502,830 having reached American ports, and 1,409,789 remaining overseas. But no matter how many men had already been discharged or how quickly they returned to the United States, it could not be as many or as soon as the men themselves or those who waited for them at home would wish.[4]

As figures reached the public, the War Department announced that it would immediately discontinue the direct release of casualty lists to newspapers. On

April 2, Secretary of War Baker, describing new procedures, expressed his gratitude that "the price of victory, in human life and limb, was not great- er." Commending the press for its service to the community, he praised the prompt and accurate publication of the lists by which "the supreme sacrifices made by the officers and men of our forces abroad might be known to their friends and relatives at home." The policy during the war had been for the War Department to send telegrams to the families of all casualties with simul- taneous release of the same information to press associations for distribution to newspapers. The revised procedure, which primarily affected the press, called for immediate release only of verified names of men killed in action or by disease, with information on all other casualties being sent by mail. As a result of this shift in policy, the daily casualty lists in newspapers also became a relic of a war era that had reached its final stages. On the same day as the announcement, Private Ralph Dismario, of the Tacony section of Northeast Philadelphia, was reported as previously missing but now killed in action in a brief article that added that his relatives on Cottman Street had been notified of his death. But if more information was sought on him, contrary to what was implied by an overeager newspaper account, it was clear that confusion still plagued the reporting of casualties. Dismario was born in Teramo, Italy, on May 29, 1893, living in Parnassus, Pennsylvania, and working as a laborer for the Union Collieries in Renton, Pennsylvania, when he registered for the draft on June 5, 1917. He died as a member of Company H, 318th Infantry Regiment, 80th Division in action on October 6, 1918, and was buried three years later in Arlington National Cemetery. If he had ever lived in Phila- delphia, Dismario had moved far away from his relatives in Tacony by the beginning of the war. But it is also possible that he never lived there at all. In either case, instead of being one of the last men reported as a Philadelphia Italian to be killed in action, he is more accurately described as an Allegheny County miner who went to war in a regiment of men mainly from Virginia, West Virginia, and the western counties of Pennsylvania.[5]

With growing impatience over the lagging return of troops, public offi- cials debated which state had contributed most in manpower or had suffered the most casualties during the war. In his protest over the failure of men to be promptly brought home, Camden's Mayor Ellis had claimed that New Jersey had provided the largest number of troops in proportion to its population than any other state and that it had suffered the largest number of casualties. He contended that Camden County had furnished the bulk of the 400 men lost by the 29th National Guard Division, decimated in the Sedan sector of the Meuse-Argonne offensive. In early March, however, the *Evening Public*

Ledger reported that Pennsylvania had incurred greater losses than any other state, about one-tenth of all casualties of the American Expeditionary Force. The figure reported on that day alone showed Pennsylvania, with 60 men, surging to one-sixth of the total of 404 for the entire nation.[6]

By spring 1919, while politicians argued in a manner that may have been more self-serving than out of concern over the welfare of troops, more descriptive newspaper coverage gradually replaced the casualty lists. Although the incidence of cases had greatly declined, sad episodes were still unfolding. On March 21, Private Frederic F. Belli, of North 19th Street, appeared among four Philadelphians on that day's official list. Having been classified in the lowest category of eligibility because of extreme family hardship, he had waived exemption from the draft and was called to Camp Meade for basic training. After three weeks, he volunteered to join other men in filling the ranks of the 109th Infantry, making its way from Fort Hancock to Hoboken for deployment overseas, and reached France in May 1918. Within two months, he was reported as missing, then wounded in action in the Marne sector on July 15, before dying on the following day. Four months after the end of the war, Belli remained among the men whose status was still to be confirmed. Only 28 years old at his death, he was first buried at the village of Sézanne before being reinterred at Aisne-Marne American Cemetery, among 34,000 American soldiers who would eventually rest in overseas cemeteries, of the more than 120,000 men who were killed or missing in action or died of other causes.[7]

A week after Belli's case was reported, the unique saga of Dr. Vincent M. Diodati, who had practiced medicine at his office on South 12th Street before a remarkable military career, appeared on local newspaper pages. Born in Philadelphia on July 15, 1889, to Fernando and Felicia Diodati, he graduated from the Catholic High School (now Roman Catholic High School), before receiving his degree as a medical doctor, at not quite 22 years old, from Jefferson Medical College in 1911. He had served as a physician and surgeon affiliated with the Howard Hospital at Broad and Catharine Streets; the Southeastern Dispensary; and the Italian Hospital in South Philadelphia, and the medical officer of about 20 Italian fraternal and beneficial societies for about seven years. On the day that the United States declared war, Diodati enlisted in the army. Commissioned as a first lieutenant in early June, he shipped out with a detachment of 70 American medical officers two months later, assigned to British forces as the first American troops to be sent overseas. In March 1919, a newspaper recognized his unmatched accomplishment: "To have been more constantly under fire than any other man in the American army is certainly an enviable distinction to have won in this war, but this is the claim made by a Philadelphian." But without knowing if other men in this first group of Americans to serve in the war had remained in action, it negated the claim that Diodati had made—of having been in action longer than any other member of the U.S. Army. Despite the qualification, it remained a robust introduction to one of the great tales of the entire war.[8]

Henry M. Neely, another Philadelphian, writing from London while involved in the work of postwar reconstruction, provided further details of Diodati's service, largely based on information provided by the latter, for the *Evening Public Ledger* in March 1919. The young doctor had arrived in London with the American medical detachment assigned to Southwark Military Hospital in August 1917. Placed in command of the 35th Royal Army Medical Corps, the first American to be given such an appointment, he received commendations during the influenza epidemic and the worst air raids that England had suffered up to that point. Sent to France with the 142nd Field Ambulance of the Royal Army Medical Corps in March 1918, he served in the Arras sector and Somme area, "and bloody places they were," where only 14 men of the 220 soldiers of his original contingent survived. Transferred to the northern sector of the Western Front, Diodati could not escape from a German offensive at Locon, Vieille-Chapelle, and a place identified as Pacut Wood. On April 10, after being gassed at Annequin, he refused to go to a hospital, carrying on his work despite his own injuries, from which he would twice suffer hemorrhages. A little more than a month later, Diodati was wounded again on May 27 at Lillers in the Bethune sector by a bomb that pierced his leg during an air attack. He treated others at a dressing station under enemy fire until he could no longer perform his medical duties. After only four or five days of rest, he hobbled back to his work. In July and August, Locon and Pacut Wood as well as Aubers Ridge, an area where more celebrated but ill-fated efforts by British troops had occurred in 1915, once again became the scene of battle. From there, his unit reached the city of Lille, which Diodati claimed to have been the first American to enter. Gassed again at Marquain and wounded by a piece of shrapnel, Diodati again refused to go to a hospital in the final days of the war in early November.[9]

In Neely's cautious account, Diodati claimed that he was the only one of the original 70 members of the medical detachment to have been under fire every day during his service in France and to have remained in action until the Armistice ended the war. With all other men wounded, killed, disabled by illness, or transferred, he was the only one left who could make the claim. Supported by honors and recognition from the British government, the details of his military record, including his citation by General Sir Douglas

Haig and awarding of the Military Cross by King George, were afterward reported in American medical journals. Appointed as an assistant surgeon in the U.S. Public Health Service, Diodati served as a staff physician, still caring for former comrades in arms at the Veterans Administration at the U.S. Naval Hospital in Philadelphia at the start of the next war. When these pieces are assembled, the final picture is a remarkable saga of an extraordinary life.[10]

Along with the last casualty lists, the reporting of more tragedy continued in spring 1919. On April 3, the two-day roster of casualties included Privates Nazareno Felicotti and Angelo Gezzo of Philadelphia, both wounded slightly, and Giuseppe Beanchionnelle of Philadelphia and Private Vincenzo Catini of Chester, both dead from an accident or other causes. Two days later, an extensive article described the narrow escape from death by Sergeant Louis Martini. He had worked as a tailor and lived with his parents on Passyunk Avenue before becoming a soldier. In 1918, as a member of Company D, 304th Supply Train, Martini would see action at Verdun, Saint-Mihiel, the Meuse, and the Argonne Forest. Listed as wounded, he reported his well-being with occupation forces in Germany in a letter to his family that gave details of recent experiences. In early October, after being assigned to a detachment bringing a supply truck to the front, an enemy barrage, which destroyed the vehicle and killed four men under his command, left him unconscious and unable to speak for the next 12 hours. With a badly injured leg and suffering from shell shock, Martini slowly recovered in a base hospital for the next four weeks before rejoining his company. But a lighter twist accompanied his story. With an ability to write musical parodies, he had composed his own version of the popular song "Smiles," using the return of the Yanks to the United States as its main theme, which the men of his company enthusiastically adopted. While its entreaty was soon to be realized, Martini's composition would be lost to posterity.[11]

Along with Martini's tale, the worst of news came on the same day, in an almost buried paragraph that reported the death of a less fortunate Philadelphian, Private Michael Scioli, only 18 years of age, of Company B, 110th Infantry. After having been listed as missing in July, a later War Department telegram brought the news to his family on Kauffman Street in South Philadelphia. But despite that message, and the failure to receive any mail from their son in many months, Scioli's disbelieving parents still hoped that their son was somehow still alive.[12]

Demobilization

The mixture of elation and celebration over the end of the war, demobilization and homecoming, along with the absence or contradiction of information regarding men whose fate was still unclear, remained all too common. In May, as the returning men of the 28th "Iron Division" paraded on Market Street in Philadelphia, after arriving at Camp Dix, the members of the 79th "Liberty Division" waited at Nantes and Saint-Nazaire for the orders to board ships that would bring them home. Although not scheduled to be part of occupation troops, the long-awaited news of their embarkation was not expected to come until late June. While they waited, General Pershing and Major General Kuhn distributed medals to men of the division, among them Privates Spadafora and Masciarelli, who undoubtedly preferred to be marching on Market Street. But even so, they remained more fortunate than their fallen comrades who would be left behind in the recently announced cemetery near the site of their most important victory at Montfaucon in the Argonne Forest. From one family to another and one neighborhood to the next, throughout Philadelphia, anxious expectation and joy were mixed with inconsolable grief and sorrow.

The end of war meant much more than transporting soldiers from the zone of military operations back to the United States. The entire apparatus by which the nation had implemented the military effort was now being dismantled. With the Armistice, Secretary Baker ordered an almost immediate end of operations by the Selective Service System. The mobilization of personnel by the army would end on November 11 and for the navy two days later on November 13, 1918. District draft boards were closed on November 13, 1918. On November 19, 1918, the order came to close local boards not later than December 10, 1918. And state headquarters, which began shutting down on November 28, were closed by May 21, 1919. By March 31, 1919, all local, district, and medical boards were closed. The Office of Provost Marshal General, which oversaw the entire system, was terminated on July 15, and the Selective Service System of World War I had officially ended.[13]

By mid-April 1919, the casualty lists had been further reduced from a daily feature to intermittent appearances. And when the word "casualty" appeared in a newspaper article, rather than an accounting of war-related incidents, it was more likely to refer to an injured athlete who was unable to play in an upcoming athletic match. And even the cherished and sacred phrase of honor roll, once reserved for those who had lost their lives in military service, was now being applied, without shame, to the athlete who had recently worn the uniform of a soldier. It was a fitting indication that peace had been restored.[14]

Neither the cessation of recruitment nor the elimination of the casualty lists would be sufficient to end the misreporting and uncertainty that lingered about men who had served in the war. The absurdity of some situations was well reflected a full year later when former Private Michael Iannelli applied to the Red Cross for compensation for having been gassed on the battlefield but was rejected on the grounds that he had died in the war. Although documentary "evidence" in the form of an official certificate of his death was available, Iannelli offered the former Miss Ida Tursi, his bride, with whom he was now living in West Philadelphia in support of his own claim that he was actually very much alive. Iannelli's irrefutable protestation also affirmed the steadfast denial by his defiant mother after a telegram from the War Department had brought news of his death in late December 1918.[15]

If clarifying the status of men in the U.S. armed forces proved to be a difficult task, the reservists who had become members of Italy's army provided an even more daunting challenge. By 1922, the War Department was still belatedly exculpating Italians who by leaving the United States had become identified as draft evaders. Among Philadelphia's Italians, Vincenzo Garafolo, unable to return his questionnaire to the Selective Service Board, thus placing his name on the list of draft dodgers, served a machine gun company of the Italian infantry, which he had joined in 1916. Narciso Limosino, a Sicilian-born immigrant laborer for the Pennsylvania Railroad, who after registering on June 5, 1917, failed to report to a local draft board in September, enlisted in the Italian army in November, which he served until his honorable discharge in July 1920. Antonio D'Alessandro, also cited as a slacker, was one of the "lions" of the Piave, who wore his uniform as an Italian soldier until being discharged in August 1919. While cleansing their status from draft evaders to honorably discharged veterans had restored their respectability, the stigma of being renitenti would remain for others. And undoubtedly, many other men who followed similar paths had fallen into these almost forgotten channels.[16]

But Are They Yet Americans?

The undeniably heroic sacrifices of men like the 18-year-old Scioli whose parents had waited in vain for his return and others like Iannelli whose survival came as a welcome surprise for his family were not the only consequences that mattered. The war had left a wide range of issues that remained to be solved. In early 1919, Dr. S. E. Weber, superintendent of Public Schools of Scranton and president of the Pennsylvania State Educational Association, speaking on Americanism at its annual convention, addressed the importance of educating the foreign born. He recognized, like Ottavio Neyroz, the Presbyterian minister at Camp Lee, and many others, the considerable part that Italians and other groups in "our foreign population" had played in the war, claiming that they had comprised one-fourth of our fighting strength. He gratuitously saluted them by declaring: "How remarkable their loyalty to the land of their adoption." But somehow, it had not been enough. For despite their contributions, Weber was disturbed that one-third of the aliens in the first draft had been unable to speak the English language. He asked: "In the light of our recent experience caused by the handicap of language, shall we not agree among ourselves as a common country, a common state, a common community, that hereafter the language of instruction in the common branches in the elementary school, both private and public, shall be the English language—the chosen medium of expression of the entire county?" While giving the impression of a widespread preference for foreign language in classroom instruction, it was an obvious straw man because such an alternative was virtually nonexistent. Beyond the instructional needs of children, Weber sought the Americanizing of their foreign-born parents, particularly their mothers, by encouraging them to attend afternoon classes and night schools. His basic aim, which only began with the specious issue of language in the classroom, was a comprehensive assault on the presence of "foreign" culture in America. Far from alone in making this argument, it was part of a groundswell of opinion during the course of the war that America had to be saved from alien influences. Buried within it was the premise that despite the great contributions made by the soldiers of "our foreign population" whom he so lavishly praised, it was necessary to erase what they carried of their own cultures. Weber's sentiments, which would be widely repeated by influential voices throughout the nation, expressed what awaited these veterans and their families in the very near future and what would ultimately to be implemented by public policy on immigration.[17]

Within a broader context, naturalization had played a role but did not by itself represent the full and final picture. In the closing months of the war, the effort to grant citizenship to foreign-born soldiers had not only gained great momentum but produced formidable results. In June 1918, the passage of a new law facilitated citizenship for men in military service by greatly reducing the required period of residence in the United States before submitting their declaration of intention and by allowing certification of their loyalty by two officers. As a result, at Camp Dix alone, the court had conferred citizenship on 11,000 men from Allied and neutral countries. By summer 1919, even with the war over, naturalization courts at military sites were still in operation. In July, an editorial in the *Evening Public Ledger* expected that the 2,000 alien soldiers who had been naturalized in the past three months would make good citizens. It solemnly noted that "they have learned in a practical school what Americanism stands for. And if they have suffered for the country of their adoption they will love it even more. Sacrifice is the mother of patriotism." But while offering a rationalization for the price that aliens had paid by choosing to wear American uniforms, it also reminded them that naturalization would not be enough to be more fully accepted as Americans. Reiterating the sentiments that Weber, the Scranton educator, had expressed a few months earlier, "Americanism," even in "liberal" minds, required the rejection of diversity.[18]

For men who had served in the military, the expected outcome of their recent experience was ceremonially displayed when 28 recent graduates, identified in newspaper coverage as "aliens," of the Recruit Education Center at Camp Upton, New Jersey, arrived in Philadelphia in October 1919. Over the next three days, the special detachment, known as the "Americans All" unit, presented marching and drill demonstrations on the Parkway from city hall to the Museum of Art and other sites throughout the city. Along with some formerly illiterate native-born Americans, the men, representing 14 other national backgrounds—Spanish, Lithuanian, Italian, French-Canadian, Norwegian, Finnish, French, Polish, Russian, Armenian, Greek, Dutch, Yugoslav, and Danish—were said to have been unable to speak English, read a newspaper, or write in their own dialects three months earlier. But now as a result of their training, they could do all of these things. As a caption over their photograph described them, they were the "Melting Pot Soldiers of Uncle Sam's Army." Their more personal stories followed a common narrative, often with tragic subplots, of an inspiring minidrama of coming to America and becoming an American with a climax of naturalization. They themselves probably found the apogee of their visit in having lunch at the august Union League, before giving another demonstration in front of its building on South Broad Street in the center of Philadelphia. They embodied precisely what their experience as members of the U.S. Army was supposed to have done for them, and perhaps it truly had. As an archetype, the tale of one of these men concluded, "He came to America, heard of the Recruit Educational Center, and today he is an American soldier and citizen." But the answer to the question of what had these recent years done for America as a society remained far more complicated and elusive.[19]

While reducing the urgency of naturalizing aliens, the end of the war did not altogether eliminate them as a problem. A few months after the "Americans All" unit had marched in testimony to the capacity of America to assimilate, as the focus shifted to the civilian scene, it could also recognize what the foreign born were contributing to the nation. In February 1920, Reverend John Nelson Mills, a well-known Presbyterian minister from Washington, DC, speaking before the Christian Americanization Conference, declared: "This good old Quaker city of Philadelphia, which we are in the habit of regarding as distinctly American, has a population that is more than one-quarter foreign born. More than one-third the remainder of the people are children of the foreign born." For the nation as a whole, its 10,000,000 aliens, larger than the combined population of Holland and Belgium, or of Norway, Sweden, Denmark, and Switzerland, represented one-sixth of the population; when counted with their children, it rose to 35,000,000 or one-third of the entire population. But it was largely an urban affair, with 72 percent of the foreign population found in American cities, and only 5 percent of residents of the 57 cities of 100,000 persons or more being Americans. Despite the great perils of ignorance and un-Americanism, Mills recognized that the foreign born were undeniably important for economic productivity. Asserting that "we are immensely dependent on these foreigners for the daily necessities of our life," he offered a laudatory litany based on census data. Immigrants and their children manufactured 95 percent of the clothing worn by Americans; refined 95 percent of the sugar; and made 95 percent of all cotton goods. They comprised of the workforce: 35 percent of meatpacking; 80 percent of all furniture making; 75 percent of our woolen production; 50 percent of our collar, cuff, and shirt production; and 70 percent of our bituminous coal mining. Yet, for all their indispensable labor, workers from the foreign population had received, until lately, an average of less than $600 in annual wages. Shifting to the plight of immigrants and their children, Mills argued for the necessity of Americanization not out of xenophobia but with a compassionate understanding of their material value to America and their intrinsic worth as human beings. He was presenting the "other side" of the argument for Americanization.[20]

The argument for Americanization gained further momentum from a widely shared, almost ecumenical perspective. In May 1921, Rabbi Harry W. Ettleson, director of Education at Rodeph Shalom Synagogue and one of the most respected voices in the Jewish community, expressed a point of view similar to any enlightened Protestant leader in Philadelphia. In his opinion, both immigration and naturalization were good for America but had to offer more inspiration to the newcomer in order to achieve the best results. While the great diversity of population in itself made naturalization more important to America than to any other nation, our institutions, as elements of a democratic society resting upon the character of its citizens, further reaffirmed it. Yet, Ettleson argued, America had a less well considered, clearly defined, or constructive policy on citizenship than almost any other nation. The Selective Service had revealed the great number of residents who had never taken out their first papers or had neglected to follow the process to its completion. While disavowing extremism that defined immigrants as a "menace" but acknowledging that some of them might not be desirable,

Ettleson maintained that "America must not be considered as a boarding place, on which the alien is to sponge, take all the advantages and give nothing in return." Of those migrants who worked temporarily before returning to native lands, he concluded: "They are probably more useful to the country doing certain work that is required of them, and for a time they would be an asset, but not a permanent one." Since some aliens did not hold citizenship in high regard because they recognized that politicians used naturalization for corrupt purposes, he called for "a warm-blooded, inspiring ceremonial" in the final granting of citizenship, which, along with more rigorous preparation, would invest this critical moment in the life of the immigrant with greater dignity. But while Ettleson and other clergymen had embraced the meaning of citizenship and the protocols of the naturalization process, not all of his colleagues supported the immigrant. Having learned during the war how to make an American soldier out of an alien recruit, the nation, with the return of peace, had returned to the task of making an American out of an immigrant civilian, or at least one who was deemed desirable. But for Italian veterans, as the arc from Felice the street musician to Diodati the physician showed, it was a challenge with a wide range of possible outcomes.[21]

Celebrating the Italian Victory—Fuori Italia

A s the war in Europe approached its conclusion, Philadelphia's Italians, buoyed by distant events, appeared to be heading for halcyon days in its aftermath. But after a fleeting moment of exuberant celebration that brought recognition for their contributions, they would become embroiled in internal dissension as well as afflicted by the isolationist politics of a U.S. government exhausted by international affairs—until being briefly distracted, if not rescued by General Armando Diaz, the hero of the Piave, an unanticipated visitor received with great acclaim in the final scene of Little Italy's engagement with the Great War. A reconstruction of the sequence of those events is worthwhile.

Raising the *Tricolore*

By early November 1918, Italy's forces had penetrated deeply into enemy territory, recaptured the Asiago Plateau, and raised the *tricolore* over Trento and Trieste. On November 4, Philadelphia's Italians, after weeks of mounting anticipation, burst into celebration with news of victory over Austro-Hungarian forces "in a way that is new to Philadelphia, but demonstrative of the true spirit of the land from which they came." Mindful both of those left behind in their native land and the army of volunteers sent back, "the entire Italian born population of the city launched a joyous celebration that will continue until their voices can no longer ring in song and cheers and until their arms grow too weary to support the flags of the Allied nations they carry." It began with the gathering of groups on dark street corners of Little Italy at 3:00 A.M., growing within a half hour to about 200 men and women, and falling into line behind a band. By 8:00 A.M., many men and women had decided that something more important than their daily work was at hand, while others already at places of employment would soon join them. But the day had only begun.[1]

As morning unfolded, thousands of local Italians, declaring "a virtual holiday," had abandoned their work and forced the closing of factories, banks, and other businesses, as throngs, carrying flags of Italy and the United States, sang and cheered in spontaneous demonstrations on city streets. Before the day ended, every Italian band in the city appeared to have joined in the celebration. A reporter declared that it was "impossibile descrivere l'entusiasmo sollevato nella Colonia Italiana di Philadelphia" (impossible to describe the enthusiasm raised by the Italian colony of Philadelphia) at the news that Trento and Trieste were occupied, Austria had surrendered, and an armistice sanctioned the aspirations of Italy. As employees poured out of Snellenberg's Department Store, they paused under the windows of the *Evening Public Ledger* in a gesture of appreciation, before assembling at the Italian consulate where official Italy reunited with overseas Italy in a shared moment of unrestrained joy.[2]

The celebration, however, was far from over. In the afternoon, Mayor Smith issued a proclamation calling for the display of the banners of the United States and Italy from homes and places of business. In the evening, several thousand Italians converged at 7th and Carpenter Streets, marching from the heart of Little Italy to Broad Street, then up to Chestnut Street in Center City, and east to Independence Square. The main speaker, Signor Gaetano Poccardi, a familiar figure after returning to the city for his second tour as royal consul, announced that he had sent messages to President Woodrow Wilson and King Victor Emmanuel III on behalf of Philadelphia's Italians. In his words to the president, linking Jefferson and Mazzini, then Washington and Garibaldi, he declared that Wilson's leadership had made possible the victory for which Italians now expressed "their devoted and grateful thoughts." To the king of his own country, he reiterated the memorable words of an earlier Italian monarch, "We are here and we are going to stay." While alluding to the taking of Rome by nationalist forces nearly a half-century earlier, Poccardi could have been referring to the more recent capture of neighborhoods by Philadelphia's Italians.[3]

If Italians needed to go beyond their own reasons to find pride in what had transpired, Philadelphia's newspapers richly embellished Italy's military success. An editorial, linking the Italian victory to the glories of ancient Rome, stated that the "superb campaign of Diaz" after Caporetto had "something of the high Roman fashion to it." But while evoking Cato, the Gracchi, Marcus Aurelius, and Julius Caesar, it even surpassed them, for nothing had ever been more decisive than "this wonderful accomplishment on the Piave, the Tagliamento and in the Trentino." Having salvaged victory from disaster, the salute continued: "Even in the blackest days of Caporetto it was impossible to conceive that she who had found the New World should lack the ardor and energy to help redeem the Old." As it galloped through historical references, it found resonance with more recent eras: "Renaissance—rebirth, a superb quickening, a heroic fulfillment—now symbolizes Italy in the chronicle of arms." Of the unexpected reversal, the tribute declared: "In all the pages of history there is nothing quite like the magnitude of titanic recovery which the last year . . . has revealed on the Venetian plains." The Risorgimento provided further inspiration: "The flame of Mazzini, most intellectual of liberators, and of Garibaldi, deliverer of sturdiest blows for freedom, burned into the hearts of unyielding Italian armies, steadfast at last on the Piave . . . Austria's final effort in June was heroically humbled . . . the redemption of Venetia, the recovery of Trent and Trieste, the two chief cities of the soil once pathetically called 'Irredenta,' and finally the armistice coup de grace whereby Austria is literally hurtled out of the war—these are the accomplishments of our triumphant ally, heir of the immortal spirit of still civilizing Rome."[4]

With press dispatches bringing more details, the estimated number of Austrians captured exceeded 500,000, with more than 3,000 square kilometers of territory and over 1,000 villages recovered, gains that had surpassed the losses of Caporetto. Despite being a smaller force than their enemy, Italian troops had advanced an average of about 31 miles, while exceeding 60 miles over winding roads during each of the 10 days of the final assault. The first effort to negotiate began on October 29, when an Austrian captain, under a white flag, approached Italian lines south of Rovereto but was rejected for bearing insufficient credentials. On the next day, nine Austrian officers accompanied by orderlies and heralded by bugles were placed in cars and escorted to Diaz's headquarters near Padua. While awaiting final surrender, Italian troops advanced over the next four days before the end finally came. A press service reported another especially cherished piece of information: "The victory was obtained by the Italians virtually single-handed, only five Anglo-French divisions and one American regiment aiding them." From Washington, General Guglielmotti, military attaché at the Italian Embassy, described the choice of the right moment; the efficient direction of the attacks; and the rapidity of execution as crucial factors in the events of October

24 to November 4. With the retreat on the Western Front, along with the withdrawal of Bulgaria and Turkey, Austria, although superior in number, had been left to face Italy alone. But bad weather and swollen streams, impeding both sides, also narrowed the Italian front of attack, while rendering enemy counterattacks almost impossible, as Diaz moved troops with utmost speed to divide enemy forces on the plains from those in the mountains. For anyone seeking a more grounded interpretation, Guglielmotti had more plausibly explained the outcome without any reference to ancient Rome, Renaissance, or Risorgimento.[5]

With celebration renewed across the city and nearby communities of Pennsylvania and New Jersey, revelers, in a familiar Italian manner, found their way to cafés and restaurants—the fashionable Leoncavallo on South 12th Street and the Caruso Italian Café on South 16th Street—invited by newspaper ads to "Celebrate the Great Italian Victory!" and further encouraged by news that the great influenza epidemic was also over. And one observer facetiously noted: "If any one went to bed last night unaware of what the Italian national anthem is, it was his own fault."[6]

As local Italians continuing to celebrate recent news, whether disseminated by an American newspaper or in their own foreign language press, or among those who could only be told about it because they were unable to read in any language, the *Evening Public Ledger* warmly saluted them:

> Nobody organized the demonstrations in which the folk from Little Italy marched about town yesterday to sing their hearts out because of the things that have just happened to Austria. Their spirits captained them.
>
> We who have lived always in the mightiest land on earth will never know just how the news from the front touched the men and women who marched and sang. We shall never be in a far place to hear of an enemy swept after bitter fighting from the soil we knew—of the deliverance of places and people greatly loved.
>
> Italy has endured more than the world realized. The crowded cables haven't told half the glory of the Italian campaign.
>
> The wonder isn't that Little Italy marched and sang. The wonder is that the rest of us didn't march and sing and whoop it up with Little Italy.[7]

With support of Italy as the *madrepatria* and America as the chosen land, these events on the streets, in churches and meeting halls, and especially among families with husbands, fathers, brothers, and sons in uniform provided reminders of Little Italy as a distinctive home front contained within the boundaries of an even broader one. It had first emerged when Italy declared war on Austria; it remained throughout the war; and it would continue well after the war had ended. But while testifying to allegiance to both countries, it would soon be undermined as public policy in America shifted to a perfidious rejection of immigrants no longer welcome, if they had ever been.

Victory on the Western Front

Local Italians found another opportunity to celebrate with news that the kaiser had abdicated and revolution was sweeping Germany. At the conclusion of his Sunday Mass, Father Terlizzi again led the congregation of Our Lady of Good Counsel onto Christian Street, then on a now familiar route up Broad Street and east on Chestnut Street. Behind a mounted patrol, a police band and Italian fraternal groups with their own musical ensembles joined the procession. Aged women in gaudy scarves or only plain white handkerchiefs, hobbled along, gay in demeanor, if not as spry as in their earlier years. Men carried babies in their arms, while younger women led groups of children on foot. Families marched together. Veterans carried torn and tattered battle flags. The men and women of organized labor fell into line. And with evident joy, six "pallbearers" dragged an effigy of the kaiser, clad in a faded blue uniform, with a frankfurter protruding from his mouth. At Independence Square, a predictable slate of Congressman William S. Vare, the political boss of South Philadelphia, Baldi, and other prominenti delivered expectable oratory. And Signor Ferruccio Giannini, the local tenor, sang his own composition, "The Yankee Boys in Italy," accompanied by his son Victor, while the crowd echoed with their own national anthem, then the Star-Spangled Banner, and waved Italian and American flags.[8]

On the following day, when more Philadelphians converged on Independence Square with news of the Armistice on the Western Front, exultant Italians returned with them. Hundreds of them, again carrying the flags of two nations, one of birth and another of adoption, had begun to march by six o'clock in the morning from their downtown homes to Center City. They again paraded around the most sacred edifice of early American history and stopped to serenade with cheers and shouts at the offices of the most esteemed newspaper in the city. And throughout the day, as trolley cars arrived from all neighborhoods of the city, amid a persistent roar, strangers grasped hands and offered congratulations to one another, and waited for the Liberty Bell to be rung, as Italians, joining others in shouting "To Hell with the Kaiser," were momentarily assimilated into another massive crowd as fellow Philadelphians and Americans.[9]

With festivities erupting across the nation, Italians at Camp Meade, easily overlooked in the extraordinary din, were arranging a suitable program at the cantonment where their conationals had been trained for military service on the Western Front. While anticipating only a celebration of Italy's defeat of Austria, recent events had broadened the scope of their agenda, which now encompassed the entire Allied victory. For sons of Italy, as one observer wrote, "Old Rome will howl with a vengeance, for there is surely going to be one hullabaloo of a good time." For Umberto "Bert" Cavallazzi, a 26-year-old Berlin-born member of a family of circus acrobats who came to the United States as nonimmigrant aliens in 1908, the celebration held special meaning. In June 1917, registering for the draft as a West Side Manhattan resident, he had already submitted his declaration of intention for American citizenship. Claiming that as a trapeze performer in Germany he had often stuck out his tongue to ridicule the kaiser, Cavallazzi may have been taking advantage of the moment. But another aspect of his life as well as for his fellow recruits was more certain. Cavallazzi and some 1,100 other aliens had recently been granted American citizenship in the final naturalization procedure at Camp Meade. While intending to bring Italians together to observe his birthday and new citizenship, both occurring within the span of a few days, victory over Austria and Germany called for an even broader event. The indefatigable Cavallazzi promised to denounce the kaiser in Italian, German, English, and other languages. But for all Italians, whether as soldiers in camp or civilians on city streets, their naturalization as citizens and exuberant participation in victory celebrations reflected their new allegiance.[10]

Celebrating Philadelphia

Meanwhile, the city of Philadelphia basked in self-congratulations for its role in the war. With unabashed praise, one assessment insisted: "Philadelphia stands pre-eminent among the cities of America for its contributions to humanity's cause." Although similar praise could be claimed by other cities, expanded by defense production, Philadelphia's industries had earned singular distinction. American soldiers wore uniforms produced by factories in the city, carried arms and ammunition manufactured here or in neighboring locations while waiting to go "over the top," and were protected by barrages of heavy guns and shells as well as gas masks from local plants. Philadelphia-made vessels shipped locally manufactured locomotives from the city's port to haul men and supplies over steel rails produced in other parts of Pennsylvania to the front. Beyond industrial productivity, military leaders with residence or family roots in the state had contributed much by their role in battlefield operations. And Philadelphians had heavily supported the financing effort by purchasing about a billion dollars' worth of bonds during Liberty Loan campaigns. But Philadelphia's greatest contribution had been the 60,000 men from the city who had entered the service during the past 19 months—leaving a record that was "written in letters of flame in the history of the great war." It was difficult to disagree with that conclusion.[11]

The early municipal plan for remembrance also called for recognition of Italy's contribution. On the day after the Armistice, Mayor Smith announced plans for a monument commemorating Philadelphians who had lost their lives in the war, which would be located on the recently opened Fairmount Parkway in Center City. Meanwhile, the *Public Ledger* proposed that the principal streets be renamed for wartime leaders, with Pershing, Foch, Haig, and Diaz being among them. Smith enthusiastically praised both proposals as expressions of "the love and admiration for the men who went into the war to secure freedom for the world," and "the noble women who have served so faithfully and energetically both abroad and at home." But no cenotaph or memorial on the envisioned scale would be erected, and no streets would be renamed. With the failed hope for a public gesture, the sculpture of such places as Holy Cross cemetery in suburban Yeadon would become the enduring monuments to the sons of Little Italy.[12]

Not quite two weeks after the armistice on the Italian front, a more ephemeral memorial announced "Triumphant Italy" on the pages of the *Evening Public Ledger*. The full-page broadside offered inset photographs of President Wilson, medallions of Savoy and the United States, at the top, flanked by King Victor Emmanuel III and Field Marshal Foch, and portraits of General Diaz and General Pershing on the sides and British Field Marshal Haig at the bottom. Its florid text extolled Italy, in "the greatest struggle of humanity," for having rescued Europe and humanity from "the threatening danger of kaiserism and subjugation" and for having risen from the struggle "with the old glory that was Rome." Beyond this ambitious claim, it added: "No longer is she the land of museums and the mecca of tourists," but as the oldest child of Rome and youngest of the modern nations, while the land of beauty and freedom, she had delivered to the "brute forces of might the death blow in the valley of the Piave and on the peaks of the snow-clad Alps." And with reproduction of a cable message sent by Wilson to Victor Emmanuel III on his birthday, the names of well-known members of the Italian community

FIGURE 14.1 "Triumphant Italy." (*Evening Public Ledger* [November 16, 1918].)

endorsed its sentiments. But as much as proclaiming the Italian effort in the war, the poster also reflected their voice in the city.[13] (See Figure 14.1.)

In ensuing days, celebration blanketed the surrounding region. Within the city, neighborhoods presented programs in observance of victory, while communities beyond its limits similarly saluted the troops and nation. Along with solemn ceremonies, other scenes were more boisterous demonstrations, and some were more like political vaudeville. But as events became command performances, Italians cast themselves in leading roles. Nearly a week after the Armistice of the Western Front, some 10,000 Italians from Philadelphia, Camden, and towns of Burlington County were expected to converge for the mock execution of the former kaiser, but now just plain "Bill Hohenzollern," planned for Beverly, New Jersey. A parade would begin the proceedings, with a contingent of 200 marchers carrying the flags of Italy and the United States, escorting an effigy of the "Kaiser that was" in an open truck, drawn by mules and guarded by 10 Italian soldiers from nearby Camp Dix. Some participants preferred hanging the former ruler from a tree before setting him on fire to convince onlookers of his "death," while others, believing that even lynching was too kind, entered "a polite but determined request that the doomed man be buried alive." The extremity of such observances measured the intensity of hatred toward the recent enemy.[14]

As the celebration continued, Philadelphia industries, with an "abundance of patriotism," joined into recognition of the Italian role in the war. In late November, several hundred workers gathered at the east side yard of the Baltimore and Ohio Railroad at 37th and Jackson Streets to cheer at the unfurling of American and Italian flags at an event honoring fellow employees who had served in the war. And to confirm that many of them were Italians, a "Neapolitan Band" provided music for the program. But such celebrations were also found in loftier venues. A few days after the railroad workers salute, some 200 Italian members and their guests gathered at the Manufacturers' Club, profusely decorated with potted palmettos and cut flowers, bunting and flags, and portraits of the king and queen of Italy, for a special Thanksgiving celebration of the victory. Organized by Luigi Rienzi, proprietor of a fashionable Walnut Street women's clothing store, and a committee of local Italians, a formidable roster of speakers included William Potter, the former U.S. ambassador to Italy; Edward E. Beidleman, the lieutenant governor–elect of Pennsylvania; J. Hampton Moore, U.S. congressman and future mayor of Philadelphia; Anthony Caminetti, U.S. commissioner general of immigration; Judge John M. Patterson, president judge of the Court of Common Pleas; Gaetano Poccardi, royal consul of Italy; C.C.A. Baldi, and other orators. In his first public appearance as archbishop of Philadelphia, the newly appointed Dennis J. Dougherty, seeking to ingratiate himself, greeted the crowd in Italian, "Essendo fra voi, sento di essere uno di voi" (Being among you, I feel that I am one of you), and earned a rousing ovation. He declared that no other immigrant group had assimilated as well, before praising its women as being more pure and noble in their thought and deeds than any other women. For the prelate, it was an auspicious beginning that would hold him in good stead for another 15 years, until his decision to close Our

Lady of Good Counsel, their largest national parish, would all but destroy his popularity. But on this night, speaker after speaker offered only extravagant blandishments for Italy and its soldiers, people, and immigrants, with endless toasts to King Vittorio Emanuele and President Wilson amid cheers and the singing of national anthems. And after operatic selections, from Verdi rather than Wagner by the Giannini sisters, their brother Victor's music and father Ferruccio Giannini's words once again pried the audience to its feet by a rendition of "The Yankee Boys in Italy."[15]

The return of peace enabled the entire city to observe a traditional holiday as a unique moment in its history. A newspaper proclaimed: "This is the most wonderful Thanksgiving Day in America's history. . . . Philadelphia is observing the day as never before." But another item captured something more when it noted: "For one thing, the 'boys' are coming home." Among various events in public squares and parks, one program, organized by the Council of National Defense, consisted of the national anthem, prayers for peace, and the reading of a presidential proclamation. And flooding the streets in seemingly unending demonstrations, Italians again found an opportunity even on this singularly American holiday to praise their own heroes. Following fraternal societies and musical bands through another of their neighborhoods, they placed an honor roll of 115 names of men who had served, included 2 who had lost their lives and 36 who had been wounded, into a glass-covered wood case on a corner at 29th Street and Allegheny Avenue in North Philadelphia. In the afternoon, members of the Sons of Italy marched on Christian Street, then north on Broad Street to a local version of the Statue of Liberty placed at city hall, before proceeding to Independence Hall for another program of speeches by Consul Poccardi and other dignitaries. And Margaret Diodati, the wife of Dr. Victor M. Diodati, who had played such an extraordinary role by his service on the Western Front, took her place as "Italia," on a float depicting "Victory over Austria." Her presence reaffirmed the note that had been sounded by the press—the widely shared anticipation of reunion for the boys who were coming home to their families.[16]

If Philadelphia's Italians had reason to rejoice at news that their sons would soon be returning, another announcement brought quieter elation. On December 19, the office of the Italian royal consul, almost entirely unnoticed, declared that Italians in the United States would no longer be required to register for military service. While the call up had already been halted, the many reservists who had ignored the summons of their government, officially making them *renitente alla leva*, could begin to feel a measure of relief, although their status remained uncertain. While serving with distinction with the U.S.

Army on the Western Front, many of them had become citizens of the United States. And by that choice, they had also repositioned themselves from temporary migrants, seeking to accumulate savings from their labor before returning to Italy, to permanent immigrants who would find their future in America.[17]

The celebration of victory did not dismiss concern for victims of the war. In early December, another "Victory Banquet" at the Adelphia Hotel sought to raise funds for relief in devastated areas of Northern Italy, "whose hardships and privations during the Austrian occupation have recently become known." The program, expected to attract an audience of about 500 persons, called for operatic selections and patriotic songs by Enrico Caruso, as well as "Professor Giannini and his two talented daughters," and speeches by the now familiar mix of immigrant prominenti, local politicians, and Italian government representatives, which again included Smith, Guglielmotti, Poccardi, Baldi, and others. But not lost were the ringing claims, as former governor Charles R. Miller of Delaware had expressed at the earlier program at the Manufacturers' Club, that "every son that Italy can spare with the return of peace is now thrice welcome in America" and that Italians in America now faced a new and brighter era. And from the clamor that arose at such events, it would have seemed so.[18]

Italians and other Philadelphians who were unlikely to attend gala events at grand hotels or exclusive clubs found their own opportunities to celebrate in rapidly proliferating restaurants whose proprietors invited guests to dine on Italian cuisine. Since before the war, such places, bearing names of famous composers, performers, or geographic locations had offered Italian menus. While the well-known Leoncavallo Restaurant had been a popular choice for some time, the recently opened Venice Restaurant on Walnut Street and the Caruso on South 16th Street, a few steps below Market Street, were now attracting patrons in Center City. The Savoy, which had been on South 11th, would announce its "new, enlarged and elaborate headquarters" in a remodeled colonial house located on South 12th, just below Market. The more intrepid diner who ventured further into Little Italy could find the Mascagni Restaurant, Curatolo's Restaurant, or the Tenaglia Bar and Restaurant within the same corridor of the 700 block of South 8th Street. Another dining site, the Diaz Italian Restaurant on 13th Street, at its opening in late December, advertised itself as "unsurpassed for its Italian cuisine . . . a new rendezvous for the epicure located within the heart of the shopping district," offering "famous a la carte" selections. Despite its premature claim before having opened, it was undoubtedly the most opportunistically named restaurant of the moment. Such establishments, however, were much more than merely places to eat or even to celebrate the end of a war. By introducing other Philadelphians to an increasingly popular cuisine, they offered a portal to the Italian colony and its culture. At a time when Little Italy was evolving beyond its earlier stage as a foreign and foreboding enclave and becoming another neighborhood in the city, its institutions could be more easily embraced by other Americans. And especially by providing another setting to celebrate not only Italy's triumph but America's victory as well, Italian restaurants facilitated the integration of an immigrant people. At no time was it more visible than during this period of great civic euphoria and unity.[19]

The Mutilated Peace

Apart from celebrations, the still unsettled matter of irredentism, too important to be left to diplomats, would become a cause of internal disruption. The lingering memory of what had brought a homeland into war and the later flush of victory renewed commitment to Italy's interests. In early December, a committee met at Columbus Hall in South Philadelphia to form a local chapter of "Italia Irredenta," a New York City–based initiative seeking to promote Italy's interest in the disputed land from the Alps to the Adriatic. Prominent business and professional men, Protestant clergymen, and representatives of the disputed provinces were among the participants. After presentations by Maestro Ettore Martini, a well-known conductor and composer, and Reverend Thomas Malan, rector of the Saint Saveur French Episcopal Church and sometimes minister to Italians, the group composed a message in English and French to be sent to President Wilson and representatives of other Allied governments. Three weeks later, Italia Irredenta offered a program at the new Shubert Theater that featured speakers defending Italy's claims, along with the latest film depictions of the war. Ignoring even the approach of Christmas, the committee's priorities had directed attention to an issue that would preoccupy efforts during the postwar reconstruction of Italy.[20]

Italians did not stand alone but were joined by scholars, such as the highly respected Italophile William Roscoe Thayer, and public officials who endorsed Italy's territorial agenda. When Italia Irredenta held a grand banquet at the Leoncavallo Restaurant in early February 1919 to honor General Ugo Pizzarello and other war heroes, it was also to express support for Italy in the upcoming Peace Conference. Judge Eugene C. Bonniwell, magistrate of the Municipal Court and principal speaker, hailed Italy for having saved the world by coming to the aid of the Allies. If Italy had joined the Central Powers, "there would have been no civilization left to save before England could have landed a single soldier on French soil." Arguing that once Italy's role became better understood, public opinion would turn in favor of her demands at the Peace Conference, Bonniwell concluded: "Italy not only has the right to ask, but she has the right to demand guarantees against further aggression from the north." Other speakers, Thomas Daly, the local humorist; Harold D. Eberlin, a noted architectural historian; Leslie M. Miller, head of the Pennsylvania Museum and School of Industrial Art; and William C. McClellan, dean of the Wharton School at the University of Pennsylvania, concurred. Master of ceremonies, and lawyer, Eugene V. Alessandroni, succinctly summarized the mood of the evening by observing that although the war had been won by the intervention of the United States the greatest victory had been achieved by Italy.[21]

While knowing the "interior life" of Philadelphia's Italians of the past remains a task whose answer lies beyond our reach, their response to the so-called mutilated peace, the disputed territorial claims of Italy, playing out in American foreign policy, is somewhat accessible. Returning to a familiar forum, Charles M. Bandiere, who had earlier commended the *Evening Ledger* for using Italian in reporting the war, now defended Italy's postwar claims. Appealing to a sense of fairness, he questioned the motives of journalists who condemned Italy, when it had not only been the true savior of the Marne but had rescued the Allies from defeat several times. He asked why Italy should be blamed "for grasping the opportunity offered to all the Allies through their united victory?" Against the contention that it had betrayed noble impulses of other Allies, Bandiere compared Italy's aspirations to France's claim to Alsace-Lorraine. Against the allegation that Italy had sordid motives, he asked if the United States, having waited while Belgium was being crushed, the Lusitania sunk, Serbia engulfed, and Romania reduced to a mere geographic expression, had pursued a purely idealistic objective. He posed the question: "If . . . we answered to the call of civilization only, then why did we not act when civilization was first attacked?" And against the sentimentality cleansing other nations, Bandiere noted that opponents discerned flaws only of Italy. After approval for Italy's attack on Austria and forbearance for Yugoslav claims, critical propaganda now elevated "infant states, not yet born, to aspire to equality with man-grown, mature democracies, whose liberties and culture have been dearly bought through years of national anguish and bloodshed." And the ardent, loyal, desperate defenders of the Hapsburg dynasty of yesterday had somehow been transformed into "liberty-loving, freedom-shouting, time trampled Slavs." He asked why Italy should be singled out when England and France had made their own secret pacts involving control over far greater parcels of territory. Bandiere added that Italy's aspirations, through adversity, defeat, and silent suffering, had become sacred and inspirational in creating a modern nation. And after bitter defeat at Caporetto, Italy had achieved the most decisive victory of the entire war. From a population of 26,000,000, it had put some 5,500,000 men into the field. To feed them, starvation came to her civilians. Almost deserted by her allies, Italy somehow ran her industries without coal. Leaving Alpine peaks stained with their blood, her soldiers had fought against great odds, while sailors performed deeds unequaled in any war. Wounded Italy had become the subject of severe, unsympathetic propaganda from formerly friendly powers opposing the acquisition of sought-after territory while applauding the repatriation of Alsace-Lorraine by France and the ceding of formerly German colonies to England. Bandiere had raised numerous issues, but he was not alone in stepping forward with his argument.[22]

Another young Italian, Ralph Rubino, a pharmacist, contended that if France recalled how Italy had protected her from being overrun by Germany, she should offer little opposition to Italian rights. But despite the victory, France and the other nations were favoring Austria over their former ally. Having paid a great price in their capture, Trent and Trieste, he insisted, should forever remain under Italy's control. And in the current political crisis within Italy, with Bissolati and Nitti having already betrayed the nation, Sonnino, although favoring a bad war, would still bring a satisfactory peace, despite the refusal of France and the United States to grant a just reward to the Italian people. While Bandiere and Rubino may have inflated what was owed to Italy, their arguments, which banquet orators had previously proposed, reflected a widely shared consensus within the Italian community.[23]

In February, a larger effort sought to convey the views of Philadelphia's Italians to President Wilson. Responding to a reporter ostensibly inquiring about his health, Giuseppe Di Silvestro, the head of the Order Sons of Italy in America (OSIA), insisted that if the president's return from Europe entailed arriving at the port of Philadelphia, local Italians had to organize a program to honor him. If such a plan was not feasible, they had to find another means to remind him of the historical, geographic, and ethnological reasons that Italy must be reshaped along the lines of Irredentist demands. Calling for a general assembly of OSIA lodges, Di Silvestro intended to involve the entire "colonia Italiana di Filadelfia." In an unprecedented display of unity, representatives of most Italian organizations, meeting at the Sons of Italy headquarters at 7th and Christian Streets, would set aside their differences. Venerables and grand deputies of the Sons of Italy; officials of the rival Independent Sons of Italy; Frank Roma, president of the Italian Committee of the Liberty Loan; Maestro Ettore Martini, president of the regional chapter of Italia Irredenta; Roberto Lombardi, president of the Circolo Italiano; and John Queroli, president of the Societá di Unione e Fratellanza Italiana, the venerable flagship of voluntary associations, responded to Di Silvestro's invitation. With only the Federation of Italian Societies being conspicuously absent, the participants agreed to hold a rally, open to all Italians in the city, at the Alhambra Theatre in South Philadelphia on the next Sunday. As Di Silvestro had proposed, the agenda would honor Wilson but also prepare an endorsement of Italy's claims to the unredeemed territories to be sent to him before he returned to the Peace Conference.[24]

In early March, more than 3,000 Italians filled the Alhambra Theatre to voice their defense of Italy's claims. Along with representatives of the organizations that had planned the meeting, the rank and file of province- and town-based societies added their enthusiastic presence. After Reverend Tommaso Della Cioppa, of the Italian Episcopal Church of L'Emmanuello, offered an invocation, attorney Giovanni Di Silvestro, chairman of the program, speaking first in Italian then in English, delineated "the just and sacred aspirations of Italy" in a speech often interrupted by applause. But Judge Bonniwell, again delivered the principal address, extolling the Italian cause to his zealous audience. Consul Poccardi and others took their turns at the podium before the program reached its main purpose of ratifying the complicated Order of the Day, which reaffirmed allegiance to the nation; recalled the sacrifices and sufferings of Italy and Italians, especially those who served in the military struggle of democracy over autocracy; reasserted the territorial claims of Italy, as they related to the future of democracy; and reassured Wilson of continuing support. And with unanimous approval of the document, the rally came to its end.[25]

The program at the Alhambra Theatre, like similar events, with uncertain impact on the priorities that President Wilson carried to the Peace Conference in Paris, raised more questions than it answered. Were the efforts of immigrant prominenti more a matter of ethnic vaudeville, which placated their constituencies but had little or no influence on higher levels of leadership? Or were they representative voices that an American president had to seriously heed? And what weight did Italians in particular carry as a political constituency? While such questions are not easily answered, they can be tentatively woven into a broader context at every level—from the internal order of the immigrant community up through international relations. The range of participating organizations suggests that a highly unified colony had been mobilized, but the absence of the Federation of Italian Societies, particularly of C.C.A. Baldi, who ordinarily assumed a conspicuous role on such occasions, was significant. With an ongoing struggle among factions within the Italian community, an anti-Baldi coalition had taken control of the rally. For city and state politics, the choice of Bonniwell as principal speaker had even broader significance. Repudiated as a candidate at the urging of national committeeman A. Mitchell Palmer by the Democratic Party, allegedly for being planted by Republican boss Senator Bois Penrose and liquor industry interests, Bonniwell had been soundly defeated by William C. Sproul in the gubernatorial election of the past November. As the first Catholic to run for the office, he was rehabilitating his reputation among Italians and the general electorate. When Captain Alessandro Sapelli, chief of the Italian Information Bureau in New York City, vice chairman of the Federation Italia Irredenta and former governor of the Italian Somaliland came to Philadelphia a month later to similarly advocate Italy's territorial claims, it had become clear that state and local concerns remained highly sensitive, if they had not become even more fully subordinated, to the agenda of a foreign nation.[26]

Immigration Policy and Little Italy

The efforts of the U.S. Congress to enact an effective policy to regulate or, more precisely, to restrict immigration provided an issue far closer to home that would disturb Italians in Philadelphia and other cities. Far more likely to be aware of Wilson's benign remarks on his arrival in Rome in January 1919 than to know what he had earlier written as a scholar at Princeton, Italians, who also recognized their own need of friends in high places, still held the president in high regard as concern turned to the future of immigration. The eventual legislative outcome, which disregarded any contribution during the war, reflected not only apprehensions of other Americans about the real and imagined flow of immigration but a generally hostile sense of the impact of Italians on their adopted nation. When some 16,000 more people left than had entered the United States, emigration exceeded immigration for the first time in the nation's history in March 1915. For some Americans, the voluntary departure of aliens, seeking to serve the military needs of their native lands, had accomplished what Wilson's recent veto had prevented the provisions of an unsuccessful immigration bill from doing. And by proving that many of them still had greater allegiance to their countries of birth "even after they come and settle in the land of the free," it could be argued that "the only really valuable additions to our numbers are those who become citizens and make this their country in fact as well as in theory." The "receding tide of immigration," therefore, was not bad but good for America, because it brought "a welcome respite from the flood of immigration which gave us so many new-comers who could not be readily assimilated."[27]

Even before America had entered the conflict, some scholars feared that a surge of postwar immigration would restore less favorable consequences. In 1915, Professor Emory Johnson, an economist at the Wharton School of the University of Pennsylvania, warned that the end of the war would bring a great increase of criminals, unskilled workers, and illiterates from Poland, Austro-Hungary, Russia, the Balkan states, and Italy. He called for the strict enforcement of present laws to prevent their arrival. Four years later, in January 1919, when the Committee on Immigration and Naturalization of the House of Representatives opened hearings on proposed legislation, it was widely assumed that the suspension of immigration during the war would produce the long-feared explosion of undesirable newcomers in the near future. On its first day, John B. Densmore, the director of the Federal Employment Service, testified that, although the balance in the labor market had not yet been disturbed, he expected that the demand for workers would rise as industries returned to peacetime production, with wages and prices remaining high. But if a great increase in numbers was not enough to incite opposition to immigration, another piece of information was more certain to do so. In a headline grabbing addendum, Densmore claimed that former Austrian and Italian "war prisoners," almost as if they were a special class of criminals, would soon be swarming to America in search of work. Although declining to say whether prohibitions on immigration contained in pending bills were necessary, his testimony implicitly suggested the answer.[28]

On the next day, several witnesses from Philadelphia offered their views on immigration to the hearings. Congressman J. Hampton Moore called for action that would allay the fears of coal operators and manufacturers in Pennsylvania of a shortage of capable workers for their industries. Speaking even more directly against restriction, C.C.A. Baldi and Joseph P. Bartilucci, representing the Federated Italian Societies of Philadelphia, protested that even without any imminent threat of large-scale immigration from Italy, restrictive legislation would abandon policies on which America had developed as a nation. Another witness noted that the 1,500,000 casualties incurred by Italy during the war would require about five years without any emigration for the nation to make up its lost manpower. While failing to dissuade Congress from passing restrictive legislation, such testimony would bear more heavily on Italians who intended to return to the United States after serving their native country along with those who sought to enter it for the first time.[29]

In April 1919, Philadelphia's Italians, along with their concern over irredentism and immigration, joined in the Victory Liberty Loan campaign to subsidize the war even after the Armistice had ended it. Although Italian subscription was reported to have reached $1,000,000, participation was also vividly reflected by other activities. Some 200 Italian organizations marched behind "a forest of silken banners" in a grand parade up Broad Street. Some 200 Italian children, said to be the sons and daughters of men who had died in the war, brought a profound silence to the procession. At the Academy of Music, when Dr. Clarence P. Franklin, the Philadelphia physician who as a lieutenant colonel had led the U.S. Army Ambulance Service in Italy for 11 months, opened the program with a shout of "Avanti Savoia!" the audience roared its approval. Speaking briefly, Consul Poccardi shifted the moment to a reassertion of irredentism by declaring: "Peace will come, and with it should come the possession of Fiume, for geographical, moral and historical reasons." It would be described as "perhaps the most enthusiastic demonstration ever held in Philadelphia by citizens and by residents of Italian birth or parentage."[30]

Such events also offered a glimpse into the ambiguous juncture that Philadelphia's Italians had reached in their adjustment. During the war, proponents of Americanization had urged, indeed demanded, that residents of foreign origins abandon their national ancestry. There was no room for hyphenated Americans even as partners in a shared struggle on the battlefield. At the same time, the entry of Italy into the war had revitalized the allegiance of immigrant Italians toward their homeland. Reservists had dutifully reported themselves to consular offices and gone to serve their native land. Some of them who had once sought a future in Philadelphia would not return to the shores of the Delaware River but die on the Italian front. In July 1921, when Philadelphia welcomed General Pietro Badoglio, the strategist of the final counterattack, the program would commemorate not only the recent victory but earlier moments of Italian history. In September, Italians in Germantown similarly celebrated the past by observing the 600th anniversary of the death of Dante Alighieri. In October, the Columbus Day program included an evening torchlight street parade, followed by an address by Italian consul general Luigi Sillitti. The observances were reflections not of immigrants who had divorced themselves from a homeland but of a people still fervently attached to it. Whether recalling icons of more distant history or events of the recent past, Italians were also asserting their presence in an adopted city and nation.[31]

As a benefit program for blind veterans at the Alhambra Theatre in early October 1921 would show, events in the Italian community were sometimes easily disrupted by political differences. Anticipating a possible disturbance, 40 policemen had been assigned to preserve order. And when Consul Sillitti attempted to introduce Giuseppe Bottai, a war hero and the youngest member of the Italian Parliament as the main speaker, audience members interrupted with cries of "Shut him up" and "Don't let him speak." After about 30 protesters were removed for distributing anarchist literature and urging repudiation of the Italian government, Bottai delivered his speech. Baldi, chairman of the event, blamed the disorder on Socialists and Nationalists in Italy and Socialists in America who sought to hamper Bottai's efforts. The sponsors of the program, the Circolo Dante Aligheri, claimed that the dissenters were not from the local Italian colony but Socialists from New York who came with the intention of breaking up the meeting. Outside of the theater, police from three districts arrested one woman and took control of a crowd of several thousand Italians. On the next morning, along with a West Philadelphia resident charged with passing out anarchist material, demonstrators were charged with inciting a riot. While the undeterred Bottai would be honored by the Circolo Dante Aligheri and other Italian societies, the affair had shown that events in Little Italy continued to reflect the tensions of a divided community. But by featuring a rising Fascist, the occasion also presaged the future.[32]

Diaz Captures Philadelphia

Within another month, in November 1921, greater consensus prevailed when General Armando Diaz, the main hero of the Italian front, came to Philadelphia. On his arrival at the Broad Street Station, it briefly appeared that his visit would be disrupted by a crowd that swept over railings, shoving, stumbling, and crushing forward in an effort to get as close to the general as possible. With order restored, the City Troop, the pride of the city since the War for American Independence, escorted the distinguished guest and Ambassador Vittorio Rolandi Ricci to city hall to be greeted by Mayor Moore. After reviewing a parade of Italian societies as they marched up North Broad Street, without any interruption other than enthusiastic cheering, Diaz addressed a largely Italian audience at the Metropolitan Opera House. Beyond honoring a military hero, the event became another tribute to immigrant Italians, separated from their homeland but not yet disinherited by assimilation, who had taken up residence in Philadelphia. Describing the event, a journalist astutely recognized its meaning:

> A typical Philadelphia Sunday, austere, workless, mirthless, colorless, was torn wide open yesterday in a wild Italian welcome to General Armando Diaz, hero of the Piave and dear to the Italian heart as the saviour of Italy. Broad street from City Hall to Poplar Street was a triumphal court, lined with red, white and blue of the United States, and

the red, white and green of Italy. Gaily-garbed school children sang songs of victory, while thirty-four bands alternately shrilled from brazen throats the Italian Royal March and The Star-Spangled Banner.

It was a welcome to thrill not only the demonstrative Italian hearts that made it, but the more repressed races that came as spectators to the glorious show. Through it all, a small slight man in silver gray, with dark gray eyes and iron gray hair beamed his appreciation. When Mayor Moore welcomed him formally on the north plaza of City Hall, the dark eyes of the hero of the Piave flashed in sudden radiant understanding and friendship. When two children, one garbed as Italy, the other as America, stepped from the wings at the Metropolitan Opera House later and twined their arms about each other in symbol of Italian-American unity, the dark eyes suddenly closed behind lids from which escaped a sudden rush of tears.

Sentimental! Yes. Dramatic! Of course. But the sentiment and the drama was of the heart, not of the theatre. Here was no Anglo-Saxon restraint, no banking of the fires of emotion. Here was a man of his people, a Neapolitan risen from the bottom, who looked through the glowing eyes of Philadelphia Italians deep into their ardent hearts and answered them in kind, unashamed alike of smiles and tears.[33]

After comments by Mayor Moore, Rolandi Ricci, greeted by cheers, shifted the message to the value of public school education, habits of thrift, and a fuller appreciation of American citizenship. He asserted that the good that comes from life in America brought benefits not only to men and women of Italian birth who live there but to Italians in Italy as well. But the waiting audience exploded at the introduction of Diaz, who seemed to be momentarily shaken by the unrestrained response accorded to him. Regaining composure, he began his remarks: "As I look into your hearts, I am back home. This wonderful reception brings me back to that one which greeted me in my native Naples when I returned at the end of the war. Then, as now, I recognized it as a tribute, not to me, but to the valiant army of Italy, thousands of whom rest in heroes' graves. To you I bring a salute from your brothers in the old country, a message of affection and understanding."[34]

Having recognized the origins in the Mezzogiorno of most of the audience, Diaz affirmed his personal connection as a Neapolitan with them, before presenting a detailed analysis of the war and the expectations of Italy in its aftermath. At the end of his comments, when two girls symbolically representing America and Italy approached him, Diaz, with more passion, declared: "I am no orator. My tongue cannot speak what is in my heart. Thus only may I show it." As he stooped to kiss the child of Italy, before raising the one of America in his arms—a thunderous response echoed off the walls of the opera house.[35]

With the occasion, Philadelphia's Italians reached a climactic moment in their long history as residents of the city. On the second day of his visit, after ceremonies at Independence Hall and a luncheon given by the mayor at the Bellevue Stratford, Diaz toured Italian sections of South and West Philadelphia. With neighborhood houses decorated by colorful banners, a band saluted him in front of the Italian Federation on South 8th Street. When Diaz departed for similar events in other cities, the final celebration of Italian victory, as well as the reception for its great hero, came to an end. For Philadelphia's Italians, festive observances would serve more routine needs of community life. When Consul Sillitti and other prominenti again gathered, at a masked ball, it was for the benefit of a planned Italian hospital in Philadelphia in April 1922. And with the annual Christmas program of the 8th Street Business Association in December 1922, a more mundane atmosphere had returned to Little Italy. Yet, as Italians mimicked Anglo neighbors with programs that generated the illusion of belonging and acceptance, they could also venture into a vaudeville house where performers, singing not the praises of Diaz but of the foibles of Tony the Barber, offered a different impression of them. It was of a presence that soon would be challenged by the rise of Fascism, resonating even in American cities, in another rapidly approaching chapter in the political history of Italian Americans.[36]

Epilogue

Being Italian; Becoming American

It has often been argued that the Great War, particularly in the aftermath of Caporetto, unified Italy for the first time in its modern history. But beyond the impact on Italy and its people, a similar question can be raised about consequences on Italians in the immigrant colonies of American cities. Since the 1880s, Italians had come to America as "birds of passage," seeking to earn enough money to improve the living condition of families left in the "old country." They remitted portions of their meager earnings through postal services and community banks to families from which they had been separated but whom they had not forgotten. And as they toiled, these sojourners looked forward to a triumphant return to a life in Italy purchased by their labor in the American economy. But as their aspirations became subverted by assimilation, and they themselves were being transformed from temporary migrants to permanent settlers, global politics that changed the course of history would also redirect their lives.

Scappa, che arriva la patria!
(Run, the Fatherland Is Coming!)[1]

Italians, even as immigrants in foreign locations, could not entirely escape from events that were internal to Italy itself. The outbreak of war in Europe in August 1914, while not yet involving Italy directly, provided an impetus for the state to increase efforts to promote greater national unity. Italy, after roughly a half century of sovereignty, still sought to consolidate a population separated by varying local dialects, customs, and history. As an emerging state, it had yet to validate its rights over its citizens. Meanwhile, Italians as members of the polity, rather than passively acquiescing to demands, pondered their obligations to the state. The call up of recruits to serve in the military asked them to raise their highly localistic consciousness as *paesani* to a newer identity as Italians and their social bonds from their *paesi* to Italy as a nation. It tested the legitimacy of the state and the strength of nationalism. But it was something that many immigrants, having removed themselves from the constraints of a vulnerable state and traditional society, were incapable or unwilling to accept. Meanwhile, the rigors and disappointments incurred by emigration had also imposed what they had left behind as an incentive on their actions. But whether their commitment would be to their original town, an inchoate nation, or another land remained to be determined.

The renitenti who chose to ignore their military obligation also confronted a new truth about modern societies at war. Whether in their country of birth or their adopted nation, being a resident and citizen had opened the question of how much anyone "belonged" to the state, or to what extent does that state have control over the individual. It was an issue that swept beyond reluctant Italians in 1915 and could be raised about the citizens of any modern nation. In a provocative essay in March 1917, Philadelphia's Agnes Repplier, one of America's most popular writers, in support of universal military training as a means of preparedness on the eve of its declaration of war, argued that any young man belonged, after God, to the state even before his family. But while the acerbic essayist, unmarried and childless, could easily afford to express her own "patriotism," pacifists and conscientious objectors would not share it. And the renitenti had also implicitly rejected it.[2]

Complicating matters further, Italy had sought to remind them of their obligation to a national loyalty at the same time that the United States was trying to Americanize them. For their part, many Italians had been willing to "assimilate" if it meant only to learn enough English to enhance the working skills that made them employable but not necessarily to abandon their original identity and customs. And Americans were similarly willing to "assimilate" Italians but without erasing all boundaries or allowing them to fully penetrate American institutions or to transform American culture. In short, "assimilation" itself remained an ambiguous term. These uncertainties began to play out almost immediately.

In August 1914, Italians, jolted by fears of violence and a sense of separation from "the Italy of family and friends," began moving in a massive self-imposed repatriation from other countries of Europe that had provided employment before suddenly becoming venues of warfare back to their homeland. With Italy's declaration of war in May 1915, the flow, mainly through the Swiss Alps, steadily increased, reaching more than four times as many as the number departing, until it all but stopped by the end of the year. In the United States, after an early surge of reservists answered the call issued through the consulates, the large number of renitenti who had ignored the order remained a problem when the Italian War Commission arrived at Washington seeking support in June 1917. During negotiations, Major General Guglielmotti, Italy's military attaché, revealed that his government would no longer seek the return of Italians already enrolled in the U.S. armed forces but continue its efforts to recruit men who were not yet naturalized as American citizens. It was a compromise partly based on the mutual understanding that Italian workers were needed to avoid a possible labor shortage in the United States. But such concessions neither resolved the status of reservists who had abandoned their obligations to Italy nor alleviated the burdens of their families. In March 1918, Major General Hugh L. Scott, attempting to redeem the reputation of 250 men under his command as members of the U.S. 78th Division, unable to secure passage to their native land and labeled as "deserters," with their families assessed a tax by the government, announced his intention to submit their names to Italian officials with a request that their classification be changed to "patriots." Whether expecting redress from Italian authorities or to ingratiate himself with Italian recruits, Scott's proposal would soon be settled by other means.[3]

The status of Italians eligible for conscription in America, as well as for Americans in Italy during the war, was settled by a treaty defining the rights and obligations of citizens of both nations, signed by U.S. secretary of state Lansing and Italian ambassador to the United States, Count Vincenzo Macchi de Cellere, in Washington, DC, on August 24, 1918. Article I of the agreement stated that male citizens of both nations, unless they had returned to enlist in the armed forces of their own country, would be subject to military service under the laws and regulations of the place where they presently were. Article VI suspended provisions of a nearly half-century old treaty on commerce and navigation established between the United States and the Kingdom of Italy in February 1871. The chronology of the new pact, making all Italians between 20 and 44 years of age eligible for the draft, provided a curious footnote to the new agreement. After ratification by Italy on October 2, the U.S. Senate voted approval on October 24 and President Wilson signed the document on November 2. Two days later, the war on the Italian front ended with the surrender of the Austro-Hungarians on November 4; and the war on the Western Front ceased with the Armistice of November 11. The treaty on conscription went into effect on November 12. On November 18, President Wilson, with the war over, officially proclaimed it to be obsolete. From the initial signing by Lansing and Macchi de Cellere to its cancellation by Wilson, its life span had been a mere 12 weeks and 2 days, with an enforcement period of only 1 day. The agreement had not only been short lived but would prove to be unnecessary.[4]

While the military service of Italians on the Western Front during the great deployment leading up to the Armistice is easily recognized, the record of their contributions on the home front is more difficult to document. In early 1919, George Creel, former chairman of the Committee on Public Information, pointed out that Italians, although constituting about 4 percent of the total population, represented 10 percent of the casualty lists. Moreover, the 300,000 Italians reported to have served on battlefields and inner lines of defense had clearly demonstrated their devotion to an adopted country. But Creel also praised Italians as civilians whose labor in the domestic economy had been so essential as to warrant exemption from military duty: "There was no shipyard, ammunition factory, airplane factory, steel mill, mine, lumber camp, or dock in which the Italians did not play a large part, and often the most prominent part, in actual and efficient work. In some places, such as mines and docks, the Italians reached fully thirty *per cent.* of the total number of employees, working at all times with full and affectionate loyalty toward the Government of the United States."[5] Despite the unflattering view of Creel held by later scholars, his praise, while prompting the question of whether an underlying motive was being served, provides a neglected footnote to the immigrant experience.

While their service under American colors is well documented, the record of immigrants as reservists in the Italian army, beginning with how many of them reported, remains to be more fully examined. In May 1918, Antonio Stella, a physician and president of the Roman Legion, an organization formed by the Italian Chamber of Commerce of New York City, claimed that over 100,000 Italian reservists, presumably from the United States, had responded to Italy's call. By February of the next year, newspapers in Italy, implying an even higher number, reported that 200,000 demobilized reservists were preparing to return to America while another 100,000 men still awaiting discharge held similar plans but did not specify to which continent. But despite encouragement inspired by the territorial promises of the Treaty of London and the entrance of Italy on the side of the Allies, relatively few of them had actually returned to their homeland. In 1923, the Commissariato Generale dell'Emigrazione, long the official source, found that of approximately 6,000,000 Italians living abroad at the outbreak of the war, only part of them were obligated to answer the call. As Piero Melograni has noted, with the illusion of rapid victory, most of them had returned in the opening months of Italy's involvement in the war, before their numbers steeply declined. Of nearly 304,000 reservists who obeyed the order, some 191,835 of them did in 1915, then 51,812 more in 1916; followed by 25,457 in 1917; and, finally, 34,815 in 1918. Some 155,387 came from the Americas; another 128,570 from other countries of Europe; 19,529 from the Mediterranean basin (Egypt, Algeria, Tunisia, and Morocco); and a handful of 433 others from Africa, Asia, and Australia. But the reservists, whether reporting for duty or as renitenti who turned their backs on Italy, had further implications for immigrant communities in the United States.[6]

Becoming Italian American

The transformation of Italians from transient sojourners to permanent residents and the parallel transformation of immigrant colonies into more enduring Italian American communities has usually been attributed to an often vaguely described process of assimilation. But the course of action taken by the renitenti reveals a more definite mechanism by which this transition occurred. By ignoring their military obligation, the renitenti had become fugitives from Italian justice. While remaining safe from prosecution by staying in America, they had sacrificed any possibility of rejoining their families in Italy. And if they became naturalized as American citizens, while expanding opportunities for employment in American industries, they wrapped themselves with even greater protection against prosecution from Italy for their defection from military obligation. But it also eventually made them eligible for conscription under the Selective Service of the United States. From having been isolated and insulated within the confines of Little Italy, they would find themselves integrated with other recruits at cantonments where they encountered not only basic military training but more American ways of thinking, speaking, and acting. And clad in khaki as Yankee "doughboys," they would be soon on their way to the Western Front, no more or less reluctantly than if it had been to the Asiago Plateau. In some sense, they had been trapped, or perhaps had trapped themselves, into becoming less Italian and more American. From the point of view of critics who condemned the renitenti for failing to answer their homeland's call at a moment of great crisis, it was not only a dereliction of duty to the state but an act of betrayal to Italy as their mother. And even if amnesty in postwar Italy erased their legal culpability, it did not exonerate them of their moral failure. The defection of this immigrant aggregate, now a permanent part of the American population, was a demographic and cultural Caporetto, analogous in its impact on Italy to what had happened on the Isonzo.

A comparison of the intentions of Italy and the United States in mobilizing armed forces as well as the consequences for national unity is instructive. Italy, a state resting on an ancient but disunited society sought to imbue military recruits with a more nationalistic consciousness as a means of placing a cohesive force in the field against the enemy. It succeeded in constructing a facade of nationalism, convincing on the surface but less successful at a deeper level of personal identity and group cohesion. The United States, nearly a century older as a state than modern Italy, but still attempting to absorb great waves of recent immigrants, similarly sought to organize an integrated military force. Emigration had drained Italy of its excess population, without ameliorating divisiveness among its people; in contrast, immigration enlarged the United States in population and expanded cultural complexity while moving toward greater unity. The two nations faced a challenge that shared some aspects but differed as well. In each case, pluralism both presented a problem and reflected a source of vigor. In contrast to Italy, where success in war would become usurped by a Fascist dictatorship, the United States would rise to the pinnacle of international political and economic power.[7]

When Italy entered the war, Italians in America made an uneven response. For some, it partly rested upon their motives for emigration. Years later Italians who had been participants in this stage of history could willingly admit that they had left Italy to avoid being conscripted into its army. But, in America, their patriotism was capricious. Audiences at movie houses politely applauded the flags of other nations, before more warmly greeting the banner of the United States, then bursting into enthusiastic cheering at the *tricolore* of Italy. When war reached their homeland, Italians overseas, safe from the dangers of actual warfare, demonstrated their loyalty by observing the *Venti Settembre* as a national holiday or by honoring such historical icons as Mazzini and Garibaldi. But Italians of longer tenure in America were more likely to manifest nationalistic fervor than recent arrivals for whom conscription loomed. After an early burst of allegiance by Italians reporting to consular offices, which received widespread attention from the press, their readiness to go to war diminished. And in glaring contrast to their willingness to express loyalty in movie houses and on streets of America, many reservists would remain as renitenti. It was, however, partly due to the inability of the Italian government to provide the financial means and ships to bring them home. In the end, while working in defense industries in the United States at greatly inflated wages, they still faced an ambiguous future. But against the hopes of avoiding the war entirely, the U.S. government, with enactment of the Selective Service Act of 1917, provided an answer for many of them.[8]

With the mobilization of troops by the United States, the fulcrum of identity and cohesion for Americans, and no less for the aliens and citizens of Little Italy, shifted to the Western Front. The participation of Italians in the American army was a turning point in their acculturation and assimilation. Entering military life as Italians who required Americanization, they returned from the war as veterans of the American armed forces. The war was a crucible of their transformation. They proved not only that they were willing to serve as Americans but that they could bleed and die alongside other Americans. And many of them would be buried in military cemeteries along with their comrades in arms. The United States needed Italians and other immigrants as soldiers. It conscripted them into the army. After the war, the nation welcomed them home as soldiers who had been willing to become citizens by naturalization. Meanwhile, on the home front, their families grieved for those who had not returned and rejoiced with those who had come home. While immigrant soldiers had been "Americanized" in their legal status through the granting of citizenship by the naturalization courts, their families and private lives remained foreign, thus leaving them fragmented by their marginality.

Emigration and Immigration after the War

With the end of the war, a formidable flow of migration from Italy to the United States as well as in reverse from American ports back to Italian destinations had begun. In late October 1919, the *Europa*, a steamship of the Italia America line became the first passenger ship to reach Philadelphia from Italy since the beginning of war. Among 507 steerage passengers, some 200 "foster sons" who had answered the call as reservists to serve in the Italian army were returning to their adopted nation. With some clad in civilian clothes but other men still in their uniforms, they were described as "a happy group . . . despite weathered faces and scars which told of long and bloody struggles in the Alpine snow." Among the many passengers who would be joining relatives in final destinations further west, one woman who arrived with two children said that her husband had been killed in the war. Several other women were being met by men to whom they would be quickly married at the Gloucester, New Jersey, detention station.[9] (See Figure E.1.)

When it left Philadelphia a few days later, the return voyage of the *Europa* carried a different story along with its 1,600 passengers bound for Italy. With most of them searching for higher pay and lower prices than they had found in America, a newspaper account tersely noted: "They may not have found the ties that bound them to Philadelphia very strong." These "foreign-born

FIGURE E.1 Italian reservists returning to America. (Underwood and Underwood [March 1920].)

optimists" were abandoning a cloudy, dry, and extravagant Philadelphia with high hopes that Italy had turned into Arcadia during their absence. Reflecting a scene that was found in other ports of departure, not every Italian wanted to become an American. Having already worked too many days in mills, mines, and factories and slept too many lonely nights, they had been unable to fulfill the elusive fiction of an "American dream." The eager visage of one of them in a photograph as he waited to board the *Caserta*, bound for Genoa and Naples, almost seemed to speak for itself in autumn 1919.[10] (See Figure E.2.)

By another year, with most of these disappointed workers having returned to Italy, millions of prospective emigrants across Europe were again reported to be seeking to enlist in America's "great industrial army." While the end of war had been expected to diminish incentives for emigration, just the opposite seemed to have occurred. A foreign correspondent for the *Evening Public Ledger* claimed that from 5,000,000 to 6,000,000 workers were prepared to immediately leave Europe for America if they were given the chance. Meanwhile, an anonymous official of the Italian government, who offered "Italy's point of view," asserted that with unemployment being the leading cause of labor unrest, emigration remained a vital question for Italy. But the plight of thousands of Italian workers who had left America to fight for their country and were now being denied permission to return by authorities in Washington, DC, had created much bitterness against the United States. It was, moreover, widely believed

Off for Italian Home

FIGURE E.2 An eager Italian prepares to join 1,200 others on the steamship *Caserta*, bound for Genoa and Naples, at the Vine Street wharf of Philadelphia for his return to Italy in September 1919. (*Evening Public Ledger* [September 24, 1919].)

that these workers were being punished for their loyalty to Italy while fellow workers who had succeeded in evading conscription and remained in America had enjoyed well-paid employment and economic security. Along with the failure to support the territorial claims of Italy, it provided Italians with another reason to believe that they were being singularly treated with hostility by the American government. Italy's "witness" tersely ended his explanation with the observation that "this feeling may be wrong, but it exists."[11]

The prospect of restrictive legislation by the U.S. Congress further prompted a surge of immigration from Italy. With a backlog caused by the war and national boundaries expanded by the acquisition of the Trentino and Alto Adige, Italians enlisted in an army of immigrants hoping to reach America before its gates closed. By 1920, more than 1,600,000 Italians ranked second only to Germany as foreign-born residents in the United States. In Philadelphia, nearly 64,000 natives of Italy, almost 16 percent of all the foreign born, placed them behind only Russia and Ireland. With over 20,000 already naturalized and another nearly 6,000 having filed their declaration of intention, about one-third of them had already begun the legal process of becoming Americans. And with the census reporting mother tongue and foreign parentage, Philadelphia's nearly 137,000 "Italians" now included not only immigrants but also second-generation children and third-generation grandchildren born in America.

Community and Identity

By 1920, South Philadelphia, with 44,000 Italian-born residents, more than any other foreign population, and the peak for any period of their history, constituted a nearly complete society within the larger city. While the area was never exclusively occupied but shared with other ethnic and racial groups, it offered retail stores, restaurants, schools, churches, hospitals and pharmacies, theaters, funeral homes, banks, real estate offices, employment agencies, and other services that catered to the special needs of Italians and their families. And like other communities, not free from internal tensions but disrupted by regional and political differences, it easily cast the impression of being an Italian city, which it virtually was, and one of the largest anywhere in the world. But beyond the row houses of South Philadelphia, their largest contiguous area of residence in the nation, they had also become conspicuous parts of other sections of the city: West Philadelphia, North Philadelphia, Nicetown, Mayfair, Manayunk, Germantown, Chestnut Hill, and Southwest Philadelphia—as well as other locations of the metropolitan area: Norristown, Bristol, Strafford, Chester, Conshohocken, Coatesville, Marcus Hook, Narberth, Ardmore, and Bridgeport, and in the formidable settlement that had spilled across the Delaware River into South Camden. Even farther away in South Jersey, Italians continued to operate their own farms or to work as seasonal laborers in the fields and orchards of Vineland, Hammonton, Bridgeton, and Landisville, cranberry bogs of Burlington and Ocean Counties, and in smaller sites with such evocative names as "New Italy." Their enclaves were sometimes "satellite communities," partly dependent on the hub in South Philadelphia, while other more self-sufficient colonies were rooted in their own local setting. Across the landscape of urban America, Italian immigrant colonies, under the impact of social forces altering group life, were being transformed into Italian American communities.

Reexamining subsequent events in relation to the recent war, however, readily leads to a disappointing conclusion about promises and policies. By their willingness to accept military service, to work in defense industries, and to join in public celebration, Italians had not only demonstrated their loyalty in ways that had not been previously available but enabled themselves to become active participants in their own assimilation as Americans. But it would be betrayed in vision and aspirations by postwar immigration policy. With enactment of the Johnson-Reed Act of 1924, slashing the quota of Italians permitted to enter the United States to 3,845 per year, mass immigration from Italy ended. Falling to 6,000 by 1925, the flow of Italian immigration had quickly become, as it had been decades earlier, only a trickle. Italians now also knew that they were no longer the "birds of passage" of earlier years but caged by new immigration laws that denied them the fluidity of the past. If they returned to Italy, almost certain to be barred from reentering the United States under the new quota system, they would have seen America and its abundant economy for the last time.

As assimilation replaced the statistics of migration in scholarly and public concern, the large foreign population remained a problem. And while military and civic life had given Italians a sense of participating in their own Americanization, it was part of an illusion from which they would soon be disabused. In 1921, a well-assimilated American of Italian origin, John D'Antonio, the secretary of naturalization and immigration for the YMCA, and a spokesperson for the Americanization movement, described what was believed to still be necessary. Since an adult immigrant, unwilling to surrender old associations, habits, and traditions rarely became "naturalized," it was perhaps too much to demand that he should. Nevertheless, D'Antonio argued that "if we can teach him our language and make him understand at least what sort of beings we are, we can make him acquainted with an America that is larger than his factory or his section gang, his cult or his provincialism." But attempts to "Americanize" by conscious and intentional efforts would be made unnecessary alongside the inherent and inevitable results of daily life in America. It was not the citizenship classes of settlement houses or the agenda of the Chamber of Commerce but baseball, motion pictures, radio, and jazz that would mold children of immigrant families into Americans, different from their parents, and becoming even more so with each passing day.[12]

For Italians, cut off from the renewal of life and language that more immigration could have nourished, America was their home and American culture was becoming their blueprint for survival. But none of them ever went to bed one night as an Italian and woke up on the next morning as an American. It was a process with slow and uncertain results. Forced to ask, "Who am I and where do I belong?" Philadelphia's Italians had transcended sectional differences in redefining their identity and cohesion. By expanding their sense of *paesani* from its original localistic reference to a more inclusive and nationalistic meaning, immigrants and their American-born children increasingly thought of themselves as "Italians." The war, particularly for those men who had served in the U.S. armed forces, had encouraged them to think of themselves as "Americans." By being partly assimilated in a hybrid Italian/American community, they were no longer fully Italian nor quite yet entirely American, leaving them marginalized, as a German officer had once recognized, as "semi-Americans." Decades later, historians and sociologists would still be calling them Italian Americans. It is within this context that their experience during the war must be seen and understood.

Notes

INTRODUCTION

1. *Discography of American Historical Recordings*, s.v. "Victor matrix B-22289. When Tony goes over the top / Billy Murray," accessed August 23, 2017, available at http://adp.library.ucsb.edu/index.php/matrix/detail/700007419/B-22289 -When_Tony_goes_over_the_top; *Discography of American Historical Recordings*, s.v. "Columbia matrix 78085. When Tony goes over the top / Van and Schenck," accessed August 23, 2017, available at http://adp.library.ucsb.edu/index.php/matrix /detail/2000025866/78085-When_Tony_goes_over_the_top.

2. Eric Hobsbawm, *The Age of Empire 1875–1914* (New York: Vintage Books, 1989), 324; David M. Kennedy, *Over Here: The First World War and American Society* (New York: Oxford University Press, 1980), 17.

3. Nancy Gentile Ford, *Americans All! Foreign-Born Soldiers in World War I* (College Station: Texas A&M University Press, 2001).

4. David Laskin, *The Long Way Home: An American Journey from Ellis Island to the Great War* (New York: Harper Collins, 2010), xx.

5. Christopher M. Sterba, *Good Americans: Italian and Jewish Immigrants during the First World War* (New York: Oxford University Press, 2003).

6. Jennifer D. Keene, *Doughboys, the Great War, and the Remaking of America* (Baltimore: Johns Hopkins University Press, 2001).

7. Agostino De Biasi, "Le relazioni degli Italiani verso la terra d'origine e verso quella d'emigrazione," *Il Carroccio* 2, no. 2 (January 1916): 1–15.

CHAPTER 1

1. For this history, see Richard N. Juliani, "The Origin and Development of the Italian Community in Philadelphia" in *The Ethnic Experience in Pennsylvania*,

ed. John E. Bodnar, (Lewisburg, PA: Bucknell University Press, 1973), 233–262; and other works by the same author, including *The Social Organization of Immigration* (New York: Arno Press, 1980); *Building Little Italy: Philadelphia's Italians before Mass Migration* (University Park: Penn State University Press, 1998); and *Priest, Parish and People: Saving the Faith in Philadelphia's "Little Italy"* (Notre Dame, IN: University of Notre Dame Press, 2007).

2. Robert F. Foerster, *The Italian Emigration of Our Times* (Cambridge, MA: Harvard University Press, 1924), 3. This seminal work remains basic for all subsequent work. The comment by Marx is found in Eric Hobsbawm, *The Age of Capital 1848–1875* (New York: Vintage Books, 1996), 202.

3. Philip Taylor, *The Distant Magnet: European Emigration to the U.S.A.* (New York: Harper Torchbooks, 1972), 66.

4. Ibid., 189.

5. Ibid., 187–189.

6. Without systematic data or even personal memoirs, the self-perception of Italians remains unknown, but the war was likely to have reshaped their identity and consciousness.

7. "Mayor Will Soon Name Committee for Envoys," *Evening Ledger* (May 29, 1917). The figure of 150,000 for the Italian population appeared in newspapers at the time of the visit of the Italian War Commission in the spring of 1917. Officials of the Italian government and leaders of the immigrant community repeatedly claimed that lower figures provided by American sources fell short of the actual number of Italians in the city and region.

CHAPTER 2

1. Among scholars who have argued that the assassination could have been addressed by means other than war, see René Albrecht-Carrié, *The Meaning of the First World War* (Englewood Cliffs, NJ: Prentice Hall, 1965), 42.

2. Ibid., 56–57.

3. "Reservists Sail for Italy," *Evening Ledger* (September 18, 1914); "1,900 Reservists Sail," *Evening Ledger* (September 19, 1914).

4. "Not a Hyphenated Country," *The Inquirer* (April 5, 1915).

5. "Says Absorbing Alien Is War's Real Problem," *Public Ledger* (February 14, 1916).

6. "Little Italy Undisturbed," *Evening Ledger* (March 11, 1915); "Italians in Fever as Reservists Sail," *Evening Ledger* (March 23, 1915).

7. "Non-Inhalable Spaghetti Foils Bohemian Diners," *Evening Ledger* (March 17, 1915); "'Padre' Off to War, While 'Madre' Weeps," *Evening Ledger* (March 24, 1915).

8. "An Appeal to the American People," *Public Ledger* (April 5, 1915); "An Appeal to the American People," *The Inquirer* (April 5, 1915); "Asks U.S. to Stop Munitions Exports," *Public Ledger* (April 5, 1915). On the same day, while Philadelphia reeled under the heaviest snow to occur in April for the past 17 years, Jess Willard would knock out Jack Johnson and win the heavyweight boxing championship in the 26th round of their fight in Havana, Cuba.

9. "A Polyglotted Appeal," *Charlotte Daily Observer* (April 6, 1915); "Hammerling Is Again in Limelight," *Wilkes Barre Times Leader* (April 7, 1915); "An Advertising-Crusade against Our Traffic in Arms," *Literary Digest* (April 17, 1915), 861–862.

10. It is difficult to determine how many of Philadelphia's Italian journalists signed the appeal. With some exceptions, the geographic locations of the newspapers were not provided. Although several titles correspond to papers once published in the city, the same names appeared in other cities as well.

11. Agostino De Biasi, "Our Free Alien Press," *New York Times* (September 24, 1915). Hammerling remained a controversial figure throughout his life. Having lost his citizenship, itself a matter of uncertainty and contention, he died under mysterious circumstances, falling from a window of his apartment in New York City on an April morning in 1935. See Berkley Hudson and Karen Boyajy, "The Rise and Fall of an Ethnic Advocate and American Huckster: Louis N. Hammerling and the Immigrant Press," *Media History* 15, no. 3 (August 2009): 287–302.

CHAPTER 3

1. "Italian Physicians Here Offer Services for War," *Public Ledger* (May 22, 1915); "Physician Here Receives Call to Italian Colors," *Public Ledger* (May 23, 1915).

2. George M. Trevelyan, *Scenes from Italy's War* (Boston and New York, Houghton Mifflin, 1919), 17–19.

3. "War Wave in Little Italy; 25,000 May Join Colors," *Public Ledger* (May 21, 1915); "Italian Physicians Here Offer Services for War," *Public Ledger* (May 22, 1915).

4. Charles M. Chapin, "From Tripoli to the Trentino," *Evening Ledger* (May 20, 1915).

5. "Italian Physicians Here Offer Services for War," *Public Ledger* (May 22, 1915); "War Wave in Little Italy: 25,000 May Join Colors," *Public Ledger* (May 21, 1915).

6. The feast day of Saint Mary Magdalen de Pazzi, May 25, celebrated on the nearest Sunday, fell on May 23, 1915. It was also the date of the declaration of war by Italy. Father Antonio Isoleri, pastor of Saint Mary Magdalen de Pazzi, for 56 years, from 1870 until retiring in 1926, would have probably not been chosen for the position if Bishop James A. Wood had known of his nationalistic leanings and enthusiastic support of the Risorgimento. His poems, "Il Risorgimento d'Italia," written as a seminarian in 1864, followed by an even more bellicose one in 1866, "Esortazione a liberare la Venezia dai Tedeschi," urged Italians to take up arms against the enemy. For events of this day, see R. N. Juliani, *Priest, Parish and People: Saving the Faith in Philadelphia's "Little Italy"* (Notre Dame, IN: University of Notre Dame Press, 2007); "Italian Physicians Here Offer Services for War," *Public Ledger* (May 22, 1915); "Italian May Procession Brings Prayers for Success of the Fatherland's Arms," *Public Ledger* (May 24, 1915); "Austrian Uses Knife on Italian," *Evening Ledger* (May 24, 1915).

7. "Italian May Procession Brings Prayers for Success of the Fatherland's Arms," *Evening Public Ledger* (May 24, 1915).

8. Antonio Isoleri, "Il 24 Maggio 1915—Viva l'Italia!" What Isoleri most likely had seen and described were the effects of rings caused by atmospheric dust

around the sun, which had been reported by other people as well. See the letter "Rings around the Sun," *Public Ledger* (June 27, 1915).

9. "Austrian Uses Knife on Italian," *Evening Ledger* (May 24, 1915).

10. Ibid.

11. Ibid.

12. Ibid.

13. "Italian Volunteers Throng Consulate," *Evening Ledger* (May 26, 1915).

14. Ibid.

15. "Italy Is Expected to Provide Ships for Patriots Here," *Evening Ledger* (May 25, 1915).

16. "Italian Officers Here Called Home," *Evening Ledger* (June 2, 1915).

17. "Italians Here Called to the Colors," *Evening Ledger* (June 3, 1915); "Italian Reservists in U.S. to Register," *Public Ledger* (June 4, 1915); "2300 Hundred Reservists to Sail," *Evening Ledger* (June 3, 1915); "Italian Reservists Start for Home," *Public Ledger* (June 5, 1915); "Viva l'Italia," *Public Ledger* (June 6, 1915); "3000 Italians to Sail for War," *Public Ledger* (June 8, 1915); "Italian Reservists Sail for Home Today," *Public Ledger* (June 14, 1915); "New England Italians Ready to Join Colors," *Public Ledger* (June 16, 1915).

18. "3000 Italians to Sail for War," *Public Ledger* (June 8, 1915).

19. "1000 Sons of Italy Sail to Serve the King," *Evening Ledger* (June 14, 1915).

20. "Italian Reservists Leave on Ancona," *The Inquirer* (June 15, 1915).

21. "Ancona to Dock Here Today," *Evening Ledger* (July 20, 1915); "700 Italian Reservists to Sail for Home Today," *Public Ledger* (July 22, 1915); "1000 Italians to Fight for Country," *Evening Ledger* (July 23, 1915). The daily news, both in English and Italian, regularly reported the action at the battlefront. See "La Vittoria E' Vicina Per Le Forze Italiana," *Evening Ledger* (July 22, 1915); "La Baionetta Italica Il Monte S. Michele Sul Carso," *Evening Ledger* (July 22, 1915).

22. "'Final Call' to Italians Here," *Public Ledger* (July 29, 1915); "Last Call to Arms Excites 'Little Italy'," *Evening Ledger* (July 29, 1915); "Italian Colony Will Send 30,000 to Front," *The Inquirer* (July 30, 1915).

23. "Pledge Support for Reservists' Families," *Evening Ledger* (August 6, 1915).

24. "Italians Observe Feast of St. Rocco," *Public Ledger* (August 17, 1915).

25. "Italian Reservists Hasten to Enter," *Public Ledger* (August 18, 1915).

26. "No Passports from Italy until Reservists Take Arms," *Public Ledger* (August 1, 1915).

27. "Citizenship Refused if They Go Back and Fight," *Public Ledger* (August 2, 1915); "Reservists Face Arrest in Leaving Families Here," *Public Ledger* (August 5, 1915); "Exile or Jail Faces Puzzled Reservists," *Evening Ledger* (August 5, 1915).

28. "No Funds for Reservists," *Evening Ledger* (August 12, 1915); "Italian Reservists Rush to Register for Army," *Evening Ledger* (August 18, 1915).

29. "Italians Mob I.W.W. Leaders," *Public Ledger* (July 26, 1915). The Socialist Club had been initially identified as the Circolo Ferrari. Giuseppe Ferrari (1812–1876), a scholar, politician, and advocate of equalitarianism and federalism, had played an important role in Italian politics in the mid-nineteenth century. But this turned out to be a case of a mistaken organizational identity.

30. Ibid.

31. "Italian 'Reds' Will Fight War," *Public Ledger* (August 11, 1915).

32. Gino Speranza Papers, 31–32, Immigration History Research Center, University of Minnesota, St. Paul, Minnesota.

33. Ibid., 32.

34. Ibid., 32.

35. Ibid., 35. Alexander L. Torrelli, quite likely the same person, was listed as a purchasing agent in the Medical Department of the American Red Cross in Rome from December 1917 until January 1919. See Charles M. Bakewell, *The Story of the American Red Cross in Italy* (New York: The Macmillan Company, 1920), 245. Torrelli can be found as a clerk at the Hudson Street Hospital in New York City in 1909. See "Surgeons Say Young Did Not Shoot Himself," *New York Times* (April 5, 1905). He also was a superintendent at the Italian Hospital, with his residence at 114 East End Avenue. See the New York City Directory (1916), available at Ancestry.com.

36. "Italians Strum Guitars as They Sail to Fight," *Public Ledger* (July 29, 1915).

37. Speranza Papers, 33–34.

CHAPTER 4

1. For an example of this omission, see David M. Kennedy, *Over Here: The First World War and American Society* (New York: Oxford University Press, 1980). While not entirely ignoring immigrants in America, this work views them more in regard to the problems that they posed than in terms of their own internal order.

2. Ibid., 12, 17–18.

3. "Italian Residents Here Mark Capture of Rome," *Evening Ledger* (September 20, 1915); "Columbus Day Stirs the Patriotic Fever of the City," *Evening Ledger* (October 12, 1915).

4. "Third Call for Men Made by Italy Here," *Evening Ledger* (October 5, 1915).

5. "Honor for 'Little Italy's' Son Who Died Fighting in the War," *Public Ledger* (November 16, 1915); Ancestry.com: U.S., World War I Draft Registration Cards, 1917–1918.

6. "Tom Daly's Column Begins Monday," *Evening Ledger* (October 30, 1915); "Grand Affairs of Barbers to Take Place Tonight," *Evening Ledger* (February 21, 1916); "Juliet of 13 to Wed Romeo of 26 Here," *Evening Ledger* (March 3, 1916); "Bomb Wrecks Steps of 'Little Italy' Home," *Evening Ledger* (February 3, 1916); "Little Italy Startled by an Explosion," *Evening Ledger* (April 27, 1916).

7. "Little Italy Here Not Excited nor Worried by Austrian Invasion," *Evening Ledger* (May 26, 1916).

8. Ibid.

9. Ibid.

10. Ibid. Although well intentioned, Baldi had obviously forgotten the actual outcome of the episode on Breed's Hill in Boston in 1775.

11. "Conference on Citizen Making, to Begin Today," *Public Ledger* (January 19, 1916); "Americanization Delegates Open Sessions Today," *Public Ledger* (January 20, 1916).

12. "Roosevelt Gives His Preparedness Plans to Philadelphians," *Public Ledger* (January 21, 1916).

13. Ibid.

14. Isoleri Papers, "Peace Sunday" (May 21, 1916). Isoleri may have been confused in identifying this day as "Peace Sunday," a title used a year before for a program in Rome. But it does not seem to have been used again when the Archdiocese of Philadelphia sponsored a military mass on May 21, 1916. The Isoleri Papers are available at the Catholic Historical Research Center of the Archdiocese of Philadelphia.

15. Ibid.

CHAPTER 5

1. "Italy Crosses the Rubicon," *Evening Ledger* (May 19, 1915). Founded in 1906 *L'Opinione* was the principal Italian language newspaper serving the immigrant community. Published on weekdays and Sundays, it received news from Italy by direct telegraphic service.

2. The Public Ledger Company was the parent corporation of two newspapers with different titles and editorial policies. The *Public Ledger*, published since 1836, one of the most respected newspapers in the nation, provided daily morning and Sunday editions. The *Evening Ledger*, introduced in September 1914, with daily weekday editions but no Sunday edition, sought to reach a broader public through more innovative features of modern journalism. With its edition of December 3, 1917, the *Evening Ledger* became the *Evening Public Ledger*. On July 1, 1918, Cyrus Curtis, president of the corporation, announced purchase of the *Evening Telegraph*, which after 55 years, was being merged into the *Evening Public Ledger*. Although formally the *Evening Public Ledger and the Evening Telegraph*, we shall refer to it simply as the *Evening Public Ledger*. While the *Public Ledger* ceased publication in 1934, the *Evening Public Ledger* survived until it was absorbed by *The Inquirer* in 1942.

For the 1915 earthquake, see "L'Italia Flagellata da Uno Spaventoso Terremoto," *Public Ledger* (January 14, 1915); "Dal Fucino al Liri L'Italia È Devastata dal Terremoto," *Public Ledger* (January 15, 1915). For the events of May 1915, see "Italian Deputies Empower King to Declare War," *Evening Ledger* (May 20, 1915); "City Excited by Spectacle of Dark Rings around Sun," *Evening Ledger* (May 20, 1915); "Tutto In Italia E Pronto Per La Guerra Contro L'Austria," *Evening Ledger* (May 20, 1915); "Rumania, Bulgaria e Grecia Saranno A Fianco Dell'Italia," *Evening Ledger* (May 20, 1915); "I Negozii di Roma Chiudono in Segno di Gioia Nazionale," *Evening Ledger* (May 21, 1915).

3. While the articles by the two papers in Philadelphia probably exceeded this figure, no attempt has been made to determine whether newspapers in other cities also presented news in Italian.

4. "The Point on Which Italy Goes to War," *Evening Ledger* (May 20, 1915); "Italians Shot by Austrian Troops in Dalmatia Capital," *Evening Ledger* (May 21, 1915).

5. "L'Italia nella Vortice della Guerra," *Evening Ledger* (May 21, 1915).

6. Adalberto Caporale, "Between Giolitti and Salandra," *Evening Ledger* (May 18, 1915); Adalberto Caporale, "Italy's Envoys Impressed by Philadelphia's Greeting," *Evening Ledger* (June 22, 1917).

7. Adalberto Caporale, "Immigrants Fighting Italy's War," *Evening Ledger* (June 2, 1915). For the decline in remittances, as well as revenue from tourism, during the war, see John Gooch, *The Italian Army and the First World War*, (Cambridge: Cambridge University Press, 2014) 129.

8. These biographical details are easily available at Ancestry.com.

9. "Triumphant Italy," *Evening Public Ledger* (November 16, 1918).

10. See "Brand New Babies," *Evening Ledger* (October 27, 1916). For the photographs of Francis Caporale, see "Back from the Shore," *Evening Ledger* (September 26, 1917); "Young America, Deeply Patriotic, Gives Vent to Its Impulses in Various War Activities," *Evening Public Ledger* (May 18, 1918).

11. "Tom Daly's Column: Da Candidate," *Evening Ledger* (June 14, 1917).

12. "Reader's Viewpoint: Why Not Italy's Flag, Too?" *Evening Public Ledger* (May 23, 1918).

13. "Show Italy's Colors!" *Evening Public Ledger* (May 23, 1918).

14. Adalberto Caporale, "What Italy Has Done," *Evening Public Ledger* (May 24, 1918).

15. Ibid.

16. "Italian Consul Praises Work of Evening Ledger," *Evening Ledger* (May 24, 1915); "Bravo for Your News," *Evening Ledger* (May 24, 1915); "Appreciation by Italians," *Evening Ledger* (May 24, 1915).

17. "War News from Italy," *Evening Ledger* (May 26, 1915).

18. Ibid. Each letter appeared under a different subtitle on the same page. In his letter, Luigi Corona had referred to Leonida Bissolati, one of Italy's most important politicians, whose name was egregiously misspelled here.

19. "Liked by Businessmen," *Evening Ledger* (June 2, 1915).

20. "Enthusiasm for Evening Ledger," *Evening Ledger* (May 27, 1915). Charles M. Bandiere, the author of this letter, was born in Pennapiedimonte, province of Chieti, on May 29, 1892. Arriving as an immigrant at the age of five on July 4, 1897, he first lived in Philadelphia and attended Central High School and Temple University. After moving to Baltimore, he worked in automobile sales and real estate, and eventually pursued a very active public life, being elected as a Democrat to the Maryland House of Delegates from 1943 to 1950. See Maryland State Archives, *Maryland Manual* 163 (1950), 164. Available at http://aomol.net/000001/000163/html/am163--164.html. His letter "Unredeemed Italy" (January 11, 1919) is also cited in this study. He died in December, 1984.

21. "A Resolution of Thanks," *Evening Ledger* (May 29, 1915).

22. "Italian News in Italian," *Evening Ledger* (May 29, 1915).

23. Mark Thompson, *The White War: Life and Death on the Italian Front* (London: Faber and Faber, 2008), 207–216. For similar issues elsewhere, see Martin J. Farrar, *News from the Front: War Correspondents on the Western Front 1914–18* (Stroud: Sutton, 1998).

24. William Bell Clark, "Philadelphia's War Chronology," in *Philadelphia in the World War, 1914–1919* (New York: published for the Philadelphia War History Committee by Wynkoop Hallenbeck Crawford, 1922), 15.

25. John L. Murray, "Column, Right: The Philadelphia Newspapers and the War," in *Philadelphia in the World War, 1914–1919* (New York: published for the

Philadelphia War History Committee by Wynkoop Hallenbeck Crawford, 1922), 515–516.

26. "Servizio di Vapori Tra Phila. E L'Italia," *Evening Public Ledger* (July 30, 1919); "Await Italian Warship," *Evening Public Ledger* (October 4, 1919).

27. William Roscoe Thayer, "Italy's Refusal to Join Germany and Austria," *Public Ledger* (January 18, 1915). George B. McClellan Jr., "Italy's Big Price for Maintaining Her Neutrality," *Public Ledger* (March 28, 1915); George B. McClellan Jr., "Italy's Dogs of War Eagerly Strain at the Leash," *Public Ledger* (May 16, 1915); George B. McClellan Jr., "Italy Engaged in War for Practical Purposes Only," *Public Ledger* (July 4, 1915); Harvey M. Watts, "Italy's 'Manifest Destiny' after a Century of Struggle," *Public Ledger* (March 21, 1915); Frank H. Simonds, "What Can Italy Do in the Great War," *Evening Ledger* (May 21, 1915); "Guglielmo Ferrero, the Famous Italian Historian Points Out the Startling Effect on the Shaping of the Future of Mankind if the Kaiser Succeeds in Holding Belgium's Coal and France's Iron Mines," *Public Ledger* (February 28, 1915); Guglielmo Ferrero, "Europe a Universal Barrack—Should Germany Win," *Public Ledger* (March 7, 1915); Guglielmo Ferrero, "Partition of Germany Possible if the Allies Win," *Public Ledger* (March 14, 1915); Guglielmo Ferrero, "Long Peace in Victory for Allies, Asserts Ferrero," *Public Ledger* (March 21, 1915); Guglielmo Ferrero, "Century of Peace to Succeed Era of Pride and War," *Public Ledger* (March 28, 1915); Vincenzo Di Santo, "Love of War Inspired by Historical Reading," *Public Ledger* (April 25, 1915). For a biographical sketch of Di Santo, see Publications of the University of Pennsylvania, *Proceedings of Commencement* (June 21, 1916), 48.

28. "War-Gloom Tonic in Italian Movies," *Evening Ledger* (September 4, 1917).

29. "Young Italian Hero Feature of Cinema," *Evening Ledger* (September 8, 1917); "Italy's Chieftain in Battle Movies," *Evening Ledger* (September 8, 1917).

30. "Theatrical Indicator for the Coming Week," *Evening Public Ledger* (September 21, 1918); also see classified advertisements in the same newspaper. For its reception elsewhere, see "It Is Creating a Big Sensation," *El Paso(TX) Herald* (September 26, 1918); "Movie Fans Seeing More of War Than Do Fighters," *Ogden (UT) Standard* (October 5, 1918); "'Italy's Flaming Front' Drawing Large Audiences," *Moving Picture World* 38, no. 2 (October 12, 1918): 252; "Budget of Filmdom News from Iowa: Palace Shows 'Italy's Flaming Front,'" *Moving Picture World* 38, no. 2 (October 12, 1918): 269.

31. "Zowie!" *Our Navy* 12, no. 7 (November 1918): 61.

32. "Just Gossip about People," *Evening Public Ledger* (September 26, 1918). While anecdotes fail to fully measure the impact of *Italy's Flaming Front* and similar films, they show that audiences reacted in different ways to them. If they encourage further study, even these fragmentary items have value.

CHAPTER 6

1. Thomas Nelson Page, *Italy and the World War* (New York: Charles Scribner's Sons, 1920), 293.

2. "Mayor Will Meet Envoys in Capital," *Evening Ledger* (April 25, 1915); "Italy Will Send Two Missions to the United States," *Evening Ledger* (April 25, 1915).

3. "Capital Greets Italian Mission," *Evening Ledger* (May 23, 1917); "Italian Envoys Seek Only Economic Help," *Evening Ledger* (May 24, 1917).

4. "Un Grande Vittoria Italiana sul Carso: La Missione Italiana," *Evening Ledger* (May 24, 1917).

5. "Italians of City Plan War Purse," *Evening Ledger* (May 23, 1917); "Mayor in Washington to Invite Italians," *Evening Ledger* (May 24, 1917); "Philadelphia Invita la Missione Italiana," *Evening Ledger* (May 24, 1917).

6. "Italians Will See Much of This City," *The Inquirer* (May 29, 1917).

7. "Italians Prepare to Greet Envoys," *Evening Ledger* (May 28, 1917); "Mayor Will Soon Name Committee for Envoys," *Evening Ledger* (May 29, 1917); "What's Doing Tonight," *Evening Ledger* (May 29, 1917); "Italians Donate $2000 for Envoys," *Evening Ledger* (May 30, 1917).

8. "Italy in War to Safeguard Civilization," *Evening Ledger* (May 29, 1917).

9. "Marconi Says Italy Reveres Liberty Bell," *Evening Ledger* (May 29, 1917).

10. "Another $1,000,000 Loan to Italy Likely," *Evening Ledger* (June 2, 1917).

11. "Italy's Offering to World Politics," *Evening Ledger* (June 2, 1917); "Great Work of Italy in the War," *Evening Ledger* (June 2, 1917). See also: William Kay Wallace, *Greater Italy* (New York: Charles Scribner's Sons, 1917); E. Alexander Powell, *Italy at War and the Allies in the West* (New York: Charles Scribner's Sons, 1917).

12. "Our Debt to Italy," *Evening Ledger* (May 29, 1917); "The Voice of the People: Display the Italian Flag," *Evening Ledger* (May 29, 1917).

13. "Italians Give Freely to Help Envoys' Fund," *Evening Ledger* (June 2, 1917).

14. "To Arrange Plans for Envoys' Visit," *Evening Ledger* (June 4, 1917).

15. "Prince Udine Better, but Italian Tour Deferred," *Evening Ledger* (June 5, 1917); "Envoys Delay Visit; Reception Plans Go On," *Evening Ledger* (June 5, 1917); "City Italians Ask Envoys for a Day," *Evening Ledger* (June 6, 1917).

16. "La Questione degli Italiani," *Evening Ledger* (June 6, 1917); "To Enroll 300,000 Alien Italians under U.S. Flag," *Evening Ledger* (June 6, 1917). General Emilio Guglielmotti was erroneously identified as Enrico Guglielmatto in this article.

17. "Want Italian Mission to Stay Here 24 Hours," *Evening Ledger* (June 7, 1917).

18. "Italians Push Canvas for $50,000 Udine Fund," *Evening Ledger* (June 8, 1917).

19. For such advertisements, see *Evening Ledger* (June 7, 1917).

20. "Tom Daly's Column: Who'll Buy a Painting," *Evening Ledger* (June 9, 1917).

21. "Italians Urge Great Reception to Mission," *Evening Ledger* (June 11, 1917); "Italian Mission's Visit to Be Made a Gala Event," *Evening Ledger* (June 12, 1917).

22. "Italians Perfect Plans to Entertain Mission," *Evening Ledger* (June 13, 1917); "What's Doing Tonight," *Evening Ledger* (June 13, 1917); "Big Reception Planned for Italian Mission," *Evening Ledger* (June 14, 1917); "Italian Mission Given Royal Welcome South," *Evening Ledger* (June 13, 1917).

23. Editorial, *Evening Ledger* (June 14, 1917).

24. "Just Gossip about People: Tag Day for Italian Red Cross," *Evening Ledger* (June 15, 1917).

25. "Exclusive Photographs of the Great New Italian Offensive against the Austrians," *Evening Ledger* (June 16, 1917).

26. "Italians of City Ready for Envoys," *Evening Ledger* (June 18, 1917); "Oversubscribed!" *Evening Ledger* (June 19, 1917).

27. "Italian Envoys Get Rousing Welcome to Philadelphia," *Evening Ledger* (June 20, 1917); "Compatriots Cheer Envoys from Italy in Delirium of Joy," *The Inquirer* (June 21, 1917)

28. "Una Folla Enorme Ha Salutato la Missione," *Evening Ledger* (June 20, 1917).

29. Ibid.

30. "Italian Envoys Get Rousing Welcome to Philadelphia," *Evening Ledger* (June 20, 1917); "Compatriots Cheer Envoys from Italy in Delirium of Joy," *The Inquirer* (June 21, 1917); "Tumult When Envoys Appear upon Balcony," *The Inquirer* (June 21, 1917).

31. "Italian Envoys Get Rousing Welcome to Philadelphia," *Evening Ledger* (June 20, 1917); "Nabbed as Pickpocket in Crowd near Envoys," *Evening Ledger* (June 20, 1917).

32. "Italian Envoys Get Rousing Welcome to Philadelphia," *Evening Ledger* (June 20, 1917); "Compatriots Cheer Envoys from Italy in Delirium of Joy," *The Inquirer* (June 21, 1917). While the *Evening Ledger* ignored the disruption that occurred when the Italian Mission reached the park, *The Inquirer* gave it detailed attention.

33. "Italian Envoys Get Rousing Welcome to Philadelphia," *Evening Ledger* (June 20, 1917).

34. "Welcome, Italians," *Evening Ledger* (June 20, 1917).

35. "Tom Daly's Column: The Barber on Baseball," *Evening Ledger* (June 20, 1917).

36. H. T. Craven, "Italy's Glory Like Old Rome's," *Evening Ledger* (June 20, 1917).

37. "Nice Things Said of Columbus at Italian Envoys' Banquet," *Evening Ledger* (June 21, 1917).

38. "Envoys Echo Mayor's Hope of Pact Here," *Evening Ledger* (June 21, 1917).

39. Ibid.

40. "Tom Daly's Column," *Evening Ledger* (June 22, 1917).

41. "Envoys Echo Mayor's Hope of Pact Here," *Evening Ledger* (June 21, 1917).

42. Ibid.

43. Ibid.

44. "Cadorna Cattura 936 Prigionieri in Trentino," *Evening Ledger* (June 21, 1917).

45. "Italian Envoys Impressed by Philadelphia's Greeting," *Evening Ledger* (June 22, 1917).

46. "Italy's Army Not to Claim Italians Here," *Boston Journal* (June 6, 1917).

47. "Italian Envoys Visit Garibaldi Island Shrine," *Evening Ledger* (June 22, 1917); "Mother Prizes Dead Son's Hero Medal," *Evening Ledger* (June 22, 1917).

48. "Italians Eager to Help Homeland," *Evening Ledger* (October 31, 1917); "Italians Rush to Enlist," *Evening Ledger* (November 6, 1917).

49. "Philadelphia to Rush Ships to Aid Italy," *Evening Ledger* (October 30, 1917).

50. "Italy United in Faith, Premier Wires Cadorna," *Evening Ledger* (October 31, 1917); "Italians Plan to Aid Native Country," *Evening Ledger* (November 1, 1917).

51. "Sign of the Cross Reflected by Moon," *Evening Ledger* (November 1, 1917); "The War in Italy," *Evening Ledger* (November 1, 1917).

52. "The Voice of the People: Italy's Fateful Hour," *Evening Ledger* (November 8, 1917). After graduating from medical school in June 1918, De Caria would practice medicine in Bradford, Pennsylvania, until his death in August 1945 at the age of 55. See "Bradford Doctor Dies," *Pittsburgh Press* (February 6, 1945); "County and Vicinity," *Portville (NY) Review* (February 8, 1945).

CHAPTER 7

1. William Bell Clark, "Philadelphia and the 28th Division," *Philadelphia in the World War, 1914–1919* (New York: published for the Philadelphia War History Committee by Wynkoop Hallenbeck Crawford, 1922), 95–101.

2. "Pershing's Army Called 'Finest,'" *Evening Ledger* (February 7, 1917).

3. George M. Trevelyan, *Scenes from Italy's War* (Boston and New York, Houghton Mifflin, 1919), 139.

4. Clark, "Philadelphia and the 28th Division," 95–101.

5. "Nation-Loving Multitude Makes Liberty Shrine Ring Cheering Loyalty Addresses," *Evening Ledger* (March 31, 1917); "Patriotic Airs Sound Again at Liberty Shrine," *Evening Ledger* (March 31, 1917); "France Hails Patriotic Meeting in Philadelphia as World Event," *Evening Ledger* (March 31, 1917); "200,000 Parade through Streets," *Evening Ledger* (March 31, 1917); "Aged Garibaldi Offers Services to U.S.," *Evening Ledger* (March 31, 1917).

6. "Americans, Native and Alien, Must Stand by Flag, Says Ex-Gov. Stuart," *Evening Ledger* (March 31, 1917); "American Citizenship Assumes New Glory in Hour of Peril," *Evening Ledger* (March 31, 1917).

7. "State Takes Lead in U.S. Recruiting," *Evening Ledger* (April 25, 1917); "Big Recruiting Parade Today," *Evening Ledger* (April 28, 1917); "House Kills Volunteer Army Plan: Vote 279–98," *Evening Ledger* (April 28, 1917).

8. "La Folette Squelched; Selection Bill Passes," *Evening Ledger* (May 1, 1917); "Sending of U.S. Troops to Europe Will Be Determined in a Few Days," *Evening Ledger* (May 1, 1917).

9. "873,000 in State Liable to Service," *Evening Ledger* (May 11, 1917); "Uncle Sam's New Plan to Raise Armies for War against Germany," *Evening Ledger* (May 11, 1917).

10. "Pershing Prepares to Leave for Front: Millions Ready to Enroll—War Machine Hums," *Evening Ledger* (May 19, 1917); "President Issues Proclamation Calling for Army Draft," *Evening Ledger* (May 19, 1917).

11. "President's Proclamation Calling for an Army Draft," *Evening Ledger* (May 19, 1917)

12. "U.S. Decides on Plans for Draft Exemptions," *Evening Ledger* (June 11, 1917).

13. "Big U.S. Army Drive Set for Next Week," *Evening Ledger* (June 23, 1917); "'Paper Bombs' Spur Recruits," *Evening Ledger* (June 25, 1917); "70,000 Men Wanted for Army This Week," *Evening Ledger* (June 25, 1917).

14. "'Paper Bombs' Spur Recruits," *Evening Ledger* (June 25, 1917). "General Evasion of Draft Denied," *Evening Ledger* (June 25, 1917). The birthplace of these men is easily available at Ancestry.com.

15. "'Paper Bombs' Spur Recruits," *Evening Ledger* (June 25, 1917).

16. "Regulars Parade to Spur Recruits," *Evening Ledger* (June 26, 1917); "Recruiting Campaign Grows in Intensity," *Evening Ledger* (June 29, 1917).

17. "May Be Early Draft to Fill Out U.S. Ranks," *Evening Ledger* (June 28, 1917); "Forty Join the Army within Two Hours," *Evening Ledger* (July 2, 1917).

18. "The Work of the Draft Boards," *Philadelphia in the World War, 1914–1919* (New York: published for the Philadelphia War History Committee by Wynkoop Hallenbeck Crawford, 1922), 126–133; "Men of 32 to 36, Youths 19 and 20 to Be Sent First," *Evening Public Ledger* (September 10, 1918); "Big Registration for City Hails U.S. Drive," *Evening Public Ledger* (September 12, 1918); "Recruiting Station Closes," *Evening Public Ledger* (September 20, 1918).

19. "The Seal of Freedom," *Evening Public Ledger* (September 11, 1918); "Big Registration for City Hails U.S. Drive," *Evening Public Ledger* (September 12, 1918).

20. "N.G.P. May Receive Call by June 15," *Evening Ledger* (May 11, 1917).

21. "The Great Day," *Evening Ledger* (June 4, 1917).

22. For the 1871 treaty between the United States and the Kingdom of Italy, see *Treaties, Conventions, International Acts, Protocols and Agreements between the United States of America and Other Powers,* compiled by William Malloy, 61st Cong., 2nd Sess., S. Doc. No. 357, Volume I (Washington: 1910), 961–977; for discussion in Congress at the time of the draft, see Calendar No. 97, 65th Cong., 1st Sess., S. Rep. No. 94, "Selective Draft of Aliens" (July 30, 1917); and 65th Cong., 1st Sess., H.R. Rep. No. 15, "Drafting Subjects of Allied Countries" (August 1, 1917).

23. "The Voice of the People: The Spirit of Liberty," *Evening Ledger* (May 18, 1917).

24. "Patriotic Italians Are Prompt to Register for Service in War," *Evening Ledger* (June 5, 1917); "Camden Reports Big Registration," *Evening Ledger* (June 5, 1917).

25. "830,507 Register in Pennsylvania," *The Inquirer* (June 17, 1917).

26. "Sectional Army Cry Raised by Senators Who Direct Probe," *The Inquirer* (July 17, 1917); "Only a Few Figures Delay Draft Now," *Evening Ledger* (July 18, 1917). Brandegee and Lodge would remain staunch advocates of immigration restriction, as well as isolationists opposed to United States membership in the League of Nations.

27. "Leading Citizens Chosen by Mayor for Draft Boards," *The Inquirer* (May 28, 1917). Within a few days, Governor Martin G. Brumbaugh ordered that Philadelphia be reorganized into 51 districts for the conscription process. "U.S. Starts Probe of Bogus Cards Held by Slackers," *The Inquirer* (June 14, 1917).

28. At registration for the Selective Service program of World War II in 1942, Pasquale Albanese (with his name corrected), an unemployed 50-year-old, was living on Passyunk Avenue and Dominic William Zurzolo, as a native of Messina, was self-employed and living on Chestnut Street. In each case, the date of his birthday confirms his identity. Military records, on file at the National Archives and Records Administration, are easily available at Ancestry.com.

29. "Draft System Launched: America Aims Justice to All, with Summons Effective," *Evening Ledger* (July 2, 1917); "President Starts Gigantic Machinery to Draft U.S. Army," *The Inquirer* (July 3, 1917).

30. "First Man Called Seeks Exemption," *Evening Ledger* (July 28, 1917).

31. "Delay in Notifying Board Here May Hold Back Quota," *The Inquirer* (July 24, 1917).

32. "Jersey Towns Protest Anti-Alien Draft Rule," *Evening Ledger* (July 17, 1917); "The Voice of the People: Aliens Should Fight," *Evening Ledger* (August 3, 1917).

33. "Predicts Bloodshed if Draft Is Ordered," *Evening Ledger* (April 21, 1917); "Only a Few Figures Delay Draft Now," *Evening Ledger* (July 18, 1917).

34. "Can't Finish Drawing before 3 A.M. Tomorrow, Latest Estimate Shows," *Evening Ledger* (July 20, 1917); "Drafted Alien Not Subject to Service," *Evening Ledger* (July 20, 1917).

35. "Senate Attacks Draft Method on Eve of Drawing," *New York Tribune* (July 19, 1917); "Congress Plans to Order Draft of Aliens," *Evening Ledger* (July 25, 1917); "Draws Bill to Deport Alien Slackers," *Evening Ledger* (July 25, 1917); "U.S. Would Legalize Drafting of Aliens," *Evening Ledger* (July 26, 1917); "Would Get Consent to Conscript Aliens," *Evening Ledger* (July 30, 1917).

36. "Italy Refuses to Let U.S. Draft Subjects," *New York Tribune* (July 17, 1917). Burnett, previously a member of the U.S. Commission on Immigration, popularly known as the Dillingham Commission, would later become one of the principal advocates of a literacy test for the admission of immigrants to the United States.

37. "City Quotas May Be Revised: First Men Up in Draft Test," *Evening Ledger* (July 30, 1917); "Three-Fourths Ask Exemption," *Evening Ledger* (August 3, 1917).

38. "Only One Man in Every Four Landed in Army," *Evening Ledger* (August 6, 1917).

39. "Draft Tests Lag: Only 500 Total of Day," *Evening Ledger* (August 7, 1917).

40. Ibid.

41. "Draft Boards Smash Records; Take 1400 Men," *Evening Ledger* (August 10, 1917).

42. "City's Youth Pass Draft Acid Test," *Evening Ledger* (August 4, 1917). In Italy, while "imboscati" sometimes referred to military personnel who held more privileged and protected positions, it was also applied to draft dodgers or those termed "slackers" in America.

43. "Aliens Taught to Avoid Draft Is New Charge," *Evening Ledger* (August 15, 1917).

44. Ibid.

45. Ibid.

46. "Says Notary Is against Draft," *Evening Ledger* (August 22, 1917).

47. Ibid.

48. "The Voice of the People: Would Exempt Aliens," *Evening Ledger* (August 30, 1917).

49. "Threatens to Tie Up Draft Board Work," *The Inquirer* (September 21, 1917); "Threat to Tie Up Draft Board Work," *Evening Ledger* (September 21, 1917); "Questions U.S. Right to Draft Aliens," *The Inquirer* (September 28, 1917); "Court Considers Draft of Aliens," *Evening Ledger* (September 27, 1917).

50. "Most of Pa. Quotas Now in Camp Meade," *The Inquirer* (September 22, 1917); "Threatens to Tie Up Draft Board Work," *The Inquirer* (September 21, 1917); "Italians to Test Power of U.S. to Draft Them," *Evening Ledger* (September 24, 1917).

51. Rawle and Henderson claims to be the oldest continuing law firm in the nation. Founded by William Rawle in 1783, it became Rawle and Henderson, with the latter becoming the first nonfamily member of the firm shortly after his graduation from Harvard Law in the summer of 1913, when Henderson became a partner under the new name in 1917. More information available at http://www.rawle .com/225th-anniversary/. For Landberg, see the manuscript pages of the U.S. Federal Census, easily available at Ancestry.com as well as newspaper items, accessed by using his name, available at http://chroniclingamerica.loc.gov/ and http://www.newsbank .com/readex/?content=96. For Judge Dickinson's presiding over the naturalization court, see "Naturalize Alien Soldiers," *Evening Ledger* (May 27, 1918).

52. "Italians to Test Power of U.S. to Draft Them," *Evening Ledger* (September 24, 1917).

53. "Threatens to Tie Up Draft Board Work," *The Inquirer* (September 21, 1917); "Threat to Tie Up Draft Board Work," *Evening Ledger* (September 21, 1917); "Court Considers Draft of Aliens," *Evening Ledger* (September 27, 1917).

54. "Will Hold Aliens, Crowder Decides," *Evening Ledger* (September 25, 1917).

55. "Aliens Subject to Army's Call," *Evening Ledger* (October 13, 1917). The identities of the plaintiffs in this case are difficult to determine. A newspaper identified the five Russian Jews, although only referring to them as Russians, as David Cohen, Abraham Miller, Abraham Cooper, Max S. Gitzen, and Menashe Leinerovitch. See "Threat to Tie Up Draftboard Work," *Evening Ledger* (September 21, 1917). The summary of the decision in the *Federal Reporter* lists the case as *United States ex rel. Troiani v. Hepburn, Sheriff, et al. and United States ex rel. Kilinsky v. Swift et al.* Nos. 9, 10 (Dist. Ct. E.D. Pa. October 13, 1917). The text is introduced as: "Two proceedings in habeas corpus—one, on the relation of Giovanni Troiani against John E. Hepburn, Sheriff of Delaware County, and another; the other, on the relation of Abraham Kilinsky against Edward Swift and others, members of the Local Board for Division No. 8, City of Philadelphia." The name Kilinsky did not appear in the newspaper account cited above. The names of the attorneys, the wording of the decision, and the date of the decision further confirm the entry as the same case. See *Federal Reporter*, vol. 245, November 1917–January 1918 (St. Paul: West, 1918), 360–362.

56. "Alien Slacker Bill Held Up," *Evening Ledger* (October 13, 1917).

57. "Would Draft Aliens into U.S. Army Ranks," *Evening Ledger* (September 6, 1917); "Bill for Drafting Aliens Said to Be Assured," *Evening Ledger* (September 8, 1917); "Congress to Finish Labors in 3 Weeks," *Evening Ledger* (September 17, 1917).

58. For an informative analysis of the early state militia, see Joseph J. Holmes, "The Decline of the Pennsylvania Militia 1815–1870," *Western Pennsylvania History* 57, no. 2 (April 1974), 199–217.

59. "Forty Join the Army within Two Hours," *Evening Ledger* (July 2, 1917); "City's Troops Will Be in France by Autumn," *Evening Ledger* (July 5, 1917).

60. "President Calls Guard Out to War," *Evening Ledger* (July 10, 1917); "N.G.P. Ready to Go to Atlanta in 10 Days," *Evening Ledger* (July 14, 1917); "City Armories Hum with Troops," *Evening Ledger* (July 16, 1917); "16,952 of Pennsylvania Guard in U.S. Service," *Evening Ledger* (July 20, 1917).

61. "State Guards Merge into U.S. Army Tonight," *Evening Ledger* (August 4, 1917); "U.S. Calls Last 75,745 Guardsmen," *Evening Ledger* (August 4, 1917); "Guard Recruiting Taken Over by U.S.," *Evening Ledger* (August 6, 1917); "5 Companies of First Ordered Back to City," *Evening Ledger* (August 11, 1917); "Division Designated for National Army," *Evening Ledger* (August 14, 1917).

62. "Training Corps Shows New 'Trickling' Attack," *The Inquirer* (August 6, 1917).

CHAPTER 8

1. "City to Honor Its Young Defenders," *Evening Ledger* (August 30, 1917).

2. Ibid. General J. Franklin Bell, a West Point graduate, after serving with the Seventh Cavalry during the Indian Wars, was accused of war crimes and genocide during his command of troops in the Philippines. He was later appointed as chief of staff of the U.S. Army under Presidents Theodore Roosevelt and William Howard Taft. During World War I, he commanded the 77th Division at Fort Upton, New York, but was rejected for overseas service after a physical examination. On his support of singing in military training, see "A Singing Man Is a Fighting Man," *Carroll (Ia.) Herald* (September 12, 1917), available at http://news.google.com/newspapers.

3. "Philadelphia Pays Honor to Hero Sons," *Evening Ledger* (September 1, 1917).

4. Ibid.

5. "National Guard Units Stir Throngs to Laugh," *Evening Ledger* (September 1, 1917).

6. "Philadelphia Pays Honor to Hero Sons," *Evening Ledger* (September 1, 1917).

7. "Phila. Honors Men Selected to Wage War for Freedom," *The Inquirer* (September 2, 1917); "Sidelights, Grave and Gay, on Great Martial Display," *Evening Ledger* (September 1, 1917); "Popular Tunes Win Cheers from Throngs," *Evening Ledger* (September 1, 1917).

8. "Philadelphia Pays Honor to Hero Sons," *Evening Ledger* (September 1, 1917).

9. "362 Drafted Men Leave Tomorrow," *Evening Ledger* (September 18, 1917); "Half of First Draft Quota Leaving Today," *Evening Ledger* (September 19, 1917).

10. The dedication, "'Over Here' affectionately dedicated to the officers and men preparing for 'Over There,' Camp Meade, MD," appears in *"Over Here" Preparing for "Over There," Camp Meade, Maryland*. Designed and printed by Horn-Shafer Press, Baltimore, MD. Available at http://www.314th.org/camp-meade.html.

11. *History of the Seventy-Ninth Division A.E.F. during the World War: 1917–1919* (Lancaster, PA: Steinman and Steinman, 1922), 8–9; "Expect Gen. Kuhn to Join Pershing," *Evening Ledger* (October 30, 1917).

12. "Stop Peace Talk, Urges Gen. Kuhn," *Evening Ledger* (September 8, 1917); "Expect Gen. Kuhn to Join Pershing," *Evening Ledger* (October 30, 1917). The headline of the first article went somewhat beyond what Kuhn was quoted as actually saying.

13. "Letter from a Selected Man at Camp Meade to His Mother," *Evening Ledger* (September 20, 1917).

14. "First Big Contingent of Local Draft Men Move on Meade," *Evening Ledger* (September 22, 1917).

15. "Local Men Get Noisy Welcome at Camp Meade," *Evening Ledger* (September 22, 1917).

16. Photo, *Evening Ledger* (October 1, 1917). More on John Aloysius Festa, available at Ancestry.com. The "Molino and Farina" listed on his draft registration card was probably not the name of a firm but a reference to Molino Farina, a highly preferred flour used in making pasta and pizza. He listed his residence as 1238 South 15th Street. In a 1917 alumni catalog of the University of Pennsylvania, his address was 740 South 12th Street. In the 1920 federal census, he was a revenue clerk at the post office, living with his parents on South 15th Street but at a different number than previously given. Among immigrant families, frequent changes of residence were not unusual.

17. "Aliens Dropped at Camp Meade," *Evening Ledger* (October 5, 1917).

18. "Letter from a Selected Man at Camp Meade to His Mother," *Evening Ledger* (September 27, 1917); "Letter from a Selected Man at Camp Meade to His Mother," *Evening Ledger* (September 21, 1917).

19. "Letter from a Selected Man at Camp Meade to His Mother," *Evening Ledger* (October 17, 1917).

20. Ibid. Private Nicola da Dario was badly wounded and suffered the loss of a leg in October 1918. He would die of pancreatic cancer shortly after his 54th birthday at the Naval Hospital in Philadelphia on February 25, 1948, and be buried at Holy Cross cemetery in Yeadon.

21. Ibid.

22. Ibid.

23. "Letter of a Selected Man at Camp Meade to His Mother," *Evening Ledger* (October 26, 1917). "Bob" had apparently erred in giving the name of the Eopolucci brother at Camp Meade. Contrary to his account, articles in various newspapers identify John Eopolucci as the sailor who had died earlier and William Anthony Eopolucci as the more recent draftee. "Mrs. Eopolucci to Wed Another Naval Man," *Evening Ledger* (May 9, 1917). See, for example, "Heroic Death of Eopolucci May Exempt His Brother," *Washington Times* (July 22, 1917). Their grandfather, Antonio Eopolucci, and their father, Samuel, had been members of the U.S. Marine Corps Band. See "Hopeful for Son's Safety," *Washington Herald* (April 4, 1917); "Eopolucci among 28 Dead on Aztec," *Washington Times* (April 6, 1917). For the memorial, see *Washington Times* (April 6, 1917). William Eopolucci would die in France one year after leaving Camp Meade. The Secretary of the Navy praised their mother: "She gave more than the richest man in America could give in money, for she has given her sons." See "Two Gold Stars Are Shining for Brave Eopolucci Brothers," *Washington Herald* (February 27, 1919).

24. "Letter from a Selected Man at Camp Meade to His Sister," *Evening Public Ledger* (January 12, 1918).

25. "Need of Gas-Mask Training Finally Realized at Meade," *Evening Public Ledger* (June 29, 1918).

26. For more on this point, see Paul Fussell, *The Great War and Modern Memory* (1975; repr., New York: Oxford University Press, 2000), 28.

27. "Censor's Lid Augurs Movement at Meade," *Evening Public Ledger* (January 14, 1918); "Man at Camp Hancock Writes of Holidays in Dixieland," *Evening Public Ledger* (January 14, 1918).

28. "Third of Draftees Fit after Army Test," *Evening Public Ledger* (January 14, 1918).

29. "Last Quotas of First Draft Leaving City," *Evening Public Ledger* (February 6, 1918); "292 More City Men Are Called in Draft," *Evening Public Ledger* (February 13, 1918).

30. "600 More 'Boys' Leave for Camp," *Evening Public Ledger* (April 2, 1918).

31. "Soldier Wins Praise for Snappy Salute," *Evening Public Ledger* (April 2, 1918).

CHAPTER 9

1. "House Will Push Alien Slacker Bill," *New York Tribune* (August 3, 1917).

2. "Aliens, Ashamed, Register Today," *Evening Public Ledger* (February 4, 1918).

3. Ibid.

4. "Naturalization Court Crowded with Aliens," *Evening Public Ledger* (February 4, 1918).

5. "Alien Slacker Bill Is Passed," *Washington Herald* (September 13, 1917).

6. "Alien Slackers' Bill Suffering Setback," *Washington Herald* (September 25, 1917); "Fights Alien Slacker Bill" *Washington Herald* (September 27, 1917).

7. "Alien Slacker Bill Shelved in House," *Washington Herald* (September 28, 1917); "Alien Slacker Bill Fails," *The Sun (NY)* (October 7, 1917).

8. "Alien Slacker Bill Held Up," *Evening Ledger* (October 13, 1917).

9. Ibid.

10. "Italians Dodge Home War Call," *The Sun (NY)* (January 6, 1918). Giovanni Preziosi, widely respected for his research on immigrant colonies, had lectured at Harvard on his first visit to the United States in November 1907. On his next visit in March 1908, he received a letter, while staying with the Augustinian priests at the rectory of Our Lady of Good Counsel in South Philadelphia, threatening that he would be murdered unless he paid $1,000. The seriocomic letter read: "You will never see Italy again if you do not give $1,000 to the person that pinches you after he salutes you. . . . Carry it with you always and remember that I am more powerful than the police and your God." Decorated with a tombstone and skull, it was signed "Black Hand." Although not believing that he was in any great danger, Preziosi reported the matter to the police. He regarded the Black Hand as a myth that was being used by individual blackmailers to frighten their victims. In this case, he dismissed it, saying "I'm not going to worry about it." See "Black Hand Demands $1000 from Italian," *The Inquirer* (March 10, 1908). Among his many works on immigration, his most important was *Gli Italiani negli Stati Uniti del Nord* (Milan: Libreria Editrice Milanese, 1909). In 1913, he founded a periodical journal, *La vita italiana all'estero*, devoted to the study of Italian migration. Unfortunately, his life and career had begun to take a different direction. After leaving the priesthood in 1911, Preziosi eventually became an influential member of the Fascist Party, well known for his anti-Semitic views, be-

fore committing suicide by plunging together with his wife from a window in Milan in March 1945.

11. "Italian Order Has 1600 Stars" (photo), *Evening Public Ledger* (January 2, 1918).

12. "Congress; What It Did Yesterday," *Washington Times* (February 7, 1918); "The Wrong Way to Go about It," *New York Tribune* (February 12, 1918).

13. "Alien Slacker Bill in House Dropped," *New York Tribune* (February 14, 1918); "Alien Slacker Bill Dropped at Government's Request," *New York Tribune* (February 14, 1918); "France and Italy Agree to 'Slacker' Treaty," *New York Tribune* (February 27, 1918); "Alien Service Approved," *The Sun (NY)* (February 27, 1918); "Bill to Deport Slackers Passes House," *New York Tribune* (February 28, 1918); "Alien Slacker Bill Passes the House," *The Sun (NY)* (February 28, 1918).

14. "Impatient and Uncivil," *New York Tribune* (March 1, 1918).

15. "Alien Slacker Bill Has Slow Negotiation," *Washington Herald* (March 17, 1918); "Million Alien Slackers," *Evening Public Ledger* (June 5, 1918); "Says Lansing Lets Aliens Dodge Draft," *New York Tribune* (June 6, 1918); "Bars Slacking Aliens," *Evening Public Ledger* (August 30, 1918).

16. "To Prepare Aliens for Naturalization," *Evening Public Ledger* (September 30, 1918).

17. "Brothers Naturalized after Enlisting," *Evening Public Ledger* (May 1, 1918). After the war, Hugo worked as a clerk at the Main Post Office at 30th Street and lived in the Kingsessing section of Philadelphia, while Armando's success as a decorator brought him and his family to Wynnewood, an affluent suburb on the Main Line, until his death in 1988.

18. "Aliens at Meade to Become Citizens," *The Inquirer* (May 24, 1918); "$12,000 P.E. Chapel to Open at Meade," *The Inquirer* (May 26, 1918).

19. "200 Camp Crane Men Given Naturalization," *The Inquirer* (May 27, 1918); "Meade Aliens Keen for Citizenship," *The Inquirer* (May 28, 1918); "364 Alien Soldiers Become U.S. Citizens," *The Inquirer* (June 1, 1918); "Aliens Swore in for Camp Meade," *The Inquirer* (June 4, 1918); "Citizenship Denied One Meade Soldier," *The Inquirer* (June 8, 1918).

20. "Camp Meade Aliens to Be Naturalized," *Evening Public Ledger* (September 18, 1918).

21. "Camp Lee Fights Foe Propaganda," *Evening Public Ledger* (September 20, 1918). For Reverend Ottavio B. Neyroz as a religious leader among the Italians of Schenectady, see Robert R. Pascucci, *Electric City Immigrants: Italians and Poles of Schenectady, N.Y., 1880–1930*. In particular, see chapter 4, on "Protestant Evangelism." Fortunately, it is online, available at http://schenectadyhistory.org/resources/pascucci/.

22. "Camp Lee Fights Foe Propaganda," *Evening Public Ledger* (September 20, 1918).

23. "Serving Their Country," *Evening Public Ledger* (March 15, 1918). After the war, Pessolano resumed a medical career that lasted for many years until his death on October 12, 1979, in Greenwich, Connecticut, at the age of 90. Further details available at Ancestry.com.

CHAPTER 10

1. Simeon Strunsky, "Nemesis on the Western Front," *Evening Public Ledger* (August 17, 1918). Strunsky later served as an editor for the *New York Times* for 24 years as well as the author of articles and books before his death in 1948.

2. "Depleted Ranks of Allies Must Be Filled by U.S.," *Evening Public Ledger* (April 29, 1918); "Baker Says U.S. Troops Are on Way to Italy," *The Sun (NY)* (May 25, 1918); "U.S. Soldiers in Italy Soon, Says Baker," *New York Tribune* (May 25, 1918).

3. "Per a Celebrazione dell 'Italy Day,'" *Evening Public Ledger* (May 24, 1918); "Italians to Mark Flag Day," *The Inquirer* (May 24, 1918).

4. Charles M. Bakewell, *The Story of the American Red Cross in Italy* (New York: The MacMillan Company, 1920), 157–160; John R. Smucker Jr., *The History of the United States Army Ambulance Service with the French and Italian Armies, 1917–1918–1919* (Allentown, PA, 1967). See, especially, chapter 5, "The Italian Contingent, 'Columbus We Are Here,'" available at http://www.ourstory.info/library/2-ww1/Smucker/usaacTC.html.

5. "'USAACS' Present a Crackerjack Show," *Evening Public Ledger* (April 9, 1918); "Allentown News Notes," *The Inquirer* (April 9, 1918); "Allentown News Notes," *The Inquirer* (April 20, 1918); "Camp Crane Play a Recruit Winner," *Evening Public Ledger* (April 24, 1918); "Brumbaugh Speaks to Allentown Men," *Evening Public Ledger* (April 29, 1918); "Brumbaugh Addresses Camp Crane Soldiers," *The Inquirer* (April 29, 1918); "Consegna di una Bandiera al Corpo di Ambulanza Che Parte per l'Italia," *La Libera Parola* (May 25, 1918); "Flag Is Presented to Ambulance Men by Sons of Italy," *Wilkes-Barre (PA) Times Leader* (May 20, 1918); "Enlists as Interpreter," *Evening Public Ledger* (May 15, 1918); "200 Camp Crane Men Given Naturalization," *The Inquirer* (May 26, 1918); "Talking Machine Gift to Allentown Soldiers," *Evening Public Ledger* (May 25, 1918); photograph, *Evening Public Ledger* (May 27, 1918); "Un Dono ai Soldati di Camp Crane Partenti per il Fronte Italiano," *La Libera Parola* (June 1, 1918). The actual figure remained elusive, partly because of the ambiguous use of the phrase "Italian contingent" to refer to the entire body of soldiers being readied for deployment in Italy and the number of Italians within that group.

6. "La Bandiera dell'Ordine Figli d'Italia Sventola in Patria," *La Libera Parola* (August 24, 1918).

7. "Dalla Zona di Guerra d'Italia," *La Libera Parola* (September 21, 1918).

8. "Just Gossip about People," *Evening Public Ledger* (August 8, 1918).

9. "Una nobilissima lettera dall'Italia," *La Libera Parola* (October 19, 1918).

10. "Lettere dal fronte," *La Libera Parola* (November 30, 1918); "Saluti da Padova," *La Libera Parola* (January 11, 1919); "Lettere dall'Austria," *La Libera Parola* (March 1, 1919). The War Merit Cross eventually became a widely distributed honor. From its inception in January 1918, over 1,000,000 recipients had earned the honor by 1927. See Michael Shackelford, *Medals of Italy* (1998), available at http://www.gwpda.org/medals/italmedl/italy.html.

11. "Saluti dall'Italia," *La Libera Parola* (May 24, 1919); "Saluti Graditi," *La Libera Parola* (May 31, 1919); "Il Ricevimento del Generale Guglielmotti," *La Libera*

Parola (December 27, 1919); Harold Speakman, *From a Soldier's Heart* (The Abingdon Press, 1919), 156.

12. "Onore al Valore," *La Libera Parola* (February 8, 1919); more information is available at Ancestry.com. Di Lauro spent the rest of his life as a self-employed printer in suburban Philadelphia before his death at the age of 81 in February 1975.

13. Information on the Protevi family is readily available at Ancestry.com. See also "City of Philadelphia," *Eighty-Ninth Annual Report of the Board of Public Education for the Year Ending December 31, 1907*, vol. 89 (Philadelphia, 1908), 147; *The Metronome*, 35 (August 1915), 7.

14. Smucker, *History of the United States Army Ambulance Service*; "Deaths of a Day—Gino Protevi," *Evening Public Ledger* (January 9, 1919); "Gino Protevi Muore in Italia," *La Libera Parola* (January 18, 1919).

15. "Philadelphia Lieutenant Killed," *Evening Public Ledger* (June 19, 1919); "Deaths—Protevi," *Evening Public Ledger* (June 28, 1921); "Died—Protevi," *The Inquirer* (June 28, 1921); "I Funerali di Gino Protevi," *La Libera Parola* (July 3, 1921). After the war, Captain Adolfo Caruso, a native of Rome, remained in Philadelphia as the general manager of the San Carlo Opera Company, which performed at the Metropolitan Opera House, at Broad and Poplar Streets in North Philadelphia. In November 1922, he married Josephine Lucchese, a highly regarded opera singer, in a ceremony at Saint Rita's Church on Broad Street. He also served as the business agent for Josephine who was often featured in programs of the San Carlo Opera Company. She was the daughter of Mr. and Mrs. Sam Lucchese, of San Antonio, Texas. Her father designed and manufactured high-quality western-style boots, which are still sold in cities of the American West today. A vintage photo of Captain Caruso, easily accessible online, shows him in the uniform of the 332nd Regiment, with its distinctive shoulder patch depicting the lion of Saint Mark. It is somewhat anomalous as he was attached to the U.S. Army Ambulance Service, not the 332nd Infantry Regiment. See the photo, available at http://www.loc.gov/pictures/item/ggb2006006689/.

16. "Enemy Always Ran, Says Lieutenant," *Evening Public Ledger* (April 15, 1919). Carl H. Trik III, "Reminiscences," in *Ohio Doughboys in Italy*, ed. William Wallace et al. (n.p.), 74–89. For general histories of the regiment, see Joseph L. Lettau, *In Italy with the 332nd* (n.p.: Youngstown, OH, 1922). Lieutenant Trik came to the 332nd Infantry after training in the Reserve Officers Corps at Fort Harrison, Indiana. Although born in Philadelphia, he had apparently moved from his family home. The address in the article was that of his German-born parents, who had previously used the name von Trik. While employed as a mining engineer, Trik remained in the army reserves before he reentered active duty in World War II. He reached the rank of lieutenant colonel as a reserve officer; he died in California in August 1954. More information is available at Ancestry.com.

17. "Giuseppe the Guide," *Evening Public Ledger* (August 2, 1918).

CHAPTER 11

1. "Wants Italian Immigrants Impressed into Service," *Evening Public Ledger* (April 25, 1918).

2. For the remark by the German officer, see *Second Report of the Provost Marshal General to the Secretary of War on the Operations of the Selective Service System to December 20, 1918* (Washington, DC: Government Printing Office, 1919), 86.

3. "Two More City Boys Are Dead in France," *Evening Public Ledger* (April 13, 1918). For a brief history of the 19th Engineers, with an emphasis on its origins in Philadelphia, see Lieutenant W. Frederic Todd, 19th Engineers (Railway), "Other Philadelphia Units," in *Philadelphia in the World War, 1914–1919* (New York: published for the Philadelphia War History Committee by Wynkoop Hallenbeck Crawford, 1922), 158–164. "Brothers in Service," *Evening Public Ledger* (July 20, 1918). While other sources identify the brothers as Domenico, Alessandro, and Giuseppe, the Anglicized form appeared in the article.

4. "Two U.S. Soldiers Killed in Action," *Evening Public Ledger* (November 19, 1917); "Addressless List of Casualties Given," *Evening Public Ledger* (March 9, 1918); "Help Us Identify U.S. Soldiers," *Evening Public Ledger* (April 12, 1918); "Legal Leeches May Feast on Casualties," *Evening Public Ledger* (April 12, 1918); "A Great Red Day," *Evening Public Ledger* (April 12, 1918); "Read That List," *Evening Public Ledger* (April 17, 1918); "Marine Corps Brigade Has Lost 278 Men," *Evening Public Ledger* (April 26, 1918).

5. "Two from Here Killed, 3 Hurt," *Evening Public Ledger* (August 22, 1918).

6. "Liberty Loan Drive Started at Meade," *Evening Public Ledger* (April 23, 1918). Among other newspapers that carried news of Viscusi's death, see "Casualties among Our Fighting Men Abroad," *New York Tribune* (April 20, 1918). In private correspondence, Dr. Jennifer Pittman Viscusi, a family genealogist, has identified Pietro and Pasqua Viscusi as the parents of Girolamo Viscusi, while also indicating that his body was later transferred from its initial burial site in the cemetery at Lunéville to Moiano, in the province of Benevento, in Italy, the town of origin where relatives still live. A poignant video of burials in the town once known as Baccarat, but now Lunéville, is available at http://www.criticalpast.com/products/location_history /Baccarat_France/1930/1932. See also W. E. Robb, *The Price of Our Heritage* (Des Moines, 1919). I am indebted to Virgil Reiter for calling this source to my attention. More information is available at http://firstworldwar.com/features/rainbowwarriors .htm and http://www.usgwarchives.org/pa/1pa/military/ww1/haulsee/wwi.html.

7. "Stirring Exercises to Mark 'Fourth' Here," *Evening Public Ledger* (July 3, 1918).

8. After Alfred V. Volpe returned from the war, he lived and worked in Conshohocken rather than in the anticipated partnership with his older brother. He is found in the U.S. census of 1940 as a self-employed "trucker" and head of a household that included his wife, Catherine, their 10-year-old son, Alexander, presumably named for Alfred's younger brother, and a nephew. His World War II Draft Registration lists his birth one year earlier in 1890 in Salerno, Italy; his employer as the Carey Magnesia Plant in Plymouth Meeting, Pennsylvania, and A. M. Volpe, almost certainly his brother, Angelo, at the same address in Philadelphia where the latter lived in 1918. More information is available at https://familysearch.org/.

9. Private James Crocco is buried at the American military cemetery at Aisne-Marne in France.

10. "Eighteen, Yet a Veteran," *Evening Public Ledger* (October 28, 1918). After the war, Bandiere endured the vicissitudes of civilian life as an automobile salesman in Baltimore before he died at the age of 100 in April 1999. His older brother, Charles, had written the letters described in an earlier section of the present work.

11. The reader may question the inclusion of some names. But rather than attempt to determine correct spelling, they have been presented as they appeared on the casualty list. When a change was obviously in order, such as replacing Musicant with Musicante, it was done. A name that did not appear to be of Italian origin was included if there was compelling evidence of an Italian background, as in the case of Bundy, whose first name was "Biagio." But such changes and inclusions were minimal.

12. These names often vary from one source to another. In this photograph, one of the men is identified as Louis Sasso; in military records, he is listed as Louis Lo Sasso.

13. Horace E. V. Fornaci was the grandson of Emmanuel V. H. Nardi, a prominent leader in the Italian community of Philadelphia. I am also indebted to Carol Klock, for providing information on Fornaci, who was her grandfather.

14. "Fell in Battle Day War Ended," *Evening Public Ledger* (January 11, 1919).

15. "'Dead Soldiers' Are Much Alive," *Evening Public Ledger* (December 3, 1918).

16. "Casualties Not Held Up, Says Baker," *Evening Public Ledger* (December 2, 1918).

17. "Yank's Lips Sealed under Boche Torture," *Evening Public Ledger* (January 14, 1919).

18. "Three Brothers in Casualty List," *Evening Public Ledger* (November 18, 1918); "Casualty Lists Again Confused," *Evening Public Ledger* (December 23, 1918); "Correct Casualties; Name City Soldiers," *Evening Public Ledger* (December 24, 1918).

19. The incongruity of the notification that the Cocozza family received was not nearly as great as another soldier who had been home for a month before a telegram arrived informing his parents in West Philadelphia that their son had died in action.

20. "15,000 Soldiers Released Each Day 'Over Here,'" *Evening Public Ledger* (December 14, 1918).

21. "Sketches of the Heroes," *Evening Public Ledger* (January 7, 1919).

22. The name "Michael Iannelli," correctly spelled on the casualty list, was "Innelli" in the "Sketches of the Heroes Item" of January 3 and under the photo, "reported dead," on the following day. His name was also misspelled in a generally reliable source, *Soldiers of the Great War*, compiled by W. M. Haulsee, F. G. Howe, and A. C. Doyle (Washington, DC: Soldiers Record, 1920). The comparable work for Italy's armed forces, *L'Albo d'Oro dei Militari Caduti nella guerra nazionale 1915–1918*, prepared by the Italian Ministry of War in 1930, is available at http://www.cadutigrandeguerra.it/Default.aspx.

23. "13 Pennsylvanians Receive War Honors," *Evening Public Ledger* (January 20, 1919); more information available at http://www.militarytimes.com/citations-medals-awards/recipient.php?recipientid=14827. Giuseppe Spadafora, Americo Di Pasquale, and Giacomo Masciarelli are also listed in Raymond S. Tompkins, *Maryland Fighters in the Great War* (Baltimore, MD: Thomas and Evans Printing Co., 1919).

24. Available at http://www.militarytimes.com/citations-medals-awards/recipient.php?recipientid=13381. For the details of his return, see: "Philadelphia's Own, Flaunting Lorraine Cross, Home Again," *The Inquirer* (May 29, 1919).

25. Available http://www.militarytimes.com/citations-medals-awards/recipient.php?recipientid=11830.

26. Available http://www.militarytimes.com/citations-medals-awards/recipient.php?recipientid=11594; http://archive.org/stream/historyofseventy0079th/historyofseventy0079th_djvu.txt.

27. Available http://www.militarytimes.com/citations-medals-awards/recipient.php?recipientid=10394. Among the men awarded the Distinguished Service Cross, Aiello disappears in subsequent years. One Antonio Aiello, a laborer at the Philadelphia Macaroni Company at 11th and Catharine Streets, who registered on June 5, 1917, as sole support of a mother, wife, and child was unlikely to have been inducted. Another Antonio Aiello registered on September 12, 1918, probably too late to be inducted before the war ended. The many men named Antonio or Anthony Aiello challenge the experienced genealogist to find one of particular interest.

28. "Camden Hero Cited," *Evening Public Ledger* (February 19, 1919); more information is available at http://militarytimes.com/citations-medals-awards/recipient.php?recipientid=10459. The official listing of the award gives his residence as Pennsgrove, New Jersey, south of Camden on the Delaware River. When Private Angelo fell upon hard times a few years later, he walked from Camden to Washington to testify before the House Ways and Means Committee in support of the promised but deferred veterans' bonus as well as for jobs in February 1931. After coming home from France, he joined the fire department of Camden, before becoming unemployed for two years. His amusing and effective testimony showed that he was, as Pershing had urged, "as brave and cool in peace" as he had been at war. See Frank Rich, "Don't Forget Me for a Job," *New York Magazine* (October 31, 2010). It is claimed that the officer whom he had rescued on the battlefield was Colonel George S. Patton. See Paul Dickson and Thomas B. Allen, *The Bonus Army: An American Epic* (Gordonsville, VA: Walker, 2004).

29. "Cronaca di Filadelfia; Nei Nostri Uffici," *La Libera Parola* (June 15, 1918); "Cronaca di Filadelfia; Partito per l'Europa," *La Libera Parola* (July 13, 1918). Further details of Esterino Crudele's life are available at Ancestry.com.

30. See *The Official History of the 315th Infantry, USA* (comp., pub. Historical Board of the 315th Infantry, 1923).

31. "Cronaca di Filadelfia; La Morte di un Eroe," *La Libera Parola* (February 1, 1919); "Cronaca di Filadelfia; Commemorazione," *La Libera Parola* (April 12, 1919). Information on the memorial in Isernia is available at http://www.comune.isernia.it/news/2016/08/2_nov_2016_gloria.htm.

CHAPTER 12

1. "Two Titled Women Describe Work of Sex in War Relief," *Evening Public Ledger* (June 3, 1918). Countess Lisi Cecilia Cipriani remains an intriguing personage of the period. Of mixed German and Italian ancestry, she came to Chicago as a child, eventually earning a Ph.D. and teaching comparative literature at the University of Chicago. "Women Bring Stories of Enemy Brutalities," *Evening Public Ledger* (October 29, 1918); "Countess to Visit City," *Evening Public Ledger* (November 21, 1918).

2. "Italian Women to Operate Tramway Cars," *Evening Ledger* (June 4, 1915); "Knitting Socks for Soldiers," *Evening Ledger* (January 10, 1916); "U.S. Ambassador Defends Italians," *The Inquirer* (July 2, 1916); "Italian Women Aid Men Dig Trenches at Front," *The Inquirer* (June 10, 1917); "Italian Women Sing in Fields, Sure Their Men Will Stay Foe," *Evening Public Ledger* (June 20, 1918); "'Equal Pay for Equal Work' Is Slogan Born of Women Doing Tasks of Men," *Evening Public Ledger* (January 14, 1918).

3. "Women of Italy Get Ready for War!" *The Day Book (Chicago, IL)* (April 4, 1915); "With the Fighters," *The Sunday Star (Washington, DC)* (March 10, 1918); "In the Fighting Zone," *The Sunday Star (Washington, DC)* (February 17, 1918); caption, "Italian Women Digging Trenches Behind the Italian Front," *New-York Tribune* (March 31, 1918); and "Wartime Activities of Women at Home and Abroad," *Evening Public Ledger* (April 11, 1918). Also see Allison Scardino Belzer, *Women and the Great War: Femininity under Fire in Italy* (New York: Palgrave Macmillan, 2010).

4. "Bridgeport Rivals Essen for Output of War Munitions," *The Inquirer* (October 3, 1915).

5. "Woman Finds Scrap O' Paper Saying Plan 'All Ready' for Destruction of Eddystone," *Evening Ledger* (April 11, 1917); "Terrified Employees Quit Scene of Catastrophe," *Evening Ledger* (April 11, 1917); "Blast Takes Father from Poor Family," *Evening Ledger* (April 11, 1917); "Stillness of Death in Wake of Great Disaster," *Evening Ledger* (April 11, 1917); "Victims of Great Explosion Located on Hospital Lists," *The Inquirer* (April 11, 1917);

"Arms Plants to Close in Respect for the Dead," *Evening Ledger* (April 12, 1917); "Blast Victims Buried in Rain as 8,000 Weep," *Evening Ledger* (April 13, 1917); "Will Name Jury in Blast Inquest," *Evening Ledger* (April 16, 1917); "Eddystone Probe May Prove Plot," *Evening Ledger* (April 18, 1917); "Coroner Seeks Facts in Explosion Probe," *Evening Ledger* (April 25, 1917); "Coroner Told of Many Plots at Eddystone," *Evening Ledger* (April 26, 1917); "Probe at Eddystone to Be Pushed Deeper," *Evening Ledger* (April 28, 1917); "Eddystone Compensation Pleas Settled by Board," *Evening Ledger* (May 14, 1917); "Eddystone Will Make Rifles for New Army," *Evening Ledger* (May 18, 1917); "Men Wanted," *Evening Ledger* (May 28, 1917).

6. "War Brings Shortage of Women Laborers," *The Inquirer* (August 7, 1917).

7. "To Inspect Camps of Berry Pickers," *The Inquirer* (June 17, 1917); "Female Help Wanted," *The Inquirer* (July 31, 1918).

8. "Italian Reservists Embark on Ancona," *The Inquirer* (March 24, 1915); "1000 Sons of Italy Sail to Serve the King," *Evening Ledger* (June 14, 1915); "Cheers and Tears for Departing Italian Reservists," *The Inquirer* (June 15, 1915); "More Ital-

ians Leave Here for the Front," *The Inquirer* (June 20, 1915); "Thousands Watch Reservists Sail," *The Inquirer* (July 24, 1915); "Italian Reservists Leave for the War," *The Inquirer* (August 4, 1915).

9. "Please Tell Me What to Do," *Evening Public Ledger* (August 20, 1918).

10. "Marriage Licenses Issued," *The Inquirer* (July 13, 1917); "Her Husband Drafted, Life Is Not Worth Living," *The Inquirer* (March 1, 1917). The spelling of their names has been corrected from the version given in the latter article. The details on Frank Bertolino's life are available at Ancestry.org.

11. "Italians Here Raise Aid Fund," *Public Ledger* (May 25, 1915); "Relief Work Begun by 'Little Italy'" *Public Ledger* (May 26, 1915); "To Assist Reservists' Families," *The Inquirer* (May 30, 1915); "Italians Seek Fund to Aid Colony's Poor," *Public Ledger* (May 30, 1915); "This Is Italian Flag Day," *Evening Ledger* (June 4, 1915); "Italians Will Help Women and Children," *The Inquirer* (June 9, 1915); "Italians Pledge Aid for $100,000," *Public Ledger* (June 14, 1915); "Italians Collect $3000 for War Relief Fund," *Public Ledger* (June 19, 1915); "More Italians Leave Here for the Front," *The Inquirer* (June 20, 1915); "Italian Festival in Aid of Poor," *Public Ledger* (June 29, 1915); "Columbus Day Stirs Patriotic Fervor of the City," *Evening Ledger* (October 12, 1915).

Ferruccio Giannini was a well-known local conductor, impresario, and proprietor of Verdi Hall on Christian Street. His son, Vittorio, would become a highly regarded composer, while Dusolina, not yet 16 years old, would become a featured performer at La Scala Opera House in Milan and one of the leading operatic sopranos in the world. His other daughter, Euphemia, had a successful career as a voice teacher at the Curtis Institute in Philadelphia, where her students would include Frank Guarrera and Anna Moffo.

12. "Society Women Are Working Energetically for the Relief of Strife-Stricken Europe," *The Inquirer* (November 1, 1914); "Increase Activities to Aid Refugees," *The Inquirer* (November 7, 1914); "$5,000 Contributed for Home Relief," *The Inquirer* (November 12, 1914); "Help for Needy Philadelphians," *The Inquirer* (December 8, 1914); "Home Relief Gives 50 More Men Work," *The Inquirer* (March 10, 1915); "Evicted Family Aided by Emergency Body," *The Inquirer* (April 24, 1915); "Emergency Aid Will Stop Work in May," *Evening Ledger* (March 19, 1915).

13. "Pa. Emergency Aid Spent $2,000,000," *The Inquirer* (July 8, 1917); "What Emergency Aid Does to Relieve War Suffering," *Evening Ledger* (September 13, 1917); "Young Italians Work for Brothers in War," *The Inquirer* (June 23, 1918); "Just Gossip about People," *Evening Public Ledger* (June 24, 1918); "Sandbags Cover Venice," *The Inquirer* (February 19, 1917); "Italians to Share Fund for Blinded," *The Inquirer* (May 19, 1918).

14. "Entertainment Funds for Italian Relief," *The Inquirer* (June 28, 1915); "Arrest Reservists Who Desert Wives, Is Advice of Ryan," *The Inquirer* (August 5, 1915).

15. "Arrest Reservists Who Desert Wives, Is Advice of Ryan," *The Inquirer* (August 5, 1915); "Will Raise Relief Fund for Italians," *The Inquirer* (August 7, 1915); "Pledge Support for Reservists' Families," *Evening Ledger* (August 8, 1915).

City Solicitor Michael J. Ryan's advocacy for an independent Ireland and his role as an anti-British speaker at German American rallies suggest views on international politics that may have encouraged obstruction of Italian efforts with the Allies.

16. "Italians Arrange Relief Efforts," *The Inquirer* (August 9, 1915); "Stirs Italian Relief Committee to Action," *The Inquirer* (August 10, 1915); "Italian Aid Body Will Reorganize," *The Inquirer* (August 16, 1915).

17. "Italian War Relief Committee Organizes," *The Inquirer* (August 21, 1915); "Italian Relief Fund Plans Perfected," *The Inquirer* (August 22, 1915); "Plan to Systematize Relief for Italians," *The Inquirer* (August 23, 1915); "Reservists Respond to Country's Call," *The Inquirer* (August 26, 1915); "Italian Relief Body Perfects Fund Plans," *The Inquirer* (August 30, 1915); "Funds for Italian War Relief Are Promised," *The Inquirer* (September 2, 1915); "Italian Committee Meets," *The Inquirer* (September 23, 1915).

18. "Bread! Bread! Pleads 102-Year-Old Woman and It Is Given Her," *Evening Ledger* (January 4, 1916); "Italian Woman 102 Years Old Begs Bread of Society," *Public Ledger* (January 5, 1916).

19. "Italian Women Organize," *The Inquirer* (August 31, 1897). This Stella d'Italia is not to be confused with the organization formed by male barbers under a similar title. "Il Circolo Italiano Dà un Ballo per i Feriti," *Evening Ledger* (February 10, 1917); "Ardent Workers for Concert and Ball to Aid Italian War Sufferers," *Evening Public Ledger* (January 31, 1918).

20. "Italian Division to Give Million for Third Loan," *Evening Public Ledger* (April 6, 1918); "Home Canvas Begins in Liberty Loan Drive," *Evening Public Ledger* (April 13, 1918); "Women Sell Total of $18,000,000 Bonds," *Evening Public Ledger* (April 25, 1918).

21. "4000 Phila. Women Awaiting War Call," *The Inquirer* (February 16, 1917); "Italians Decorate Columbus Statue," *Evening Ledger* (October 12, 1917); "Sing for Liberty Loan," *Evening Public Ledger* (April 29, 1918).

22. "To Keep Boys in Navy Supplied with Music," *Evening Public Ledger* (July 11, 1918).

23. "Men Folks Fight, Woman Translates," *Evening Public Ledger* (April 29, 1918).

24. "This Is the Day! Buy a Bond Now," *Evening Public Ledger* (October 11, 1918). See also Jacob Warner Rhine, "Four-Minute Men," in *Philadelphia in the World War, 1914–1919* (New York: published for the Philadelphia War History Committee by Wynkoop Hallenbeck Crawford, 1922), 490–496.

25. "City Employes [*sic*] to Boost Loan," *Evening Public Ledger* (September 24, 1918).

26. "Will Reaffirm Loyalty," *Evening Public Ledger* (September 15, 1918); "Italians Celebrate Day," *Evening Public Ledger* (September 20, 1918); "New Loan Drive Gets Start Here," *Evening Public Ledger* (September 23, 1918); "Foreigners Here Buy $83,000,000 Bonds," *Evening Public Ledger* (May 20, 1919).

27. "Catch U-Boat Orders on Meade Wireless," *Evening Public Ledger* (April 12, 1918); "Gli Italiani per il Third Liberty Loan," *Evening Public Ledger* (May 3, 1918). In the newspaper account, Di Leonardo's name was given as Leonardo, but becomes Di Leonardo in other documents. Similarly, his birthplace is given as Chieti

and Pianella, both in the Abruzzi region. He was among the Italians naturalized at Camp Meade in September 1917.

28. "Italians Arrive in New York to Boost Loan," *Evening Public Ledger* (October 2, 1918).

29. The same Joseph Francis Petti would serve in the U.S. Army in World War II, with two overseas tours of duty, from his enlistment in March 1941 and discharge in November 1945.

30. Although the young goddess was identified as Marie Guidice, she was more likely Maria Giudice. And while the setting is given as the Campbell-Lyons School, the Lyons School was actually another public school located not far away at 10th and Catharine Streets.

31. "Kaiser Bill 'Lynched,'" *Evening Public Ledger* (September 30, 1918).

CHAPTER 13

1. "Italian, Gassed in Battle, Returns and Grinds Organ," *Evening Public Ledger* (January 29, 1919).

2. "Bemoans Being Unlucky," *Evening Public Ledger* (February 11, 1919).

3. "Sketches of the Heroes," *Evening Public Ledger* (February 17, 1919); "Reception for Soldier," *Evening Public Ledger* (March 15, 1919).

4. "Soldier Longs for Home," *Evening Public Ledger* (February 19, 1919); "Demands Camden Heroes Return," *Evening Public Ledger* (February 19, 1919); "Army Discharged 1,513,471," *Evening Public Ledger* (April 2, 1919). Despite his surname, Luciani was not an Italian American but perhaps a Franco American, since his father, according to census information, was born in France, which makes his comment about that country interesting from another perspective. But given the massive migration of Italians into France, his family may have been of Italian origin.

5. "Casualty Lists Are Nearing End," *Evening Public Ledger* (April 2, 1919); "Additional Casualties Reported by Mail," *Evening Public Ledger* (April 2, 1919); "Tacony Soldier Dead," *Evening Public Ledger* (April 2, 1919). While Dismario does not appear among the names of the quasi-official *Soldiers of the Great War*, his personal life and military service are documented in *History of the 318th Infantry Regiment of the 80th Division, 1917–1919* (Richmond: The William Byrd Press, Inc., 1919).

6. "Demands Camden Heroes Return," *Evening Public Ledger* (February 19, 1919); "State Maintains Casualty Lead," *Evening Public Ledger* (March 4, 1919).

7. "Hero Volunteer One of 4 Killed," *Evening Public Ledger* (March 21, 1919).

8. "Phila. Man Holds Record for Times under Gunfire," *Evening Public Ledger* (March 28, 1918); for information on Diodati's earlier life, see Pennsylvania, Philadelphia City Births, 1860–1906, index and images, *FamilySearch* (available at https://familysearch.org/pal:/MM9.1.1/V1MZ-DN9, accessed October 8, 2012), Vincent M. Divdoti [*sic*] 1889. It is not known what college, if any, he may have attended. But given the age at which he received his medical degree, he may have entered medical school directly after completing his secondary education. The additional details on his life are also available at Ancestry.com.

9. "Phila. Man Holds Record for Times under Gunfire," *Evening Public Ledger* (March 28, 1918).

10. Ibid; see also "Awards of Military Cross," *Journal of the American Medical Association* 72, no. 14 (April 5, 1919): 1005; "General News Items," *Pennsylvania Medical Journal* 23, no. 7 (April 1920): 423.

11. "Three Casualty Lists Reported," *Evening Public Ledger* (April 3, 1919); "Yank Listed Missing Now Reported Alive," *Evening Public Ledger* (April 5, 1919)

12. "Yank Listed Missing Now Reported Alive," *Evening Public Ledger* (April 5, 1919).

13. For information related to the termination of the draft, see *Final Report of the Provost Marshal General to the Secretary of War on the Operations of the Selective Service System to July 15, 1919* (Washington, DC: Government Printing Office, 1920).

14. "Baseball Honor Roll," *Evening Public Ledger* (April 10, 1919).

15. "Can't Believe He's Dead," *Evening Public Ledger* (April 5, 1919). Iannelli died at the age of 81 in 1974.

16. "Not Draft Dodger," *The Inquirer* (January 20, 1922); "Served in Italian Army," *The Inquirer* (February 6, 1922); "'Slacker' Saw Real Service," *The Inquirer* (August 30, 1922).

17. "Urges Education of Foreign-Born," *Evening Public Ledger* (January 2, 1919).

18. "Dix Aliens Made Citizens," *Evening Public Ledger* (February 26, 1919); "The Making of Americans," *Evening Public Ledger* (July 30, 1919).

19. "'Americans All' in Drill Here," *Evening Public Ledger* (October 24, 1919).

20. "Says City Is Half Foreign Families," *Evening Public Ledger* (February 11, 1920).

21. Rev. Harry W. Ettleson, "Now My Idea Is This: Daily Talks with Thinking Philadelphians on Subjects They Know Best. On Immigration," *Evening Public Ledger* (May 19, 1921). Ettleson achieved recognition in *Jewish Activities in the United States*, vol. 2 (April 1921) of Henry Ford's notorious publication, *The International Jew*, for helping persuade the school board of Hartford, Connecticut, to eliminate *The Merchant of Venice* from its reading list in 1911.

CHAPTER 14

1. "La Disfatta degli Austriaci Completa," *Evening Public Ledger* (November 1, 1918); "Gli Italiani Ovunque Avanzano Vittoriosi," *Evening Public Ledger* (November 2, 1918); "Il Tricolore Issato su Trento e Trieste," *Evening Public Ledger* (November 4, 1918); "L'Entusiasmo nella Colonia Italiana," *Evening Public Ledger* (November 4, 1918); "Italians Exultant at Austria's Fall Hold Celebration," *The Inquirer* (November 5, 1918).

2. "Victory Thrills All Little Italy," *Evening Public Ledger* (November 4, 1918); "L'Entusiasmo nella Colonia Italiana," *Evening Public Ledger* (November 4, 1918); "Italians Exultant at Austria's Fall Hold Celebration," *The Inquirer* (November 5, 1918).

3. "Italians Exultant at Austria's Fall Hold Celebration," *The Inquirer* (November 5, 1918).

4. "Evviva Italia!" *Evening Public Ledger* (November 4, 1918).

5. "Italians Took 500,000 Captives," *Evening Public Ledger* (November 5, 1918); "Masterly Direction Won Italian Triumph," *Evening Public Ledger* (November 5, 1918); "Con le Armate Italiane in Campo," *Evening Public Ledger* (November 5, 1918).

6. "Celebration of Victory by Italians Continues," *Evening Public Ledger* (November 5, 1918). For the ads, see the *Evening Public Ledger* (November 5, 1918); the comment is found on the editorial page of the *Evening Public Ledger* (November 5, 1918). For an outlying colony, Williamstown in Gloucester County, New Jersey, with a large Italian population employed in the glass manufacturing industry, see "Italians to Celebrate," *Evening Public Ledger* (November 7, 1918).

7. "When the Italians Cheered," *Evening Public Ledger* (November 5, 1918).

8. "Italians Cheer Fall of Kaiser," *Evening Public Ledger* (November 11, 1918).

9. "Old State House Bell Rings Joy," *Evening Public Ledger* (November 11, 1918).

10. "Italians at Meade Celebrate Tonight," *Evening Public Ledger* (November 11, 1918).

11. "City Led Nation in Saving World," *Evening Public Ledger* (November 12, 1918).

12. "War Monument on the Parkway," *Evening Public Ledger* (November 12, 1918). Among monuments of more modest scale, the best known probably is "Over the Top" or the "Doughboy Statue" by John Paulding, in honor of men from the Sixth, Eleventh, and Twelfth Wards, financed by neighborhood residents and erected in 1920, now at the northeast corner of 2nd and Spring Garden Streets in Northern Liberties.

13. "Triumphant Italy," *Evening Public Ledger* (November 16, 1918).

14. "Bill Hohenzollern to Die at Beverly," *Evening Public Ledger* (November 16, 1918). Since 1863, Beverly National Cemetery has provided the burial ground for deceased members of the military. Some men who lost their lives in World War I may have already been, or expected to be, buried there, perhaps explaining why more intense emotion would have been found at this location.

15. "B. and O. Men Raise Flags," *Evening Public Ledger* (November 23, 1918); "Thanksgiving for Victory," *Evening Public Ledger* (November 26, 1918); "Italians Celebrate at Dinner Tonight," *Evening Public Ledger* (November 27, 1918); "Italians Feast to Mark Victory," *Evening Public Ledger* (November 28, 1918).

16. "La Parata di Domani dei 'Figli d'Italia,'" *Evening Public Ledger* (November 27, 1918); "City Bows Head in Thanksgiving for End of War," *Evening Public Ledger* (November 28, 1918); "Honor Roll of 115 Unveiled," *Evening Public Ledger* (November 28, 1918); "Thanksgiving Spirit for World Peace Brings Joy Today," *The Inquirer* (November 28, 1918).

17. "Comunicazione del R. Console Italiano," *Evening Public Ledger* (December 19, 1918).

18. "Italians to Celebrate," *Evening Public Ledger* (November 19, 1918); "Italians' Big Day," *The Inquirer* (December 1, 1918); "Il Grande Banchetto All'Hotel Adelphia," *Evening Public Ledger* (November 19, 1918).

19. These restaurants are easily found in advertisements in the *Evening Public Ledger* during these years.

20. "Comitato Regionale 'Italia Irredenta,'" *Evening Public Ledger* (December 6, 1918); "To Present Italy's Cause," *Evening Public Ledger* (December 21, 1918).

21. "Italy Is Hailed as Saving World," *Evening Public Ledger* (February 3, 1919); "Il Grande Banchetto al Gen. Pizzarello," *Evening Public Ledger* (February 5, 1919).

22. "The Reader's Viewpoint: Unredeemed Italy," *Evening Public Ledger* (January 11, 1919).

23. "The Reader's Viewpoint: To Safeguard Rights of Italy," *Evening Public Ledger* (January 18, 1919).

24. "I 'Figli d'Italia' per il Ritorno di Wilson," *Evening Public Ledger* (February 21, 1919); "Un Grand Comizio tra gli Italiani," *Evening Public Ledger* (February 26, 1919).

25. "Italians Here Protest," *Evening Public Ledger* (March 3, 1919); "Il Grand Comizio al Teatro Alambra," *Evening Public Ledger* (March 3, 1919).

26. "Democrats Read Bonniwell Out of Party Pale," *Evening Public Ledger* (September 14, 1918). For Sapelli, see the pictorial section, *Evening Public Ledger* (April 5, 1919).

27. "Receding Tide of Immigration," *The Inquirer* (March 12, 1915).

28. "Immigrant Influx after War Certain," *Public Ledger* (October 10, 1915); "Says War Prisoners Would Come to U.S.," *Evening Public Ledger* (January 14, 1919).

29. "Oppose Immigration Ban," *Evening Public Ledger* (January 15, 1919); "Italians Here Protest," *Evening Public Ledger* (January 16, 1919).

30. "Italian Residents Boost Loan $1,000,000," *The Inquirer* (May 5, 1919).

31. "General Badaglio [*sic*] Is Acclaimed Here," *The Inquirer* (July 25, 1921); "Honor Dante's Birth," *The Inquirer* (September 15, 1921); "Columbus Day Will Be Observed by Italians," *The Inquirer* (October 8, 1921).

32. "Thirty Italians Held for Rioting at Relief Meeting," *The Inquirer* (October 10, 1921); "Italian Radicals Fined for Rioting," *The Inquirer* (October 11, 1921).

33. Richard J. Beamish, "Diaz Overwhelmed in Great Welcome by Italians Here," *The Inquirer* (November 7, 1921). The journalist who wrote this article, later became secretary of the commonwealth, chief counsel of the State Utilities Commission, and director of Publicity of the Democratic Party of Pennsylvania, and coauthor of a popular history of the war.

34. Ibid.

35. Ibid; "Raise Funds for Italian Hospital," *The Inquirer* (April 20, 1922); "Christmas Rally Held," *The Inquirer* (December 30, 1922).

36. "Diaz Overwhelmed in Great Welcome by Italians Here," *The Inquirer* (November 7, 1921). It also ended a chapter of Sillitti's personal and professional life. Sillitti's later career in diplomatic service included a brief stint with the Fascist Republic of Salo, before he died in Palermo in 1961. His vice consul, Guido di Vincenzo, served several consuls until his retirement, before dying in Saranac Lake, New York, in October 1954.

EPILOGUE

1. Beginning with this admonition by a peasant woman, attributed to Francesco Jovine, a distinguished writer from Campobasso, this section is partly based on Eric Hobsbawm's chapter, "Waving Flags: Nations and Nationalism," in his book *The Age of Empire 1875–1914* (New York: Vintage Books, 1989), 142–164.

2. "Child Really Belongs to State, Not Parents: Patriotic Declaration," *Evening Ledger* (March 21, 1917).

3. Robert F. Foerster, *The Italian Emigration of Our Times* (Cambridge, MA: Harvard University Press, 1924) 32–34; "Italians in the U.S. Army Are to Be Protected by Treaty," *Jackson Citizen Press (MI)* (March 1, 1918); "Moves to Help Italians," *New York Times* (May 25, 1918); "Bliss to Aid Deserters," *The Sun (NY)* (May 25, 1918).

4. Available at https://www.loc.gov/law/help/us-treaties/bevans/b-it-ust000009 -0136.pdf (accessed February 25, 2017).

5. George Creel, "Italians in the United States," *Journal of American History* 13, nos. 3–4 (1919): 374. This publication of the National Historical Society, a patriotic organization, is not to be confused with the much later journal of the same name that has served as the official journal of the Organization of American Historians.

6. "Concert to Mark Italy-America Day," *The Sun (NY)* (May 20, 1918); "Italy Would Keep 300,000 Reservists," *Washington Herald* (February 27, 1919). For the recent view mentioned here, see Bruce White, "War Preparations and Ethnic and Racial Relations in the United States," in *Anticipating Total War: The German and American Experiences, 1871–1914*, eds. Manfred F. Boemeke et al. (Cambridge: Cambridge University Press, 1999), 97–124. For the original source of the figures, see Commissariato dell'Emigrazione, *Mobilitazione e smobilitazione degli emigrati italiani in occasione della guerra, 1915–1922* (Roma, 1923). For a later version, see Virgilio Ilari, *Storia del Servizio Militare in Italia dal 1871 L 1918*, vol. 2, Collana Ce.Mi. S.S.— Serie Blu (1990). For a recent interpretation, see Piero Melograni, *Storia politica della Grande Guerra 1915–1918* (Milano: Mondadori, 2014).

7. On a similar judgment of the effects of the war on Italy, see Foerster, *The Italian Emigration of Our Times,* 430–431.

8. For interviews in which informants mentioned flight from military service as a factor in their own immigration, see Richard N. Juliani, *The Social Organization of Immigration: The Italians in Philadelphia* (New York: Arno Press, 1980) 152. See also Foerster, 426–427. The Venti Settembre was the annual observance of the victory of nationalist forces over the Papal States on September 20, 1870. The decisive moment was the breaching of the Aurelian wall at the Porta Pia in Rome by Italian forces, under General Raffaele Cadorna, against greatly outnumbered defenders. As the final battle of the Risorgimento, it ended the Temporal Power of the Papacy. Nearly a half-century later, Cadorna's son, General Luigi Cadorna, served as supreme commander of the Italian army prior to his dismissal after the defeat at Caporetto in World War I.

9. "200 Italian Veterans Back in Adopted Land," *The Inquirer* (October 26, 1919); "Ship Unloads Aliens at Gloucester Station," *The Inquirer* (October 28, 1919).

10. "1600 Italians Sail for Native Shores," *Evening Public Ledger* (October 31, 1919).

11. "Europe's Workers Eagerly Knock at America's Door," *Evening Public Ledger* (June 19, 1920).

12. John D'Antonio, "Now My Idea Is This. On Literacy in Philadelphia," *Evening Public Ledger* (November 28, 1921).

Index

Page numbers in italics refer to figures.

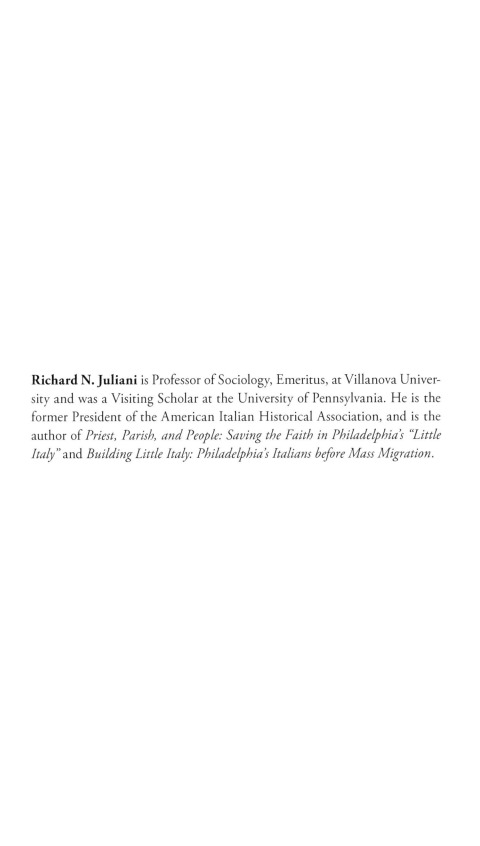

Richard N. Juliani is Professor of Sociology, Emeritus, at Villanova University and was a Visiting Scholar at the University of Pennsylvania. He is the former President of the American Italian Historical Association, and is the author of *Priest, Parish, and People: Saving the Faith in Philadelphia's "Little Italy"* and *Building Little Italy: Philadelphia's Italians before Mass Migration*.